pw

WITHDRAWN

George Rapp's
Successors and Material Heirs
1847-1916

Other books by Karl J. R. Arndt

German-American Newspapers and Periodicals, 1732–1955
George Rapp's Harmony Society: 1785–1847

Jonathan Lenz, Associate Trustee of the Harmony Society, who died January 22, 1890. He was the last of the Harmonist pioneers. Born in the first settlement, he moved with the Society to Indiana and later to the third settlement, Economy.

George Rapp's
Successors and Material Heirs
1847-1916

Karl J. R. Arndt

Rutherford • Madison • Teaneck
Fairleigh Dickinson University Press

Associated University Presses, Inc.
Cranbury, New Jersey 08512

ISBN: 0-8386-7889-0
Printed in the United States of America

Dedicated with faith, hope, and charity
to my investments in the future
of the *United States of North America:*
My son, Karl Siegfried Norman Arndt
My daughter, Carola Anne Sylvia Arndt

On the political value of being a father.—If a man has no sons, he has no full right to participate in discussions about the needs of an individual state. One must oneself together with others have risked what is dearest to one: that first ties one firmly to the state; one must have in eye the happiness of one's descendants, therefore, above all one must have descendants, in order to take a real and natural part in all institutions and their change. The development of the higher morality depends on having sons; [and daughters even more so, Herr Professor Dr. Nietzsche! KJRA] this makes a man unegoistic, or, more correctly: it extends his egoism in duration of time and permits him to follow seriously goals that extend beyond his individual life's duration.

Nietzsche, *Menschliches Allzumenschliches*

Contents

Preface

This volume is a continuation of my *George Rapp's Harmony Society*,[1] *1785–1847*, and takes the history of the Society from the death of its founder to its final legal settlement by a special act of the Legislature of the State of Pennsylvania. As the previous volume showed, the Harmony Society was the socio-economic showplace of the United States in the first half of the nineteenth century. It left its mark in international literature during that time and served as model for Goethe's *Auswandererstaat*, the emigrant state, which Goethe outlined in his *Wilhelm Meisters Wanderjahre* after the reports about the Harmony Society and Owen's attempted sequel had been reported to him by the son of his chief, the Duke of Saxen-Weimar-Eisenach,[2] who had visited Rapp's Society as well as Owen's and was profoundly impressed by the former. If Goethe had lived to complete an envisioned third volume of his great novel of development representative of his age, that volume would probably have had its setting in the New World and would have shown the mastery achieved by his hero Wilhelm Meister, after developing from apprentice, to journeyman, to master of the art of life in the New World in a sort of glorified Harmony Society.[3]

There have been so many divergent views of the embattled and disharmonious later period of the Harmony Society that only the presentation of all documentary records can answer the remaining questions about its latter days. I have here included as much of the documentary record as is possible in this narrative part of the history; the full documentation will appear in my *Documentary History of the Harmony Society,* to which convenient reference can then be made for the definitive evidence.

The first volume of the *Documentary History* is to cover the period 1785–1815, from the beginning to the end of the

Butler County period. It was begun under a grant from the National Foundation for the Humanities, but could not be completed because of shortage of funds. The second volume will cover the period from the move to Indiana to the return to Pennsylvania. This volume is now in preparation under a grant from the Lilly Endowment. Volumes three, four, and five are planned to cover the period from the building of Economy, Pennsylvania, to the legal dissolution of the Society, i.e., from 1847 to 1916. The sixth volume will be a *Biographical Dictionary* of all members of the Harmony Society from the beginning to the end, whether they died in celibate membership or left the Society to help populate these United States. Because many persons withdrew, there are many thousands of descendants of the Harmonist pioneers living in all parts of America, especially in Pennsylvania, Ohio, Maryland, Kentucky, Indiana, Missouri, Louisiana, Oregon, and Utah.

Documentation and notes in the present volume have been reduced to a minimum, giving in the text the dates and names of documents, periodicals, books, or authors cited. Those who wish to check the sources will find them in the original in the Harmony Society Archives, or presented in my *Documentary History of the Harmony Society*. Originally, this second volume included the full text of the documents I considered most important, but the economic facts of publishing have caused drastic reduction in size of the volume and allocation of many of these documents to the *Documentary History*.

I thank all my critics here and abroad for their comments on my first volume, *George Rapp's Harmony Society, 1785–1847,* their criticisms have been considered in the forthcoming new edition.

My purpose in these volumes is not to present a sociological or philosophical analysis of the Harmony Society, but simply to restore these pioneers to the memory of their and my countrymen and to remind all of what we owe to our pioneers, to their faith and to their hard work. I am concerned with their deeds and their record. Any sociological analysis, even when approved as "scientifically objective," bears the stamp of an unbelieving generation which would fit Rapp and the "bride of Christ" into Spanish boots. As much as possible, I have tried to let the Harmonists themselves, and their contemporaries who knew them, relate this history of those who succeeded George Rapp and who ultimately became his material heirs. Their written or printed record is the most accurate we have. Their spelling is maintained in its inconsistency.

For generous access to the Harmony Society Archives at Ambridge and for their encouragement in carrying out this research, I express my gratitude to Dr. S. K. Stevens, Executive Director of the Pennsylvania Historical and Museum Commission, to Director Donald H. Kent of the Bureau of Archives and History, and to Mr. Daniel B Reibel, Curator of Old Economy.

I reiterate my appreciation of the early support of this research from the American Philosophical Society and the more recent grant from the National Foundation for the Humanities, which has also helped in the preparation of this volume.

I wish to express my very sincere thanks to Mrs. Helga Bahlo and Mrs. Mathilde E. Finch for patient assistance in preparing the manuscript for the printer.

George Rapp's
Successors and Material Heirs
1847-1916

PART I

The Baker-Henrici Trusteeship: 1847-1868

These are they which were not defiled with women; for they are virgins.
These are they which follow the Lamb
withersoever He goeth. These were
redeemed from among men, being the
firstfruits unto God and to the Lamb.
Revelation XIV, iv

1

The Renewal of the
Harmony Society Covenant

CELEBRATED AS "THE GREATEST COMMUNIST OF THE AGE" BY THE
Pittsburgh *Daily Morning Post,* George Rapp had reluctantly
departed this life on August 7, 1847, the same year that a
congress of Communists in London asked two comparatively
unknown men named Marx and Engels to prepare *The Communist Manifesto,* which was published a year later. The report
of the *Post* stated that Rapp had departed "respected and honored as a truly good man, and a most venerable patriarch."
The communist and religious Harmony Society was at the
same time described as immensely wealthy and the paper stated
that Rapp's place could not be filled.

The tremendous contrast between the venerable old communist patriarch and the almost forty-year-old founder of the
ruthless materialist religion that threatens the world today is
seen most clearly by recalling Rapp's final sermon and by
studying the report of a visit to the Harmony Society a few
years later by Wilhelm Weitling,[4] an early collaborator of
Karl Marx but, unlike him, a devoutly religious man. To Rapp
religion was everything, to Marx an opium to keep the people
enslaved. In spite of this difference, however, Marx and Rapp
through the Swabian philosopher Hegel had a common heritage
in Württemberg, where the earnest piety of the people had
for generations been interested in building the City of God
on earth. Hegel was born in Stuttgart in 1770 and was not
only a countryman but also a contemporary of Rapp.

"The Lord bless you and keep you in the communal spirit!"
With these words George Rapp ended his last address to his

fellow Christian communists, whom he had led out of Württemberg into a new Canaan, and whom he had served with heart, soul, and body throughout his life. They constituted the last of seven points "from our dear Father's last address" found in the archives of the Society in numerous copies noted by many different hands as a personal memento and guide through the remaining days of waiting for the Lord's coming.

The other six main points which the dying prophet had impressed upon his followers in this last sermon preached from his bed through a window of his house to the congregation assembled outside were:

1. Suffer everything that happens to you and be patient in all sorrow, for as gold through fire so those who please God are proved through the fire of adversity.

2. All your intentions, no matter how good they may appear to you, and may be called good by every man, you should submit to the will of God, for you do not know whether they agree with his divine council.

3. Would you wish only one of our generation of brethren to remain in the clutches of Satan?

4. Never let the fire on the altar go out!

5. The warmth of your heart you must combine with the word of God, if within you it is to grow and become one with you.

6. Two worlds (the world of the senses and the world of darkness) you should fight against, one (the world of light) you should attain.

Although many newspapers and individuals hoping to sue the Society predicted that it would break up with Father Rapp's death, these prophecies were those of rationalistic men who out of their own experience could not appreciate the potent influence of an unselfish personality which itself had lived up to the ideal it preached "insofar as human weakness" had permitted. Many travelers and journalists previously had stated that Rapp was interested only in enriching himself and his family and that he would leave all his property to his own family. But he left no will and no special requests for his family. With his death his own needs had been satisfied and the property which he had enjoyed before his death remained the property of the Society, *communal property of a church that was never to be dissolved by its members but which was to remain intact until the Lord's coming, for any testament or legal provision for the dissolution of the Harmony Society by its trustees or members would have been a denial and betrayal of the basic faith of the Society in its establishment and election by Christ himself to be His bride, faithful to Him until the death of the very last member or the previous coming of the Lord in His glory.*

Der Deutsche Auswanderer (The German Emigrant), a newspaper serving especially the German emigrants to Texas, expressed the view that it was chiefly the strong and commanding personality of Father Rapp which acted as the binding force to keep together the parts of the Society, which otherwise wanted to disperse. The reporter for this paper saw inevitable death in store for the Society if the strictly upheld rule of celibacy as an institution pleasing to God were to continue as before. The paper reported that no new members had been admitted since Proli went away with about one third.

Entire rows of houses stand vacant and deserted and even in the more occupied streets lush grass is growing in the streets and the uncanny deathly silence is broken neither by the lively movement of cheerful children nor by the song and music formerly promoted and encouraged by Rapp himself. For the greater part there are only elderly and occasionally withered figures with silent and indifferent faces creeping alongside the houses and only the complete incapacity to establish and maintain themselves in the to them completely strange world outside, which is constantly moved by the restless traffic of business, holds them together as a matter of dire necessity.

All such voices, however, underestimated the binding force of the religious ideal and hope which Father Rapp had taught and in which the loyal members remaining in the Society had never lost faith. These outside voices knew nothing of the powerful influence of Father Rapp's preaching and teaching, a power which outlived him because it was concerned with eternal nonmaterial values and because it gave a satisfactory answer to the question with which the Harmonists were chiefly concerned: "What shall I do to be saved?"

Before Father Rapp's death, the discordant elements had

been eliminated. Those who remained in the Society at Rapp's death, with the exception of a family of three (the report just cited claimed there were seven), wanted to stick to the principles of the Society, that is, to keep prepared for the coming of Christ, even though physical death should precede this event. And why should they break up and leave their beautiful estate? Their leaders had given them loyal and thoroughly honest and efficient leadership. They were tested men. So when Henrici, in a moving address over the grave of the great leader, asked the survivors to pledge themselves to keep the faith of Christian communal life, he was expressing the wish of all but a few members of the Society. These few left the Society soon after, but the two hundred and eighty-eight remaining Harmonists renewed their pledge over the grave of their prophet and king, and soon after signed the following formal agreement:

WHEREAS, by the decree of God, the venerable Patriarch and much beloved founder and leader of the Harmony Society, George Rapp, has departed this life, whereas its members are deprived of his Christian fellowship and religious ministry and of his Superintendance in their temporal affairs, AND WHEREAS, in consequence of this deeply afflicting dispensation it has become necessary to the good order and well-being of the association, that some plan should be agreed upon to regulate its future affairs, promote its general welfare, and preserve and maintain it upon its original basis;

THEREFORE, BE IT KNOWN TO ALL WHOM IT MAY CONCERN, That we, the undersigned, surviving and remaining members of the Harmony Society, and constituting the same, do, severally and distinctly, each for himself, covenant, grant and agree to, and with all others thereof, and with those who shall hereafter become members, as follows; that is to say:

ARTICLE I.

We do hereby solemnly recognize, re-establish and continue the Articles of our Association, (the 6th section excepted,) entered into at Economy on the 9th day of March, A. D. one thousand eight hundred and twenty-seven, in the presence of John H. Hopkins and Charles L. Voltz, and the supplement thereto adopted at the same place, on the 31st day of October, A.D. one thousand eight hundred and thirty-six, in the presence of Charles L. Voltz and William P. Baum, except so far as the same are affected by the death of the said George Rapp, or hereinafter altered or modified; and to this extent we declare the said Articles to remain in full force.

ARTICLE II.

We hereby ordain and establish a Board of Elders, which shall consist of nine members of the Harmony Society, and their successors, to be chosen as hereinafter provided. John Stahl, John Schnabel, Adam Nachtrieb, Matthew Scholle, Joseph Hoernle, John Eberle, Romelius L. Baker, Jacob Henrici, Jonathan Lenz, shall be the first Board.

ARTICLE III.

The Board of Elders shall have and receive the following powers, to wit:

1st. To regulate and manage exclusively the internal temporal concerns of the Harmony Society; to appoint and remove Superintendents in the several departments of industry; to make regulations and give orders in relation to their business operations, and generally to take care that the members perform their duties assigned to them.

2d. To determine all disputes and misunderstandings amongst the members of the Society; to advise, and, if necessary, to reprove any member who may be in fault, or found delinquent in his duty.

3d. To admit new members into the Society, and to expel them therefrom. New members, when admitted, shall subscribe this agreement as the evidence of their membership, and of the rights acquired by, and the duties imposed upon them.

4th. To establish regulations for the maintenance and improvement of the morals of the Society, and for the instruction of its members.

5th. To appoint one or more of its members spiritual leaders and instructors, with such authority in relation to church discipline as shall be conferred by the Board.

6th. To remove from office any member of the Board of Elders, and to declare his seat vacated. Also, to remove from office either or both of the Trustees hereinafter appointed for the management of external affairs, and their successors in office.

7th. To fill all vacancies in the Board of Elders occasioned by death, resignation, removal from office of any of its members and their successors, and so often as a vacancy shall occur; to fill all vacancies in the office of Trustees, when either or both of said Trustees, or their successors, shall die, resign his office, or be removed from the same, and so as often as a vacancy shall occur.

8th. The concurrence of six members of the Board of Elders shall be deemed the act of the Board, and a legal exercise of any of the powers hereinbefore conferred on the said Board.

9th. A record book shall be kept, in which the Board of Elders shall enter all proceedings that they shall consider of sufficient importance to be preserved.

In all controversies, judicial or otherwise, in which the Society, or any of its members, may be a party, such record shall be full and absolute evidence of the facts and proceedings therein contained; and the affirmation of any Elder shall be competent evidence of the identity of said record.

ARTICLE IV.

We do further ordain and establish a Board of Trustees, for the exclusive management of the external business and affairs of the Society, which Board shall consist of two persons who shall be members of the Board of Elders, and their successors, who shall be appointed as hereinbefore provided. Romelius L. Baker and Jacob Henrici shall be the first Board of Trustees.

ARTICLE V.

The said Trustees shall, jointly and severally, have and exercise the powers following, to wit:

1st. In their own names, or that of either of them, or otherwise, to purchase and sell, deal, barter, exchange and traffic, make all contracts and bargains in the prosecution of business; to invest the funds in stocks and other securities, and make transfers and assignments; to collect debts, receive and pay out moneys, settle claims, compromise disputes, institute legal proceedings, appoint and dismiss agents, clerks and attorneys, in fact and at law, and generally to transact all the external business and affairs of the Society.

2d. To make donations to seceding and excluded members, and to the representatives of those who are deceased; and for such benevolent and charitable purposes as they may deem prudent and fit.

3d. The said Trustees shall have power jointly to purchase real estate in their own names; and, also, in their joint names to grant, bargain, sell and convey all or any of the lands and tenements now or hereafter owned by, or belonging to the said Society; and for this purpose, to execute deeds of conveyance in fee simple, or otherwise, in their joint names. But the proceeds of all such sales shall be held in trust for the Society.

4th. For the purpose of providing an effectual and convenient remedy in law, for all injuries to the property of said Society, real and personal, by trespass, ouster, detention, conversion, or otherwise, the said Trustees are hereby invested with the rights of possession, entry and action in their own names, as fully, and to all intents and purposes, as do and may exist in the said Society.

And to effectuate this object more completely, and in consideration thereof, we grant and transfer to the said Trustees all such title and interest in the said property as shall be necessary therefor. The proceeds of all suits to be brought, shall be in trust for the Society.

5th. The powers hereby vested in the said Trustees shall extend to, and embrace all the property of the said Society, real, personal and mixed, whether standing or held in the name of the late Frederick Rapp, the said George Rapp, or in any other name or form whatsoever.

ARTICLE VI.

It is hereby distinctly and absolutely declared and provided, that all the property, real, personal and mixed, which now or hereafter shall be held or acquired by any Trustee or Trustees, or person under them, is and shall be deemed the common property of the said Society; and each Trustee now or hereafter appointed, hereby disclaims all personal interest in the present resources and all future earnings of the Society, other than that of a member thereof, according to the articles of Association hereby reestablished and continued according to the present agreement.

In witness whereof, we, the undersigned, members of the Harmony Society, who constitute the said Association, have to these articles, executed in English and German, hereunto set our hands and seals, at Economy, in Beaver County, this twelfth day of August, A. D. one thousand eight hundred and forty-seven. Read over to, and signed and sealed by the several persons whose names are subscribed in the presence of us.

To give this document its full legal binding force it was signed before witnesses and properly recorded at the Beaver County Court House, on August 13, 1847, by two hundred and eighty-eight persons, who then made up the membership of the Society.

At the time of the Count Leon secession the ideal of a council of elders had first been recorded in the by-laws then adopted, but the importance of this board was overshadowed by the strong personalities of George and Frederick Rapp, and later by George Rapp alone. The agreement signed at the end of George Rapp's career recognized that the Society had suffered an irreplaceable loss and the length of the agreement reflects an attempt to provide in writing and in legal form those assurances of honest dealing and of security which were inherent in George Rapp's very personality. They also make an attempt to guard against some of Father Rapp's undue severity. Basic to the various articles is the expressed determination to "preserve and maintain it (the Harmony Society) upon its original basis." These renewed articles were an agreement to hold together until Christ should make his personal appearance, or until the death of each member.

The record book called for in the ninth point of the third article either was never kept adequately and continuously under Baker and Henrici or, like many other documents, it has disappeared. The record book showing the signatures of members to various articles of agreement, the "Book of Life," could not have been the one intended in this article. It is clear, however, from the following letter signed by Jacob Henrici and submitted to the Board of Elders on October 26, 1848, that the transition from Rapp's stern and prophetic rule to the more democratic government after his death was not achieved without difficulty: "Because of my renunciation yesterday, I likewise hereby renounce my offices as Trustee of the Society and member of the Council." Why did Henrici resign and why did he eventually resume his office as Trustee? What key to his character is reflected in this action? We must remember that he really was the most fanatical of the millennialists in the Society but that, in spite of Rapp's love for him, he was an outsider to the old Harmonists who had been through the building of Harmony in Butler County, New Harmony in Indiana, and Economy on the Ohio. He did not join the Society until the moving and pioneering were over, until they were back in Pennsylvania after having spent their years in the desert.

In a handmade notebook containing all sorts of records and notes about daily life in the Society, e.g., how much cattle and how many hogs are to be slaughtered, and how much wine, cider, and beer is to be distributed, appear the following memoranda in R. L. Baker's hand, often in cryptic and telegraphic style, here given in their deciphered form. Although it looks like anything but a Book of Record, it does bear that inscription. The last entry is dated December 14, 1850.

The Henrici difficulties reached a critical stage with the Agape celebration on October 15, 1848. Elisabeth Geiger had been excluded. This and other matters were then taken up the following Sunday evening in a private meeting of the Council of Elders in which they forbade Jacob Henrici the following matters:
1. It was wrong to exclude any person from the Agape without their knowledge.
2. They objected to his use of unsuitable texts and too long prayers.
3. They objected because he never announced a text or a hymn to the council of Elders.

Henrici obviously believed that the mantle of George Rapp

had fallen upon him. As Father Rapp in the critical days of the Count Leon revolution had firmly refused to stand for any interference in his office of priest and prophet, so Henrici felt himself, and according to this "record," told the Council he could promise nothing, because he could not say how the spirit would move him. On October 23 and 24, the record continues, Henrici was excited and ordered church for Tuesday evening the 24th. Because of Baker's absence, the Council did not take up the matter. Baker returned from Pittsburgh the afternoon of the 25th. He then had a discussion with Henrici in which he said: "Jacob, so you want to be independent in the spiritual field, whether the congregation or the companies find this to their advantage or not, and whether the Council is satisfied with this or not?" His answer was: "Yes." With that Baker left him.

On Wednesday evening, October 25, the Council met before church began, and all sorts of things were then said. Henrici then resigned his office as "Wort-Führer", i.e., Minister of the Word, and addressed the Congregation about himself and his points of view, defending his point about independence and complaining about the Council. After he had had his say, R. L. Baker also spoke the mind of the Council and complained about Jacob Henrici's despotic behavior. In this meeting the Congregation unanimously declared that it would not accept any solitary rule and confirmed the Council's plan to care for everything in common with one another; further, the Council of Elders was to know about everything, not the Minister of the Word alone. Many persons spoke out loudly, but the meeting adjourned with the decision to commit it all to God and to wait until the next Sunday.

Henrici, however, would not wait. The following Thursday morning, October 26, at five-thirty in the morning Henrici handed a written statement to R. L. Baker in which he resigned all his offices, and on the same day he moved from the "executive mansion" to Jonathan Lenz's house. On the same day R. L. Baker was designated Minister of the Word and on Sunday, October 29, was presented to the Congregation.

The matter kept smouldering for some time. During the week of December 17 to 23 discussions were held again. On

Wednesday evening, December 20, after the meeting, the Council, with the exception of Nachtrüb, met with Father Rapp's family in the council room and decided that Jacob Henrici was to recant the following points: namely, that he bore the Council a grudge and that when the same offered to settle the quarrels on October 22, he either could or would not give any satisfaction. This had resulted in the division and the resignation, and likewise had brought on the remarks about despotism. Henrici was to recant the remarks about "six men on a rope," also the statement that once before only one man was right and the Congregation wrong and that it could be that way again. At Jacob Henrici's request this proposal for recantation was submitted for approval to the "Privat Company," a special group in the Congregation entrusted with consideration of important spiritual matters. This group approved the proposal and on Sunday, December 24, in the evening, R. L. Baker made some introductory remarks stating that Jacob Henrici had erred and that he revoked the above statements. Henrici then said that he accepted this action just as if it were that of Father Rapp, and that he now had much more faith in the Congregation than before and less in himself. R. L. Baker then asked the members of the Congregation whether they were satisfied and many said yes. When R. L. Baker asked whether anyone was not satisfied, no one said a word. Baker concludes his record with these words: "Jacob promised obedience and thus finished. January 22, 1849, Jacob Henrici with the approval of the Council again moved into the "Vaterhaus" (Father Rapp's house, the "Executive Mansion").

Henrici's stubborn interlude, combined with the threat of lawsuits, contributed to adverse publicity outside the Society, with the result that correspondents the following fall began sending Baker newspaper notices of the impending dissolution of the Society. One of these reports stated that each share of a member would be eighty-thousand dollars ($80,000).

On October 16, 1849, Baker wrote Johann Georg Mayer, Sen., in regard to these reports:

Of the dissolution of the Harmonie we here know nothing. The children of the world would, of course, rejoice if Zion would also become Babel, but they will have to wait long before Christ will be defeated by *Belial*. We are still over 300 members, who, however, by far are not worth 80,000 each. That is tremendously exaggerated.

A backslider has sued us, but that does not mean he will win the suit. Many a man starts a war and wins nothing from it. It might be the same way here.

If you need something, then tell us simply without bringing errors about our wealth from the mouths of liars to our attention. This ill suits you, especially because it is not true. Herewith $5 as present.

When distorted newspaper reports continued to appear, the Society resorted to a then-popular method of reply through "a friend." In November of 1849 Wilson McCandless, an attorney, addressed a letter to the Editors of the *National Intelligencer*, objecting to an unspecified paragraph about the Society, which had been widely published, as false and extraordinary:

Its appearance in the German papers of Europe, as well as of those in America, to which our attention has been called, requires this explanation and refutation.

Our professional relations with the Harmony Society at Economy in this State, enable us to say, that since the death of its estimable and venerated *Founder George Rapp*, its social condition was never better.

Persecution in the Courts of Pennsylvania, and suits in the high tribunals of the United States, have not shaken their fidelity to their faith, which is based, in their opinion, upon the creeds of the Patriarchs and Apostles, as taught in the Holy Bible.

They are now united as one family, enjoying the largest liberty and in the possession of every personal, political and religious privilege.

The Henrici incident leaves no doubt about the fact that the new regime set up after Father Rapp's death by the somewhat revised articles of agreement was more considerate of the human weaknesses of members than Father Rapp had been. This greater consideration and patience, however, is also explained by the threats of some serious lawsuits which the Society was facing from former members shortly after Father Rapp's death. Without that threat it is doubtful whether the Trustees and

Board of Elders would have shown such patience as is found in the cases of David Aegerter, Daniel Reichert, and Dorothea Reichert.

On August 2, 1848, David Aegerter signed one of the most unusual agreements found in the archives of the Society. He confessed that he had already four times run away from the Harmony Society and that by unseemly behavior he had several times excluded himself from the Society. He confessed that he deserved to be excluded from the association of such peaceful men, but because he had experienced that he could find neither peace nor pleasure in the world outside the Society, he requested another chance, with the firm determination to improve and to give no further offence. Because his past experience had shown him that he found it difficult to keep to his resolutions and was inclined to give way to his quick temper, he gave the Elders unlimited authority to order two or three men to whip him, if necessary, to bring him back to his senses and to keep him within the human limits of morality and order. In order to protect the Society from any legal action in this matter, he also requested in advance that the Society call the help of the Constable and that he be put in the County Jail until he gave satisfaction. This document was then approved and countersigned by his Father "as means for the improvement of my son."

On February 18, 1849, Daniel and Dorothea Reichert confessed that "since the death of Father George Rapp" they had behaved in disorderly and immoral manner toward the Society and many of its members. They had been admonished by the Elders and had promised improvement, but on February 8 they entertained two relatives (from the outside) and got drunk. Daniel on that day went to Shousetown without permission, did not return until late, and during the evening, while in a state of intoxication, insulted and mistreated several men. When Daniel was called before the Board of Elders the next day he denied everything. Both then confessed that the Council rightfully decided that they were to leave the Society because they were bad people, a decision which the entire congregation unanimously approved on the 11th. The order to leave the town, they confessed, brought them to their senses, and because they "could find neither peace nor rest in the world outside of the congregation" they begged most urgently to be given another chance. They promised that they would improve, that they would be obedient to their superiors, that they would receive no further visits from their sons-in-law or from their children who had left the Society, that they would no longer give them presents or a place to stay, that in general they would hold strictly to the regulations of the Society. If they should break this promise, they stated as their own free will that the Society should have the right to call in the government (law) and drive them out of their house and the town. Both documents were written in a tone of great severity.

2

Echoes of the 1848 Revolution

THE YEAR FOLLOWING GEORGE RAPP'S DEATH WAS THE YEAR OF the 1848 revolution in Germany, and the results of this conflict were naturally felt even in Economy on the Ohio. It brought many of the refugees of the revolution[1] to America and to Economy in search of financial assistance. Among the most prominent were Kossuth, Kinkel, and Weitling.[2] Because of the worldly nature of these men and because the Harmonists were generally not kindly disposed to men who wanted to defy the order of things with force of arms, they did not get any financial assistance from the Society, although they were kindly received. How the Chief Trustee R. L. Baker felt about all these efforts of world reform is succinctly expressed in a letter of February 15, 1853, to Moritz von Friedrichs of Bremerhaven, who wanted to join the Society:

The papers always tell us what is going on in the world. The years 1851 and 1852 have produced unexpected scenes. Kossuth and Kinkel, who both seemed to bring everything to a ferment in the United States and who aroused a great interest in the liberation of Hungary and Germany, have had to be satisfied with much smaller amounts of money here than they expected for their purposes and now live in England. France as a republic, of which those men of freedom expected great advantage, has with incredible speed become a monarchy, which could also be changed just as quickly. We are more and more becoming confirmed in our faith in the word of God, that we are living in a time like that of Noah, where all human piece work, both political as well as religious, can create nothing genuine, nothing whole, whereby the Honor of God and the real welfare of mankind could be established permanently on a large scale, not until the Lord comes.

It is only natural that the reports of revolutionary men and refugees from Europe would not speak too enthusiastically of visits to Economy. In the entourage of Kossuth was a woman of great intelligence and keen observation. In the fascinating book *White, Red, Black*,[3] which contains her and her husband's observations while visiting the United States, Mrs. Theresa Pulszky thus describes her "Visit to Economy":

Economy, the successful experiment of a communistical society, had interested me long before our visit to the United States. As it is only a few miles' distance from Pittsburg, I wished to see it.

Rapp, the precursor of the French and English Socialists, and of Joe Smith, the Mormon Prophet, had in his character several features common with them all. He pretended to be a seer, an instrument raised up by Providence, like Joe Smith; and he stuck to his own schemes of political economy,—to the theory of the community of property and repudiation of commerce,—as steadfastly as Baboeuf or Cabet.

In one respect he succeeded: his community grew wealthy, and independent of the world without. They raise, grow, and manufacture everything which they require for their food, clothing, and enjoyment. But, in another regard, the experiment has failed. Religious fanaticism was the only means of keeping them together, and of excluding foreign elements from the community which might have disturbed it. This was the case so much the more, as the natural increase of the value of their land, about 5000 acres, in the very neighbourhood of Pittsburg, has increased this capital to a stupendous amount. The property was to remain among the original settlers; marriage was therefore abolished. The establishment became a kind of monastery, and as the accession by adoption was restricted, Economy assumes the character of a Tontine, to the benefit of the last survivors. During our stay in Pittsburg, I inquired, from those who could give me information, of the origin and the fortunes of this singular community.

John George Rapp, born in 1757, was a weaver and farmer in Württemberg, and came to the persuasion that the Church, in her present form, is nothing more than a police establishment, "which does not lead mankind to Christianity, but out of Christianity." He therefore refused to pay tithes to the clergy, and preached that people should return to the tenets of primitive Christianity, and, in particular, to the community of property. He soon was surrounded by disciples, principally farmers and mechanics. Worried by the persecution of the police and the law, he emigrated, with his community, in 1804, to the United States. They first bought 3000 acres in Butler County, but, as they soon found themselves implicated in serious difficulties, being unable to meet their engagements, the women had to give up even their rings and earrings, and everything costly they possessed, which had not yet entered the common stock. Nevertheless, they at length sold the first establishment with profit, and thereupon settled in the neighbourhood of Pittsburg.

When their wealth increased, Rapp introduced a new feature into the community. "Asses!" said his prophetic voice to the faithful flock, "do you mean to be wiser than our Saviour? IIE was unmarried!" And such was Rapp's authority, gained principally by the auricular confession, which he strictly enforced, that they submitted to this decree. He then divided them into groups of five to seven persons, so that every one of those should form one artificial family, where the defects of one member were to be remedied by the qualities of the other. Their fare and clothing were the same for all, and of the coarsest description.

Rapp (as the reader will anticipate) had visions and dreams. He predicted the near approach of doomsday, and therefore compelled his disciples to give up selfishness, property, and family. In 1847 he died, being ninety years old; a strange compound of a religious enthusiast and a cunning impostor. At the time of his death, the community possessed 5000 acres, with cattle, machinery for agriculture, wool and silk manufactories, and was worth two millions of dollars. His successor as prophet, was Doctor Henrizi, [sic] a scholar, who preached in the style of Rapp, and seemed more anxious that the Spartan fare should not be improved. But Bäker, [sic] another member of the community, went with the other eleven elders into the kitchen,—where the new prophet was just then enquiring into the contents of the saucepans,—and caught the sacred sleeve, exclaiming, "But now it is enough! we want better fare and less work." The community approved of this "coup d'état," and Bäker and Henrizi had to exchange positions.

Thus, the revolution of Economy was consummated, and the twelve elders, who in the lifetime of Rapp, never dared even to discuss his decrees, became thenceforth a "Consultative Body," though it is said, nothing but the form of proceedings has changed, for Bäker is so clever, that he always carries his point. And as he retains the hoarding propensities of the German peasant, there is no danger that the community should turn epicurean. Our visit was previously announced to the prophet. When our carriage arrived at the foot of the hill, where Economy stands, we were met by Bäker and Henrizi. Bäker's features are those of a shrewd, thrifty peasant, half Jew, half German. Henrizi has the expression of a Puseyite clergyman. Their hair is long and curly, such as Rabbis used to wear. They had broad-brimmed hats, silk waist-coats, and wide and long coats of fine cloth.

They accompanied us to the village, composed of about a hundred clean and neat houses. Several women of the community, in the

Suabian peasant garb, greeted us here, and told us how happily and peacefully they lived. Remembering that my poor friend, the celebrated German poet, Lenau, (some years ago he became insane and died) had paid a long visit to Economy, with the intention of himself making a practical experiment of communism, I asked Henrizi, what he thought of him? "He was no material for us," said he.

When I spoke about the communistic principle, they said: they believed that Christ is coming soon, and therefore it is better to prepare for the future world than to care for individual property, family, and the external world. I remarked to them that if they do not marry, and the day of judgment is yet delayed, their society might be centralised at last, and absorbed by one, perhaps very worldly individual, inheriting the fruit of all their toils. But Henrizi met my objection, saying, that as their motives were sacred, Providence would take care of the results.[4] They offered us wine and cake; we visited their wool, cotton, and silk manufactory. The weavers were poorly clad, and looked dismal. I asked, therefore, how it came to pass that the elders, in spite of equality, were better dressed than the workmen? Bäker answered, that it was only to do us honour, that they had put on their holiday dress; but on Sunday they were all alike.

The dinner was a substantial German peasant's fare. I enquired whether they cultivate music and song in the German way? They said, music was their enjoyment, though I heard nothing but the nasal twang of the Suabian rural communities, not German melody.[5]

We visited Rapp's house, it is like the others, one story high, clean, and nice. The adopted grand-daughter of Rapp, and her mother were clad like all the other women, and looked as some of the old pictures of Van Eyk or Hemling.

They told us, they had also a school and a library, but they did not show it. I asked why they kept a school, when they had abolished marriage? They said, that some children are adopted, and others chance to be found.

The community consists of about six or seven hundred members; the majority of them is above fifty years old.

Interesting about this report is that the Society's self-assertion against Henrici's attempt to take over the mantle of the prophet George Rapp had become such common knowledge that she was informed of it and could record it in her diary. There was then, as we have seen in the previous chapter, a considerable easing of discipline in the Society, showing that prophets like George Rapp were indeed men of unusual calibre—"giants in those days."

Also worth noting in this report by a friend of the German

poet Lenau is her assertion that he had paid a long visit to Economy, contrary to the usual reports of Lenau scholars regarding his stay in the Harmony Society, which, in fact, marked a turning point in his life and proved to be highly productive in his later poetic work.[6]

Less intellectual and warmer is the report of a visit to Economy on November 21, 1851, by Wilhelm Weitling, another refugee of the 1848 revolution and once collaborator of Karl Marx. Weitling by this time had come to a bitter parting of ways with Marx, mainly because he felt convinced that the latter came from too comfortable economic circumstances ever to be able to feel properly the distress and hardship under which the workers had to live. Weitling at this time was busily engaged in establishing a worker's "Harmony Society" in Iowa, which was called "Communia."[7] It was to have all the advantages and none of the defects of the Harmony Society. The description of Economy which he wrote for the readers of his communist journal, *Die Republik der Arbeiter*, seems to exist only in two copies, one in the Library of the Historical Society of Wisconsin and the other in the New York Public Library, which obtained its copy, together with the Weitling papers, from the Weitling descendants. The following account is translated from the issue of December 6, 1851. (Vol. II, p. 34.)

Economy, Pa., November 21, 1851

How happy I was when I discovered yesterday that since very recently a railroad runs to the Rapp colony! Now it would be possible to pay a visit to that peculiar society without much loss of time. For that reason I set out for that place this morning. A thin covering of snow which was spread over hills and meadows had changed the scenery and clothed the bare wintry meadows and forests in a new borrowed garment. One of the elders of the colony sat in the same car with me, but on a seat at some distance and least accessible to the rest of the group. He had that nauseating Pittsburg paper, the socalled "Freiheitsfreund" (Freedom's Friend), in his hand. I tried to get into a long conversation with him by beginning with the exchange of newspapers and by reference to the concert at which I had seen him last night. I thereby hoped to be able to make up for the lack of a written or oral recommendation. As I discovered later, however, this recommendation was not necessary with this man, who now presides in the house of Rapp. Having arrived in the vicinity of "Oekonomie" I noticed more order and beauty of arrangement in the fields and fences, wherefor I called to the member of the Board of Elders, Mr. Lins [Lenz]: Does this land already belong to the colony? He confirmed this. There is a railroad station near the city and from it a well paved street leads gradually up to the bank which lies about 100 feet above the Ohio. Economy lies close to the edge of this high bank, on a level plane surrounded by hills. I immediately went to the store. I there found Mr. Henrici with three or four other elders. But they were very busy, partly with farmers, partly with conferences with each other. I therefore decided first to make a little tour through the little city. According to the description given me beforehand, all the houses faced the street with a bare wall, since all doors and windows opened upon the garden. I found the latter to be so in the case of most houses, but every house had windows opening on the street, as everywhere in our cities, so that this arrangement did not seem the least bit strange to me. On the contrary, I was highly surprised about the beautiful city which I found here. I had already read and heard much about the beautiful and clean buildings of Economy and had pictured it to myself accordingly, yet that picture was never as pleasant in its representation as the reality which I found here. The reader should not, however, imagine some fairy temple, but merely a very common, clean, and tastefully built garden city with factories, and at the edges of town the incidental buildings needed for farming. All streets are beautiful and broad, and the sidewalks are shaded by trees. All houses are two stories high and each seemed to me to have space for at least four large rooms: for each house in front showed two rows of four windows each, and on the sides—if I am not mistaken—just as many windows, also toward the back, in short windows on all sides. Some houses were of brick, some of wood. Some few houses were broader and higher than others, e.g. the Economy Hotel, the Post Office, the Store, the Meeting House, Rapp's House, the Factory, and the Church. Toward the back each house stood as if in a garden, these gardens, although subdivided, together formed a common large garden of one city square, being limited by the houses forming the front on the four streets enclosing the square. The houses were surrounded up to the gable with grapevines.—I thought: Ah, if only the *Arbeiterbund* [worker's union] had this city! In half a year all the workers of Pittsburg and in one year most of the army of workers in the States would belong to our association [Bund].—The streets here were very empty. I walked around in them if per chance I might at last get to know the people here. In the distance I now and then saw several women hurrying across the street, but near me nothing stirred. Finally I discovered a pair of old women at a spring. Like in Württemberg, Baden, Switzerland etc. these springs have a watering trough (Waschtrog). "Hi, little women, tell me," I began, "where are all the men here? I cannot find a single one."—"Yes, we do not know that." was the short reply.—"How many

of you are there still in Economy?"—"Well, there you will have to
ask more important people than we are. Go down there to the store,
they will tell you." I walked one block farther and saw a house which
looked like a factory. Curious to see the inner part of the houses
also, I entered, but found no one in the yard. Through the window
I saw a machine run by steam. In a hallway I finally met a woman,
she seemed to me to be about between thirty and forty years old,
and she looked quite awake. She told me that I was in the washhouse
and at my request took me into the washing hall to an old man who
explained the machinery to me and told me that they washed there
every day and that every family washed its own clothes, but that
this was regulated according to certain days, so that each day was
the washday for a designated number of families. In this old man
I found a good and willing informer and therefore used his loquacious-
ness until the bell rang for eating. He told me that they did not eat
in a common dining hall but that each family had its own kitchen
and carried on its own household, just as at home in Swabia. Whatever was needed for this purpose each woman got from the store,
the butcher, etc. Each week they butchered an ox and sometimes
one in fourteen days.—*Rapp's communism then has not availed itself
of the savings which would be possible in housekeeping and kitchen*
and in spite of this has achieved the heaping up of a tremendous
property. But under such conditions this could be done only *because
Rapp's fanaticism through saving the time necessary for the bringing
up of children* obtained for the society a ten times greater economic
advantage than through the possible savings of a common kitchen.—
How it became possible for Rapp to persuade his followers to get
rid of child production and to hold them to this, is all the more of
a riddle to me since I have been in Economy. I had formerly imagined
some sort of segregation of the sexes, but that is by no means the
case. Men and women live together as girls and boys, just as they
do with us everywhere. Each individual, however, is morally obligated
to sleep alone, the women upstairs and the men downstairs. Otherwise they all mingle with each other as freely that one can say very
definitely that the Rappites were able to make this great sacrifice
of celibacy only by overcoming themselves. A great number of cases
of the defeat of these attempts at overcoming oneself have also
become known. Quite a few have left, others have been expelled,
because they could not withstand the flesh. And if it were written
on the forehead of each present inhabitant of Economy how often
and to what degree he has failed in this manner, then, I believe, the
public would have some interesting reading matter. They say that
instances occurred that girls from Economy drove to Pittsburg with
the coachmen who often stop there, and that they then returned
but were turned away. Others have gone to Pittsburg with young
men from the colony, married there and then returned. These were

received again, but Rapp then forbad them to sleep together. And when even this did not help, they were expelled. There are several fathers in the colony whose sons and daughters were expelled for this reason. If such an economic misstep was made between man and woman the wasters were called before Rapp and he then gave them a coarse lecture, without regard for the often advanced pregnancy. Of Rapp no one knows that he ever broke his own rules. In a series of forty years and in the battle with so many enemies and dissenters this certainly would have become known. But nothing of that sort has so far been heard. Since so many rumors circulate in the public about every extraordinary event, most of which prove to be false, I mention the following only because they came to my ears so often, which does not mean that I believe them. According to these, sexual intercourse in Economy was formerly permitted once every seventh year and now once each year. This much is certain that celibacy was not so strictly demanded at the start of the settlement as later, for the colony was founded in 1807 [sic] and therefore consists almost exclusively of children of the first settlers. Now the colony has a total of two children, both of whom belong to the physician of the colony, who has not permitted himself to be denied sexual intercourse and who was not on that account expelled, since he is the only physician the colony has.[8] This physician was born in the colony and studied at its expense.—According to all probability the entire property of Economy will fall to these children and their descendants in from twenty to twenty-five years. When I asked the Economites what would happen after their death and told them that it was a pity that this estate which was won by poor workers should fall into the hands of speculators, they answered me: whatever happened after their death did not bother them. These temporal goods were not the goal of their life, etc. I told three different persons this and asked them the same question and three times they gave me the same reply. Two women in the hotel, probably cooks and waitresses, almost seemed to be piqued somewhat by this question. After they had answered like the others they added: "We cannot give our property away, we still need a lot and do not even know if anything will remain, and we might live many years longer. There are several there who will perhaps live forty years longer." I took this woman to be the wife of the physician, for it was noon and the twelve-year-old boy of the physician was with her in the dining room. When I later spoke with the innkeeper (also a member of the Board of Elders) about this point, and when he also wanted to present this matter as something that was indifferent if after the death of the colony its property should fall into the hands of the rich, I became excited and told him: This is not an indifferent matter, it would be a sin and a shame for the colony if all that which the industry of the poor had created for the community of goods would again return into the hands of speculators and would again become new instruments of oppression. It was the Christian duty of the colonists, I told him, to lay these riches at the feet of the Apostles before their death, i.e. to leave them to the poor who were struggling for justice, to those who would not use them to improve their own position in life but who in turn would use them as a means to establish a brotherhood of all men (Bruderreich für alle Menschen). Thereupon the man became thoughtful and asked me all sorts of questions, especially when I told him about the colony Kommunia, a thing which seemed to interest him very much. He asked me some covered questions, which, however, let me guess what he really wanted to know. I told him the truth and asked what I owed him for the dinner. "Twenty-five cents" was the answer. But the meal there was something exceptional. The Economites— at least those in the hotel—know how to cook. I doubt whether they eat that well everywhere in Economy. Upon leaving the hotel the innkeeper suggested that I go to the store and speak to Mr. Becker. Mr. Becker is the storekeeper and since Rapp's death also the speaker of the colony. I went to the store but again found Mr. Becker too busy, wherefore I turned to Mr. Henrici. Contrary to my expectations I was received in very friendly manner by him and taken into Rapp's house and garden, into the church and up to the tower, and was treated with fruits and with old wine of their own make, the kind that is produced in Economy by Catawba which has been cultivated.

In that little town these people can live as if in paradise. From the tower I could overlook the entire little town in the beauty of its symmetrical architecture, and also the region around. It is true, the beautiful season of the year was lacking, but my imagination completely made up for that which was lacking and I am convinced that everyone who was here in the most beautiful time of the year will agree with me about the almost unsurpassably beautiful situation of Economy.—The interior of the church is as simple as possible. In it there is neither pulpit nor altar, no pictures, no coat of arms, no hangings. The only luxury which I noticed is the cover over the piano, if such a cover over a piano can be considered a luxury in church or in another place. Instead of a pulpit a broad, un-varnished writing desk stands on a platform and opposite it is another platform for the piano and the singers.

The dress of the people in Economy is still exactly as it was in Swabia, only somewhat finer. They wear their hair just like that combed behind the ears to the nape of the neck. The elders I saw all have winning and intelligent physiognomies, those with whom I spoke all made upon me the impression of noble human beings who are not hypocrites, but who do everything that they do out of principle and who firmly believe that Rapp's doctrine is the best of all those they might have followed.—The city has about 100 houses and 280 inhabitants, among these only two children. Several years ago they were 1400 strong. Disunity and death have reduced them to this small figure. Their property is estimated at from 12 to 14 million dollars. Already 15 years ago it is said that they invested $500,000 in banks etc. Interesting details are related about their industry. The women work much in the field and during harvest on the way home pick up all sheaves which they see lying about. Silk culture also was women's work. The English language was not taught in the schools. Now the Economites are gradually letting up on work. Silk culture has been discontinued. Half of their acres they have rented out for half the harvest. Agriculture in recent years had always brought in less and less, so that Rapp had said that silk culture alone, or the weaving alone, brought in more than all the agriculture. But now they say: *"Stocks bring in more than all this working. It is best if we change everything into stocks."* Formerly they also had a fine museum, now they have sold it. Occasionally they give concerts and have feasts, such as harvest festival, Agape (Liebesmahl, Love Feast), etc. but they place no emphasis on these.—It is impossible to imagine how much they have had to suffer from the attacks of malicious lawsuits. One lawsuit follows another and each costs heavy sums of money, whether they win or lose. We in the worker's association (Arbeiterbund) will not have to fear as much in this regard because, when our property increases, our number of members must also increase relatively. The temptation of the individual to divide will therefore fail because of the very tremendous number of equals. When Count Leon, however, separated from Rapp with his followers, Rapp had to pay out over $100,000 to him. At present another lawsuit is pending by a man who is 43 years old and who was born the first year of the colony. This man was expelled from the colony several years ago merely because he had spoken with the followers of Count Leon. Rapp kept such a discipline in his colony. This expelled man for thirty years had worked in the colony at one time as farmer and another time as hatter, and he now demands a share of the common property amounting to $60,000. They are very intensely interested in the outcome of this lawsuit, for several might still come and bring suit for a share of $60,000 if this plaintif should win.[9]

Rapp's dwelling and garden make upon the stranger the impression of a beautiful country home which a rich city man has arranged for his relaxation. Henrici, who now inhabits this house, is an exceptionally well suited man for the reception of strangers because of his friendly manner. I gave him a clear insight into my different views in matters pertaining to religion and marriage, but this did not in the least change his friendliness. Kinkel had also been here, but revolution as a means of liberation find no sympathy with these people, although Kinkel also enjoyed the most friendly reception. They gave nothing for the national loan.

Mr. Henrici accompanied me to the railroad station. We still spoke about the revolution. Then Henrici concluded that the Lord Jesus would not always so quietly look on to all evil. He would certainly come one day himself and judge and punish. And that might happen very soon. In answer to this I could say no more than that it was rather cold today. The locomotive rolled along and I sat down in the coach enriched with new experiences.

If now someone asks me whether I could live among such people, I must admit: Yes! If I had nothing else to do, if I would not have to live in my sphere of activity, I would be able to live among these people, in spite of all my views and their diametrically opposed peculiarities, and I do not believe that I would then have reason to regret it.

But I do not consider it impossible that after some time I would be expelled by them.

So the report of the German utopian Communist, who until then was better known than his former fellow-worker Karl Marx, but also French communist circles were informed about and interested in the Harmony Society. This we see from the works of Cabet and from records of the Harmony Society.

In the year 1854 Heinrich Albrecht of Chicago, Illinois, approached the Harmonists in an attempt to obtain their support for Cabet's Icarian movement. This movement, incidentally, had become tremendously popular in France, especially after Cabet in May, 1847, had published in the *Populaire* his call "Allons en Icarie!", a call which brought all the greater response because the *Populaire* supported this romantic call with factual accounts of the phenomenal success of George Rapp's Harmony Society in America. As old George Rapp had been cautious in advising others about the road to communist success, so Jacob Henrici reacted to Albrecht's enthusiastic letter. Under date of October 7, 1854, in the name of the Board of Elders, Henrici gave him a very sobering reply to what had been a highly enthusiastic letter. I translate as follows from the original German, for many of Cabet's enthusiastic followers were German:

Your honored letter of the 18th of last month was properly received. We thank you for your friendly attitude toward our Society.

There are few people who have such favorable views of communal life as you. With your natural kindness of heart and your flaming good will for suffering mankind you, however, are in danger of becoming prejudiced with a blind preference for such a way of life, and we are very much afraid that sooner or later you are bound to experience bitter disappointment. For for fallen and non-regenerated man there is no system under which he could be truly happy, just as for the truly regenerated, loyal follower of Jesus there can be no condition under which he can be really unhappy. For not that which a man *has* or does *not have,* but that which he *is* or *is not,* makes out his happiness or unhappiness. We are fairly well acquainted with the principles of Icaria, and in general have little confidence in the tenability of the same as in those of Robert Owen. To be sure, we are not inclined to harbor or express hard and unkind judgments about any religious or social community; but when we are asked to take an active part in any kind of undertaking, then we are compelled to express ourselves about it. The following two main reasons, therefore, compel us most definitely to give your well-meant request a negative reply:

1. At the present we have invested all our funds;
2. We have no faith whatever in the religio-social principles of Icaria. Hoping firmly that you will not take ill our caution, which is based on many a bitter experience, I remain respectfully, Your friend, Jacob Henrici, Trustee. By order of the Council of Elders.

3

Three Important Lawsuits

WHILE FATHER RAPP'S DEATH HAD INSPIRED THE HARMONISTS TO greater resolve to finish the course upon which they had started, this event also was the signal for several lawsuits brought by or against previous members of the Society. The most bitter of these were between close relatives within and outside of the Society. The foundation for all the suits had been laid during the life of Father Rapp, and in one case the suit had already been started before his death. These were the suits involving Jacob Wagner, Elijah Lemmix, and Joshua Nachtrieb. They went through several courts and the last went to the Supreme Court of the United States before it was settled. All three suits resulted from the bitter feelings which existed between the Harmony Society loyalists and their former brethren who had departed with Count Leon, and from the fact that the former members of the Society during the course of their sheltered existence within the Society had never become aware of the serious *legal* consequences arising from their action. In all three cases the former members were thinking in terms of justice and fairness within the Christian context of the Society in which they had lived in a spirit that was generally more generous than that of justice under the law, just as all Christian theology is based on law and gospel with the gospel of grace and love to redeemed men surpassing the requirements of the law. They did not realize that their cases would be settled in the world outside on the basis of fine points of law and without any regard for the naïve attitude of these unfortunate souls who scarcely knew what they were doing when they signed carefully

worded legal documents placed before them, but had absolute
faith in their pastor. Two of the cases at least would never have
been fought if the individuals concerned could have remained
in the Society and without social stigma have satisfied their
strong urge to hand on the spark of life to children. All three
cases should have been settled out of court on the basis of
Christian justice and love, but all parties had already hardened
their hearts. This would have been in harmony with one of the
beloved hymns in their hymnal: "In diesen heil'gen Hallen,
kennt man die Rache nicht, und ist ein Mensch gefallen, führt
Liebe ihn zur Pflicht."

What a world of grief and what costs might not have been
saved Jacob Wagner and Romelius L. Baker if the former had
been gifted with greater lucidity and calm, and if the latter had
been less of a zealot! Jacob Wagner had left the Society with
Count Leon, not because he was tired of religious communism
but because he wanted to have a family *and* religious communism. After the first months of greater freedom with Count
Leon had also revealed to him that they had made too easy a
settlement with the Harmony Society, he overlooked the fact
that their relationship with the Society now was entirely on the
basis of LAW of the world and that this by no means was
synonymous with Christian charity or justice. In the excitement and anger that grew out of the confusion and misunderstanding of the legal settlement, he had joined the group that
marched on Economy and in his spirited manner had broken
down the door of the tavern and the bar, and had later even
tried to break into the residence of Father Rapp. He obtained
no satisfaction because he had made a legal settlement and the
law of the land was against him. Quite understandably he tried
to obtain indictments against the Society, all without avail. He
did, however, cause the leaders of the Society much trouble,
but only succeeded in making himself the symbol of opposition
of the Leonites and thus in concentrating the "righteous" wrath
of the leaders of the Harmony Society upon his head. He was to
pay dearly for this in his legal battles with R. L. Baker.

In June 1844, Jacob Wagner came to Economy and exhibited
a letter which he had just received from his brother Jonathan
in France, announcing to all his relatives in Philippsburg and

Economy the death of his uncle John Huber. John Huber and Father Rapp had been schoolmates in Iptingen and both had made their mark in later life. Huber had gone to France and had become a wealthy banker in the town of Honfleur near Le Havre. He had never married and his lawful heirs were eight children of his sister Maria Bentel, deceased, and five children of his sister Anna Maria Wagner, deceased. Both sisters and their families were members of the Harmony Society at Economy. Four of the Bentels and one of the Wagners were then still members of the Society, but the other four of the Bentels and four of the Wagners had left with Count Leon in 1832 and settled at Philippsburg. The names of the four seceding Wagners were Jacob, David, Simon, and Jonathan. The last-named had gone to France in 1832 to reside with his uncle. John Huber had in this way heard about conditions within the Society, particularly about celibacy. He had written George Rapp one of the most vehement epistles he had ever received, indicating in no uncertain terms that he would never repeat what he had done, give presents to his relatives now that he knew that private property did not exist in the Society. Just how strongly he felt on the matter of celibacy as a sin against nature is seen from the fact that he did have illegitimate children who had received individual presents and gifts before his death. These children, now, however, threatened to bring suit for the recovery of their father's property.

John Huber had died intestate and in this situation it was urgently advised that all the legal heirs in the United States join and send Jonathan Wagner a general power of attorney to administer and settle the Huber estate. The desired documents were sent to Jonathan Wagner and by Fall of 1845 he was ready to complete the execution of his trust. He asked that Jacob Wagner be sent to France "to inspect and examine all and to receive your money, be it in cash or Bills of Exchange." Jacob Wagner was accordingly sent to France and upon his return to the United States informed his relatives at Economy that the share of each of the Bentels amounted to $2558.55 and the share of each of the Wagners to $4093.70, but that Uncle Huber had directed that no part of his property should go to his Economy heirs unless or until they left the Society. Unfortunately, he had no written record to prove this, although circumstantial evidence was certainly entirely in his favor. Huber's letters clearly showed his attitude toward the Society and its communistic policy, not to mention the fact that Jacob and Jonathan claimed that Huber had stated before witnesses that none of his estate was to go to the Harmony Society common fund. The situation was involved enough as it was, but the Economy heirs made matters much worse by appointing R. L. Baker their attorney in dealing with Jacob Wagner. R. L. Baker had always been in the background even when the first discussions about this matter took place, and, from the beginning, his feelings toward Jacob Wagner were strongly biased. He certainly must have known about the seething letter that Huber had sent to Rapp, for it had been carefully preserved, and that letter would have been sufficient evidence in any court to support Jacob Wagner. Devout Christian that he was, however, this situation proved too much of a temptation. His letters to his lawyer Walter Forward reveal his "righteous" hatred for Jacob Wagner, the enemy of the elect of God. Acting for the heirs at Economy he claimed that since Huber had died intestate his verbal declaration could be of no effect. It is very clear from the existing record that Jacob Wagner was a very honest man and that he certainly did not want to deprive his fellow-heirs of a cent of their inheritance, but he did want to keep this inheritance out of the common treasury of the Harmony Society. Jonathan Wagner had written that Huber would have disinherited all his heirs in the Harmony Society if he had not promised him to take care that the share would be secured to them until they left the Society, in order that they might have something for their old age. For this reason he had asked Jacob not to send them their share by Bills of Exchange. Because Jacob Wagner refused to pay out the amounts and because he had been talking about moving to the Red River region to join the followers of Count Leon there, Baker feared that the money would be lost to the heirs in the Society. He grew excited and in Pittsburgh swore out a statement to the effect that Jacob Wagner owed heirs in the Society $14,327.90 "which sum he refuses to pay" and that he "intimated a desire to remove to Red River near Texas where some of his acquaintances reside." The next day, December 16, 1845, the warrant was served on Jacob Wagner in Pittsburgh charging that he "has property which he fraudulently conceals, for the purpose of defrauding his creditors, and that he is about to remove his property with the intend to defraud his creditors." Wagner was arrested and put in jail but released on bail through the kind efforts of Frederick Kahl, who had been Count Leon's attorney when he came to America and who then lived in Pittsburgh.

How mean this Trustee of the divinely established Harmony Society could be toward a former brother in Christ is best revealed in his own report of the matter to his fellow trustee and fanatic, Jacob Henrici, which I translate:

Pittsburgh, December 16, 1845.

Today at 12 o'clock Judge Hepburn granted the five warrants of arrest, at 2 o'clock they were completely written out and in the sheriff's hands. The *Michigan* landed at 1 ½ o'clock when I received my adversary Jakob Wagner at the banks with considerable tension. He immediately wanted to get down to business, and we agreed to meet at 2 at the store of our friend Wm. Baum, where we also did meet, but he came first, wherefrom Baum also benefitted.

The three of us now sat in the back room, where, as usual, Jacob had most to say. The Sheriff had been ordered to stand outside in the store until his time came. When all necessary things had been discussed I told him, here is a letter from the heirs in which they demand their money, and I now stand before you in their names as agent to receive it. He hesitated and read, after reading he stubbornly said, I do not recognize you as their agent. But, said I, here is also their power of attorney given to me. Read it, Mr. Baum! Wagner answered even more stubbornly and more insolently than before: I do not want to hear them, I will have nothing of it, and rushed out of the room into the store to leave. In that moment I called: Sheriff, this is Jacob Wagner!, who immediately arrested him, read the 5 letters of arrest to him and without delay took him into the Court House to Judge Hepburn.

This quite unexpected action surprised the proud crude fellow tremendously. His red color became pale in the face, he looked straight ahead rigidly, not a word passed his lips, and as a prisoner he marched behind the Sheriff to the Court House. After a half hour he was here called up, where he, as usual, repeated his verbal authority. The Judge said, if Huber made no will you cannot keep the money from the heirs, you must give it to them, even if the next day they throw it into the water: but you have three choices: either leave the money with a third person or give satisfactory bond, or you must remain in the hands of the Sheriff. His lawyer Heidelberg advised him to choose the last; until tomorrow afternoon at 3 o'clock when his trial takes place. After this the Sheriff took him away and the Court broke up. How things will now go, can be expected. I am happy about McCandles. He is a General in his business. He laughed very much and said, this is the most beautiful arrest I have ever seen etc. So far all has gone slowly but step by step and regularly, which cannot be otherwise because of the letter of the law. It is very enjoyable that right is on our side, and that the communal spirit so far has been victorious and triumphant. But I also find myself much supported by you. A powerful magic is at work which gains strength the more it suffers, and thus the Universal, namely our free surrender, is applicable to all cases of life and an unfailing guide on our life's course until eternity.—Miller and Ricketson order 3 bbls same old Whisky They had before. Also send the 2 bbls for Jamison to Baltimore.

By thus resorting to force, Baker compelled Jacob Wagner to pay out the full sum, which was then loaned to an individual outside of the Society, who in turn paid interest for the sum. The capital was not made a part of the common fund, and the ultimate fate of the Huber fund continues to remain a mystery. On September 28, 1854, Baker wrote to R. P. Roberts: "Miss Wagner will not leave our Society, if the whole of the Huber money and tentimes more were given her for doing so, therefore we consider said money a foreign matter, so guarded by Huber that our Society shall never get it." In 1905 C. F. Straube, attorney for some of the heirs, looked into the matter and discovered that the papers relating to the settlement had disappeared from the court record. When he took the matter up with Susie Duss, the last Trustee of the Society, she claimed complete ignorance of the entire matter and stated that she knew nothing about the case and could find nothing on it in the Society records. In view of the voluminous record on the Wagner-Baker-Huber suits still found in the Archives today, that reply was an understatement, to say the very least.

Wagner's arrest did result in the release of the money, but it did not end the battle. Being put in jail hurt Wagner deeply and as an honest but helpless man he was furious. In various places he told people that he had been put in jail because Baker had sworn a false oath. He made the remark in German in various places, and considering the facts as the full records show them, namely, that he had never refused to pay the inheritance due according to the conditions stated by Huber, which conditions he knew to be entirely in accord with Huber's attitude toward the Society, Baker actually had sworn a "false" oath in saying that he refused to pay, only Wagner did not know or consider that the strong language "fraudulent" was the legal language of the warrant. Baker in turn felt that the entire Society's honor was at stake if he were silent to such a charge of what he believed to be perjury, so he sued Jacob Wagner for libel and asked $5000 damages. He was awarded the sum of nine hundred dollars damages, but the case was taken to the Supreme Court of Pennsylvania. During the course of this bitter litigation Wagner, through Baker's lawyer, made earnest attempts to get a peaceful settlement, and even Baker's lawyer favored such a course, but Baker believed that a peaceful settlement would stamp him a coward and in writing to his lawyer, Walter Forward, later Secretary of the United States Treasury and Ambassador to Denmark (1850), even indicated in very strong terms that he would change lawyers if he would not prosecute "with courage and vigor to carry out my rights." Forward had long represented the Society in its many lawsuits, and since it probably was the best paying client he had, he made no further attempt at a compromise. Since Wagner used the word "falscher Eid" and not "Meineid", he should never have been fined, but although Wagner knew the difference and deliberately had not said "Meineid," which meant perjury, it did not occur to the Court to call in a Germanist to settle the point objectively. The circumstances show clearly that Wagner's remark "false or incorrect oath" did not imply moral turpitude and that Baker was humanly very eager for revenge against a "ringleader" of the Count Leon rebellion.

From the point of view of historical interest, the suit of Joshua Nachtrieb against the Harmony Society (Romelius L. Baker and others) was the most important in the history of the Society. This action was begun in 1849, by a bill in equity in the Circuit Court of the United States, for the Western District of Pennsylvania, and afterwards carried by appeal to the Supreme Court of the United States and decided by that Court in 1856. No previous lawsuit had caused the Society so much trouble and expense as this one. In a letter of November 28, 1854, Baker expressed his views on the subject to Jacob Silvan at Zoar, Ohio, the representative of the other Württemberg group of communists with which the Harmonists were on intimate terms. The Zoar community at the time was itself engaged in complicated litigation resulting from the death of the head of their Society. They had been asked to give a complete inventory and accounting of their property. In reply to Silvan's letter giving this information, Baker stated that during the fifty years of its existence the Harmony Society had never been asked to give an accounting or to render an inventory "until the court in its decision in Nachtrieb's suit three years ago ordered and forced it." Baker then added that they disliked very much to do this and that they almost refused to give an accounting but that the command of St. Paul to be obedient to the government combined with the exaggerated claims about the magnitude of their wealth persuaded them to comply. The result had shown that their property amounted to a little under a million dollars. In all things, Baker assured his friend, they lived by the principle expressed in the Bible that they possessed goods as though they possessed them not.

Joshua Nachtrieb had long been a faithful and popular member of the Society. In the Count Leon secession he voted to remain with George Rapp, although relatives of his at that time took their leave. One day in June of the year 1846 Joshua Nachtrieb went to Beaver County Court to serve on a jury. While he was there he met three men who used to live in Economy. These men asked him if he had not heard Rapp say something about a delegation that had been sent to him the preceding April to inquire whether the seceders could not obtain more money than they had received upon their departure. Nachtrieb did not have much time to talk with them because the bell was about to ring calling him to his jury duty, so he informed them that if they would come to Legionville Run, near Economy, on the following Sunday sometime after three o'clock he would bring some other Harmonists who could give the desired information. At the designated time four former Harmonists, one of them Jacob Wagner, came to the appointed place on Harmony Society property to meet the men Nachtrieb would bring there.

Nachtrieb was accompanied by his friend Elijah Lemmix, whose case will be discussed later. Others who had promised to come did not appear. As they sat there under a large tree waiting for them, they could not talk of anything because their minds were so disturbed. They felt that something was wrong because the others did not come. What happened next is best told in the court testimony of Joshua Nachtrieb in the case of *Elijah Lemmix* v. *The Harmony Society,* a case which parallels that of Nachtrieb:

Two other gentlemen came down, and we did think then that they came down to watch us—that they knew something and came down to watch us. There was nothing done. There was nothing more said there than what I told them before in Beaver. Then, on Monday following, Mr. R. L. Baker came in my house and told me I should come in Rapp's house, and my uncle with me. I went to Rapp's house with my uncle. When I came there, there was a pretty large assembly. Rapp asked me first, as Rapp said I was the leader or the cause of our going down there, what we went to Legionville for? I told him as well as I could, and then he asked Elijah Lemmix the same question. Then he began to scold us so that we could not say much more, and told us we must give up our keys to the shops, and leave the Society right away. I went home from there and took my hoe and went to hoeing corn that afternoon; and as I passed the carpenter shop Elijah Lemmix fought for his key before his shop. He did not want to give it up. He was forced to give it up there; and Daniel Shriver was sent home from the cornfield to take charge of the key and the shop of Lemmix.

The sworn testimony of Lewis Kast in the Nachtrieb case gave an authentic account of the events that followed the above scene insofar as Nachtrieb was concerned. Kast was sixty-five years of age at the time of the testimony. He had been a member of the Society for thirty-one years and had known Nachtrieb for forty-eight years. He had left the Society on the second of February, 1848. Kast stated that Nachtrieb conducted himself well and that nothing could be said against him, but that the circumstances of his leaving were as follows:

He had gone out and talked to some of his friends. I cannot say when he spoke to his friends; he was ordered away by Rapp. I never heard of any other charge brought against him, except that he talked to his friends. Nachtrieb wanted to remain at Economy, and said so publicly; he wanted to remain a member of the Society. I was present at the Wednesday evening meeting, the last meeting at which Nachtrieb was present. After the religious exercises were over, Rapp enquired whether Joshua Nachtrieb was present; Nachtrieb then arose and said, Yes, father, I am here. Rapp then said, Why what are you doing here yet, I thought you had left. Nachtrieb replied, Well father if it had not happened, it should not happen again. Rapp replied: Why, any fool can speak so—you must leave, thy father too, don't want you any longer. Nachtrieb's father was a member of the society. From Monday to Wednesday it had been rumored all through the Society that Nachtrieb had been, or that he would be ordered off, and John Schnable, one of the defendants and one of the elders, came out into the meadow where we were moving, between Monday and Wednesday above spoken of, and said to the plaintiff's uncle Adam Nachtrieb, to tell Joshua that he was not allowed to work any more, that Rapp had so ordered. Adam told Schnable to tell Joshua that himself. After Rapp said to Nachtrieb "any fool can say that, you must leave, thy father too, don't want you any longer," nothing was said by Rapp that I know of. The meeting then broke up. What Rapp said to Nachtrieb was in a loud voice in the presence and hearing of the members of the Society, so that every body could hear it. He was a man of strong voice.

In its defense, the Harmony Society denied that Nachtrieb had been expelled. It presented evidence in which it tried to prove that Nachtrieb was thinking of leaving the Society before this incident occurred. It also presented testimony from men of importance in their vicinity stating that the officers of the Society were men of greatest integrity and honor, but these men were business friends of the Society who had no reason to complain about their dealings with the trustees of the Society and who were quite ignorant of life within the Society. The strongest evidence presented by the Society against Nachtrieb was the following document which he had signed at Economy on June 18, 1846:

To-day I have withdrawn myself from the Harmony Society, and ceased to be a member thereof. I have also received from George Rapp, two hundred dollars as a donation, agreeably to the contract.

That Nachtrieb was by no means aware of the full meaning of this *legally*, is clear from the letters he wrote to the Society after his departure and previous to his lawsuit. Under date of

September 19, 1847, he wrote R. L. Baker as follows from Wooster, Ohio:

Because Father, when I went away from you, promised to give me something more, for I did not want to go, until he said, only go with what I am giving you now, and spend this first, when you have a place where you want to settle, I shall help you, it does not suit now etc. Then I took what you gave me, signed a Receipt in Confidence of Father. It would never have come into my mind, that you would say, as you should have said to one; forsooth we have got Joshua away with little etc. Be this as it may, the principal point is, several opportunities offer themselves at present to buy something, particularly from the partner of my Brother, who has laid out much this Summer for Lot and house building. Now his stock in the shop not being large say $1000 that would be a small present for one. . . . You know all well yourself, it is a good while, since you stretch'd me the Pants, when John Baker kept school in Father's upper house in old Harmony. I was with you A.D. 16 and 26, [meaning he helped build Harmony, Indiana, in 1816 and Economy in 1826] when the birds let fall upon the dinner plate, of which old Mr. Forstner is witness. But now I should have one thousand dollars, that I could buy out the one above mentioned, can you not bestow it to me, then we pray you for a loan of five to ten years, and you shall have good security. There is another hatter here who wants to sell out, which would be the second chance to buy something. In short now it is time that I should have one thousand dollars in any way, as aforesaid. For to do journey work goes too hard, as I am as old as many among you, therefore help me to something, you will not regret it.

Baker gave the following reply to this letter under date of September 24:

In answer of your letter 19 inst. I mention, that we have no money to loan at present. The Factories and mechanics are not in opperation, therefore we take in but little. Like other seceders you have received a present in money agreeably to your contract which you made with the Society, we can do nothing farther. Your father, uncle, sister and cousin are in health as usual.

By coincidence, the extra fee alone of only one of the lawyers, Henry Stanberry, who helped take the case to the Supreme Court of the United States, was one thousand dollars. This sum was to be paid him above his regular fee in case the Society won the verdict. Under date of January 5, 1857, Baker wrote Stanberry an effusive letter of thanks for his services and enclosed a check for one thousand dollars: "I believe this to be in full of the agreement between us." But that is only a preview of the later part of the story.

The evidence presented to the Court by Nachtrieb was so overwhelming that it resulted in a decree by the United States District Court for Western Pennsylvania in November 1851 that the Society must render an account. For this purpose it appointed a Commissioner in Chancery, who spent much time taking testimony for a full and complete account of the possessions of the Society when Nachtrieb became a member and when he "withdrew." As a result of this order of the court there was prepared and preserved for posterity one of the most thorough and accurate accounts of the financial state of the Society in June 1819 and in June 1846 that could be wished for by any historian. The "Master's Report," as it was called, is an invaluable source of information about the economic, religious, and social status of the Society in these years. It is of primary importance, however, to understand that even this comprehensive report managed to evade the most important source material of all, the writings of George and Frederick Rapp. And yet, in no other documents is the true meaning, the very semen from which this celibate organization developed so clearly and decisively pictured, as in the letters and sermons of Father Rapp. To read them, however, was beyond the ability or scope of the Master and to inform him or the Court of their contents was beyond the honesty of R. L. Baker, for there is in religious fanaticism a strange mental reservation or blindness to justice which permits the purest and most conscientious children of God to withhold from a worldly power such information as might be injurious to its cause. In this respect Baker was a true follower of Father Rapp, who had dealt similarly with the German government in some of his troubles there.

On December 23, 1853, in a letter to E. D. Rogers, the friend and agent of the Society at New Harmony, Indiana, Baker gave an up-to-date account of the status of the Nachtrieb litigation, saying that if in any way the verdict should be over two thousand dollars, the Society would carry the case to the Supreme

Court in Washington, "as we did not get a fair trial in the District Court." In view of the arguments successfully presented to the Courts a half century later in support of the legal right of the then members of the Society to divide the property of the Society into individual shares, it is most interesting to note that Baker and his attorneys in this case argued with all the force at their command that according to the Articles of Agreement of the Harmony Society under which Nachtrieb claimed partition, distribution, and individual enjoyment, "All the property of the Society, real, personal, and mixed, in law and equity, and however contributed or acquired, shall be deemed, now and forever, joint and indivisible stock." Baker's letters during this period frequently informed his correspondents that the property of the Society was "now and forever, joint and indivisible stock." Following this reasoning, A. W. Loomis, one of counsel for the Society, in his brief presented the excellent solution that the Society be compelled by the Court to restore Nachtrieb "to the bosom and privileges of the Society, a full, complete and adequate support by the Society, under the order, direction and supervision of the Court or its officers."

For a number of reasons the trial was drawn out over a long period, during the course of which one of the judges involved was appointed to the Supreme Court in Washington. On May 15, 1854, Baker confided in Jacob Silvan of the Zoar Community in Ohio[1] the full figures resulting from the Master's investigation. The value of the Harmony Society property on June 16, 1846, the day of Nachtrieb's departure, amounted to $901,000 (actually, $901,723.42). From this the sum of $368,000 (actually, $368,690.92), the value of the property in June, 1819, when Nachtrieb became a member, was deducted. "Of the rest, viz. $533,000, the complainant could, (if our articles permit, which will be vigorously opposed), be awarded the 321st part, which would be about $1691.00." It was not until a year later that Judge Grier sent the Harmony Society a copy of his verdict in the Nachtrieb suit. On May 16, 1855, Baker informed Jacob Silvan of Zoar that Judge Grier had concluded that Nachtrieb had been forced out of the Society, and that he was therefore awarded a share of the entire property with interest from the date of his exclusion, $3,890 and costs. As previously decided, the Society appealed the decision to the Supreme Court of the United States.

Meanwhile another lawsuit had been started against the Society in 1852 by Elijah Lemmix[2] in the same court and for the same reason given by Nachtrieb. The evidence in this case is also voluminous and likewise preserves for posterity an important record of life within the effective but invisible walls of the Harmony Society. Lemmix's background was completely different from that of his friend Nachtrieb, and the case which he presented was not so strong. Elijah was the son of Isham Lemmix, a man of indigent circumstances, who had a large family of children. While the Society was in Indiana he had been in the employ of the Society and had cleared land for compensation, not being a member. In 1818 his wife died, having given birth to a large number of children. Soon afterwards Isham Lemmix came to the Society and stated that it was the dying request of his wife that their younger children should be placed in the Harmony Society for care, nurture, and protection, if the Society would consent to receive them. Isham was in cordial agreement with this request. The Society was moved by these requests and by their destitute circumstances and helpless condition, and received the nine youngest of Isham's children, Elijah being the eldest of the nine. One child died in infancy but all the others were fed, clothed, and educated by the Society. When Elijah became twenty-one years old, although he had no property and contributed nothing to the funds of the Society, he was admitted to full membership. This was in 1826, after the Society had moved back to Pennsylvania. When the Count Leon secession developed, Elijah remained loyal to George Rapp and stayed at Economy, where he was principally employed in manufacturing cloth in the woolen factory. He sometimes worked as a carpenter and made carding machines and all other kinds of machinery for the factory.

The immediate cause for Lemmix's departure from the Society was the fact that he had participated in the meeting which Nachtrieb had arranged. On the day after Nachtrieb's departure Lemmix also received two hundred dollars as a donation from George Rapp, the same amount Nachtrieb had received, and signed a statement containing almost the identical wording of that Nachtrieb had signed. The arguments and the evidence presented in his case in the Circuit Court of the United States for the Western District of Pennsylvania parallel those in the Nachtrieb case, only it seems that the Society presented better and more conclusive evidence that he had been interested in leaving the Society before matters came to a climax by his participation in the Legionville Run conference. On February 7, 1855, R. L. Baker received the opinion of the U. S. District Court in Pittsburgh, which was in favor of the Harmony Society "with costs." No appeal was made in this case.

The Society did not have to put up with the trouble and delay in the Supreme Court which had caused Baker so much irritation in the years that had passed. The case was argued on December 5, 1856, and decided very simply on the basis of Nachtrieb's signed receipt on December 16 of the same year. The validity of the agreements of the Society and the circumstances which led to the "voluntary withdrawal" of Joshua Nachtrieb were not discussed at length in the opinion. Although Judge Grier, who had rendered the decision in favor of Nachtrieb, was now a member of the Supreme Court, he was reversed. Whereas in Pittsburgh the weight of public opinion was probably a factor working in favor of Joshua Nachtrieb, the situation in Washington was such as to be distinctly in favor of the Harmony Society as an influential political and big business organization. This view inevitably forces itself upon the reader of Baker's letters to Jacob Henrici, written from Washington while he was attending the hearings before the Supreme Court. Apart from the important light which they shed upon the powerful influence of the Society in the circles of the mighty of the nation, the letters provide a very interesting picture of life in Washington one hundred years ago.

Baker's first Washington letter is dated November 30, 1856. He had found comfortable quarters in Willard's Hotel on Pennsylvania Avenue "between the house of the President and the Capitol." On the day of his arrival he took a hack and drove around to see the "President's House, Treasury Buildings, Patent Office, Post Office Department, Capitol, Smithsonian Institution, Congress Burying ground, Washington's Monument etc." He was impressed with this evidence of a rich and mighty nation "to which we also externally belong, and in which we therefore participate as citizens. The beautiful works testify to the greatness of man in his fallen state, what will he first become when he has been elevated from the Fall and united with God and will apply his strength and talents to the honor of God and the welfare of man!"

The next day brought a visit to the halls of the Senate and Congress and meetings with the following old acquaintances: Senator Trumbull of Alton, Ill., Senator Wade of Ashtabula, Ohio, Mr. Bingham, Member of Congress from Cadiz, Ohio, "and nephew of our old friend," Mr. Horton, Member of Congress from Pomroy, Ohio, "Partner in Law of W. Forward during our revolution 1832," Purviance of Butler, Mr. Ritchy of Pittsburgh, Martin of Westmoreland, and John Allison, all Members of Congress, Col. R. L. Baker, Captain Sanders, and Major Grisp, "these three former residents of Pittsburgh," Mr. Rockwell, a brother of the President of the Cleveland and Pittsburgh Railroad, General Quitman, "who distinguished himself in the war with Mexico is also a Member of Congress and an old friend of Mr. Loomis" (attorney of the Society in the Nachtrieb case). On the second of December Baker attended the first full session of the Supreme Court and witnessed the disposal of three cases.

When I see Judge Grier and lawyer Stanton I feel the spirit of the dragon on 1832, as also of the dark night of April 2, 1833 and the scenes that followed in Beaver Court 21 years ago in 1835, which spirit again expressed itself strongly in the years 1852 and 1853, when the testimony for Nachtrieb's suit was taken. With all my confidence to God a deep worry and concern fills my heart which is like the 22nd Psalm, verses 3. 4. 5. 6. 12. 13. 14. 17. 20. 21. 22. These verses are now really being fulfilled, so that as the halls of the court houses of Beaver and Pittsburgh resounded loudly about us, so the halls of the Supreme Court of the U S. will resound about us, whether the outcome at present be favorable or unfavorable for us we commend to God.

On December 4th Baker reported the opening arguments on their case and stated that it would require four of the seven to concur to reverse the judgment of the court below. Two of the nine judges apparently took no part in the decision, so Baker was much concerned because one of the seven had become sick. After court Baker was busy renewing old friendships and making new ones. He mentioned Ex-Gov. Bigler, Senator Lewis Cass of Pennsylvania, Mason of Virginia, Captain Nailer of Mexico memory, Isaac Blackford "former judge in Indiana and now judge in the Court of Claims, an old friend, he is the man who corrected the English translation of Father's paper on the Wabash," [*Thoughts on the Destiny of Man* (New Harmony, 1824)] Col. Wooley, formerly of Pittsburgh, Mr. Dick, Member of Congress from Meadville, "who told me that Judge Baldwin's only son was in the Patent Office, where I visited him today," Mr. Campbell, P. M. General, First Assistant P. M. General King, Mr. Offitt, Chief Clerk in the Auditor's Office, Attorney General Cushing, etc.

Baker's report of December 4, the day of the concluding arguments, was very confident, with only a worry about the fact that the number of the judges to decide the case was *seven,* a number about which he had some mystic misgivings. He was well pleased with the performance of his attorney, Mr. Loomis, especially when he came to speak about the character of George and Frederick Rapp, the Harmony Society in general, and that of "R. L. B." Mr. Stanberry, another of his attorneys, also was greatly pleased with Mr. Loomis and assured Baker that "the Court is on our side" and added that he was "very intimate with Justice McLean." Baker expressed his surprise at the presence in Washington of so many of their friends and remarked that their old law friends, Judge Blackford and John Allison, attended the hearings together with other members of Congress. "According to my present feelings I sense victory, but I wish that our good friends in Economy would not cease praying and imploring God the Almighty—as I myself do—that he might turn our disgrace from the honest founder and His Congregation and lay it upon the heads of the scorners." With such a victory, he felt, Gertrude Rapp would be moved to compose a beautiful symphony on the 18th Psalm, because it showed that David even 3000 years ago had prepared a verdict for the Harmony Society which would then be in agreement with that of the Supreme Court. To this symphony Henrici would sing the *Primo* and "Paulina" the *Secondo* while he and many happy members would make up the audience.

The most interesting of all the Washington letters is that of December 7 in which Baker reported how he spent his Sunday. First the old legal friend of the Society, Judge Blackford, took Baker to a church, where he was greatly impressed by the refinement of the audience and the form of service. After church the Judge took him to dinner at his private boarding house, where he dined "with Justice McLean and Lady," one of the seven to decide the Nachtrieb case the next day, and Mr. Allison, another old legal friend. "It was really a refined social gathering," he wrote, "quite a few things were said about us and I had an opportunity to explain our principles. After dinner I spent another hour with the two judges and Allison—later another hour with Blackford and Allison alone, where we talked about old and new things." He concluded this letter with the remark that his lawyers did not want him to leave yet because his presence was valuable. He also found that it was better for them that he was there alone and not in the company of another Harmonist because everything was in such high style that he himself did not really know how to behave. In his letter of December 8 Baker reported the departure of his attorney Stanberry and that he had given him a check, presumably for one thousand dollars, for in the same line he added: "If we win he still gets $1000. If we lose, then he is paid." Loomis remained to visit friends and to find out the sense of the Court, while Stanberry was sure the decision of the lower court would be reversed. On the following day Baker was also taken to the President's "Levee" by an old acquaintance, Mr. Whittlesay, the first controller of the U. S. Treasury, and presented to "President Pierce and Lady."

The rest of the story of the Nachtrieb case was told in Baker's letter to Henry Stanberry of January 5, 1857, in which, immediately after his statement that he was enclosing the check for one thousand dollars on the Bank of Pittsburgh Baker added the note marked "Confidential": "After you had left Washington the Court held their consultation as we were told on Monday the 8th. Mr. Loomis in his modesty could not approach any one for information. But on Tuesday on his way to dinner was overtaken by Justice Grier, who had the frankness to tell him that he had been reversed in the Nachtrieb Case."[3] Baker stated that they had received the printed opinion a few days previously through the politeness of the Honorable John Allison, the Member of Congress from their district. The decision "is just what we wanted, and I do hope this decree will put a stop to all those dishonest and restless excitements and expectations of our enemies." Baker's only concern in this letter was quick action "to look to Nachtrieb's bail for costs without losing more time."

The Harmony Society had won a victory over one of its former most loyal members, whose study of the Bible, not unlike Luther, had led him to new truths, but the financial cost of that victory alone was from five to ten times higher than the amount he had humbly requested as a present or even a loan in his letter of September 19, 1847. No person could possibly read the reasonable and Christian letters of Joshua Nachtrieb before and even during the trial and not feel that in this reversal of the verdict of the lower court a great social and legal injustice was committed.

Like George Rapp, R. L. Baker knew the noblest passages and commandments of the Bible backwards and forwards, but when it was a question of applying these in his dealings with former Harmonists who had signed the legal paper of withdrawal from membership, then his otherwise clear judgment was completely blinded by a furious hatred which was all the greater because his Bible told him that he was now dealing with the worst kind of enemies that the Bride of Christ could possibly face, namely, backsliders—men who had belonged to the elect and had fallen from grace. To Rapp's and Baker's way of thinking any Harmonist who had once put his hand to the plow and looked back was no longer worthy of the Kingdom of Heaven. "And Jesus said unto him, No man, having put his hand to the plough, and looking back, is fit for the kingdom of God." (Luke 9: 62)

Whosoever transgresseth, and abideth not in the doctrine of Christ, hath not God. He that abideth in the doctrine of Christ, he hath both the Father and the Son.

If there come any unto you, and bring not this doctrine, receive him not into your house, neither bid him God speed;

For he that biddeth him God speed is partaker of his evil deeds. 2 John: 9–11.

4

From Communal Work to
Communal Investments

THE TWO DECADES FROM GEORGE RAPP'S DEATH TO R. L. BAKER'S
death (1847–1868: from the founding of Brook Farm, influenced by the Harmony Society, and the writing of the Communist Manifesto to the first commercial use of the Sholes
typewriter) mark a rapid change from communal work to communal investment, and also the period of the Society's greatest
material prosperity. Contrary to a frequently noted trend in
history, this period of highest material prosperity is also marked
by an equal religious and spiritual fortitude. Material prosperity at best was an uncalculated byproduct or accident of the
old policy of seeking first the kingdom of God and its righteousness, and it was always received as a gift of the Giver of
all things. Least of all was this prosperity the result of any
carefully designed application of "Weltweisheit" (worldly
wisdom), but the result of many internal and external influ-
ences and factors. The period under discussion is full of national and international tensions. Within America the frontier
phase of history, which because of communal problems incident
to the opening of primitive areas to civilization was more favorable then to a communist economy, had moved far westward
and the new communist groups like the Amanaists, the Mor-
mons, the Hutterites, and the followers of Pastor Keil had
accordingly settled in Iowa, Utah, the Dakotas, and Oregon.
The exhortation to young men to go west applied also to
the newly arrived or newly organized Christian communist
churches. Above all, the membership of the Harmony Society

during this period not only aged considerably but declined from a total of 288 in 1847 to 146 in 1866, the last census available before Baker's death.

On the first of March, 1862, R. L. Baker wrote his co-trustee Henrici:

Yesterday noon David Kant died quietly and peacefully. He is the last family father of the earlier migration, a loyal member, a firm disciple of Father Rapp and of the congregation in general. His death brings to an end the roll of the old, honorable fathers of the Harmony Society in this world. They as he, and he as they enjoyed little here, but they suffered a lot, showed a great deal of love, and accomplished a great deal. May their fine example remain as model before the eyes of those who have remained behind so that they also may live in their virtues and also end as he did, namely in the faith of the Son of God who showed us such great love.

But not only the old timers were being called to their eternal reward; the number of virile young men was rapidly declining. When the Civil War draft came, only five members of the Society were of eligible fighting age, and that was not because the others were too young. Since the law at this time allowed hiring substitutes at as low a figure as $250, however, the Society did not suffer any loss in manpower from this cause. The years were beginning to tell even on the second generation of Harmonists not only in declining physical strength but in increased income from the investments made by the Society during the time of its youthful vigor. The returns from the investments resulting from the communal labor of their hands were then communally put to work just as are the dollars of contemporary capitalists who dwell within an individualistic system. Communal work had been, or was rapidly being, succeeded by communal investments. This transition was noticed, as mentioned above, by the former friend and close collaborator of Karl Marx himself, the then internationally famous Wilhelm Weitling.

To what sort of a development was Weitling referring when he said that the stocks of the Harmonists paid more than their work? An examination of the Society records—incomplete as they are—shows that during these two decades their trustees began to spend more time than before acting as salesmen on

the road, attending to lawsuits, collecting bad debts in places
as distant as Texas, and taking care of their financial affairs
outside the limits of Economy. A voluminous correspondence
developed between Jacob Henrici and R. L. Baker, and between Baker and Jonathan Lenz as each followed the growth of
the Harmonist capitalist empire. They went to Pittsburgh and
New York to attend board meetings with great individualistic
capitalists, to Chicago and Cleveland to break into the coal
trade there, and to the Tidioute area in order to become firmly
established in America's youngest, most promising, most com-
petitive, and most dangerous industry—oil. At home agricultural pursuits continued to occupy the simple folk, keeping
them happy raising chickens, picking apples, and making jam,
or planting wheat and similar crops, and keeping up the vege-
table and flower gardens, but even this was more and more
turned over to hired labor. The farms were rented out on
shares and there was quite a bit of business in cattle, because
these activities always kept down the amount of money spent
and were the best ways of getting returns on the land they held.
The making of woolen and cotton fabrics had been discontinued by 1864, when R. L. Baker wrote to the Amana Society[1]
intending to buy the supplies the Harmonists would need from
them. He explained that they had given up manufacture, lacking workers because so many of their members were too old
and had died. They had decided that they would prefer buying
clothes to hiring strangers to manufacture for them, "for the
Lord Jesus says: 'He that is not with me, is against me; and he
that gathereth not with me scattereth abroad.' (Matt. 12:30;
Luke 11:23) On this account and also because we have heard
that in Amana you are carrying on more manufacture than in
Ebenezer, we wanted to request you to send us some patterns
. . . with cash whole sale rates." As further reason for this order
he stated that goods now available in the cities were usually
made for the purpose of "swindle, sale, and fashion" and that
at Amana they expected to find a more durable and honest
product. Baker's letter also gave a brief description of the Society at that time, consisting of "200 souls who carry on the
communal work and celibacy, according to the first plan and
our conviction. We have no descendants and the spirit of the

times with its wild freedom and selfishness is so strange and
hostile to the communal spirit that it does not produce any
worthwhile persons upon whom we could depend. Hence our
decline."

Several years before these manufacturing industries were
given up, the Society had ceased to make silk, an industry in
which it had pioneered in the United States but which proved
to be unprofitable, as cheap labor within the Society ceased to
exist. Rye and other types of whiskey, wines, and beer continued to be made, but in quantities which diminished as
rapidly as the membership became incapacitated or died. The
prices quoted to Dr. C. Secret of Milford, Illinois, and to J.
Bristol of Xenia, Ohio, on May 15, 1858, would bring tears
of longing for the good old days to the eyes of any American
scholar and gentleman:

Pure Rye whiskey 3 year old @ $1.00 per gallon by the Bbl.
Pure Rye whiskey very old $6.00 for 12 bottles boxed.

Pure old apple brandy cost no more than very old rye, and
each bottle was approximately the size of the post World War II
fifth. This price was the delivered price, and the whiskey made
by these deeply religious celibates then had a national reputation which now would equal that of the famous products of the
Benedictine monks or of the monasteries at Etal and Andex,
where beer is still brewed under the crucifix.

Beginning with the year 1850, the Society began to invest
more and more in the development of the railroads of this
country. Soon thereafter, Henrici became director of the Darlington Cannel Coal Rail Road Company, and on November 1,
1853, the Harmony Society offered to furnish two hundred
thousand dollars for the purchase of income bonds of the Ohio
and Pennsylvania Railroad at seven percent, free of taxes. "The
money is ready at Economy in English sovereigns," they wrote,
since they preferred to make payment at Economy, but only on
condition that they would get as favorable a rate as they could
get in New York City. The Society had been of special assistance in the construction of this road. In 1856 Henrici had
added to his many other duties the Presidency of the Little Saw
Mill Run Rail Road, which really belonged to the Harmony
Society. In light of Henrici's particularly strong chiliastic and

ascetic views it seems especially strange that he rather than R. L. Baker should have been the Society's specialist in railroad affairs. But even this involvement in railroad construction work had its religious motivation. Henrici and Baker were no more shaken in their chiliastic hopes by modern technical development than Father Rapp had been, for like Rapp they saw in all technical development the hand of God, who was using these means to advance His plan of ultimate restoration of harmony (Harmonie) and unity throughout the world.

The following letter written by Baker and Henrici on November 21, 1851 to the President of the Ohio and Pennsylvania Railroad, General Wm. Robinson, reveals their millennial thinking:

Your kind offer for giving a Rail Road ride to our people has been so far accepted and enjoyed that three companies each male and female of about twenty in number have visited Pittsburgh and New Brighton and were much delighted with the enterprise, which was carried to completion in so short a time for the public good, (if it should interfere somewhat with private comforts). Please accept our thanks for your friendly offices!

Rail Roads!

A fair commencement of the fulfilling of the following prophecy, Isaiah 40:4.

"Valleys shall be exalted"
"Mountains and Hills brought low"
"The crooked made straight"
"and the rough places plain"

To what a degree chiliasm permeated all of Henrici's thinking is also illustrated in a letter written to Baker from New York in which he reported a visit to the "gigantic ship" Great Western.

The same is built entirely of iron and carries 25,000 tons, is almost 700 feet in length and from 80 to 120 wide and could carry 10,000 soldiers or 4000 passengers overseas. When one observes the magnificence of the entire structure, its tremendous steam engines and besides the outer majestic, giant size also the inner wonderful construction, where everything is so powerfully and well assembled that practically not a drop runs through, . . . when one considers and admires all this, one cannot help but consider that this wonderful gigantic work with its entire splendor and magnificence had to exist first in finished and completed form in the mind of a fallen man, before it could be started. Who would not be compelled at such a sight to think of the greatness of man who can produce such miraculous works even now in his low, fallen state? What will he be able to accomplish then when he has been restored to his original dignity and when he will apply his sanctified and practiced powers of creation for the honor and glory of God his Savior and to the welfare and pleasure of his beloved fraternal family (Bruderfamilie).

With such an attitude toward technology it is not at all surprising that Henrici, even after Baker's death, continued to invest Society funds very heavily in the construction of other railroads. This is best shown by the participation of the Harmony Society in the construction of the Pittsburgh and Lake Erie Rail Road, of which Henrici became president, and of its subsidiary, The Pittsburgh, Chartiers & Youghiogheny Railway. The building of these roads, for which the Harmony Society was very largely responsible, was of invaluable importance to the industrial development of the entire Pittsburgh area. To clarify the part played by the Society in these ventures it becomes necessary to carry this narrative chronologically beyond the period covered by the Baker-Henrici trusteeship.

Because the transportation conditions in Pittsburgh and the Pittsburgh area prior to 1876 were so inadequate that the business and industrial development of the area was being retarded, a committee of representative Pittsburghers was created in 1874 to promote the building of a railroad with a view to bringing much needed relief. Their first plan failed because of lack of support given by the Baltimore and Ohio Company. Two years later another committee was created by Pittsburgh interests for the specific purpose of promoting the building of a line of railroad from Pittsburgh to Youngstown, in order to connect at this point with the Lake Shore & Michigan Southern Railway (later the New York Central) and the Atlantic & Great Western Railway (later the Erie), both of which roads had lines extending to the Great Lakes as well as through lines between New York and Chicago. As a result an interesting prospectus was published on December 21, 1876, setting forth the reasons why the Pittsburgh & Lake Erie Railroad should be built. It read in part:

The estimated cost of the Pittsburgh & Lake Erie railroad for the line complete is $4,000,000; $2,000,000 of stock and a like amount of bonds. We believe it will be more profitable than our best bank stocks. But what is of vastly more importance to us all is the great want supplied to our suffering business. With rents reduced, houses empty, mills idle, and our strongest firms struggling against the low freights given to other cities and the exorbitant freights taken from us, this becomes of paramount importance. Let it be built at once. Then let every manufacturer, merchant, real estate owner, capitalist, clerk, mechanic and laboring man join in this most important work. If you cannot subscribe much, subscribe a little. Let us again call your attention to the fact that this is not a "branch", with its business yet to be made, but a link in a great main line with the business already made awaiting its completion.

In the construction of this important railroad line the Harmony Society was a most important factor. Much of the land through which the road was to pass belonged to the Society. It not only most generously granted free right-of-way through its lands, saving the venture large sums of money, but subscribed to $650,000 worth of the company's stocks and bonds. The Harmony Society also took an active part in the affairs of the Lake Erie Railroad, and was, during its early struggles, its real backbone. Jonathan Lenz, then Henrici's fellow-trustee, took great interest in the construction of the road. It took tremendous effort on the part of the first directors to get the road under way, and when the first pay day after construction had begun came around, the directors found they could not raise enough money to pay their men. They consulted with Jacob Henrici, who then saved the day. It will be remembered that Henrici had been George Rapp's trusted agent and assistant at the time he was determined to collect and bury the fund which he believed he should have on hand as part of his preparation for the Second Coming of Christ. Henrici would not have touched this religious fund without the inner conviction that the building of this railroad was another link in the chain of events which would bring on the glorious day when man would be restored to the original image in which God had created him. Accordingly, Henrici had the money which Father Rapp had buried for that special purpose brought up to the directors' meeting in the Monongehela House. The boxes containing the money were emptied of their contents in the center of the room, forming a large pile of silver, all of which had to be cleaned before it could be put back into circulation. From January 12, 1881, to January 14, 1884, Henrici was president of the railroad the Harmonists had helped build by their investments, but the obligations of his office were very hard on him. On January 14, 1884, the Vanderbilts took over the railroad and the Harmony Society sold its interests to the new owners for $1,150,000.

The Society also, as stated above, was the main power in the building of the Pittsburgh, Chartiers and Youghiogheny Railway, in which they owned the controlling interest until, early in the 1890s, they sold their shares. This subsidiary line of the Pittsburgh & Lake Erie extended from McKees Rocks and Neville Island, through Carnegie, to coal fields southwest of Carnegie. Although a short line, it was of much importance to the Pittsburgh district because of its strategic position and because of the great industrial development which followed along its line of road. Control of the road passed into the hands of the Pennsylvania Railroad. Aside from its interests in these main railroad developments, the Society helped finance and further the development of a railroad from Ann Arbor to Caseville, Michigan, where it was interested in the development of colony lands which it owned. All this is such a vast and involved part of the Society's history that a book could be written on this phase alone, based upon the railroad records of the Harmony Society.

The Harmony Society had always been interested in the availability of coal whenever it considered moving, but it did not seriously go into the coal business until 1849, when it engaged a prospector to search for coal in lands which it held. Several years later it entered vigorously into the coal business at Cannelton and Darlington, and by 1859 the Society was the owner and worker of the principal coal mines near Darlington, Pa. By special agreement with the President of the Cleveland

and Pennsylvania Railroad, a friend of the Society, coal was shipped and sold in Chicago and Cleveland. Henrici began visiting the gas companies in the principal eastern cities to persuade them that "Extra Economy Cannel Coal" was better and cheaper for their purpose than the coal they were then importing from England. He proved to be an excellent salesman and obtained orders and endorsements from Cleveland, Albany, Buffalo, and even New York. During all these travels he reported regularly to the Society back home, and while the letters are full of reports of his business transactions, the dominant concern of all his thinking remained the longing for Christ's return in order that man might be returned to the original perfection in which God had created him and from which he had so miserably fallen. Whenever it was possible to visit a community or a church which promised to present some religious teachings like those preached by Father Rapp, Henrici used the opportunity to go there and would give a full report of his experience to the brethren back home. Scarcely could a young bridegroom love his bride more or show more concern for her than did Jacob Henrici, the builder of railroads, love his Lord and long for union with Him.

While the building of railroads and the mining of coal were an important source of income to the Harmonists during the Baker-Henrici trusteeship, these business interests were surpassed by their pioneer work in the American oil industry. They not only were among the very first to drill for oil, but they also pioneered in the refining of oil and in laying an oil pipe line.

The story of the beginnings of the American oil industry has been treated almost exhaustively by Professor Paul H. Giddens in four books on the subject, but beyond one rare photograph of the Economy Oil Wells—with a brief statement that during 1868 the society sold about 100,000 barrels of oil and drilled seventy-six wells between 1860 and 1873, the largest of which produced 250 barrels a day, and with four bibliographical references, one giving the capacity of the Economy oil refineries—the contribution of the Harmonists as pioneers of the American oil industry is passed over. It is unfortunate that the voluminous records of the Economy Oil Company in the Harmony Society remained hidden from this extensive research on such an important chapter of American industrial history, for the reports of the Society's manager Merkle and engineer Henning and the letters of Henrici, Baker, and Lenz on the subject would have stood in interesting contrast to the turbulence and greed found there. It must be left to a later period to give as full an account of the Economy Oil Company as the records in the Harmony Society Archives justify, but within the limited space of this history the story must be summarized. Because this story is not yet free from controversy, the following account, which well illustrates the business acumen of the Harmonists, closely follows in detail an official statement on the subject published by Baker and Henrici, a statement supported by many affidavits of noted Pennsylvanians of the time.

Situated on the eastern side of the Allegheny river, and partly opposite Tidioute in Warren county, Pennsylvania, there was a large body of land consisting of eleven tracts, containing in all upwards of twelve thousand acres and reaching down the river between seven and eight miles, the lower end reaching into Venango County. The tracts were patented in 1798, by George Mead, and conveyed to Walter Grossett, of Stockholm, Sweden, who devised them to his daughter, Mrs. De Kantzow, of Berlin, Prussia, who by her agent B. R. Brandford, Esq., of New Brighton, Beaver County, Pa., in 1850, by articles of agreement, sold nine thousand acres, consisting of all that remained unsold, or was not in possession of squatters. Brandford agreed to assign all unpaid balances on former sales to William Davidson, of East Bridgewater, in said County of Beaver, for the sum of eight thousand five hundred dollars, if paid within four months, or nine thousand dollars, if paid within a year from date of agreement.

Mr. Davidson, who was at that time with comparatively small means, carrying on a large business in Beaver County, with his flour and saw mills, and who had not long before suffered heavy damage by fire, was in somewhat embarrassed circumstances, but by mortgaging his real estate and in other ways, he succeeded in raising the money within the appointed time, and conveyances of the nine thousand acres were made to him, and also all balances of former sales assigned to him.

Before his purchase, all the good land in the three river tracts had been purchased by others, or settled upon by squatters, who surveyed their pieces out of the tracts as pleased themselves, and left the residue in illshaped remnants. Furthermore, during the fifty-two years that the land belonged to the absent owners, nearly all the valuable timber, convenient to the river, had been taken off by squatters, under pretended settlement rights, or by trespassers.

Three of the tracts were river tracts and eight were hill tracts. Number 5277, the uppermost river tract, commenced about a mile above and extended down opposite Tidioute and was in 1852 divided into four pieces, as follows: one hundred and twelve acres had been conveyed to Henry Magee; one hundred and fifty-nine acres, improved and considered the best part of the tract because the only suitable place for depositing and rafting the timber of the best back tracts, to John Magee; and six hundred acres to Wm. Davidson, together with the unpaid balances on the Magee pieces. The six hunderd acres had been stripped of all valuable timber; were rough, hilly, and unimproved, and were considered the refuse of the tract, but after 1861 these became the seat of the Economy oil wells. The lower end of the tract was owned by W. S. Cohill.

In 1856 the Society bought the John Magee piece for twenty-one hundred dollars, and thus enabled him to pay his unpaid balance of purchase money to Mr. Davidson. In 1857, an action of ejectment was instituted by Hayden and others for the whole of No. 5277, on the strength of an old tax title.

About six hundred acres, the residue of the next river tract, No. 5278, conveyed to Davidson, was then held by a party who claimed it by virtue of an old tax title. The remnants of No. 5280, the lowest of the river tracts, were partly in Venango County. The parts of the two hill tracts nearest the river tracts, conveyed to Davidson, were in 1854 divided by him into several two-hundred-acre lots for himself and his sons, but four hundred and fifty acres of it, being the best-timbered parts, he afterwards sold to one John Ross.

Not having any timbered land left near the river, he had to look to the back tracts for reimbursement of the money paid by him for the large body of land, which had been in market more than half a century before he purchased it. He therefore made a road from the John Magee place through tract No. 5205 to 5206, which was well timbered, built a sawmill, and for a while carried it on successfully, and then sold the whole tract to John Ross, on time. The two other timbered tracts, Nos. 5204 and 5205, of eleven hundred acres each, and also the best-timbered part of No. 5208, he sold for cash.

In 1854 the Society bought from John Ross the mill tract No. 5206 for eight thousand dollars, and thereby enabled him to pay Davidson the purchase money he owed him, and about the same time the Society bought from Davidson tract No. 5222, the next back of 5206, and paid him six thousand dollars for it. It was considered the best timbered of the eleven tracts. The Society purchases of the De Kantzow lands that had been conveyed to Davidson, including the one hundred and sixty acres of John Magee, amounted to sixteen thousand dollars, cash. Thus Davidson, within three-and-a-half years after his purchase from De Kantzow, had realized in money a good deal more than all the land and his improvements had cost him, and had over four thousand acres left. That which he had left, except what he had laid off for himself and family, was worth but little, in fact was then almost valueless, scarcely worth the taxes.

About the time the Society made these purchases, Mr. Davidson took a lively interest in a joint stock glass manufacturing company just started in Bridgewater, Beaver County, Pa. Since it did not have sufficient working capital, this company applied to the Harmonists for aid, in the form of a subscription to stock and a loan, to both of which they agreed after a good deal of hesitation. Because the men running the company lacked the special knowledge and experience necessary for that peculiar branch of business, serious errors were made and the company was compelled to stop operations. Davidson and two other partners then bought out the stockholders and made a fresh start. Again the company got into trouble and Davidson bought out his partners and continued on his own, but within a year the business of the glass works had largely failed. The Society had meanwhile at various times furnished him considerable sums of money to aid him in his business, therefore he again approached the Society for financial aid, offering various securities which included real estate in Beaver, Warren, and Venango Counties. The Society made a written agreement with him by which it promised to furnish him the means needed to carry on his business, he to give the Society judgment notes to secure their advance. Soon after this some of those who had judgments against him lost patience with him and forced a Sheriff's sale. The Harmonists, by far his largest creditors, were willing to accept a proposition he made to his creditors to prevent the sale, but the other creditors would not agree to any time-extending arrangement. Before the sale of his dwelling house and mills, Mr. Davidson, against the advice of the Society, left for Missouri, and was absent at the time of the sale. At his son's request the Harmonists redeemed the dwelling-house, accepting his guarantee that he would repay the money they gave for it, and in this way a home was secured to the family. Other assistance was also given to help the family in its distress.

Because nobody would bid any higher, the six hundred acres in Venango County were bid off for the Society by its attorney at what they considered below their value, but that purchase, if considered cheap, was overbalanced by what they paid for the six hundred acres of tract No. 5278, of which they never got possession and which they conveyed to Mr. Davidson for but a nominal consideration. The Society obtained the depreciated, ill-shaped remnants of Davidson's land in Warren County by bidding more per acre than Davidson had previously paid per acre for the whole body with its fine timbered lands.

After everything was sold a large number of debts remained unsatisfied and without any reasonable prospect of ever being paid, unless Mr. Davidson should be started in some business that he was known to be fully competent to manage. Accordingly, some of his sympathizing creditor friends in Pittsburgh proposed to furnish him all the machinery necessary for a good saw and shingle mill if the Harmonists would give a site for it on the Big Beaver Creek on property of his that they had purchased at Sheriff's sale. Since they knew from experience that a sawmill at that place would not be profitable, they offered to build a new sawmill on the Ross tract, in Warren County, which the Davidson family might carry on for a certain share of the lumber and shingles, while they would also employ him to take care of their Warren County property and give him a liberal percentage on sales of land he might make for them. His family expressed an unwillingness to move to such a rough, cold country, so the Society granted the site on the Big Beaver at first cost, on easy terms of payment. Although the Society bought timber for stocking it, which they sawed on terms proposed by themselves, they did no better than the Society had expected and could not do much more than make a living.

It was in December 1857 that Colonel E. L. Drake visited lands of the Pennsylvania Rock Oil Company on Oil Creek near Titusville and began drilling for oil. After nineteen months he finally struck oil at sixty-nine feet on August 27, 1859. This was the first time that petroleum had been tapped at its source and gave the first proof of the existence of oil reservoirs within the earth's surface. It was also the first time that pipe driven to bedrock was used to prevent the filling of the hole. Only a few months after this, soon after the first discoveries of rock oil had been made, the attention of some parties at Tidioute was attracted to a small oil spring on the shore of the Harmonists' river tract, No. 5277, and they concocted a plan by which they expected to purchase that tract from the Society at a very low figure, under cunningly invented misrepresentations, and they appointed two of their party, well fitted for such a business, to visit the Trustees. Fortunately for the Society, however, Mr. Michael Merkle, a German friend and relative of the Society, to whom they had sold a piece of land in order to have someone in whom they could confide on the spot to look to their interests, happened to discover the scheme almost as soon as it was formed, and by mail informed the Society of it in time to defeat it.

In the early part of the summer of the same year some good oil wells were struck immediately below their tract, which created great excitement, and many persons wanted to buy or lease from them; if it had not been for a pending lawsuit they would probably have either sold or leased.

In 1857, soon after they had purchased the John Magee piece for $2,100, one Hayden instituted a suit for the whole of No. 5277, including the two Magee pieces, the Davidson six hundred acres they had bought at Sheriff's sale, and the lower corner owned by Cohill. The plaintiff had raked up an old tax title, but although it was without legality or merit, an effort was made under this title to force the Society to compromise, which they refused. And until there was a decision in their favor, they decided to neither sell nor lease.

If oil had not been discovered, it is questionable whether the case would ever have been brought to trial. During the summer of 1860 the Society collected all necessary testimony and the case was put down for trial at the September term of that year. When the court met, the Society was ready and pressed for a trial, but their opponents had it continued. The Society then immediately took actual possession of the tract, located wells in five different places on it, made contracts for drilling them, and engaged hands for a vigorous development of the property.

The first two wells were total failures; the third had a pretty good show of oil but finally proved to be nearly worthless. After about three months' hard labor, and the expenditure of a large amount of money, they had for it only about one dozen barrels of oil. The prospect of success was gloomy enough, but they hoped and worked on, and unexpectedly, at a depth of about one hundred feet, the tools struck a large crevice, sank some eight or ten inches, and in a few moments large quantities of oil and water were thrown high up in a continuous stream, showing that a flowing well had indeed been struck.

Because the deep, large, flowing wells of Oil Creek had not yet been discovered, the Society's well attracted great attention, and many visited it who wonderfully overrated its production. Only about six percent of what it threw up was oil; the rest was salt water. The oil being of excellent quality, the flow constant, and the price at that time good, the well soon became an object of special attention to those interested against the Society in the lawsuit. They paid the Harmonists frequent visits and frequently asked how soon they would give up the well to them. The invariable reply was, whenever they convinced them that their right to it was better than that of the Society.

This well flowed constantly for about six months, the oil

not varying in quality but decreasing in quantity; then it stopped, and would flow only periodically. At the end of nine months it wholly ceased flowing, and the only recourse was to pump it.

In December 1860, the plaintiffs in the suit entered a rule to choose arbitrators, and in January 1861, the arbitrators having been chosen, the case was tried before them. The majority found against the Society, from which it appealed. When in the following summer the case was tried in court, the Society won without difficulty.

A still well, which they had sunk near their oil spring about the time they struck the flowing well and which had made but a poor show, was not pumped until February. After it was pumped awhile it proved to be a very good well and continued to be a good producer for more than six years. During the spring of 1861 the Harmonists continued drilling until they had finished eight holes, four of which were failures and four good shallow wells, not more than one-hunderd-and-fifty feet in depth.

From the beginning of the Society's oil operations, either Henrici or Lenz, an excellent mechanic and later fellow-trustee with Henrici, was nearly always present. Henrici had acquired a good deal of experience in the oil business from his connection with the Cannel coal oil works, in which the Society had a large interest. These two superintended, directed, and with head and hand aided in the successful prosecution of the new undertaking. The Society always had good mechanics in its employ and at this time they were also enjoying the services of B. C. Henning, who had been educated by the Society and who had served his apprenticeship with them. He was the chief engineer at the wells and later put in their pipeline.

The Harmonists began their work in the Pennsylvania oil region in a perfect wilderness, with not a square foot of improvement on the whole six hundred acres of land. In March 1862, eighteen months from their beginning, they had four good wells, had erected a number of buildings, had three good engines, and had made roads and constructed wharves, had a cooper shop, a blacksmith shop, a carpenter shop, and all necessary tools, also a large stock of dry firewood for the engines and several thousand barrels in which to send their oil to market.

About fifteen months after they had struck their first good well—and were convinced by the result of the lawsuit in their favor and the testimony they produced on the trial that they held a good title, and after they also had everything at the wells in the best working order, they consulted together and agreed among themselves that, although under no obligation, they would do something for Mr. Davidson and his family and creditors. From the beginning of their oil operations they had employed Mr. Davidson, who was then out of business, and his son William, but they wanted to give him another opportunity to make a strong financial comeback.

Mr. Davidson at the time was unable to do business in his own name because of the many unsatisfied judgments hanging over him. Therefore, in pursuance of their determination, the Harmonists gave what they considered and what was in fact a very liberal lease to William, his eldest son, who had borne himself honorably toward his parents in their affliction. Under the lease, they put him in possession of all their wells, engines, dwelling houses, shops, tools, barrels, fire wood, and so on, and furnished him with the money necessary to commence business. He was to pay them in their own barrels at the wells one-fourth of the oil produced. The lease was for a term of years, with a proviso that either party could terminate it upon three months' notice to the other.

At the beginning under the lease the price of oil was low, but it soon went up, and the business was profitable. By agreement, outside the lease, the money realized by the lessee under the lease was to be applied, first to the support of the family, then to the redemption of the homestead in Beaver County and to payment of what was still due on the saw and shingle mill to the Pittsburgh creditors who had furnished the machinery, and to payment of the note William had given the Society for various items, and then to other debts, the total of which amounted to $35,000. Through the kindness of this lease Davidson was enabled to pay all his debts and free himself from all pecuniary liabilities. After this had been accomplished the Harmonists began, on behalf of Davidson and family, to invest their share of the proceeds of the oil in United States Five

Twenty Bonds. When the lease under notice had nearly expired, the Society had for him in its possession $40,000 in such bonds and offered to extend the lease three months longer, but the Davidsons refused to accept the extension and proposed another plan. This convinced the Harmonists that there was something brewing among them that they did not consider right, after the substantial proofs of friendship they had shown them.

Upon investigation, the Harmonists learned that the Davidsons had determined to deny their right to the property and forcibly withhold possession from them. They then immediately resolved to institute legal proceedings to regain possession, but some of Davidson's friends, when they learned the true state of the case, advised them to arrange the matter peaceably. Because the Society held the $40,000 in bonds in its hands for the faithful fulfillment of the conditions of the lease, one of which was, that at its termination peaceable possession of all the premises leased was to be delivered to the Society, it had full indemnity if legal measures were resorted to, which could not result otherwise than in the Society's favor. Through the persuasion of mutual friends the Society offered to let Mr. Davidson have a lease of the property for six months, on the same terms his son had had. This offer he gladly accepted, and executed and delivered to the Society a release of any supposed right or interest he professed to have in the property, which release the Society placed on record in Warren County. At the expiration of the new lease, he gave the Society peaceable possession of the property, and withdrew to Beaver County, with an additional sum of at least $40,000, cleared during the six months of that lease. Thus, in about twenty-seven months, Mr. Davidson was freed from his debts, amounting to over $35,000, and was, with his family, after a state of near destitution, in possession of about $80,000 in United States Bonds and money, besides much valuable property. But during the twenty-seven months that the Davidsons had leases of the Harmony Society property, although they had promised to sink new wells, not a well and not a gallon of oil was added to what the Harmonists had already developed.

In the entire Davidson account there is no mention of the

amount the Society made during this period out of the Economy Oil Company. To determine that total would require an exhaustive study of the records of the Economy Oil Company in the Harmony Society Archives, a project not within the scope of this history. Nevertheless, from the figures given for Davidson some conclusions can safely be drawn as to the income derived by the Society during this period. It is characteristic of the Society's ideals that it acted as it did toward Davidson, just as the following declaration in their statement is characteristic of their attitude toward their wealth:

We scarcely made cost and interest out of all his (Davidson's) real estate purchased by us in Beaver County, and out of the glass and glasshouse made less, and lost all our time, labor and trouble. Nothing that we purchased at Sheriff's sale, that was once his, has realized us any profit, except our oil tract; and that, we feel in duty bound to acknowledge, as a special gift from Him, who is the real and sole owner of the whole earth, and all that is therein and thereon, and who giveth when, to whom, and as much as He pleaseth.

It was He, the great author and giver of all good, who led our simple-minded, honest German friend to discover the cunningly laid plan of certain speculators, through misrepresentations, to obtain our oil tract for a grossly inadequate price. It was He, who directed our minds, and guided our steps, when we located our wells at proper places, and has given us sufficient wisdom to adopt a policy in carrying on our oil operations, and in treating our wells and territory so as to make our oil works a source of blessing, profit, and pleasure to all who have worked honestly for, under, and with us.

The Economy oil wells were considered a model institution for other oil works in the oil region. Fortunes were invested all around them by companies and individuals without obtaining a barrel of oil. A great deal of oil territory around Tidioute, once considered better than that of the Society, was in a short time totally ruined by the way it was operated upon, so that Tidioute was for a while almost deserted, and might have remained so, notwithstanding the immense hidden treasures of oil that were developed there around 1866, had not its name, and to some extent its fame, been kept alive by the never-failing little Economite wells, whose product rated highest in the market on account of its quality, purity, and the good order in which it was prepared for sale.

From the "Correspondence of the Pittsburgh Commercial" the following account, published in the *Titusville Morning Herald* under date of August 14, 1867, is here reprinted as a contemporary account:

The finest oil field in this region belongs to our friends the Economites, and the country has reason to be glad that it is in the hands of men so prudent and far-seeing. Their lands are on the opposite side of the river from Tidioute; their possessions start from the shore and take in the hills for miles, and on their land are six producing wells; some of these have been yielding oil for six years; and show few signs of decay. So long as the injunctions and regulations of the present trustees of the society are in force, their territory will be an inexhaustable source of revenue and wealth. On these lands there are built most comfortable houses for the laborers and agents, and, as we might know, the warmest barns and stables for their horses and cattle; and even the pigs have rooms which would be a palace to an Irishman. Around these houses are neat, white picket fences, the cleanest gardens, shrubbery and vines. Thus our good friends carry order and comfort, plant the germs of good fruits and prosperity wherever they place their feet. Some persons whom I have met are under the impression that the Society retained these lands in violation of a covenant, made with the gentleman who owned them before they came into the present possession. But these lands were taken for debt due the Society long before oil discoveries, when they were thought to be valuable for timber only, and the Society paid much more than their then value. An investigation of the case on the ground has convinced me that the Society violated no pledge, and disappointed no just expectation—but dealt most magnanimously with Mr. Davidson, aiding him to escape from many entanglements which reverses and misfortunes had woven around him, and lifted him from poverty to comfort and affluence. Few men who experience disaster fall into hands equally generous.[3]

The truth of this report is substantiated not only by the evidence already presented but also by the instructive collection of photographs published by Paul Giddens in his volume *Early Days of Oil. A Pictorial History of the Beginnings of the Industry in Pennsylvania,* Princeton University Press, 1948. Nothing could give the reader a more vivid account of the sort of environment in which the Harmonists operated their oil business than this volume. Against all the wild boom activity, the operations of the Harmonists and the very appearance of their wells stood in great contrast. Preachers in the oil regions, who were having a difficult time making headway against the lively competition of gambling men, wicked women, and other ruthless individuals who would stop at nothing to get oil, were greatly cheered and comforted by the presence of the Economy Oil Company, whose religious silence, spread over their wells each Sunday, testified to and supported their cause.

As millennially minded Jacob Henrici was the Society's railroad genius, so he was the Society's big oil man. If it had not been for Henrici's fearless determination, R. L. Baker would surely have disposed of the Society's oil properties in 1864. On November 9, 1864, he received a threatening letter containing a "Minni Rifle" bullet from Venango County. It was not the first time that the trustees of the Harmony Society were threatened with murder, but the violence of the oil regions somehow seemed more impressively real than that of the Wabash territory. How Baker spent the following night is clear from these remarks which he addressed to Henrici the next morning:

Last night after an earnest prayer the following points vividly presented themselves for observation and consideration. Because the world spirit and the fire element [a concept taken from Böhme] are not favorable to us, because we are no longer suited to take care of many far reaching affairs, because we are old and have as much as we need etc., would this letter not be a sign of what might happen? Would it not be better if we sold the oil wells with a part of the land, now that everyman wants to buy? And should we not set a price which would include the petroleum rights so that we would be free of much trouble etc?

Baker was so convinced of the wisdom of his plan that he wanted to present it to the council, but not until Henrici and he agreed. Henrici's reply on November 14 was very calm, although he was right in the area from which the bullet-laden letter had come. He felt he was in God's hands "without whose will not even a hair on our head can be touched." Ever since he discovered how hostile the Davidson family had turned out to be, he had committed the entire problem to God in prayer "and asked him for wisdom and strength to recognize His will and to fulfill it most exactly to the fullest extent of my ability." No letter on file in the Harmony Society Archives shows as well as this letter the religious and clean spirit in which the Society's trustees, Baker and Henrici, arrived at important business decisions, and no letter reveals better the harmonious spirit under which these trustees acted, even at such a critical time when they held opposite views.

As far as the external business affairs and investments are concerned which we have carried out since our dear Father's death, it is entirely possible that in spite of our best will and intention important mistakes have been made. The difficulties created by this, of which I rightly had my share, in the course of events have forced me to many a heavy sigh and have caused me many a cold sweat—and have driven me to many a serious prayer. But no matter how difficult and hopeless many things at times appeared, everything went better than we had feared, and not one of our important undertakings until now has failed completely. In all things that we have undertaken, we have never applied so little of our own calculation and wordly wisdom (Weltklugheit) as in this very oil business, and none by far contains as much potential to be turned into great profit through proper care, as just this. When I then consider how this property against our will came into our hands and was kept there only by difficulties connected with it, then I cannot come to any other conclusion than that the gracious God, in return for many cares, because of losses suffered or feared, which through our wisdom and with our best will and intention we could not hinder, wishes to give us rich recompense by this gift of His, that He has given us this preferential blessing as a special preference over our neighborhood, and that he thereby wants to put us into a position to place the family which was His vehicle for this act of bringing this property into our hands into a state of wealth never before experienced and to repay them abundantly for the suffering which came over them entirely without our fault.

Henrici was convinced that everyone, especially the Davidsons, would be very displeased if they should sell the property, and he also pointed out that they would never be able to get a decent price for the land because they would not be able to give a General Warranty Deed. Although Lenz was also inclined to sell the oil lands or to return them to Davidson, Henrici's religious logic won out and the Tidioute oil lands remained one of the most valuable assets of the Harmony Society almost until its end. Long before the lands were sold, the Harmonists built a sawmill on these lands and started the

Economy Lumber Company, another paying business, which also was a means of assisting another group of religious communists, the Hutterian Brethren, whom the Harmonists later helped in their move from Russia to the United States.

When in 1869 it was reported that Colonel Drake, the petroleum pioneer, was in great financial distress and sickness, the Harmonists were among the first to support the move to obtain relief for him. Through its representative, Wm. Merkel, the Harmonists did their generous share to bring him assistance.

As a last word on this subject of the Society oil interests, a glimpse into the Senate Chamber of the State of Pennsylvania in the spring of 1868 shows that a bitter battle was going on over oil pipe bills which sought monopolies for powerful financial interests and would have crushed the Economy Oil Company. Under date of March 28, 1868, Senator Taylor from the "Senate Chamber" wrote the following revealing letter to the attorney of the Harmony Society:

Private

Dear Sir,

Geo K. Anderson is here and defiantly tells me that he will pass his pipe bill and will make no exceptions in favor of the Economites or any body else.

I replied that he should not pass that bill & if he persisted in annoying me, he should not pass any bill, for any purpose while I remained in the Senate. This of course opened the fight. He will start a bill in the House and pass it; but I will defeat it in the Senate—I write this so that our friends in Economy need not be alarmed when they hear of its progress in the House of Rep.

Anderson talks like a man who means business & the State treasurer (Kemble) is at his back; but it requires *votes* as well as *cash*, to pass bills. Col McClure once told a Senator that the devil couldn't beat seventeen votes in the Senate—if that be true, I am reasonably safe in saying that George K. Anderson can't beat 20 votes with all his *cash* & McClures personage thrown in—

Show this to Mr. Henrici but to no one else.

Mail closes in two minutes—

Yours etc
Taylor

P.S. I may possibly need your aid here next week. T.

The pressure of the oil pipe men increased the next week and a most determined effort was made to pass a "huge monster in the shape of an exclusive privilege bill for the counties of Venango and Warren," but although these powerful interests gained control in the House, the friend of the Harmony Society, Senator Taylor, made good what he had stated in the above letter. On March 27, 1869, the House and the Senate approved "An Act to authorize the Harmony Society to carry their oil across the Allegheny river," provided that the pipes be so placed or laid on or beneath the bottom of said river as not to interfere in any way with the navigation of the same and provided that the said society shall not enter upon or interfere with the rights or property of any other person without first procuring the right and privilege of so doing. On March 22 of the same year the same Senate and House had passed an act to incorporate the Western Oil and Pipe Company *"Provided,* That nothing in this act shall be so construed as to prevent the Harmony Society and their lessees from conveying the product of their own oil wells in their own pipes or other conveyance."

The Harmonists were no longer communist workers, yet the Lord certainly had not forgotten His elect. If they were now communist capitalists, they were still the Philadelphian Church which kept the faith.

5

The Civil War and
the Last Years of R. L. Baker

ONE OF THE REASONS THE HARMONISTS GOT THEMSELVES INTO difficulties in old Württemberg during the days of Napoleon's drive for a European Army was that they considered it incompatible with their faith to serve in the armed forces of their country. Strictly speaking they were not pacifists. With all their attachment to Jacob Böhme and the Book of Revelation, they were too rational, realistic, and intelligent to believe that natural man could live without wars. Their quarrels with the government in Württemberg during the Napoleonic upheaval and later with democratic Americans in Butler County during the war of 1812 were owing to their difficulty in communication. They failed to get across the idea in Swabia and in Butler County that they did not mind having others participate in the wars which natural man—a concept which did not include them —would always have to fight just as surely as natural man would answer the call of a natural urge to create children, but that they as men devoted to the imitation of Christ just did not have in them the stuff that made desirable soldiers. Thus on May 11, 1853, Baker wrote to J. M. Mayer, a friend and former member of the Society who had told him of his family troubles:

Since you have fulfilled the Old Testament command [instead of the New] "Be fruitful and multiply and fill the earth," you must also put up with the results which the nature of this business imposes on you. Your children and theirs are natural men and as such selfish and by nature cannot fulfill their duty toward a sickly, and because of this perhaps ill-humored, father in such a manner as they should.

They probably could have persuaded a psychologist connected with the draft board in our time, but in those days America was of too rugged and uncomplicated a mind to pay much attention to psychology. There was, however, a much easier way out; one had only to have the price to pay some more sanguine adventurer to take one's place in uniform. In Butler County the Harmonists still found it difficult to follow this easy way out of a difficulty, partly because money was not plentiful and partly because they did not yet know their way around well enough. And there was one more very important consideration: at that time they did not have the communistically invested capital on hand, and perhaps at stake, as they had when the Civil War began. The official attitude of the Harmony Society leadership toward the Civil War, therefore, is a matter of great importance to their history.

Under date of April 28, 1861, Baker wrote Jonathan Lenz, then taking care of the Society's oil wells near Tidioute:

Since my last letter of eight days ago the news continues that the South is going on with its plans to fight against the North and to get the upper hand. From Washington there is no news that anything has been done there. East and South Virginia have joined the South, the western part of the mountains to the Ohio is still undecided, Kentucky would like to remain neutral but still remain the medium of getting food supplies and ammunition to the South from Louisville by way of the Ohio River, etc. Maryland and Baltimore also are more with the South, but this will soon be decided fully. If Maryland and the western part of Virginia go over completely to the South, then Pennsylvania will be a boundary state along its entire length from Beaver County on the Ohio to the Delaware River, therefore great preparations are being made for Home Defence, especially Pittsburgh is immeasurably busy in organizing all capable men who have not left as volunteers into a Home Guard. There is drilling everywhere, men like our friend Baum and even older men are practicing with weapons and gathering contributions of money for the volunteers and to support the families left behind. Meetings and speeches are held everywhere to encourage the people to prepare against an attack by the enemy. We have also given a fine contribution for Beaver County. ($2500) In Pittsburgh they collected $25,000 in one day. In New York it is reported that one Stewart gave a million and rich Astor three millions as contribution to the cause. Also other smaller sums have been given by many others. We also find it necessary to use caution, for which reason we have appointed

Stump and Killenger as constant night watchmen equipped with guns and dogs. These stand watch at night and rest during the day as much as they wish. Before dinner and supper each family should read a psalm, song, or chapter and otherwise not forget prayer, just as today's text Luke 18 demands that one should always pray and not become cold. The widow is praying humanity, the elect may still in part be in time and in part yonder in eternity: for the entire large congregation is not yet gathered as long as the coming of the Lord and the resurrection has not yet happened. Also the promises which have not yet been fulfilled yonder are being held before God, that he make haste, and He must still patiently listen to the many particular prayers until His universality has been completed and the time has come. This morning the 27th Psalm was taken as text, which deals with confidence in God and with seeking the face of the Lord.

As in all things, so here also Baker interpreted current events in the light of the mystical theology of Jacob Böhme. To this letter Jacob Henrici added a factual note dealing with oil, lumber, the inevitable rise in the price of oil because of the war, the New York money market, Ohio shipping, mill construction at the Oil Wells, and lawsuits. War and the coming of the Lord never were an excuse to give up work and business.

On May 6 Baker wrote Lenz about the Home Guard companies that were being formed everywhere, three of which had come to Economy to drill. The Harmonists had given them eat and drink, and presented flags, which they had ordered in Pittsburgh, to two of the companies. Business was very slow as the entire area prepared for war. More funds were collected for war and Baker urged Henrici, who had gone on a trip, to bring back all the cash he could because the Society would again have to contribute to war drives. An old friend of the Society, Bishop Hopkins, was at this time collecting money for the building of a seminary and he also addressed the Society and asked for a donation. He had previously been a lawyer and as such had defended the first serious case of the Society in 1821–22. Usually the Society was very liberal about donations for worthy causes, and they surely would not have turned down the Bishop at another time, but they did write him that they had already given so heavily "for home defences and other war Purposes" that they could not contribute to his cause, "particularly when our Country is in great trouble and an early bright future cannot be expected." The terminology of Jacob Böhme in this time permeated all the letters of Baker to Lenz. Even the entire chronology from Abraham on was interpreted by Baker in the light of Böhme, Stilling, and the Berleburger Bible in his sermons to the Harmonists, and these sermons with the exegesis he had given were always fully reported to Lenz or Henrici if they happened to be away.

After the defeat of the Federal Army at Bull Run on July 21, 1861, Henrici expressed the attitude that this would serve as a good lesson that "the old hero General Scott will be better followed. There can be no doubt about the final victory of the North, unless Providence has decided otherwise."

Because of the poor state of business in this time, the developments in oil were a boon to the Society's finances, as they were invigorating to the North as a whole, but these developments were offset by heavy losses occasioned by the complete destruction by fire of the Society's oil works near Darlington and further heavy losses by floods in the fall of 1861. In December of the same year the Society suffered another heavy loss when fire completely destroyed their oil refinery and much of their oil, just as a Pittsburgh broker was about to conclude a deal for 600 barrels of their refined oil. Fires at the time were quite common because the workers had not yet learned enough about oil and gas. Boilers were not yet tight and firm enough. Thoughtless men would walk about at night with a lantern looking for gas leaks. At a later date the Society lost one of its junior trustees when he went with a lantern to look for a leak in the Society's gas main and found it.

It is strange and ironical that the U. S. Deputy Marshal during this period was Jacob Henrici. As such it was his duty to draw up the militia lists of Harmony Township and inform those who were liable to military service, and also to participate in courts of appeal. Henrici performed his duties conscientiously, but for the few men of the Society who were drafted, releases were obtained by finding substitutes. One of the men thus freed from service was the physician of the Society, Dr. Benjamin Feucht. But the Trustees of the Society, although not ready to participate personally in fighting the war, were very active in its interest. This is seen very clearly from their actions when Congress was discussing the selection of a site for a U. S. Armory in Western Pennsylvania. On January 6, 1862, Baker addressed a letter to the Honorable D. Agnew at Beaver in this matter. One James Patterson, against whom the Society at the time had a claim, was doing everything possible to locate the Armory there, hoping in this way "to make something out of Brighton for himself, after our claim is paid." Henrici had already been to Beaver to see Agnew about pushing this matter in Washington but did not find him at home. They were wondering whether they should engage some suitable person or persons to go to Washington to urge the claim of Beaver County. "We have already spent a good sum of money through Mr. Patterson and will do more for sake of the County, if others would join in the same interest."

The position of the Shakers during this war was far more difficult than that of the Harmonists, partly because of their less compromising attitude and partly because their greater number, about 6000 at the time, exposed them more to the call to arms. The Harmonists since the days down on the Wabash had been on good terms with them and had done some business with them. Of special interest, therefore, is a letter which Baker wrote to one of their leaders, Mich. Eades, in South Union, Kentucky. The Harmonists were greatly concerned about the description Eades had sent of the state of things around them, and they prayed that "divine protection will be extended to your good People now, in days of trouble as heretofore."

A very heavy Judgement is down upon the American People, their Glorious Union and their Constitution for self Government is on Trial. Pride, Extravagance, faithlessness, immorality and infidelity, are Witnesses against the Nation. We must await the Verdict and sentence from the Supreme Judge above. All good people within the States must suffer more or less, directly or indirectly with the bad, yet we believe that your people as a Whole and our people, gave little or no Cause of this universal Calamity of Civil War. You have not transgressed against the law of God or Man, you have done your duty as good Citizens and good Christians, you have not encouraged nor practised Pride, Extravagance, immorality nor infidelity, but you have like ourselves cultivated Peace, Virtue, honesty, and purity of heart, Soal & Body, and it is a great Trial for our peaceful feelings, in the Evening of Life thus to be disturbed. But the Will of God be done; He has ever made use of hard Probations towards his People, of which we have many Examples before us in holy Writ, Daniel among the Lions, his three Friends in the Furnace of Fire, and all came off Victorious, depending on the God of their Fathers. In treating these two Texts in Church yesterday, We also read your letter openly, and at the same time encluded the whole of you in our Prayer with much Feeling and Sympathy from the whole Congregation.

Baker in this letter then asked how man could be improved and how world unity might be restored. Would it be by legislation, fire, sword, powder, thousands of preachers with baptized and confirmed Christians,

or can it be done, and when, by the Society of Shakers, who after Eighty years duration, number about 6000 life members, can it be done by the Harmony Society who at one time numbered 750 and now about 300??? The Prospects from those sources are indeed gloomy! Therefore we are still, as we have been expecting soon to see in its fulfilment what is written in the Word of God about the second Coming of Christ, and what is clearly expressed in Revelation, Chap. 19. Verse 11 to 16. In this 2nd Coming we hope to see a General Reformation to take place, which is indispensible to place man on a better and happier foundation free of sin and evil, which all power of Earth so far has failed to accomplish on a large scale.

A careful consideration of the above reasoning will explain why Baker's faith was not shaken by the events in the world and why three days later he could write an encouraging letter to Colonel R. P. Roberts of the 140th Rg Pa V. 3rd R., a friend of the Society who had just written. Roberts had "been conspicuous in subduing a base enemy" and he hoped soon to shake hands with him. Baker expressed the confidence that spring would improve the roads and chance for military action and was sure that Roberts was in a good cause. In an obvious reference to the two substitutes of the Society, he concluded: "Give our greeting to our two Boys. Tell them to be good and obedient and do their duty."

In April of this year another letter was written to an old friend, F. Shiras, who was about to move with his corps "with the main Army to attempt to put down the rebellion, which is very desirous." To help along in this situation the Society was taking care of Shiras's parents by providing living quarters for them in the Economy Hotel. Several weeks later Frank Shiras had sent them a realistic report of a battle in which his corps had been engaged and in which there had been a heavy loss of life. To this letter the Trustees immediately sent an encouraging reply expressing their satisfaction over the news that in spite of the destruction the soldiers were still in good spirits "to fight for the good cause to its ultimate termination which a Kind Providence may soon bring upon this once happy land."[1]

To their Kentucky Shaker friends who were living in the line of battle, the Trustees continued to write letters of encouragement. On June 17, 1863, they reported that the railroad cars frequently brought Union Soldiers and rebel prisoners past the Society lands to be sent East.

Last week quite a mixed lot, old men with spectacles and many boys. A neighbor of ours who enlisted for three years now at Fort Delaware writes on the 12th inst. "We have another crowd of Grey Backs Rebels numbering 2200, and such an appearance as they make, it is horrid to think of, Vermin dirt and every filth that can be thought of, oh too horrid for discription" Similar statements might most likely be given from Union men as prisoners in the hands of the Rebels, such is the fruit of War and Rebellion, when will it end?

On Sunday last information came to Pittsburgh 18 miles above Economy that a large Rebel Force had entered the State of Pennsylvania with a design to take and destroy the City and arsenal, Cannon founderies etc. Great Excitement took place, and Rifle Pitts and fords [were] commenced and worked on as fast as possible ever since. Report says a Rebel Force has entered Chambersburg and were aiming for Harrisburgh the Capital of this state. Should the Rebels get to Pittsburgh we may be called in too, to find out the bitterness of the War Cup, upon the whole it will be well for all of us to pray for one other to be delivered soon from all evil and the War too.

The Harmonists were in communication not only with the Southern Shakers but also with those of the North. It was the northern group which was particularly insistent in inviting them to visits and doctrinal discussions. In the summer of 1863 another such invitation had been received at Economy, and it received an answer which contained much of the smugness of New England. "The Earth, the Hills and Valleys, Streams, Towns and Cities etc. etc. being really all the same in the main, if you see one, you see all. Mankind too, any where and every where is the selfsame Compound of good and bad, mostly far from the true aim for which they were Created, of which we have no lack to see around us every day fair and sufficient Examples without travelling." If they were in the habit of visiting, he wrote, they surely would visit the Shakers and the Amana Society first, and they surely would visit the Shakers if they ever got up that way, being fully aware of a kind welcome, just as the Shakers would always be sure of a kind welcome at Economy. "But the grand Point is, you cannot make Shakers of us, and we cannot now make Harmonites of you." With this Baker and Henrici took up the military matters which were of such concern to both. The last session of Congress had passed a law requiring all who were drafted and who would not go in person or find a substitute to pay the sum of $300. The War Department had stated that this law would be carried out to the letter. Next the Trustees state the position of the Harmonists.

We are enroled as non Compatants, we have not over six members, subject to draft, which as We just hear escaped being drafted yesterday by the proper officer. We have ever since the formation of our Society in 1805 paid Militia Fines, which in the agregate do amount to a large sum, rendering to Caesar what he exacts, and we give them in Consideration of the Civil protection we enjoy, (as well as other Taxes). Up to this Time we have not been overrun by any raid nor Army, for which we are very thankful—However when the Rebels entered Pennsylvania, it was stated that western Pennsylvania and Pittsburgh, (where many canon and Ball are made) was a point aimed at by them. Pittsburgh at once Commenced to fortify, much work has been done, our position would be similar to south Union Ky, and a like treatment would be expected. We do not believe that we will be thrown into the Power of the Enemy, without just cause. Should the Allmighty see cause for our Probation and purification, we pray for your folks and ourselves that we may retain Faith Hope and Love to submit to his Will.

Practically the same ideas were expressed to the South Union, Kentucky, Shakers several months later (January 19), with an additional defense of the case of the North because it had not entered the battle with an aggressive interest in territory but simply to maintain the constitution and the form of government under that constitution. "Had the north not opposed the South, the latter would have subdued the whole of the North long before now. If your Societies and ours had not defended themselves in law against malitious seceders, they would have broken up our Union without a doubt before this time." Scarcely a month after writing this letter the Society again contributed one thousand dollars to the Home Defense for fortifications.

Economy at this time was living in considerable uneasiness about the possibility of Rebel raids. Pittsburgh was a target as an important arms center and from there the Rebel troops would surely have found a way to the deep cellars at Economy which were still well stocked with excellent wine, beer, and the best whiskey in the nation. (Even in the days of the WPA these treasures were soon found and appreciated far more than the Society records.) When J. W. Maddox of Vincennes at this critical time requested the Society for another donation to complete his church, he was informed that the Board of Trustees two years ago "passed a resolution not to do any thing by way of donation to Churches as long as the War lasts, which is a very expensive burthensome customer, requiring funds all the time in one way or another. You will please therefore to excuse us on that point."

During this same period another German communist colony in Michigan, Ora Labora, was placed in a very critical position because its leader, Emil Bauer, had been drafted. He applied to the Harmonists for assistance and advice. In reply they told him he would have to go or get a substitute and urged him to look around in Detroit where he surely would be able to find one for from $300 to $500.

By May 11, 1865, the Harmonists felt safe in expressing to their Southern Shaker friends the view that the war in the main was over and that the leaders of the Rebellion were concerned only with saving themselves from that point on. "The assassination of President Lincoln and his death is a great sacrifice required at our hands, one we did not think of, and we cannot fully see the ways of Providence in this matter. We must submit in mourning and wait."

It was in August of this year that the Society suffered a shock which was probably harder on the Trustees than all the events of the war: Dr. Benjamin Feucht, the Society's physician, took leave and got married. His father before him had shocked the Society and especially Father Rapp by leaving the Society with Hildegard Mutschler to get married. Father Rapp, over the objection of Frederick, had sent after them and brought them back, although Conrad Feucht refused to adhere to the regulations of celibacy until several children had been born. This was clearly contrary to Rapp's preaching, as Frederick had stated in his letter, but Rapp tolerated this backsliding because of extraordinary obligations which he felt to Hildegard's parents for kindness shown him in his difficult days in Württemberg. Out of that marriage Benjamin Feucht had been born. He had been brought up in the Society, had been educated as a physician by a German physician-tutor who took him along on his sick calls and ultimately gave him a complete medical education. Another duty of Benjamin Feucht had been to lead the band, a system which seemed to go back to the earliest days of the Society when the physician was also band leader. Thanks to this "elopement," a record shedding important light upon the latter days of the Society has been preserved outside the records of the Society. For the events to come, the correspondence between the Feuchts and Hennings, both very confidential and illuminating, are of great importance.

On August 16, 1865, Benjamin Feucht was back in Economy tending to his business, evidently without any intention of resigning his interest in the Society. After all, something had been learned since Nachtrieb. On this date he wrote his wife a beautiful letter, beginning: "My Dear little Wife. (Mein Liebes Weibchen) How strange these three words sound! I must often think hard to decide whether the past week is reality, whether I am awake, or whether everything is a beautiful dream." He was ready to bear anything that might come because the thought of his wife made everything light. "I am almost the only one who is not excited. What people fear is that I will go

away from here, but when they once know that this is not the
case, everything will pass. . . . You must not worry about me.
I will come through, I am ready for everything. You have taken
this step with the full consciousness of its consequences and you
were ready to take the entire blame upon yourself and you
have risked everything out of love for me, while I would not
have sacrificed everything for you, because I would rather have
lost you than break my given word to serve the Society. Now
I can, however, pay you in love, because I may bear all the noise
alone to which you voluntarily would have exposed yourself."
Feucht mentioned two persons in this letter whose attitude
toward his marriage would be particularly ugly. The first was
Gertraut Rapp, the only daughter of George Rapp's only son.
Concerning her he wrote: "I have not yet met Gertraut, but
will see her soon, and am prepared for a tempest." The other
person was Jacob Henrici, concerning whom he said: "I wish
a week had already passed so that Henrici would be home, he
will make the biggest noise of all when he comes, but it does
not matter, it also will pass." The next day Feucht was still confident that he could arrange to bring his wife back and live with
her at Economy as though nothing had happened, and he was
sure he would never be driven into a corner by the Trustees:
"Baker is really very kind to us and you will have a good support in him, as I hope. Until now he has really acted in a very
fatherly manner. His kindness is almost more difficult for me to
bear than the anger of the rest of the people." But Feucht had
been too optimistic. On August 21, 1865, he sent a Western
Union Telegram to his wife in Wooster, Ohio: "Dont send box
meet me at Wooster Station nine oclock that evening." On the
same day he signed a statement that he had "voluntarily" withdrawn from the Society and had received a present of two
thousand dollars. Not until September 2, 1865, was the explanation given in a letter to his brother, stating that Baker and
Henrici had informed him that it was a question of whether he
wished to remain the victor or whether he wished to have the
"basic principles of the Society be victorious and give all honor
to God. This was saying in other words: we cannot send you
away if you will not go voluntarily, but we would prefer to
have you go because marriage opens a door for others which we

could not close again." Celibacy at this critical stage of world history was now the law of the Society.

Later events will bring a return to this interesting correspondence, but for the purposes of the present chapter these revelations are sufficient to show that celibacy was still the iron-clad rule of the Society and that not even a descendant of a founder who had been given special dispensation could at this time expect a change in policy unless he were willing to fight for it in a nasty legal way, or endure the constant religious criticism of his fellow Harmonists. Feucht had tried to be wiser than Nachtrieb but had failed.

Feucht's dear little wife had not only cost him his membership at this strategic time when many young and clever men of many faiths were selling their souls in the hope of becoming members and sharing in the wealth that was awaiting those who should survive Baker and Henrici, but when he rejoined the Society shortly before Henrici's death it was to cost him the Trusteeship, for which he had been groomed, and the potential full inheritance of the Society's millions, for Gertrude Rapp and Jacob Henrici, the most extreme celibates and chiliasts in the Society, never forgave him his marriage, although Henrici later blamed this on himself for not teaching Feucht better. This attitude is more readily understood when one realizes that Gertrude Rapp and Jacob Henrici for many years had been very much in love with each other and that they had lived under the same roof without surrendering to the flesh but giving victory to the Lord and to "the basic principles of the Harmony Society," as Baker and Henrici had expressed it to Feucht. Henrici had become reconciled to loving Gertrude as a sister in Christ, and, as Dante loved his fair Beatrice, from a distance and afar. If the poets of that age of chivalry were right in believing that love could not exist in the married state, then the very celibate state of the Society was responsible for the long duration of this love, which became so obvious that travelers visiting the Society wrote about it, and it was celebrated in literature and verse at least twice. The first literary notice of the affair was recorded in the November 1879 issue of *Scribner's* magazine by a man who signed himself Jacob F. Henrici.[2] The author is not known but he must have been greatly interested

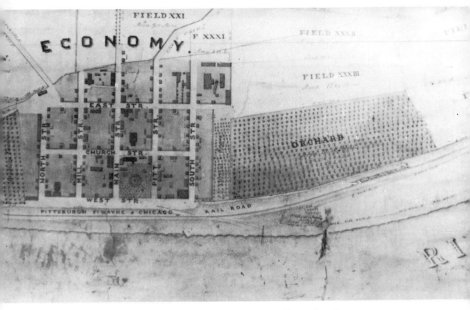

Plan of Economy and surrounding land.

Church Tower at Economy

House in which Lenau lived, as seen from Rapp's garden.

From left to right: Town Hall, Trustee's house as seen from Rapp's garden.

Former Main Street

Typical house and garden at Economy. All were built far apart for fire protection, all had gardens, all had vines trained along the walls facing the sun, and grapes flourished here.

Economy Hotel, showing vines along wall facing sun.

Old Economy Whiskey label.

Jacob Henrici. From photograph taken in 1892 by Mitchell Creese.

A street view in Economy.

Father Rapp's house, Economy.

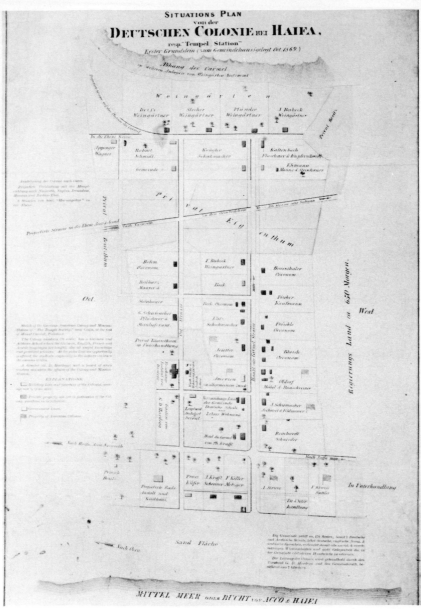

Harmony Society investments on the slopes of Mt. Carmel and Bay of Haifa. They were practicing Zionists long before Theodor Herzl founded the movement; in fact, they offered to sell New Harmony to Mordecai Noah for his Jewish colony project, which he then located upon Grand Island in the Niagara River.

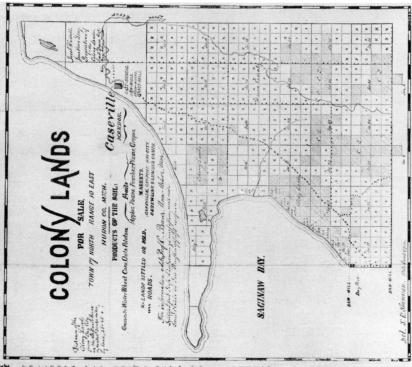

Map and advertisement of Harmony Society lands in Michigan.

Economy Lumber Co

Saw Mills, near Tidioute, Pa. land at Economy, P

Economy, Pa. Deober 21.

Economy Lumber Co

DOORS, WINDOW SASH, LATHS, MOULDING, BLINDS, FLOORING BOARDS, SIDING, RAILING, PICKETS, ETC.

SAW MILL.

PLANING MILL.

MS: _____ days.

Economy, Pa. _____ 189

OFFICE OF THE

Economy Oil Company.

Tidioute, Pa., _____ 1870.

Harmony Society letterheads showing some business interests.

in biology, judging by the comparisons used in the poem. The next issue, incidentally, contained a long article about Johns Hopkins University with illustrations showing a class in biology. The text of the poem was headed by a sketch showing an old man, dressed not unlike Henrici in those days, calling an old maid's attention to a microscope on the table before him. The text of "A Microscopic Serenade" by "Jacob F. Henrici" follows:

O, come, my love, and seek with me
A realm by grosser eye unseen,
Where fairy forms will welcome thee,
And dainty creatures hail thee queen.
In silent pools the tube I'll ply,
Where green conserva-threads lie curled,
And proudly bring to thy bright eye
The trophies of the protist world.

We'll rouse the stentor from his lair,
And gaze into the cyclops' eye;
In chara and nitella hair
The protoplasmic stream descry,
Forever weaving to and fro
With faint molecular melody;
And curious rotifers I'll show,
And graceful vorticelledae.

Where meli certae ply their craft
We'll watch the playful water-bear,
And no envenomed hydra's shaft
Shall mar our peaceful pleasure there;
But while we whisper love's sweet tale
We'll trace, with sympathetic art,
Within the embryonic snail
The growing rudimental heart.

Where rolls the volvox sphere of green,
And plastids move in Brownian dance,—
If, wandering 'mid that gentle scene,
Two fond amoebae shall perchance
Be changed to one beneath our sight
By process of biocrasis,
We'll recognize, with rare delight,
A type of our prospective bliss.

> O dearer thou by far to me
> In thy sweet maidenly estate
> Than any seventy-fifth could be,
> Of aperture however great!
> Come, go with me, and we will stray
> Through realm by grosser eye unseen,
> Where protophytes shall homage pay,
> And protozoa hail thee queen.

The other literary note of the Abelard and Heloise of the Harmony Society is by Rudyard Kipling, who visited the Society in the eighties and in his letters from "Sea to Sea" wrote:

And last of all that quaint forgotten German community, the Brotherhood of Perpetual Separation, who founded themselves when the State was yet young and land cheap and are now dying out because they will neither marry nor give in marriage, and their recruits are few. The advance in the value of their land has almost smothered these poor old people in a golden affluence that they never desired. They live in a little village where the houses are built Old Dutch fashion with their front doors away from the road and cobbled paths all about. The cloistered peace of Musquast (Beaver) is metropolitan beside the hush of the village. There is too a love tale tucked away among the flowers. It has taken seventy years in the telling, for the brother and sister loved each other well, but they loved their duty to the brotherhood more. So they have lived, and still do live, seeing each other daily and separated for all time. Any trouble that might have been is altogether wiped out of their faces, which are as calm as those of very little children. To the uninitiated those constant ones resemble extremely old people in their garments of absurd cut, but they love each other.

Benjamin Feucht was the son of a physician and he, too, was a physician. Judging by the letters which each wrote to his wife, love in each instance endured even in the married state with great tenderness and devotion as long as they lived. Neither father nor son was ready to desert his young wife, and because Benjamin Feucht was too honorable a man to remain in the Society, which he loved over the objection of the leaders and members, he had to leave. He had overestimated the generosity of the leaders and underestimated his ability to resist social and religious pressure. His departure, in spite of the two thousand dollars given him as a departing present, caused him great hardship, for he found it difficult to establish a medical practice. He wandered about, went to Zoar, the fellow communistic society of the Harmonists, and finally settled in Allegheny, where he was much liked by fellow physicians and where he wrote many prescriptions to be filled by the *Deutsche Apotheke* of F. H. Eggers on *Ohio Strasse*. He kept in constant touch with the Society through his brother, his sister, and Casper Henning at Economy, and B. C. Henning, engineer of the Economy Oil Wells. Because direct correspondence between members of the Society and persons outside was prohibited and watched over so carefully at this time that writing paper was not available, Dr. Feucht suggested in one letter to Henning that he take empty pages out of books. Some of these letters were then smuggled out by Mrs. Carolina Duss, mother of the last Trustee of the Society, who had been working in Economy since March 1862. Her husband had fought and was killed in the Civil War. By his correspondence Feucht kept himself fully informed of developments in the Society. Henning's reports even included summaries of the sermons, to which Feucht attached special importance and in which he was very much interested. "Write me again immediately on Monday morning, very exactly, also what is being preached in Church, for that is the best place to find out how things stand," he wrote his brother on September 2, 1865. A Pittsburgh friend who knew the situation at Economy well wrote Feucht after his departure: "The people living there are very good people, but they do not live, they just vegetate."

Baker did not long survive Dr. Feucht's departure. He fell into bad health and on January 13, 1868, the new trustees of the Harmony Society, Jacob Henrici and Jonathan Lenz, sent out the following notice in German and English to all friends and business associates of the Society.

DIED IN THE LORD

On the morning of the 11th of January, 1868, in his 75th year, Brother Romelius L. Baker, in full trust in the all-sufficient merits of his dear Saviour, Jesus Christ, whom he loved unswervingly with his whole heart, and whom, in the person of his brethren, ever since the founding of the Society in 1805, he served unto death with unspotted fidelity. Since the lamented departure of George Rapp, the highly beloved Founder of the Harmony Society, in 1847, he was Presiding Elder, the principal Trustee, and the Religious Leader and Speaker of the said Community. He is now succeeded by Brother Jacob Henrici, who is about 10 years his junior, and who, since 1832, has been closely associated with him in similar offices, and who under Father Rapp's and his guidance, was initiated into the business of the Society. As his fellow Trustee, there was this day elected Brother Jonathan Lenz, who was born in the Society in 1807, was raised by the same, and which he always served most faithfully, and by which he was elected in 1847 a member of the Counsel of Elders, in which capacity he has served ever since with fidelity. The general business of the Society will therefore henceforward be done in the name of HENRICI AND LENZ, Trustees; and all Deeds and similar documents will be executed and signed in the names of JACOB HENRICI AND JONATHAN LENZ, Trustees, in conformity to the Articles of Association, duly recorded in Beaver Co., Pa.

Like Frederick and George Rapp before him, Brother Baker had served the Harmonists with all his being. He was often hard and even cruel in his letters and actions to those who had left the Society, but he gave his best defense for all such actions when he justified the Civil War by comparing it to the legal battles he had fought to preserve the unity of his first and last love, the Harmony Society.

Many papers sang his praises, but the article which impressed the Society most was written by the Reverend George C. Seibert, D.D. and published in the *Americanische Botschafter* of New York City. Fifty copies of the German and several copies of the English version of the article were ordered by Henrici, who in the same letter referred the paper to Aaron Williams's book on the Harmony Society for information. He promised to give any further information desired "insofar as our religious regulations permit." It is unfortunate that not a single copy of the *Americanische Botschafter* of this issue has survived, neither in the Archives of the Society nor in the Libraries of America. Other lengthy and favorable accounts of R. L. Baker's life and character, accounts which certainly seem dependable, were published by Louise Weil—later Zehnder—in three German books:

> *Aus dem Schwäbischen Pfarrhaus nach Amerika.* Stuttgart, Franckh'sche Verlagshandlung, 1860. *Geläutert.* Freuden

und Leiden eines Schwabenmädchens in Amerika. Stuttgart, D. Gundert Verlag, 1891. *Das grosse Los.* Stuttgart, Verlag von D. Gundert, 1896.

Louise Weil knew Baker and the members of the Society well because she lived with Baker's sister at Economy while she taught school there. (The children in school were mostly orphans adopted by the Society.) She came to America in 1854 and the three books mentioned not only describe daily life and customs of the Harmonists in her time, but also her experiences in America as a whole. Much truth and fiction about George and Frederick Rapp survive in her interesting accounts. For many years after leaving Economy—she found it difficult to stay there as a young person because she was surrounded by persons so much older than she was—she kept up a correspondence with Baker and Henrici. Upon hearing of his death she wrote a poem in his memory which she published and distributed widely. The last three verses of the nine-verse poem dedicated to the Harmony Society are quoted here:

Verzaget nicht, Ihr meine fernen Lieben,
Ihr steht nicht einsam, nicht verwaiset da,
Des Theuren Segen ist Euch ja geblieben,
Mit seiner Liebe ist er Euch noch nah;
Und nimmer dürfen hoffnungslos wir weinen,
Es ist ja Gottes Wille nur gescheh'n,
Er wird uns droben einstens froh vereinen,
Denn auf die Trennung folgt das Wiederseh'n!

Wohl habet, Freunde, Ihr gar viel verloren,
Jedoch der Herr verlässt die Seinen nicht;
Ein neuer Hirte ist für Euch erkoren,
Der treu erfüllt die übernommene Pflicht.
Und willig wird er seine Heerde waiden,
Die ihm des Höchsten Hand hat zugeführt,
Und wird mit Lieb' und Gottvertrau'n sie leiten,
Dass nicht Gefahr und Sünde sie berührt.

Schon lang hat Henrici Euch angehöret,
Hat als ein Bruder unter Euch gelebt;
Und nie hat Weltlust je sein Herz bethöret,
Denn nur nach höh'rem Gut hat er gestrebt.

D'rum bitt ich Gott, dass er ihm möge schenken,
Viel Jahre noch Gesundheit, Kraft und Ruh,
Damit er freudig möge weiter lenken,
Die Harmonie dem ew'gen Ziele zu.

Dr. Benjamin Feucht on hearing of Baker's death wrote the following note to a friend: "Now Baker has died and the entire direction of the Society still depends on Henrici, and as soon as he dies the entire Society will dissolve because no one will be found who knows anything, especially since the entire Counsel of Elders consists only of fools and blockheads. What can these prescribe to Henrici, how he is to act, much less call him to account." Henrici, the uncompromising antagonist of fallen man and his bestial method of reproduction, Henrici the chiliast, was now in control of the Society, but the Board of Elders was not so unrealistic that it did not vote to make Jonathan Lenz his associate.

PART II

The Henrici-Lenz-Wölfel-Duss Trusteeship: 1868-1892

Watch therefore: for ye know not what hour your Lord doth come. But know this, that if the goodman of the house had known in what watch the thief would come, he would have watched, and would not have suffered his house to be broken up.

Matthew 24: 42, 43

6

Life Under Henrici and Lenz,
Last of the Harmonist Pioneers

IT IS SYMBOLIC OF JACOB HENRICI AND HIS FAITH IN THE INDELIBLE character and mission of the Harmony Society that upon the death of R. L. Baker, he undertook nothing, beyond the official notice just quoted, to renew and record anew the Harmony Society Articles of Agreement, legally stating who the new trustees of the Society were. The matter of accounting within the period of the Henrici trusteeship was generally handled according to the Second Book of the Kings, as George Rapp had done within certain restrictions, and Henrici never freed himself of the thought that he had in fact inherited Father Rapp's mantle.

When Jacob Henrici and Jonathan Lenz took over the direction of the affairs of the Harmony Society there were one hundred and forty members still living. When Lenz died in January 1890 there were less than twenty living members of the Society; within this period of almost a quarter of a century, most of the second-generation Harmonists went the way of all flesh without leaving any descendants to take their place. That this second generation existed at all was due in part to the early attitude toward marriage. When the second generation of Harmonists was born, the Society had not yet progressed sufficiently on the road to the imitation of Christ, who, they were frequently reminded, died a bachelor. To this less elevated Christianity, men like Lenz owed their life. Lenz was born in the society in 1807. He was the last of the Harmonists who had seen life in all three settlements. By all rights he

105

should have become the chief trustee upon Baker's death, and this undoubtedly would have happened if the close personal devotion of Henrici to George Rapp had not elevated Henrici to a position of importance in the lifetime of George Rapp. While Henrici saw the beginnings of life only in the *third* of the Harmonist settlements, Lenz remembered his earliest years in the first, in Butler County, and upon the Society's return to Pennsylvania he frequently visited the place of his birth. He was particularly fond of the place on the Wabash where he had spent a happy boyhood. His and his fellow Harmonists' love for the Wabash is seen from these remarks written to their friend Mr. Maddox in October 1868, after Lenz had returned from a visit to the old home on that river:

I arrived at my house at Economy in safety, and in good spirits. My brother Trustee Jacob Henrici, and all the rest of my brethren and sisters were very eager to hear from the old home, where we had worked hard for ten years in order to change a wilderness into a pleasant habitation, where people could prosper, be happy and enjoy good health. My brethren came one evening into our meeting room, where they listened attentively to my narration. I told them how things looked, what was still the same and what had changed, and there was no street, building or spot in and around New Harmony, somebody was not inquiring about, I also told them, how hospitably and friendly I was received by all as one of the pioneers, and all was pleasantness in that meeting.

As long as Lenz lived, he kept up a correspondence with friends on the Wabash and kept friendships alive by personal visits. These were often connected with the Society's concern for the peaceful and respectful preservation of the cemetery where they had buried their dead.

This is shown in the following letter by Lenz written to E. I. Rogers in New Harmony on February 19, 1869:

Your kind letter dated January 11th was received by me. This is just the day, on which Mr. Baker died last year. Many a time I remember with pleasure the journey I made to New Harmony. It was a very interesting journey to me in many respects. I was so kindly received everywhere and so hospitably entertained, that I only wish I could repay at some time for all the friendship bestowed on me. I am only sorry for having caused you so much trouble in writing the history of the two brothers Maclure and Samuel Arthur, since we have not the power to alter anything in that whole affair. To your question, why we had to pay twice for the grave yard, I can give you the following answer. Philipp Bendel, formerly a member of our Society, and now living in Freedom, had just before me been on a visit in New Harmony, and had mainly spoken with Samuel Arthur. This latter showed him everything and gave him the commission, to ask Mr. Henrici and Lenz, how it came, that E. J. Rogers was made agent beside himself since he faithfully and honestly had attended to that business since the last twenty years. Bendel came to me and told me how badly the graveyard was cared for and how uselessly the lumber was cut. I myself being not posted in this affair conversed with Mr. Henrici about it, and he told me, that the grave yard had been kept back in the sale for only twenty years, and that we had to buy it back from Mr. Arthur or the church for six hundred Dollars. This sale proved to be unlawful, and we had to get possession of it through the court, which cost us one hundred Dollars more. Now the quarrel between you and Mittshel appeared in the newspaper and Henrici himself did not know what to think about it. This state of affairs caused my journey to now New Harmony. After I had made myself acquainted with everything, it was plain to me that Arthur was never appointed by Mr. Rapp or Mr. Baker and that he was not capacitated for such a business. You may therefore rely on what I said, viz. that you are appointed by the two trustees as well as by the whole Society as our agent. Whenever my business should bring me near Harmony, it will make me great pleasure to visit you again, and if you should come to the East, to buy goods, I hope you will give me a chance to entertain you for a few days in Economy in return for the hospitality I received when I was with you. On the 15th of this month we celebrated the anniversary of our Society. We were all socially united in the great hall, where we took our dinner and supper together, sung religious songs and listened to the beautiful music which our young folks were giving us with their brass instruments. The weather was until now very moderate especially during February we enjoy good health with a few exceptions and wish you the same. My best respects to you and to your Sister.

In 1874 the Society purchased the "lots and the building thereon known as the Hall" in New Harmony and donated this property and the sum of two thousand dollars in addition "to aid in erecting a School House to be attached to the North Wing of such Hall, which is to remain as it now stands." In the end this sum was increased by $3100. Also, the Society furnished brick and timber and stone in sufficient quantity to erect the desired schoolhouse. At this time Lenz also arranged to build a brick wall around the old Harmony Society Cemetery. The Harmony Township of Posey County, Indiana, under date of May 13, 1874, bound itself through its Trustee Eugene S. Thrall to the following perpetual care of that cemetery, since sadly neglected:

NEW HARMONY SCHOOL HOUSE

In memory of the gift of the lots on which it stands, and the munificent donation for the building thereof by the Harmony Society of Economy Pennsylvania through their worthy Trustees Mess. Henrici and Lenz, we the citizens of New Harmony dedicate said School House to said Harmony Society, and as a further sense of our gratitude to said Society we pledge ourselves that the Trustee of Harmony Township and his successors in office shall take good care of the German Grave Yard where said Society interred their dead when they occupied this place, and protect and guard the same from all trespasses or mutilation of the trees or fences on and around the same.

The generosity of the Society prompted Professor E. T. Cox of Indianapolis, Indiana, to suggest in 1884 that the Society establish a polytechnic institute at New Harmony, but the Society felt compelled to turn down this request because such great demands were being made upon its good will to help various projects in various parts of the world. When Jonathan Lenz under date of November 24, 1884, informed Professor Cox of their decision, he referred to his last visit to New Harmony in these fond terms:

That visit to the places and scenes once so familiar to me as a boy and young man brought to my mind many memories, some saddened with suffering and loss of dear friends, who struggled manfully for health and life, against the terribly dangerous and deadly malaria that seemed to lurk in that rich soil, but who could not resist the deadly power, and whom with sad hearts we had to lay away in that little grave yard. There were other memories, too, of pleasant events with my associates, that did so much to relieve and cheer us in the hard work of clearing off the great forest and securing from the soil, at first the bare necessities, and later some of the comforts of life. However, pleasure and sadness, joy and sorrow, are always intermingled more or less in the lot of all, but to those who like our Society undertake, as pioneers, to clear up the heavy forest, and establish homes in a wilderness, there was much of real hardship, and where the soil, though rich and productive, as there, gave off so much of poisonous vapor to be breathed in by those who undertook its cultivation there was very much of sickness, suffering and death. You know something of these things, and will not wonder that some thoughts of sadness arise in my mind when I look back to the events of those days. Those lands of the Wabash Valley are beautiful and comparatively healthy now, but those who occupy them now have but little conception of the labors, the trials, and the hardships of those who first sought to fit them for cultivation. I need not however say more about these things to you.

Under date of September 9, 1885, Robert Owen's son, Richard Owen, then in his 75th year, wrote to Henrici and Lenz in very beautiful German suggesting that the Society use $100,000 to establish "The Rappite Polytechnic" or "The Rappite Memorial Institute" at New Harmony as a living monument to their dead in New Harmony. I have not been able to find a reply to that beautifully written German letter.

The same loving regard for the members of their Society who had gone before them prompted Henrici and Lenz to have a stone wall built around the cemetery at Harmony in Butler County. Here is Lenz's accounting of the work:

August 5, 1870. Settled with Charles and George Cable for stone mason work at the cemetery in Harmonie, Butler County, Pennsylvania.

Cable's bill for all his work is	$4515.63
Work done by Elias Ziegler for digging the foundation, digging out trees, and all other work on the place	$1514.05
	$6029.68

In connection with this transaction Lenz gives the following statistics of members of the Society awaiting the first resurrection in their three resting places:

Harmonie, Butler County, died from 1805 to 1814	100
On the Wabash from 1814 to 1824	230
At Economie from 1824 to March 1874	379
	709

As long as the Lenz trusteeship lasted, all three Harmony

Society cemeteries at Harmony, New Harmony, and Economy were given the loving and respectful care that they deserved among civilized men, but with all the vast funds granted by the citizens of Pennsylvania and Indiana since then for preservation of historical monuments, few places in the entire world have been so shamefully neglected by a wealthy state as these resting places of some of our greatest American builders.

During the Henrici-Lenz quarter century many travelers visited Economy, many of these in search of help, even of a large inheritance. Membership applications continued to come in, but the Harmonists had become wise to the ways of men and during this period knew how to protect their interests and to be discerning about the manner in which they received visitors. Three such visitors may serve as example for this period. Two had the intention of visiting Economy in order to write about it.

In 1874, Charles Nordhoff made his memorable visit to the Harmony Society. He had been visiting the various communistic societies of the United States and was preparing what was to become the first authentic work on the subject. As one reads his work today one must marvel at the kindness and tolerance with which he wrote about each Society, no matter how strange its views and practices might have seemed to him personally. His letters to the Harmony Society Trustees and their replies testify to his and their gentlemanly and sincere character. He very much wanted to get Henrici and others to sit for photographs, but Henrici adamantly refused: "It is almost impossible not to do what a friend like you demands; but our religious scruples in this respect are so strong that they overpowered all other considerations. It is a consolation to know that your kindness will pardon this our non-compliance with your friendly wishes." [George Rapp himself had no such scruples!] Jacob Henrici read the proof of the pages dealing with the Harmony Society and sent Nordhoff his corrections. He assured Nordhoff that "This your late work will undoubtedly be a success" and gave a preliminary order of twelve copies. Since these corrections, which included an evaluation of their wealth, were all made by the author, the Nordhoff account presents an authentic picture of the situation at Economy in the year 1874. What were some of the points in this report[1] that are of importance to his history of the Society?

A number of Nordhoff's facts, by his own admission, were taken from Dr. Aaron Williams's account,[2] to which Henrici had referred him. Likewise he had referred him to the account of the Duke of Saxen-Weimar, from which he quotes. The usual history of the Society is given, which contains nothing new, but substantiates much that has been reported in previous pages of this history. The wealth of the Society at this time is reported to be between "two to three millions of dollars," a figure given directly by Mr. Henrici. Their creed is restated more briefly but in substantially the same form as we have come to know it. The separation of the sexes in the two Sunday services is described. With Henrici's approval it is stated that they observe as holy days Christmas, Good Friday, Easter, and Pentecost; and three great festivals of their own—the 15th of February, the anniversary of their foundation; Harvest-Home, in the autumn; and an annual Love Feast (Agape) in October. On these festival occasions they assembled in the great hall, and there, after singing and addresses, a feast was served, there being an elaborate kitchen adjacent to the Hall for the purpose of preparing these feasts, while in the two great cellars nearby there were fine large wine casks "which would make a Californian envious, so well-built are they." Nordhoff showed a fine appreciation for the architecture of Economy, for its naturally beautiful setting, and for its prevailing character of "neatness and a Sunday quiet." The industries had closed down, "and as you walk along the quiet, shady streets, you meet only occasionally some stout, little old man, in short light-blue jacket and a tall and very broad-brimmed hat, looking amazingly like Hendrick Hudson's men in the play of Rip Van Winkle; or some comfortable-looking dame, in Norman cap and stuff gown; whose polite 'good-day' to you, in German or English as it may happen, is not unmixed with surprise at sight of a strange face; for, as you will presently discover at the hotel, visitors are not nowadays frequent in Economy."

At the time of the Nordhoff visit the total membership of the Society was one hundred and ten persons, "most of whom are aged, and none, I think, under forty." There were twenty-five or thirty children of various ages, adopted by the society and apprenticed to it, and an equal number living there with parents who were hired laborers, about one hundred in number. The whole population was German, and although all the people spoke English, German was the language commonly heard. He found the Harmonists to be sturdy, healthy-looking, with an air of vigorous independence, by no means dull, and very decidedly masters of their lives. Old as they were he found that they continued to labor in the fields and orchards, partly out of habit and partly because this was thought healthful to body and soul. Waste was considered a sin, and "we live simply; and each has enough, all that he can eat and wear, and no man can use more than that." All, he found, usually attained a happy old age beyond seventy, and they died without fear, "trusting that they are the chosen people of the Lord."

Such is Economy at this time. Its large factories are closed, for its people are too few to man them; and the members think it wiser and more comfortable for themselves to employ labor at a distance from their own town. They are pecuniarily interested in coal-mines, in saw-mills, and oil-wells; and they control manufactories at Beaver Falls—notably a cutlery shop, the largest in the United States, and one of the largest in the world, where of late they have begun to employ two hundred Chinese; and it is creditable to the Harmony people that they look after the intellectual and spiritual welfare of these strangers as but too few employers do. (p. 90)

No mention is made in the Nordhoff report of the trouble that had been caused the year before because of the employment of the Chinese workers. A committee of citizens from Beaver Falls, where the cutlery works were located, had come to Economy to protest against the employment of Chinese laborers, because this action had displaced white laborers and obliged them to leave the place. The delegation demanded relief of the Society. In a widely published reply, signed by the Board of Elders of the Society, it was established that the Cutlery Company was an organized corporation, transacting its business through a board of directors, the Society being the principal owner of the stock, but having only one director on the board and only one voice in its management. The Society as such had not been informed of the plan to employ Chinese, but, without knowledge of the Society, the Board had entered into contract for the employment of three hundred Chinese laborers for a term of four years. The Chinese had been employed quite legally, but only after attempts to get other labor, without which the works would have been compelled to close down completely, had failed. The Chinese were called in only as a last resort, the Harmonists replied, and then gave indication of their belief that the very appearance of the Chinese was a further fulfilment of prophecy:

And may not we here express the hope, that aside from every other view of the question, this may prove to some of them at least, the call spoken of by the evangelical prophet—Isaiah, 55, 5: "Behold, thou shalt call a nation that thou knowest not, and nations that knew not thee shall run unto thee because of the Lord thy God, and for the Holy One of Israel; for he hath glorified thee."

To meet the objections, however, the Elders instructed their Director to bring all their share of the proceeds of the business during the next eight years before them. They would then direct the expenditure of that money for the purpose of supporting missions, schools, and the poor, with particular reference to Beaver Falls, but they would not add to the amount of Society funds invested in the business if it should not yield a profit. As for the white employees, who claimed unjust dismissal, the Society asked that they be properly and legally made to appear before a court of justice, and that they be fully compensated.

Since there had been intimations that there might be violence used by protesting elements in Beaver Falls, the Society stated that it would not only protest against such a course but would also withdraw its means not only from the cutlery works but from Beaver Falls in general. If their views were favorably received, however, and the Chinese were permitted to continue to work in peace for four years, the Society would be glad to let the citizens of Beaver Falls have the Society's interest in the cutlery works on very reasonable terms. The full and complete reply in the question of the Chinese laborers was published by the Society in German and English and distributed widely on handbills. It was the end of a very disagreeable problem, all the more so because the Harmony Society had really built Beaver Falls and had not only invested great sums of money in its development, but had been extremely generous to its citizens. This generosity had earlier been recognized by the local newspaper in a dispatch dated June 4, 1869:

An interesting event in the history of our new town transpired on Monday last. The Economy Silver Cornet Band—one of the best in the country—accompanied by Mr. Lenz and two of the Elders of the Harmony Society, came down to visit the place they have had so much to do in building up and giving it its prosperous attitude. Whatever other agencies have lent their influence thereto, the Harmony Society has been "the power behind the throne" in building up this thriving town.

The Chinese labor incident was but one example of the fact that these communists had now in fact become wealthy communist capitalists who were determined to get a return on their investments but who also were using the income from their investments for unselfish and charitable purposes. It was not only the era of capitalism but also of social welfare. During his visit in Economy, Nordhoff witnessed abundant evidence of such activity in the "Economy Hotel," where he stayed. Formerly this hotel had been a favorite winter as well as summer resort for Pittsburghers, and an important source of income for the Society. When Nordhoff was there he witnessed the following scene after he had had his supper:

As I sat before the fire in my own room after supper, I heard the door-bell ring with a frequency as though an uncommon number of travelers were applying for lodgings; and going down into the sitting-room about seven o'clock, I discovered there an extraordinary collection of persons ranged around the fire, and toasting their more or less dilapidated boots. These were men in all degrees of raggedness; men with one eye, or lame, or crippled—tramps, in fact, beggars for supper and a night's lodging. They sat there to the number of twenty, half naked many of them, and not a bit ashamed; with carpet-bags or without; with clean or dirty faces and clothes as it might happen; but all hungry, as I presently saw, when a table was drawn out, about which they gathered, giving their names to be taken down on a register, while to them came a Harmonist brother with a huge tray full of tins filled with coffee, and another with a still bigger tray of bread. (p. 66)

After this these men were given beds for the night. The next day they were given breakfast and sent on their way. From the innkeeper, Nordhoff discovered that the Society each day took care of from 15 to 25 such tramps or beggars, asking no questions, except that the person shall not have been a regular beggar from the Society. Toward the conclusion of his account Nordhoff wrote:

> The great factories are closed, and the people live quietly in their pretty and simple homes. The energies put in motion by their large capital are to be found at a distance from their village. Their means give employment to many hundreds of people in different parts of Western Pennsylvania and wherever I have come upon their traces, I have found the "Economites," as they are commonly called, highly spoken of. They have not sought to accumulate wealth; but their reluctance to enter into new enterprises has probably made them in the long run only more successful, for it has made them prudent; and they have not been tempted to work on credit; while their command of ready money has opened to them the best opportunities. (p. 94)

In taking leave of Economy Nordhoff noted that they were looking for the coming of the Lord, that they awaited Christ's appearance in the heavens, "and their chief aim is to be ready for this great event, when they expect to be summoned to Palestine, to be joined to the great crowd of the elect." It was this faith that led them to send large sums of money to the Holy Land to support the work of the "Tempelgesellschaft" there and that inspired them to give extensive financial assistance to other religious communist groups. Before covering that chapter of their national and international relationships I continue with the eyewitness account of Karl Knortz, friend of Longfellow and a correspondent of Friedrich Nietzsche.

Karl Knortz, a theologian and writer, stated in his first letter to the Society that he had studied theology in Germany and that he wished to serve them in this capacity during a fourteen-day visit. Although he was a German and would normally have been given a warm reception, Henrici urged him not to come and stated that they would be much happier if no one would speak or write about them because all publicity caused them much useless effort in replying to the many questions which then followed about their principles and about the possibility of becoming members in their society. Karl Knortz would not be turned down. He forced his attentions upon the Society and wrote three reports about it which indicate that the Society was extremely reticent about answering his questions.[3] They had discerned in advance what manner of man he was. Two reports were flippant, entertaining, and inaccurate, the reports of an intellectual whose study of theology in Germany quite naturally had made him cynical about all religion. I here translate his best and most interesting description.

A Sunday in Economy (1875)

A deathly silence, which was interrupted only by the cackling of innumerable chickens on the streets, lay over Economy when one magnificent Saturday afternoon I walked through that romantically situated settlement of the Harmonists. Not a human being was to be seen, and my intention to spend a Sunday there in order to attend a divine service for a moment lay like lead upon my soul, for the question how one would kill the rest of the time in this little city it seems was difficult to answer.

Mr. Jacob Henrici, the spiritual head of the Rappites, at the moment when I looked him up, was just occupied translating several religious hymns from English to German in order to practice them that evening with his choir, for the seventieth festival of the founding of the Society was to be celebrated in a few days, and on this occasion things were to be neither dry nor still. By his kind invitation I attended the singing practice that evening with Mr. Lenz, who powerfully assists Mr. Henrici in the administration of the extensive property of the Society. The singing society consisted of about 26–30 young people of both sexes, who had found a very pleasant home as workers or servants. There were magnificent voices among them, and the zeal with which they sang the folkish melodies which had been rendered in German with great command of form showed that they were eager to contribute their share to do away with the monotony of the silent colony, and on the other hand it brought praiseworthy testimony for the cleverness and circumspectness of Mr. Henrici, who understands extremely well to inspire the young people for song and music.

At 9:30 Sunday morning the divine service began. The church inside is without decoration; neither pictures nor crucifix are found in it, and the benches are as plain as possible. It was fairly well attended; but the audience consisted two thirds of young non-Harmonists, who in general attend the services more regularly than the very aged Rappites, who occasionally cannot leave their home because of physical weakness. Several of the old gentlemen had to be led into the church slowly; most of those present, however, of whom perhaps only very few are below seventy years old, still look as vigorous as persons of fifty, and by appearances quite a while will pass before the last Harmonist departs this world. They wore long, blue coats with yellow buttons, on which fashion has not exerted the least influence; the women wore the Württemberg peasant costumes with blue, pointed bonnets, which suits most very well. The servant girls there dressed more fashionably, but still simply enough in comparison to their city colleagues.

At nine-thirty sharp, as said, the divine service began; no one came late, for the bad manners of dress-interested women and silly dandies to direct everyone's attention to their important person and their costly clothes, does not exist in Economy for reasons readily explained. Mr. Henrici and Miss Gertrude Rapp, the grand-daughter of the founder of the colony, each took a seat before a melodion, and after a short prelude the choir sang one of the songs practiced the night before. Then the congregation sang several verses out of the songbook of the Harmonists compiled by Rapp in 1826, and then Mr. Henrici ascended a platform, sat down at a table and read a part from the New Testament, which he explained verse after verse in the strictly orthodox sense of a Chiliast. In the course of this he often spoke of the unfavorable conditions of the time which he contrasted with the organization of the first Christian congregation at Jerusalem, which also gave him the opportunity to enter upon the discussion of the advantages of the communist system. Everyone listened to his simple and understandable explanations with great interest. The "Amen" at the close was repeated in unison by all present, after which first the women and then the men left the church.

In the afternoon before the divine service beginning at three o'clock, I took a short walk through the so-called "Orchard," a well-kept garden of fruit trees covering about 25–30 acres, within which is also found the small cemetery enclosed with a white-painted fence. Not a cross is found in it and not one of the old men walking there could definitely point to the spot of Rapp's grave. It was a wonderful day in February and as warm as in May, so that many of the old Harmonists had taken to the open. Those old men were very talkative and for a long time I conversed with them about the history of their settlement and Father Rapp. The latter enjoys an almost divine veneration, and the people could not say enough about the kindness of his heart and personal sacrifice. Each day he was ready with council and for each sickness he could give an effective remedy.

The Harmonists worry little about the future of Economy. Some hope that as once before a number of families from Germany will join them and continue their work, when they are no longer among the living. All, however, are of the opinion that by permission of marriage the ruin of the Society would be brought on, and before they are willing to allow sexual intercourse they prefer death to ruin. With joy and pride they look upon the blooming condition of their colony, which gives them the most obvious proof that they have followed the right path. "How easily," one of the true old men said, "could all men find happiness, if they only wanted; but the world today no longer wants to obey, everyone wants to be his own boss, and to what misery this leads is proved to us each day by 30–40 bums who seek bread and shelter by us."

The afternoon church lasted an hour. Mr. Henrici in his address stressed the respect of the Bible, which must unconditionally be looked upon as the basis of all religion and morality, because it was directly inspired by God, and he then urged all to report such workers who express contrary sentiments. Each person, of course, could believe what he wished; the Harmonists, however, were so firmly convinced about the profound truths of the Bible and of Christianity, that they would not want to sit at one table with people, and on top of this feed them, who made fun of the book of God. When at the close of the divine service I spoke to Henrici about this remark, he informed me that a worker had said in a group of colleagues and children, that there were far more sensible books than the Bible, of which one did not even know who had written it. That man was dismissed on Monday morning after they had first assured themselves of the truth of the accusation brought against him.

In the evening I spent a very pleasant hour chatting with Mr. Henrici. When I asked whether it was true that Lenau once wanted to join the Harmonists, he remarked that that poet had lived at Economy several months in the company of a servant; but he could not remember that he had ever wanted to become a member. Lenau at that time wrote many poems, and when he finished one he usually read it to Henrici, and because he noticed a strong satirical vein in him, he advised him not to give it too much expression, because he could thereby do much harm without wanting to do so. Lenau's servant at that time was full of stories of the adventurous plans of his master and could not stop laughing about them; for he did not see the first traces of his long incurable insanity in this. When Lenau left Economy, Henrici bought the four-volume Dictionary of the German language by Hensius from him, which still is in the library of the Harmonists.

Finally I asked Mr. Henrici why the Hungarian writer Pulszky in her work "White, Red and Pink" had expressed herself in such a sarcastic manner about Economy, and got this reply: "If we were not Germans, the companion of Kossuth would surely have treated us with better manners, and then the main reason might have been,

that we refused to support the Hungarian revolution with money."—
Our conversation, unfortunately, was interrupted by the fact that
Economy has a nine o'clock curfew and that the hotel is then locked,
a rule to which there are only very few exceptions. Mr. Henrici was
so kind to take me home with a lantern; there are a few street lights
in Economy, but more, it would seem, *pro forma,* than for real use.

One of the greatest bridge-building engineers ever to come
to this country was Eduard Hemberle. He has left us an
interesting record in his *Erlebnisse und Beobachtungen eines
deutschen Ingenieurs in den Vereinigten Staaten. 1867–1885.*[4]
Among the bridges built was the Pittsburgh Point Bridge over
the Monongahela, which was to handle traffic between Pittsburgh and South Pittsburgh. Harmony Society capital was, of
course, involved in the building of this bridge. When Hemberle's firm settled accounts with the Point Bridge Company,
which was a stock company, they were partially paid in stocks
instead of cash because some of the stockholders had meanwhile
gone bankrupt. The Harmony Society owned some of the
stocks and Henrici, as one of the directors of the Point Bridge
Company, became acquainted with Hemberle in meetings of
the board of administration. Because of the diminutive ending
of the name, Henrici considered Hemberle a Swabian and was
kindly disposed to him. Hemberle states that the old gentleman
made a strange appearance in an American city wearing his
"Swabian costume," but he had great influence "because he
administered the many millions of the congregation and directed their business and factories." The American Bridge
Company now wanted to sell the stocks they had taken, and
because buyers were scarce, Hemberle was asked to try to sell
them to the Economites and to discuss the matter with Henrici
in the course of a visit which he had long ago promised to
make. For this reason he picked a beautiful day and traveled
to Economy, nineteen miles down the Ohio. This visit was
made in the Spring of 1877, when, according to Hemberle,
only seven of the old members of the Society who had a share
in the property were still living.

From the station the path leads upward to the high-lying town,
whose houses lie along a long, broad street, and the whole makes

the impression of a large Württemberg village or small country town. There were no human beings on the street for it was just work-time and there are no unoccupied people or children. I walked down the street until I came to a store, where cigars were also shown in the show case. There I entered and asked the young man who sold, and who spoke pure Swabian, for the house of Mr. Henrici. When I further asked why wine and cigars were sold while it was forbidden to use them, he said they sold everything, but only to strangers. Two stone-aged men who, unnoticed by me, had been sitting in chairs in the background now took part in the conversation and said that I would now meet Mr. Henrici in his house further up the street, opposite the church or the congregation house.

Having arrived there a feminine being came to the door to answer my ring and after hearing my request she said that I would now meet Mr. Henrici in his vineyard, where he was now at work. But since I did not know the way to the vineyard she led me into a large room and herself set out to get him. I had to wait a long time and used the time to look over the room of the little prophet. It was a simple, cleanly kept room and only the pictures on the walls were noteworthy. They were exclusively representations of acts from the Bible which should testify to the ruinous influence of woman on man: Adam, Eve, Joseph and Potiphar, etc.

Finally Mr. Henrici appeared and was very happy about my visit. Over a bottle of his self-made wine we spoke about all sorts of things. But when I wanted to speak about the sale of the stocks he begged me to spare him this, because it was a strict rule with them not to talk business in their homes. Surely a very beautiful rule, which, however, did not agree with my purpose. Nevertheless, I did succeed in the course of conversation to find a place for my wishes bit by bit. My praise of his wine brought a second bottle and some bakery on the table which he recommended as genuine home-made *Lebkuchen*. With regard to admission of new members to the Society he said that very many would like to have the advantages but did not want to fulfill the difficult duties. When I took leave he gave me another bottle of wine with the remark that I should drink it in Pittsburgh with friends, for such a good wine one could not get there. When I left the house I had the bottle in my hand, which upset him, and he asked me to hide it in a pocket or under my coat.

In the opposite direction from which I had come I left the place with the hidden bottle and by a circuitous way reached the station with a feeling that I had done something wrong.

7

Shrewd Capitalist and Santa Claus
of Christian Communists

EXCEPT FOR THE FACT THAT HIS EXTREMELY ASCETIC WAY OF life did not favor the development of the *embonpoint,* Jacob Henrici, after he had been freed from the economic brakes of R. L. Baker, looked somewhat and behaved entirely like Santa Claus. What made this sort of generosity particularly dangerous was the fact that Henrici, now that he was Senior Trustee, assumed the privilege George Rapp had usurped on the basis of 2 Kings 12:15:

Moreover they reckoned not with the men into whose hand they delivered the money to be bestowed on workmen, for they dealt faithfully.

and 2 Kings 22:7:

Howbeit, there was no reckoning made with them of the money that was delivered into their hand, because they dealt faithfully.

As an illustration I present the following part of a letter from Mother Mary Anna of the "Sisters of the Holy Humility of Mary," who, under date of November 9, 1879, thanked him for stoves he had sent to their hospital:

But now Mr. Henrici, I must own that I do not find you so wise a business man as I expected. Who ever heard of a prudent man lending such a sum as $400 on the mere asking, without witnesses, note or any security whatever? Now if I were to run away or close on this money you could never oblige me to pay it. You are really too kind to us. I should be thankful if when you write again you would send a note which I will sign and return.

It seems that Santa Claus Henrici never sent the note and that it was never signed, and probably never paid, because long ago "as rich as an Economist" had become proverbial among Americans. A few months later he sent the same Sisters of Mary a large supply of excellent medicines and liquors for which he was thanked with "constant prayers." People began to look upon the Harmonists or Economites much as the public today still looks upon Texas oil men or Arabian sheiks who control vast oil reserves.

Such generosity, which outdid even a Carnegie or Vanderbilt, with whom Henrici did business, soon became famous throughout the world, and in the Henrici period the Archives of the Society are filled with requests for aid from all over the Western World. The Sisters of Mercy, the Convent of the Good Shepherd, the Convent of Mercy, the Ursuline Convent of Louisville, Mother Superior of this and that soon got the word, and Father Henrici became such a favorite among Roman Catholic orders that the author of his biographical sketch, J. Twing Brooks, who had transacted some big financial deals with him, was convinced he was a Roman Catholic. Jacob Henrici, a nephew of Father Henrici, who knew him better, pointed out this error and showed from the record that his entire background and training were thoroughly Protestant. It was only his fanatic devotion to the celibate way of life that made him particularly vulnerable to requests from celibate Roman Catholic orders. But these were not the only ones favored. In 1880 Adolph Zucker from Starkville, Mississippi, thanked Henrici for help and advice. He had built the University and most of the other buildings there. In the same year a Dr. Emmerling of Pittsburgh approached him for help because of his "ingewohnter Herzensgüte und Menschenfreundlichkeit." A Mr. Bloom from New York City asked him whether he would "not regard me as one of God's children and help me." George Kinsberg of Mt. Airy requested help to insure their buildings, and Katharina Schweikle from Wittlensweiler, Germany, asked help to come to America. An Allegheny City church wanted help for its church, the Pennsylvania Working

Home for Blind thanked him on behalf of the "Home, toward which you are so large a contributor," a man named Thurston of Tidioute, Pa., wanted help to start a German paper to promote the Bible, Mrs. Thomas Hindman of Buffalo Park wanted help to build a Presbyterian Church, "even a little from a few men such as you who will never miss it," Mr. Samuels of Pittsburgh requested assistance for starving Silesians and Thüringians, a William Bender of a Soldier's Home and a Frau Müller wanted help and advice for her children. These are but a few of the requests that reached Henrici. Most were given assistance and patient advice in letters carefully written in Henrici's clean hand—copies of which were retained, often showing how he troubled himself writing and rewriting his reply. When his petitioners would plead poverty he often wrote in this vein: "Poverty, which strikes us through God's wise direction, must surely serve for our welfare, and if we make right use of it, it will assist us in gaining eternal riches." Although these numerous requests came from individuals, they were given the same personal consideration shown to the many requests from larger groups. Among the larger group of human beings requesting help were those who had been inspired by the great success of the Society and who wanted assistance to start a communist colony of their own. It is not an overstatement to say that probably no communist movement existed during the nineteenth century which at some time or other did not correspond with the Harmony Society, for the Harmony Society was the great center of practical communism during this period. When such letters reached them the Harmonists would carefully distinguish between those whose plans were based on the Bible as the beginning and end of all wisdom and those which were founded on a rational belief in the goodness of man apart from Scripture. Those who built their Society on the Bible as the infallible and verbally inspired Word of God were sure of getting excellent advice and sound financial assistance. Thus, without long investigation and acting simply in faith, Henrici sent several hundred dollars for the poor in an Icelandic colony. Through Dr. Luther Roth, the Pastor of Zion's Church of Lunenberg, Nova Scotia, Henrici helped this new settlement through to their next harvest.

While these individuals in need of assistance demanded much

of Henrici's time, the larger communist groups needed, and were patiently given, much more. Among the major groups with which Henrici and Lenz kept up extensive correspondence were: the Temple Society in the Holy Land,[1] which was dedicated to rebuilding the Temple in Jerusalem and to preparation for the Second Coming of Christ there; the Hutterian Brethren in Russia,[2] their former countrymen, the communist society in Zoar, Ohio; the communist congregation of True Inspiration at Amana, Iowa; the various Shaker communities; and the German communist colony Ora Labora near Caseville, Michigan. There were many others like Cyrus Teed's movement of Koreshanity[3] and the grand dream of Topolobampo,[4] Mexico, which belabored the Society in the hope of getting some of its millions. But let us first examine those who were brethren in the faith in Christ. The Harmony Society did not expect others to conform to their system of dogma and practice, but they did expect them to build upon a faith in Christ as the Redeemer of fallen man and as the only help for man in his predicament in this evil world.

In the year of Baker's death, the *Tempelgesellschaft,* a Christian Zionist movement in Württemberg, which had millennial hopes of its own and which with Jewish Zionists wanted to rebuild the Temple in Jerusalem and was generally preparing for Christ's second coming and reappearance in the Holy Land, sent two emissaries, G. D. Hardegg and Christian Hoffmann, to Palestine to prepare the way. The former believed that the best approach would be to open schools and hospitals and thus win the population there for Christianity; the latter favored a strong policy of migration from Württemberg to the Holy Land. This religious movement also found a large number of followers in the United States through its German-American publication *Die Reichs Posaune,* to which the Harmonists subscribed and which they read with much interest. One of the friendliest accounts of the Harmony Society to be published in the German press of America appeared in a series in this paper, the last of the series appearing on December 1, 1872. Among the most generous and earliest contributors to the cause of the Christian Zionist movement was the Harmony Society. In June 1869, their Buffalo, N.Y., friend, Jacob Schumacher, whose brother had been an apprentice of the Society, was chosen by the American branch of the *Tempelgesellschaft* to go to the Holy Land.

Because the Harmonists had given this Zionist movement financial support and were greatly interested in it, Schumacher immediately wrote to ask whether he could visit the Society before leaving for the Holy Land. Henrici immediately expressed the satisfaction over his election and stressed the importance of the work Schumacher was about to undertake. He continued:

We, as a congregation called long ago, believe to have our special mission, which we hope to accomplish correctly with the help of the Lord. We are, of course, firmly convinced that a far more thorough and exact preparation is necessary than is expressed in the *Reichsposaune* and the other writings of the Friends of Jerusalem, if we are to become worthy to escape that which is to take place and to stand before the Son of Man. However, we are not set up as judges. And what has not yet been recognized and required may still come. If it is the Lord's will, however, that others of his elect should be led into his new and glorious kingdom by an easier route than he is leading us, then we shall be heartily satisfied with his all-wise direction.

Schumacher visited the Society and before his departure for the Holy Land was presented with a check for $1000 in support of his important work. Soon after this, Schumacher was on his way to the Holy Land and under date of January 29, 1870, sent Henrici and Lenz his first carefully written report from Haifa (Caifa), from which I translate the following sections:

At present there are seven families here with a number of single young men, and externally are primarily occupied with the building of houses. Our colony lies 1/4 hour west of Caifa (Haifa) at the foot of Mount Carmel. Before us lies a magnificent bay of the Mediterranean Ocean. Nature has here formed a harbor, which, when prepared, would be without equal. To the northeast the mountains of Galilee and behind them Mount Hermon over 8000 feet high, whose crown is generally covered with snow, tower above us. We, of course, must struggle with no small difficulties, because one can here attach oneself to nothing lasting but must create everything new. The houses by all means must be built of stone, because first of all wood is too expensive and cannot stand the extreme heat without being torn apart, and they would offer too little protection against the heat. Stones are quarried from Mount Carmel and brought over on donkeys. Lime is burned a short distance from here and the sand is fetched from the seashore. Our place was selected with greatest care and externally combines such magnificent qualities as few places could offer. Already eighty workers, all Arabs, are occupied with bringing up materials, digging or drilling wells or cellars. (Everything must be drilled or broken through rock.) The direction of building is in my hand, carpentry work is in the hands of Brother Oldorf. Lumber comes partially from Triest and from Asia Minor. The Turkish government does not do the least here for culture, in general there is a sad ignorance, a low level of life, yes, I might say the poorest sort of life to be found among the population here, although on the other hand they mark the customs and usages of former times, as the Bible designates. Also one does not see such flat, spoiled faces as, e.g. in the finely civilized Europe or America, but even in spite of all decadence more seriousness and dignity is to be noted, also the people for their part are industrious. The Catholic and Greek Churches have established themselves well, but the Greek is in constant conflict with the Catholic, which is good for us. There is not a thought of deeper religious life among these churches, the Muslims or Mohammedans really are ahead of the Christian churches in honesty, and it is pleasant to deal with the Turks.

The report continues at length with a description of the buildings that are being constructed and the agricultural and educational activity and plans in progress. Most of the members of the Society speak several languages and all are either fluent or getting fluent in Arabic. On the basis of the prophecies which are to be fulfilled in these latter days Schumacher then suggests that the Harmonists support their project with $10,000, and that they send a delegation over to convince themselves that they are a worthy cause. Not only Schumacher but also W. F. Schwilk, the editor of the *Reichsposaune,* urged the Harmonists to remember Rapp's dying faith that he was called to lead his congregation to the Holy Land, and that he made careful financial and other material preparations to fulfill this mission. They were ready to use the old printing press of the Society to publish their *Reichsposaune* and were especially eager to make Economy with its many empty houses their educational youth center. This plan of using the assets of the Harmonists to carry out the dream of Father Rapp is in part the subject of another Schumacher letter written from Haifa on November 18, 1870. By this time their community had grown to 100 souls and the work was continuing to grow so much that they were negotiating for more land and more colonies. Schumacher continues:

Nothing stands in the path of our expansion, even the Turkish government is more than meeting us half way. I also cannot help but inform you that in recent days we have felt the help and merciful generosity of God in a special manner; some time ago we requested and suggested to the Turkish government, i.e. the Governor (Wali) of Syria, to allow us to purchase Mount Carmel, at the foot of which our colony lies. Last week at the order of Wali we were informed officially through the Consul General Weber in Beiruth, that Mount Carmel would be transferred to us as a free gift because the Wali, secretly and unknown to us, had visited the colony and could only express his complete satisfaction with us. Now imagine the change, while one can implore the Turkish government for years before it will do anything, and people have only laughed at us, and only destruction was seen in store for our work, God performs a visible miracle. . . . Mount Carmel is well suited for raising cattle and building vineyards, gardens on the Plateau, and buildings for nursing homes for sick people. I am now busy surveying it all and drawing a map which will give our boundaries. I merely add that the territory which will be given to us will stretch out over great distances.

Again Schumacher urges Henrici and Lenz to come over and see for themselves.

In spite of all this enthusiasm and success, Henrici writes Schumacher on February 8, 1871, that the Lord has not yet given them complete enlightenment convincing them that the plans of the Temple Society for the Holy Land are those He has in store for this area and mankind, but as a sign of their good will, Henrici again sent them a draft for two thousand dollars in gold.

Highly interesting in this reply is the fact that the Harmonists cannot agree with the Temple Society in improving the native Arabs and in building colonies, because

we have an unlimited confidence in the promise of God and expect a complete and unadulterated verbal fulfillment of the same. We therefore consider the descendants of that people which He, when the time was fulfilled, with strong hand himself led out of Egypt into Canaan, that these descendants are the legal heirs of the same, whom He, according to repeated promises, will, when the time is fulfilled, himself again re-instate in their legal inheritance.

But although salvation once came from Israel, Henrici believes that it will this time come in reverse order, and he then asks: "And which people would be more suited to be His tools for such blessings than the German?" The kind invitation to visit them is not accepted because the Harmony Society has another mission and they cannot come "as long as we do not receive a higher command." Henrici wrote this letter three times, carefully making many changes in wording, showing how much he struggled to find the right way to act toward this obviously very sincere people.

For the next twenty years the Harmonists were in close communication with these Christian Zionists who established other colonies at Jaffa and Jerusalem. All this was achieved largely with the help of Harmony Society gold dollars, which were sent over at various and frequent intervals. The exact amount donated cannot be determined from the existing record, but it is certain from a record in the Imperial German Consulate at Jerusalem, dated April 27, 1890, that the Harmony Society as late as 1889 loaned the *Tempelgesellschaft* the sum of $10,000 at three percent, capital to be repaid in ten years, for the purpose of buying additional land for Temple Colonies in Palestine. This loan was secured by the property of the Society of the Temple, which included title to Mount Carmel and the settlement near Haifa. There were 170 souls then living in this settlement, some of the largest land holders being American citizens. A map of the lands and a complete inventory of property had been sent the Society. In appreciation of the earlier gifts received from the Harmonists one of the main halls in the school built at Temple Station near Haifa was called "Rapp Saal" and a bronze plate in the hall testified to George Rapp's and his Society's generosity. By 1890 Jacob Schumacher had become U.S. Consular Agent at Haifa and in that capacity countersigned and sealed the record of the loan. The Imperial German Government and the Government of the United States at this time were cooperating in a very friendly manner to support a joint German and American

Christian Zionist movement. It is not to be determined, in view of the extremely confused record of the Society affairs from this time on, whether this loan was ever repaid. A report in the New York *Neue Volkszeitung* dated May 20, 1939, stated that the descendants of the Hardegg-Hoffmann colonists, although their ancestors had come to Palestine to help the Jews rebuild the Temple, had all become vigorous Nazis and had proceeded to purify their ranks of Jewish elements, but this report does not seem completely dependable either.[5] By a strange coincidence, the author of this history upon opening the Religious Affairs Office of U.S. Military Government for Württemberg-Baden in Stuttgart after the Second World War, received as his first business on the first day a request from some of these descendants who had been repatriated to Germany to be permitted to reestablish the *"Tempelgesellschaft"* and return to their *native* Palestine. The State of Israel, which had meanwhile been established, had dispossessed these native Palestinians of German race and Christian creed. They ultimately found a home in Australia.

The Hutterian Brethren or the Hutterites were another group of communist brethren who were considered worthy of extensive aid from the Harmonists during this time. They were then and are now the oldest surviving practicing communists of the world, their organization having been established by Jacob Hutter, who was burned at the stake in Innsbruck on February 24, 1536. From that time until today they have lived, worked, and frequently suffered martyrdom for their primitive Christian faith. They have lived in and been driven out of most countries of the old world, generally moving to frontier or so-called backward and underdeveloped areas to escape from the dubious and to them soul-killing blessings of progressive civilization. Although their faith and sense of values are completely different from those of the Jewish People, they have had in common with them a certain sense of exclusiveness, and surely the history of the sufferings and persecution of the Jewish people presents no more tragic a record than do the Hutterites' faithfully kept records, which have since been edited and published most painstakingly by Professor A. J. F. Zieglschmid.[6]

The Harmonists knew about these people long before they

had direct contact with them, for their library contained an interesting and fully authentic account of their life and practice while they were still in Russia.[7] According to this account, it was in May 1802, about a year before George Rapp left Württemberg to find a place for his followers, that the Hutterites moved away from their twenty-four-year-old home at Wishinky and in July of that year began building their new settlement near Roditschewo or Raditschy in the northernmost part of the Ukrain. Four months after this beginning, the head of the United Brethren at Sarepta, Johann Wygand, visited them in their new location and was surprised at the progress they had made in the short time they had been there. The account he left of their settlement reminds one of the Melish account of the first settlement of the Harmonists in the United States.[8] They had completed eighteen or nineteen homes, had established a blacksmith shop, tannery, shoemaker shop, distillery, and were well on their way toward the establishment of other industries. They carried on this activity although their and their ancestors' experience had amply proved the Biblical teaching that they were sojourners and pilgrims, and that they had here no continuing city. Just as the settlement they were building with so much zeal was not their first, so it was not to be their last, home; in fact they were destined to continue their search for new frontiers, where they would be able to live unmolested and free from compulsions and regimentations, which, in their experience, had been a concomitant of growing population and civilization throughout the world and throughout the ages. As the Harmonists had to change their abode in America, so similar circumstances were to bring these oldest of practicing communists to America as almost penniless refugees from Russia and throw them at the mercy of the Christian communists of this country.

One institution found in the Hutterian settlement as described by Wygand was not found in the Harmony Society, although in other ways the two groups were almost identical, and this Hutterian institution was its strongest link to the future, the link which explains why the Hutterians continue to live today while the Harmonists are but a memory. "On the left side of the Quarre," wrote Wygand, "are two rooms, which are now inhabited by 18 mothers, each with her infant. They remain in this house for the first year and a half; they obtain their food from the common kitchen." This institution, embodying so many ideas claimed to be the development of our age, had earlier been described in the greatest German novel of the period of the Thirty Years' War, *Simplicius Simplizissimus*,[9] in a chapter describing the life of the Hutterites while they still lived in Hungary, one of the periods of their greatest prosperity.

Wygand's report not only tells about the historical records which the Hutterites had at the time, and which Professor Zieglschmid later obtained for publication from descendants in South Dakota,[6] but also mentions the following Hutterites with whom or with whose direct descendants the Harmonists later dealt directly: Johannes Waldner, Andreas Wuzy, Joseph Kleinsasser, Jacob Hofer, Paul Glanzer, and Christian Waldner. By 1877 the Hutterites had multiplied considerably in Russia and were living in a place named Hutterthal (Hutter Valley) in South Russia, where they received advice on matters of international exchange and travel to the United States from the Harmony Society. It was and still is the practice of the Hutterians to keep their communities small and to establish new "Bruderhöfe" (communities) as their children mature and the population increases. These new communities are established with the assistance of the old.[6] Because the Russian Government at that time had passed restrictive measures against them, the Hutterites were in the process of moving to the United States. One of their communities had already been established at Bon Homme, Dakota Territory, at this time, and the earliest written evidence of relations with the Harmonists seems to begin in the year 1875.

On May 31, 1875, the entire Bon Homme community, represented by twenty-three male members, signed a document which empowered Michel and Joseph Waldner to raise a loan for the community "because the congregation is poor in money." Both in language and calligraphy it reflected the tradition found in the four-hundred-year-old Hutterian Chronicle. It is at the same time one of the most unbusinesslike and yet effective applications for a loan in the Harmony Society Archives. That it was acted upon favorably was due partly to the absolute sincerity of the Hutterians and partly to the fact that the request was presented personally by the two Waldners named in the petition. The Harmonists felt that the Hutterians, except for the matter of celibacy, were fellow believers. For this reason there was almost no limit to the patient help granted as long as the old Harmonists remained in control of their wealth. They were spiritually the closest of kin to the Harmonists, and it is a pity that before Henrici's death some provision could not have been worked out making them the material heirs of the Harmonists, for certainly no other group in America or in the entire world could at that time make greater claim to being their spiritual heirs.

On June 22, 1875, the Harmonists wrote to the two Waldners, who had received a loan of three thousand dollars and were back at Bon Homme. From this letter I translate the following:

Your letter written to us from Amana[10] was safely received and its contents carefully considered. We are very happy that the brethren in Amana showed themselves willing to support you with council and action. It was very proper that an experienced brother brought you to the man who can furnish you a good mill. We are not surprised that this costs no less than $5000 to purchase that which you can use to construct it. It would be unwise to erect such a mill which in a short time you would have to exchange with a larger one at great loss, and it is quite proper to do the thing right at the start. We are therefore willing to let you have the additional two thousand on the same condition as the three which you already have. Just write how soon you would like to have the money and we will send you a draft at the right time, payable in New York, and which you probably can convert into cash easily and without great deduction. The man who is furnishing your machine would probably accept the same as money. Soon after the middle of the month our friend Judge Hice will pay you a visit to look into everything, he could then bring the draft with him. But if you should need the money sooner, let us know that we may send the draft by mail.

If it can be done, brother Lenz will come along with Judge Hice. In any case you can now close the contract for the machinery, so that you will get your mill going as soon as possible. With hearty greetings to you and your community, we remain your sincere friends . . .

Like most of the solid buildings constructed by the Harmonists at their various settlements and at Springfield, Indiana, this mill still stands today. It has been modernized, but the additions do not seem to be so solidly constructed as the original part which was built on the advice of the Harmonists.

As is evident from a letter of September 24, 1875, Jonathan Lenz, the Junior Trustee of the Society, actually went to visit the Hutterians in Dakota that summer. He made a report to the Harmonists in which he made some criticism but still expressed the confidence that experience and the spirit of the Lord would step by step correct these matters. He was astonished to find all the Hutterians in such excellent health, no doubt recalling the difficulties the Harmonists had faced in this regard when they pioneered on the Wabash.

Lenz was deeply impressed by the sincerity and genuineness of character of the Hutterians, therefore Henrici in summarizing their situation says: "Your sincere and honest attitude toward God and the ideal of communal brotherhood (Brüdergemeinschaft) for the present is the main thing. God looks down to the bottom of the heart and if that is right, then the rest is also achieved with his help."

A week after this letter was written another "Gemeine Spruch" (community resolution) requesting another loan of $1000 for the mill construction was signed by the community and addressed to the Harmony Society. This request explains that the money loaned will not cover the expense of constructing the mill and states that they make this request of the Harmonists "as our fathers, yes we have confidence in you as we have among our own brethren." October 8, 1875, Henrici and Lenz sent the amount requested and stated that they were not surprised that the amount previously loaned did not cover the construction of the mill "and we do not expect the amount now sent to suffice, and we are ready between now and New Year to send you another thousand dollars if you need it. You need only let us know in a few words how much you need and when we should send it." In reply to such kindness the Hutterians on November 4 explained the situation in which they were and that their construction work actually was running beyond their original estimates. On November 16 another draft for a thousand dollars was sent them with this comment:

Be as economical and saving as you possibly can, for the present times are hard, and no one knows how long this can continue. It is very good that you all love industry, and that you have not accustomed yourselves to expensive foods and clothing, but that you are satisfied with that which is necessary. If you continue in this way you will certainly with the Lord's help fare well and you will soon get into comfortable circumstances. We will be very happy if you get along with the amount you are now receiving from us, but if it does not carry you through entirely, let us know in time how much more you must have. As soon as you see your way clear we will send you a bill and request you to give us a proper certificate of indebtedness for the amounts received, so that we as administrators can prove properly in which way we invest and have invested the Society's capital.

The original letter of the Hutterians must have contained considerable religious material, for Henrici's reply takes up a number of these points. The Hutterians are warned against concerning themselves too much with Spiritualism, in which there was much interest at the time and about which the Harmonists were very careful as often as it was mentioned to them. The Hutterians obviously had also expressed the wish to send out messengers to guide new recruits to their society and Henrici, obviously with the experience of Count Leon in mind, warns them against attempts at conversion or at attempts to increase their membership in other ways.

The present generation is very unreceptive for such a community life as is practiced among you and us. Above all see to it that you among yourselves now in a small way achieve something worthwhile, dependable, and tried through God's help. When the time comes that you have spiritually and physically achieved a certain independence and manly maturity in your present congregation, then you may also consider increasing your membership. For the present it seems to us to be too early and inadvisable to enter upon such things.

What you write us about organs and the like is surely well enough meant and we would not advise you to deviate from your quiet simplicity. Formerly, when we still had many young people, and were stronger ourselves, we made use of musical instruments only at special festivals, and then to the honor of God, to which he often visibly gave his special blessing. Now that our voices often are too weak to hold singing in the right harmonious tune, we use instruments to support us. So do not take offense if in faith and to the honor of God we use musical instruments, as was also done at God's command and order (Psalm 150) in Israel in the Temple service, and as is done and will be done by the harpists at the glassy sea.

Henrici urged the Hutterians to consider music in nature and to refrain from being narrow and judging everything by their standard, rather than by the standard of love, which gives to all its best possible interpretation.

On March 8, 1876, Henrici and Lenz sent a sum of one thousand dollars to the Amana Society in Iowa to pay for a debt the Hutterians owed there on the construction of their mill. On August 14, 1876, there is reference to a letter of July 31 by Michael and Joseph Waldner reporting their safe arrival in Dakota together with their new friends. The Waldners had just met some of their brethren who had come from Russia, and had stopped at Economy on the way north. There is the usual offer of a loan, this time to pay off land. All this kindness to the Hutterians, of course, spread the good news of ready cash among neighboring Germans in the Dakotas, so that many requests reached the Society for loans to individuals. These, however, were not granted and in each case the Harmonists carefully explained that they could and would help the Hutterians because their communistic way of life practically made them brethren of the same faith. In accord with God's command they reserved their help chiefly for those of the same or like faith.

In a letter of January 6, 1877, Henrici and Lenz acknowledged receipt of a book called *Rechenschaft,* sent them by the Hutterians and giving their history and religious and social regulations. This material was sent that the Harmonists might study the history and prepare the proper legal form of organization for the Hutterians. The Harmonists were concerned about the inclusion of proper articles to cover the Hutterians against those who might eventually leave them. In this connection it is revealed that the Harmonists, with the help of their legal adviser, Judge Hice, actually worked out legal articles of association for the Hutterians, based on those of the Harmony Society. These articles the Harmonists translated carefully into German and promised to send to the Hutterians for their examination and adoption. But since the careful translation of the articles would take considerable time in view of their business just then, they at once sent on the three thousand dollars which the Hutterians had just requested as a loan.

It has already been pointed out that the Harmonists advised and assisted other Hutterians still in Russia on migration to the United States. The Harmony Society by this time had become a sort of information bureau for prospective emigrants and immigrants, and they fully justified all confidence placed in them, for they knew the situation throughout the United States from this point of view much better than the transient officials of the Government in New York or Washington. Above all, people had confidence in the integrity of the Society, and always their advice and help could be depended upon. Alone for its service to the thousands of immigrants during the century of its existence the Harmony Society deserves to live forever in the history of our nation.

In the fall of 1877 the Hutterians asked the Harmonists to market two thousand sacks of wheat for them. Since this was done in their usual unbusinesslike manner, Henrici took all the trouble to write to a business man he knew in Yankton to ask about the price of wheat there, what the weight of each sack was, and whether packed in paper or cloth sacks. A few months after this the Harmonists sent the Dakota brethren a shipment of vines, locust trees, and other things intended to aid them in their pioneer work in the Dakota Territory.

In June 1878 Michel Waldner again called at Economy, bearing a letter from Jakob Hofer requesting another loan of $4000 to cover the cost of twenty new claims of land which the Hutterians had taken, and the letter stated that they had the "childlike and beautiful confidence in you dear brethren" that help would be given.

Economic conditions were very hard during these years and, to make matters worse, the Hutterians lacked good and sound business leadership in this critical period. But the Harmonists were blessed with worldly goods which the Heavenly Father had "added thereunto," and since the bridegroom had not yet appeared, although they were old and without heirs, they did not mind continuing their help. In view of the difficulties of the times just then, the Harmonists made one more great attempt to put them on their own by giving them a new start in a more favorable location.

The Harmony Society for some time had owned a great deal of land around Tidioute, Pa., the cradle of America's oil industry. Because they had been among the first in America to drill for oil in these rich fields, they had received many excellent offers to sell this land. This they persistently refused, because they were holding the land for a suitable group of Christian communists. In 1884 a tentative agreement was reached, according to which the Hutterians—especially the "Russians," who had meanwhile arrived, with the help and guidance of the Harmonists—were to move to this land, and Lenz even made several trips to Dakota to bring groups of the brethren to Tidioute.

In January 1885, finally, the Harmonists proposed very definite terms for the transfer of the Tidioute lands to the Hutterians. They gave them highly favorable terms of payment and interest, but the entire agreement depended upon the actual removal of the colony to these lands, in fact they proposed the transfer of all the Warren County lands held by the Harmony Society if the entire group of Hutterians numbering about 130 at Bon Homme and 250 elsewhere in Dakota would move unto this land. This offer was accepted, but for some unknown reason it was never fully carried through. A group of Hutterians settled on the Tidioute lands and with the help of the Harmonists did some business in lumber for quite a while, but they failed to get on their own feet. Apparently there was also trouble about selling the Dakota lands and property, and some of the brethren simply voted to stay in the Dakota Territory. The Harmonists nevertheless continued their help for many years. In 1886 Judge Hice was again sent to Dakota to aid the Hutterians in legal matters. It appears that the expense of all such travel was carried by the Harmonists.

The Harmonists certainly were patient with these new communist pioneers. That is shown not only by their many loans but also by the fact that they turned over to them some of their most valuable lands, since held by one of America's largest oil companies, and there is every reason to believe that the trustees of the Harmony Society would have turned over more of their property to them. Had they accepted celibacy, they could have become members of the Society. Henrici and Lenz loved and trusted these people, but with all the confidence they had in them they also wanted evidence proving that their brethren could manage business affairs well. Had the Hutterians given evidence of business ability, it seems quite certain that they would be the owners of much of the Harmony Society empire today. They would not have made them their heirs, because their faith in their own mission kept them from making a will, but the Hutterians surely would have become owners of the Society lands either in the vicinity of Tidioute, Pennsylvania, or near Saginaw, Michigan. In both places the holdings of the Society were extensive, and the terms for the Hutterians would have amounted to a donation. Since the Hutterians did not manage to make themselves financially independent but continued to ask for loans, the Harmonists at last, in a letter of May 5, 1887, felt themselves obliged to inform them that they had now done all they could for them and that in the future they would have to help each other along and make communism work. This by no means broke off the relations between the two groups, but with Lenz's death in 1890 and Henrici's in 1892, a complete change came in the management of the Harmony Society, one that had no spiritual understanding and much less patience with the ideals of Christian communism. The Hutterians were still negotiating with the Harmonists just before and after Henrici's death, but by that time a worldly and hard business man had become head of the Harmony Society, and although the business ability of the Hutterians by then had shown great improvement, they could not touch the heart of the man who was then plotting to become the sole heir of the Harmony Society millions.

As was pointed out previously, the Harmony Society since the time before the Civil War had given financial and spiritual support to another communist colony, which called itself *Ora Labora,* and which had chosen the frontier near Saginaw, Michigan, for the scene of its prayers and labors. A great deal of Harmony Society money went into this venture, but eventually it broke up and the Harmony Society took over its lands. The former director, Emil Bauer, a sort of "Latin farmer," who later was a Professor of German at the University of Michigan, became the real estate agent of the Society in these Michigan frontier lands. With the help of Harmony Society funds the railroad was brought up from Ann Arbor, and from that point on the individual and capitalistic development of this frontier went on rapidly. The extensive correspondence between the Harmonists and Emil Bauer contains ample material for a book in itself about the early history of virgin lands bordering on Saginaw Bay, Michigan.

The relations of the Harmonists to their fellow Württembergers at Zoar, Ohio, were always cordial, and they often exchanged visits and members. Some preferred the more leisurely piety of Zoar to the more rigid "strictest observance" at Economy, but the Trustees of both Societies had troubles in common resulting from lawsuits of withdrawing members. In such cases they always helped each other by exchanging legal information. The same was true of the Shakers, who also faced such lawsuits and gave the Harmonists the benefit of their experience. With the Shakers there was also a friendly correspondence of long standing, which originally had developed out of the hope of reaching some sort of union. This, however, failed on the basis of the Shaker teachings of Christ, whereas the Harmonists stood firmly on the Lutheran orthodox faith out of which they came.

Relations were also very friendly with Amana, from whom the Harmonists bought their cloth after they had closed down their own mills. The relations with the Shakers, Zoarites, and Amanaists were always on a basis of mutually successful Christian communists. The Shakers, Zoarites, and Amanaists were financially independent and solid, but not one of the many communist societies of the age ever reached the capitalistic heights which made the Harmonists the bankers of Pittsburgh. The names of Carnegie and Vanderbilt will live forever in

American life through the great institutions that were established through their generosity, but because the generosity of Santa Claus Henrici was bestowed according to 2 Kings, its memory, like his seed and that of the Society members has been extinguished. Their generous gifts were never named.

This is not the place to describe the influence of the Harmony Society on such highly interesting communist movements as Cyrus Teed and his Koreshanity, A. K. Owen (no relative of Robert Owen, as he carefully pointed out) and his *The Credit Foncier Movement* at Topolobampo Harbor, Sinaloa, Mexico (what romance!), and that of Wendell Willkie's forerunner, Doctor Von Swartwout, whose ancestral line dated in America before 1640 and who once ran for the Presidency of the United States on the Olombia One-Plank Platform. This was to change the name of the U.S. to the Olombia Commonwealth, which was then to become *The New Columbia United States of the World.* Alexander, Napoleon, Hitler, Stalin, and all the Communists today, were and are small and provincial in their thinking when compared to Dr. Von Swartwout! His letterhead showed his world level of operations: New York, London, Paris, Egypt, Palestine, and so on. If the trustees of the Society had accepted his offer to raise the Olombia Flag over the property of the Harmony Society, Economy would have become the first capital of the *One World* which the Republican Presidential Candidate Wendell Willkie later wrote about.

Nor is this the place to deal with the Harmony Society's influence on the founding of Brook Farm, Fruitlands, and similar movements and plans for a Utopian world. They all were inspired by the success of the Harmony Society and their leaders either corresponded with, visited, or read the widely publicized reports on, the Society. Brook Farm and Fruitlands especially, though great economic failures, live on through their literary productions, while the Harmony Society, the most successful economically and spiritually, today is practically forgotten. The Harmonists' faith was their greatest asset in life; for survival and posthumous fame it was a liability.

8

Harmonist Doctrine and Its Fundamental Prohibition To Divide Society Property or To Make Any Testament

AFTER FATHER RAPP'S DEATH, THE MEMBERS OF THE SOCIETY HAD renewed their covenant, making necessary changes. When Baker died, this was not considered necessary, and no more was done than to inform the public and those with whom the Society did business that the business of the Society would now be carried on in the name of Henrici and Lenz. Many persons outside of the Society were now more concerned than ever about the failure of the Society to make legal provision for the inheritance of its wealth, because it was rapidly losing its members to the power of death. Friedrich List had already expressed his concern about this matter to Frederick Rapp and more recently Wilhelm Weitling had used the Bible, which he knew well, to support his arguments for such a provision in his discussion with one of the elders of the Society. Although death was claiming one member after another in the Society, there was absolutely no concern about a testament within the Society, for nothing that could happen, be it war, pestilence, depression, sickness, or death, could shake the faith of the seasoned members who now made up the Society—faith in the teachings of Father Rapp; faith that the Society had been established in these latter days by God himself, according to prophecy; and faith that it was not up to man to dissolve what God had created, or up to the trustees or members to waver in their faith in God's promises to the Harmony Society by making a

141

last will and testament which would provide for the distribution of the worldly possessions of the Society. These possessions were the gift of God, held in trust for Him, and were to be placed at His feet when He came, as evidence that they had been good stewards.

The belief that the Harmony Society was established by God and was indissoluble because God had established it for a special mission which was to be realized in the Millennium quite logically precluded the making of any Society last will and testament. If God should choose not to claim his bride before the last member died in the flesh, then there was always the Commonwealth of Pennsylvania, the Government ordained by God, which would logically take over the property. In view of what happened to this property ultimately, it is important to the history of the Society at this time to consider its religious teachings as they were made public during the latter part of the Baker-Henrici trusteeship, for it was at the end of the Henrici trusteeship, after the death of the last of the Harmonists, Jonathan Lenz, that the Society developed the malignant cancer which rapidly brought spiritual death and paved the way for the impious and irreligious dissolution of the Harmony Society. As long as the Baker-Henrici trusteeship lasted, they did stand loyally by the faith and doctrine of the Harmony Society. And this was not merely a passive loyalty, for during the Baker-Henrici trusteeship there was just as active a religious life within the Society as during the time of the Rapps, with the difference that age had conquered the sexual infirmity of the flesh, and that they concerned themselves more than the Rapps had with doctrinal discussions involving persons outside of the Society. It is such religious discussion with others that documents the full explanation for the Society's refusal to make any provision for the final disposition of its property. The Society had always refused even to think of making provision for the division of its wealth or the dissolution of the Society, but it had always hesitated to explain its reasons publicly. This attitude now underwent a change, a change that is understood best through a careful review of the doctrines held by the Harmonists.

In spite of everything that has been written, sworn, or solemnly affirmed to the contrary, the Harmony Society was first, foremost, and last a *church*. As has been shown in my *George Rapp's Harmony Society*, in discussing the events which led to the founding of the Society, George Rapp and his followers considered themselves a *congregation* and a *church*, having a divinely ordained and prophesied mission. In the first articles of agreement the Society had been called a *church* and the word *church* (*Kirche*) and *Congregation* (*Gemeine*) had been used interchangeably to designate the organization. As a church it had its body of doctrine, even though this doctrine was carefully guarded as a possession which should not be cast before the swine, that is, before the curious and inquisitive and intolerant public. For this reason the Articles of Agreement made it a privilege to benefit from George Rapp's teaching. As the Society gradually made intelligent, tolerant, and genuinely interested friends in the great world, it became less secretive about its teachings. A friend of Nietzsche, Professor Knortz, who wrote very entertainingly but inaccurately about the religion of the Society during the Henrici era, never was granted access to its inner sanctum, but Dr. Aaron Williams, who by living at the Harmony Hotel became a friend of the leaders, was shown a great measure of confidence and was given assistance, particularly by Baker, in writing his book *The Harmony Society*, which was published in Pittsburgh in 1866 with a prefatory note by Baker and Henrici stating that the material had been submitted to them previous to publication, and that they found the statements correct. "His statement of our views on the various points discussed, although in somewhat different language from what we are accustomed to employ, may be received as, in the main, correct." The words they employed were, of course, the German words of their sources, and they were difficult to translate. The following survey of their doctrinal position is largely taken from Williams's two chapters on the religion of the Harmonists and from the letters of Baker and Henrici, especially those written to the Shakers during the last years of Baker's life.

Concerning the Word of God. The Society taught that the Old and New Testament were the inspired Word of God and that this was the infallible divinely revealed guide for the present and the future. The only source of the Society's religion was therefore the Bible, but in their understanding of the Bible they were guided by such famous German mystical and theological writers as: Johann Arndt, Jacob Spener, August H. Franke, Jacob Böhme, Gottfried Arnold, Bengel, Jung Stilling, Michael Hahn, the Berleburg edition of the Bible with its commentaries, and von Welling. All these were represented in the library of the Society. The last-named writer was of special importance to George Rapp in his earliest period in Germany, and the letters of Baker show that he learned much from him when he prepared his sermons for his fellow members. Von Welling's great work so interested Johann Wolfgang Goethe that he made an index to it and used some of the material found in it for his great drama *Faust*.[1] The work also was part of the personal library of Joseph Bäumeler, the founder of the communist colony at Zoar, Ohio. It was generally a work of great influence in Germany among the religious nonconformists, therefore its rather lengthy title is here given in a form that should be intelligible to English readers:

Herrn Georgii von Welling Opus *Mago-Cabbalisticum et Theosophicum,* in which the origin, nature, character, and use of salt, sulphur, and mercury are described in three parts, and, besides many strange mathematical, theosophic, magic, and mystic materials, also the development (Erzeugung) of metals and minerals is proved from the basis of nature; together with the main-key of the entire work, and many curious mago-cabbalistic figures. To this is added: a small tract on Divine Wisdom; and a special appendix of several very rare and valuable chemical pieces. Franckfurt and Leipzig, 1760.

The author states in the introduction that he had begun this secret study without any thought of publication and that the first part had been published against his will, that for that reason he felt obliged to correct and complete the publication. His intent by no means was to teach any man to make gold, "rather our goal reaches out for something much higher, namely, how one may see and recognize nature out of God, and God in nature, and how furthermore out of this perception the true, pure service of the creature flows as a thank-offering due the creator."

Gottfried Arnold's *The Secret of the Divine Sophia or Wisdom*,[2] a work also highly revered by the leaders of the Ephrata Cloisters,[3] with whom the Harmonists had much in common, was another beloved work of Baker and Henrici. The attitude which Baker took toward wisdom in his discussion with the Shakers was that of the author of this work.

In addition to the works of Jacob Böhme, cited and discussed in the first volume of this history, another work ascribed to him must be mentioned, because in 1855 the Harmonists had it printed and had a copy placed in each home of the Society. Strangely, it was a Masonic work, although the Harmonists were not Free Masons. Its title was *Hirten Brief an die wahren und echten Freimaurer des alten Systems,* Pittsburgh, 1855 (Pastoral Letter to true and genuine Free Masons of the ancient system, 5785).[4] Like von Welling's book, this pastoral letter is deeply concerned with the Fall of Lucifer, its resulting disharmony and chaos, and the order to come. As these works made liberal use of an allegorical interpretation of the Bible, so the Harmonists did, from George Rapp to Jacob Henrici. This method of interpretation was applied especially to the Old Testament to find the deeper symbolical meaning beneath the surface of historical facts. This by no means meant a denial of the literal inspiration of the Bible or of the literal verity of the historical facts; it did mean that they spiritualized the letter and in this way found the Old Testament full of the richest gospel truth. Using this method of allegorical interpretation, R. L. Baker summarized one of his sermons as follows in a letter of May 17, 1861, to Jonathan Lenz:

This morning I was in the meeting. The text was Genesis 48, where Joseph gets the news that his father Jacob is sick, and he with his two sons Manasseh and Ephraim visited him. The space from creation to the founding of the congregation of Israel under Moses belongs to Abraham, to Isaac the time from said founding to Christ, from there on as the third period of time, from the pouring out of the Holy Spirit on the first day of Pentecost until the coming of the Lord and perhaps the millennium included is Jacob's time.

The present time is also a sick time. Also the heavenly Joseph is getting news that Jacob according to nature is sick. Sickly is the unharmonious world of elements (*Elementar Welt*) in the realm of plants and animals, whereof we had sufficient proof during this changeable winter. Sickly are *customs and morals* of men, sickly is the *religious* branch of the world. And sickly are the *political* conditions of the entire world, also those of the United States. What would be more suitable than that the heavenly Joseph would soon put in his appearance, in order to reform everything. Also the first-born Manasse in the light of nature, that he might be made subject to the firstling Ephraim, so that the light of grace of Christ might become dominant in all the world. This is our wish, whether we are dealing with oil or some other thing, isn't that so?

Concerning God. The Harmonists taught the doctrine of a triune God. In the words of Baker and Henrici: "We hold God the Father as active, Christ as passive, and the operation of the Spirit as Exit (going out) of the two, as on the day of Pentecost. God the Creator, Christ the Restorer, and the Holy Spirit the Exit (going out) of both dwelling in the Restored. Therefore we shall, as we have done, expect all from and through Christ and shall look for His coming as the word of God has it." They highly exalted the character of Jesus Christ and made him all in their system of salvation. For many years they kept up a close correspondence with the Shakers and were very friendly with them because they believed that they had much in common with them, but this friendship came to an abrupt end in a letter from Baker dated May 11, 1865, informing the Shakers that they had perused some of their statements "about our Lord Jesus Christ derogatory to his divine character." "It is not our intention to invite you to a paper controversy," it went on, "or to ask explanation of the matter, it is plain enough and stands on paper in black and white."

Concerning Man's Creation. The Harmonists held those views of the dual Adam which are found in the works of Jacob Böhme. They believed that God created man originally in his exact image and in a higher sense than is usually attached to those words. As Williams stated it (p. 98):

Instead of confining the image of God to a mere moral likeness in "knowledge, righteousness, and holiness," they include in it also a resemblance in form to the person of the Godman, or God-manifest, whose "voice was heard walking in the garden," and whose visible appearances are often referred to in the Old Testament; this theanthropic manifestation being not merely anticipative of his incarnation, when he was "made in the likeness of man," but his original and normal characteristic as the Logos or God-revealed. Hence the expression, "No man hath seen God at any time; the only begotten Son, who is in the bosom of the Father, he hath declared (revealed) him." His incarnation as the son of Mary was but the subjection of his theanthropic person to all the conditions of our fallen humanity, "without sin." Thus he became the second Adam.

Man they regard as constituting the highest order of created beings, higher even than the angels, who are only "ministering spirits sent forth to minister to the heirs of salvation." This they infer also from his being the last in the ascending order of creation, as well as from the honor put upon our humanity through its assumption by Christ as the second Adam, who "took not on him the nature of angels." The passage which says, "Thou hast made him a little lower than the angels," they understand as it is given in Luther's version, "Thou hast for a little time deprived him of the angels," i.e. in the person of Christ as "Son of man," who during his incarnation was deprived of that ministry and worship of angels with which he was surrounded before he became man.

They regard Adam also as having been made a *dual being,* having both the sexual elements within himself, according to Gen. 1: 26,27, "And God said, Let us make man in our image, after our likeness, and let *them* have dominion," And "so God created man in his own image; in the image of God created he him; male and female created he them." They understand the word *them* in both these verses as applying to the dual Adam, before the separation of Eve from him, as recorded in the second chapter.

Concerning Man's Fall. The Harmonists, as Baker and Henrici informed the Shakers on January 19, 1857, taught that the first influence practiced on man by the serpent's head (or by the evil spirit) was to inflame his imagination in favor of an external helpmate when he discovered the animals before him to be male and female (Gen. 2: 19, 20). Just at this juncture the first fall of man took place by which Adam violated his own inward sanctuary and his own female function by means of which he could have been, as Gen. 1: 28 has it, fruitful and multiply without an external helpmate, after the order of a Hermaphrodite then; and after the order now, see Luke 20: 34, 35, 36. "And God saw everything that he had made, and behold it was very good" (Gen. 1. 31). "God said it is not good that man should be alone" (Gen. 2: 18). Now who occasioned this sudden remarkable difference from good to not good? Certainly not God! nay, it was man who had committed a great violation not to be mistaken, and which was punished of necessity by a separation of half, namely his female attribute. Williams states (p. 100) the same views but adds an explanation about the eating of the forbidden fruit. He also adds the explanation that the original Adam was capable of reproducing himself, i.e., a son of man and son of god, in a manner incomprehensible to us, by a certain holy mingling of the male and female elements of Adam's being with God's immediate approbation. This reproduction was without lust or pain.

With the fall of man into sin came the present disharmonious and disunited condition of our earth in which the "whole creation groaneth and travaileth in pain together until now." Because Lucifer was lifted up with pride and aimed at independence of God, Lucifer fell from his first estate and, on being banished from heaven, threw that part of the universe which he had before governed into conflagration and chaos. Our globe never recovered from this semi-chaotic condition. Its volcanoes, earthquakes, tornadoes, pestilences, and so on are all manifestations of the "groaning" of the world for deliverance. The earth now is a fit habitation only for the fallen, sinful race of beings, "waiting," as St. Paul says in Rom. 8: 19, "with earnest expectation for the manifestation of the sons of God." They also taught, however, that just as there is still much in the world to remind man of its original perfection, so in every man there still remains a divine spark of his original divinity which tends to search for light. But neither fallen man nor the fallen world will be liberated from its present sad state except by God's mighty action.

Concerning Christ's First Coming into the World. The Harmonists taught the doctrine of the vicarious atonement. To amend the great breach which Adam had brought about in the manner above described, Christ, the son of the woman, assumed human nature and suffered death as an atonement for the sins of the world, and soon after his ascension, the Father accepting the valued sacrifice and the Holy Spirit emanating from the Father and the Son as a comforter, was sent to the

Apostles (Acts 2), in a powerful manner and the church of Christ received a sudden and large acquisition, and a permanent standard. From that period to the present day the Holy Spirit manifested itself often, at times more and at times less. The Harmony Society was such a special strong manifestation of the Holy Spirit.

Concerning marriage and sexual intercourse. The Society taught a doctrine which was derived from their doctrine of the creation of man and the manner and penalty of his fall from his original high station. Since man's fall, the sexual organs have become bestial and separated, contrary to God's design. Because of this situation they regarded all intercourse of the sexes, both in and out of marriage, as polluting. While such intercourse might be allowed the lower order of man in lawful marriage, but only so far as it is related to the creation of a human being, yet the human offspring resulting from such acts of natural man is naturally conceived in sin. After his fall Adam no longer begat a son in the image of God but in his own sexual likeness. All men and women born since Adam are his sinful posterity, all have the bestial sexual organs, and all, because they represent only a half, and that a fallen half, of the original Adam, are living symbols of the disharmony brought into the world by Adam's sin. Because Joseph, the husband of Mary, was a sinful man, he could not beget a hold seed. This made necessary the miraculous conception of Jesus, in order that he might be a Son of God, and free from the taint of ordinary generation. On the basis of such views they regarded celibacy as the higher and purer state, while the concept of marriage was about the same as that held by the earlier German-American predecessors of the Harmonists at the Ephrata Cloisters in eastern Pennsylvania and described by Johann Conrad Beissel, the principal of this group, in his work *Die Ehe das Zuchthaus fleischlicher Menschen* (Marriage, the Penitentiary for Men of the Flesh), Ephrata, Pa., 1730. They made a very convincing case for celibacy and against marriage by reference to passages in the New Testament extolling the celibate state, particularly Rev. 14: 4: "These are they which were not defiled with women; for they are virgins." They also taught

that this celibate life was suited only to those who have a special calling for it, and they interpreted Matt. 19: 11, 12 in that
light: "All men cannot receive this saying, save they to whom it
was given. He that is able to receive it, let him receive it." But
all men who continued to propagate fallen man in the usual
carnal manner were not contributing to the hastening of the
Kingdom of God on earth. When the British geologist G. W.
Featherstonhaugh,[5] in discussing the results of celibacy with
Jacob Henrici, remarked that the adoption of the Society's
principles by all Christian communities would lead to the ex-
tinction of all society, he was startled by this unexpected reply:
"If men, by subduing their passions, which are the cause of so
much trouble in life, could accomplish an eternal life of inno-
cence, perhaps it would suit God's design, if we knew enough
of it, that our race should become extinct. We certainly can
comprehend that an existence in Heaven is infinitely more
worthy of our attention than an existence on earth." The same
view is expressed in Williams's account (p. 102), with the
additional explanation that by universal adoption of celibacy
the way would thus be the sooner prepared for the Lord's
coming, and for the new heaven and new earth wherein righteousness shall dwell.

Concerning the Millennium. The Harmonists taught and
believed in the ultimate restoration of man and this earth to its
original paradisaic condition. The library of the Society was
particularly well stocked with books dealing with the millennium and the restoration of the original state of all things. In
all sermons and letters of a theological nature written within
the Society, the doctrines concerning celibacy and the millennium were those most emphasized. In the theological letter to
the Shakers already referred to, Baker and Henrici stated that
they expected Christ to come soon, and they cited as proof:
Acts 17: 30,31,32; Rev. 14: 14–20; also 19: 11–16; also 1: 7;
Jude 14, 15; Matt. 25: 31–34; Acts 1: 11; Luke 21: 27; 1 Thess.
4: 15–18.

The scriptural Testimony here adduced confirming the personal
appearance, or the second coming of Christ is what we firmly always

held to, do now hold to, and shall hold to without deviation in time to come. We hold that Christ will be seen by all, he will not only walk the Streets of Harmony, but will walk all the Streets, and all places to judge mankind in rightiousness, separating error from truth, tares from the wheat and bad from good, and as Zachar. ch 14, v 9 has it: "And the Lord shall be King over all the Earth. In that day shall there be one Lord, and his name one.

To support the rationality of their argument that Christ would have to come to redeem his promise, they argued that only Christ with his divine power could straighten out man and the world in their present corrupt state. They wrote to the Shakers in this connection: "Why at the ratio you have been increasing say twenty thousand living and dead in about 80 years, you would require four millions years to convert a thousand millions now living."

Well, you say this wont do, it would take too long time, so say we too therefore, if man cannot effect the proper union, it requires the Spirit of the Lord to do it, as Ezekiel Chap 37 has it, to revive the living and the dead, and this we expect soon from the hands of the Lord. In summing up, we do believe, that the perfect, after the resurrection of the body will all be Hermaphrodite, hence a separate feminality is inadmissible. We have given you the foundation on which we stand, supported by Scripture; May the Holy Spirit lead us in the way of truth to a full union in Christ.

With St. Paul (Rom. 8: 19 ff) they taught that the whole creation was waiting for Christ's coming, waiting in earnest expectation for the manifestation of the sons of God, when "the creation itself shall be delivered from the bondage of corruption, into the glorious liberty of the children of God." In this restitution of all things they expected to see four points realized:

1. The physical renovation of this disordered mundane system, and the introduction of the "new heavens and the new earth" spoken of by the apostle Peter in his second epistle, 3: 13.

2. The restoration of the Jewish nation to the land of Palestine, according to the numerous predictions of the prophets, e.g., Ezek. 37: 21, Amos 9: 11–15, Jer. 30: 3.

3. The conversion of the Jews to Christianity, according to Zech. 12: 10: "They shall look upon me whom they have

pierced," and Rom. 9: 12–32 "And so all Israel shall be saved."

4. The resurrection of the sainted dead, and the transfiguration of the pious living, spoken of by the apostle Paul in 1 Thess. 4: 13–18.

All these things were to come to pass not with the end of the world, as most Christian churches teach, but before judgment day, at the beginning of the thousand years during which the saints are to live and reign with Christ according to Rev. 20: 4,5: ". . . and they lived and reigned with Christ a thousand years."

During the life of George Rapp, as has been noted, the Harmonists accepted the date set for the Second Coming by Jung Stilling, but their resulting disappointment, far from shaking their faith in the doctrine, taught them only to be more patient and cautious about setting a definite time in this matter. All technical developments, they believed, were further evidence that the great day was being hastened. Thus, when the Atlantic cable was successfully laid and when it seemed that the Russo-American Telegraph would soon be completed by way of Behring's Straits, they recalled the prediction of Nicolaus von Flue that the Lord would come when a cord should be put around the whole world. Because it was expected that telegraphic communication would be completed around the globe by 1867, many interpreters of prophecy were hoping for the Second Coming in that year. Further support for this belief was found in Matt. 24: 27: "As the lightning cometh out of the east, and shineth unto the west, so shall also the coming of the Son of Man be." They learned to keep in mind Acts 1: 7, with the warning that it is not for man to know the times or the seasons which the Father has put in his own power, and especially the Lord's injunction to his disciples, to "watch and pray," for "in such an hour as ye think not, the Son of man cometh." They believed and taught also that under the kingdom of the Messiah, which was to be set up, there would still be a race of men in the flesh, but that all these would be righteous, according to Isa. 60: 21. During this period, which they believed had already begun with the appearance of the Harmony Society, they looked for the literal realization of the many happy things foretold by the prophets, when the curse that was put upon the ground for man's sake would be removed, when "they shall build houses and inhabit them", when "there shall be no more curse," and "no more death."

Concerning the Harmony Society. The Society's leaders and members believed and taught what has already been expressed in the first volume through many quotations from the two Rapps, Baker, and Henrici. During the life of George Rapp the Harmonists were more hesitant to make their views about their Society known to nonmembers, for the same reason that all esoteric groups dislike to proclaim views they hold and cherish when they know at the start that these views will meet with opposition and persecution. Nevertheless, the following words of the preamble to the Articles of Association clearly testified to the divine origin of the Society:

Whereas, by the favor of Divine Providence, an association or congregation has been formed by George Rapp and many others, upon the basis of Christian fellowship, the principles of which, being faithfully derived from the sacred Scriptures, include the government of the patriarchal age, united to the community of property, adopted in the days of the apostles, and wherein the simple object sought, is to approximate, so far as human imperfections may allow, to the fulfillment of the will of God, by the exercise of those affections, and the practice of those virtues which are essential to the happiness of man in time and throughout Eternity . . .

In the discussion of Father Rapp's sermons prior to his death his teaching about the special mission of the Society has already been documented.[6] This special calling was the theme of several hymns in the Society's hymnal and it was celebrated especially in poems written for the annual celebration of the festival of the Society's organization. Baker, in a letter to Lenz on May 6, 1861, in summarizing his sermon on Isaiah 2 and 4 stated:

for we are still the branches of the harmonious stem and are continuing what our fathers founded, and because our life's role is interwoven and combined by a common bond, we are inwardly and outwardly registered among the living at Jerusalem.

George Rapp had taught from the start that the Harmony Society was the Sunwoman, the holy church of the Apocalypse with the special blessing, and that its members were elected to belong to the 144,000 who alone were to be able to sing the song of Harmony. Father Rapp had never tired of telling his people of this special mission God had in mind for them and for which they were to prepare by living the celibate life. Baker and Henrici upheld this doctrine of special election for a special mission. The faith in Father Rapp's time had been reflected in the religious fund buried by Father Rapp for the millennium, and it was continuously reflected in the determination to remain intestate. To have made a legal provision for the division of the property, the indivisibility of which they had upheld through many lawsuits, one carried to the Supreme Court of the United States, would have been inconsistent with the entire system of Harmonist doctrine. This point was not explained to the outside world during Father Rapp's time because it was then not yet so pressing an issue to men of the world as it was in the latter days of the Baker-Henrici era. In this time it was, however, stated with unmistakable clearness by both Henrici and Lenz.

Since before the Civil War, the Harmony Society had been supporting a new German communist society which had settled on a large piece of frontier land some distance from Saginaw, Michigan. This community had given itself the Latin name of Ora Labora. Its leader and representative was Emil Bauer, a well-educated German who was very close to Henrici. The new group was having a very difficult time and was continuously in search of more financial aid from the Harmony Society. The Harmonists helped them not only financially but also sent Henrici to their location in order that he might advise them on some of their problems. The Civil War and the drafting of a number of their strongest men added to their difficulties. The death of R. L. Baker prior to the second coming of Christ gave Emil Bauer the courage to renew suggestions he had made earlier about the importance of making a will. First he suggested, in a letter of November 30, 1868, that the Harmonists buy out the entire Ora Labora colony for fifty thousand dollars. Since they already had quite a mortgage on their property the Society would be making an excellent investment, and in a few years the lands would be worth double that amount. After making this suggestion, Emil Bauer carefully went on:

May the Lord keep you healthy for a very long time still in that youthful courage peculiar to you; do not forget to reflect upon this that we are but pilgrims and strangers in these huts of Mesech and that the possibility exists that, after the older members who are most capable in doing business have been called away, those remaining might have to endure Roman treatment in a Roman monastery. Is it at all wrong if the fathers make a testament? Did Christ not make one and seal it with his blood?

Although on the occasion of my visit you gave me a terrific box in the ears from the pulpit because of such inquisitiveness (Vorwitz), I am nevertheless still fearless and so free to impart to you the convictions of my heart. You are wiser than I am, but it should not be forgotten that I was your apprentice and that I marched beside you in your stockings for forty miles.

Henrici gave Bauer a detailed reply under date of December 18, 1868, from which only the significant portion pertaining to the important question of the Society's future and its testament is translated here:

I would not take the liberty to speak to the Society about a voluntary purchase of the property of the colony, as you suggest. Our Society could excuse only a forced purchase, because our people are strongly against increasing our business affairs. As far as your further advice concerning our inner Society affairs are concerned, I thank you heartily for your good intentions. But I should like to request you in future to cause yourself no unnecessary worries about our future, for we have entrusted it entirely to the wise and loving disposition of Him who before the foundations of the world were laid has calculated all our fates and who has even counted all the hair of our head. Our congregation, which was planted almost directly by Him and was cared for by Him, and which at all times has given him an unlimited authority over itself and which has given Him everything that belongs to it, and which at all times has placed an unlimited confidence in His allwise, fatherly guidance, *this (congregation), I say, cannot and is not permitted to recant or take back any of this; or again begin to worry, to fear, or to be timid because of anything that lies ahead. We are firmly convinced that the Lord himself is in His little ship, and know that even during the most violent storms we are not permitted to say: Lord help us; we perish, without justly being called (persons) of little faith by Him.*

We are not allowed to think of any kind of testament, because our congregation has the unshakeable conviction that it should not and dare not bring its temporal course to a close before the Lord creates things new. He has already set time, number, measure, weight and goal for all our fates, so that we are not allowed to interfere in his divine plan by means of any sort of testament, or to wish to prescribe anything to him. The only thing which many of our departing friends left to us as testament was: "Hold out! Remain true to our holy covenant in the exact imitation of the Lord Jesus! Our way is right; it stands the test of the hour of death."

With this we would not condemn what other congregations or individual persons feel obligated to do. Our congregation without doubt has a special calling and therefore has peculiar fates and duties. The Lord's counsel is wonderful; but he brings it to a magnificent conclusion.

Under date of September 7, 1869, Henrici wrote a Mr. J. C. Doubt of Louisville, Kentucky: "In reply to yours of the 4th instant, I have to inform you, that, according to the articles of our association, *there can never be a division of the Society's property; nor is there any desire, by any member of the Society, for such an event; and we feel sure, that such a thing will never happen.*"

To the editor of a German-American millennial paper, *Die Reichsposaune* of Buffalo, N. Y., Henrici wrote on June 30, 1869: "We as a congregation called long ago believe to have our special task, which we expect to perform rightly with the help of the Lord."

Neither Henrici nor his parents were original members of the Harmony Society; he joined the Society after it had moved to Economy and after its fame had been established. Yet no man in the Society was so close to George Rapp during the Economy period as Jacob Henrici. In the above statements there is again expressed in clearest words the firm faith of the Harmony Society in its special calling to be the Sunwoman in the Wilderness, the Congregation at Philadelphia, the Bride of Christ. This firm faith accounts for the hard attitude shown toward all seceders and, quite logically, it explains *why no member of the Society, especially no Trustee of the Society, would ever have the right to make a will disposing of the prop-*

erty of the Society, or even worse, to interfere in God's all-wise counsel by dissolving the Society. This same attitude toward the future is reflected in the letters of the Rapps, of R. L. Baker, and of Jonathan Lenz. The statement about a testament, however, was never made so clearly to the public as it was to Bauer, because such explanations belonged to the very innermost convictions of the Society and were therefore like precious pearls, which were not to be cast before the swine, i.e., the curious men of the world, the journalists, and the lawyers. When these approached Henrici or Lenz on the question of the future disposition of the Society's property, they invariably replied with a smile that the Commonwealth of Pennsylvania would eventually be well able to use their property to pay some of its debts, an answer suited to men of the world, but also an answer consistent with their policy of many years, to give unto Caesar the things that are Caesar's. In legal terms, the Harmony Society from the time of Rapp to Henrici expected the property of the Society to go to the Commonwealth, *if the Lord Jesus Christ should not return to make all things new before all had passed away.* This was certain: *"We are not allowed to think of any kind of testament, because our congregation has the unshakeable conviction that it should not and dare not bring its temporal course to a close before the Lord creates things new."* This was the faith that founded the Harmony Society and kept it strong and wealthy as long as its members and trustees lived by it.

On the occasion of the eighty-first anniversary of the founding of the Harmony Society Jacob Henrici gave an interview to some Pittsburgh reporters, during the course of which he made the following statement:

There is no truth in the story that when our membership is reduced to five our property is to be divided and our society dissolved. Our organization will be maintained till there is only one of us left and then that one will still comprise the society. We firmly believe in a visible, personal reign of Christ on earth and that His second advent will take place before the last member of our society shall have passed away. If that belief is realized, all our possessions will be laid at the feet of the Master, to be disposed of as He shall deem best. But if our belief is a mistaken one and death should wipe us out before that glorious second coming, it is highly probable that the State of Pennsylvania would be glad to employ our savings as an aid in the payment of her heavy debt.

This decision that the State of Pennsylvania, to which they had always been deeply attached, was to be the heir to their property—if Christ should not claim it prior to their death—was so generally known that even Richard Owen, son of Robert, stated it as follows in his letter of Sept. 9, 1885, from which I translate:

If I am not mistaken, the great wealth of your congregation may never be divided and if only two members remain, the entire estate will be left to the State of Pennsylvania.

This letter was addressed to Henrici and Lenz, whom Richard Owen knew very well and with whom he was on close terms as a result of his father's relations and through long-established friendship.

Jonathan Lenz, under date of February 5, 1886, in a letter to Christian Ebert in Schnaith, Württemberg, expressed the same idea, thus providing full evidence of the following points:

1. It was contrary to the religious teachings of the Harmony Society for any Trustee, member, or members to dissolve the Society.
2. It was contrary to these teachings for the Society to make a testament.
3. It was contrary to the teachings of the Society ever to convert the property of the Society into private property.
4. If Christ should not come before the last member died, then the property was to go to the State of Pennsylvania.

9

1890, the Year of Crisis

THE CHRISTMAS OF 1889 WAS NOT A PLEASANT ONE, FOR GERTRUDE Rapp, the granddaughter and last surviving descendant of "the most famous communist of the age," was nearing the close of her pilgrimage on earth. On December 29 she fell asleep and, like her Grandfather, was put to rest in an unmarked grave. Her father had still had the distinction of a gravestone, the only one, in the Harmonist cemetery at Harmony in Butler County, Pennsylvania, where it may be seen to this day. Her death seemed to make a particular impression on Jonathan Lenz, the last Harmonist trustee to have experienced the pioneer work of these great people in all three settlements. On January 3, 1890, Lenz wrote to some unnamed friends:

Since my time is so much in demand I will only briefly and in a hurry report to you what sort of fates have come over us.

At the close of the old year our dear sister Gertraut was called away by Death. At her funeral very many people, not only those who live with us but also many strangers, were present. By all the song was sung

Who knows how near my death?
("Wer weiss, wie nahe mir mein Ende.")

and Kirschbaum, with his singing society also sang a beautiful song, but no one would have believed that today on the third, they would sing the same for him, for a terrible fate overcame him.

When yesterday morning the gas pressure went down, he and the man who usually takes care of gas went into the gas reservoir (near the saw mill), and they had a lantern with them, they opened the jet too much, and the container filled quickly with gas, and Kirschbaum stood in flames from head to foot and in a minute he was burned to death.

159

Who was Kirschbaum? The Society had known him as one of their hired men years before. On April 30, 1868, he had settled accounts with the Society and had started for California. On January 3, 1869, out in Oakland, California, he wrote the Society about his uncle in the Society, then continued a migratory life until on December 20, 1877, after seven long years of wandering, he decided to apply for the spiritual and social security granted by membership in the Harmony Society. He admitted that the good germ had suffered some while he wandered about like a sheep without a shepherd, but since he knew the precepts of the Society well he felt he would find a place with them. He was born April 3, 1849, at Kirchentellmsfurth, a/a. Tübingen in Württemberg, and graduated from the usual grade school. He wrote clearly and correctly in German and English, and appears to have been an intelligent man commanding at least the forms of Swabian Pietism. Kirschbaum had joined the Society on February 15, 1879, with six others, and was being groomed for higher office, although there was strong opposition to his character. On December 30, 1889, he had written the family Merkle, the old trusted manager of the oil wells of the Society at Tidioute, Pa.

We herewith send you the news that our dearly beloved friend and sister, Gertrude Rapp, gently fell asleep in the Lord last night at quarter past six of a suspected lung collapse after scarcely three days of sickness in bed. We regret the loss of a valued and esteemed member of the Society very much, but with patience, conform to God's council and hope he will make it all well.

Kirschbaum wrote various letters for the Society, among them one to Johann Christian Metzger on August 21, 1888, at the order of brother Lenz. Metzger and his people had been hard hit by the elements up in Dakota and wanted to move. He advised him to see things through, but if that were not possible and they were determined to leave, the only asylum the Society could offer them would be their property at Tidioute, Warren County, Pa.,

which formerly was an oil region, but now considerably built up. Our Russian Menonites tried it out there without seeing it through, and thus it might be with you.

In spite of his smooth and unctious tone he seems to have been capable of being extremely crude to some of the Economites, who complained about him, but his violent death was a shock and warning to the Society. He was a Swabian, not married, had good religious form and was young enough to be of service to a Society interested in capable young followers.

When Jonathan Lenz informed his friends about the quick deaths of Gertrude Rapp and George Kirschbaum on January 3, there was not a trace of evidence in his letter that he would be the next to go, but eighteen days later the kindly Junior Trustee died himself, one of the greatest losses the Society had suffered for many years. The Pittsburgh *Commercial Gazette*, in announcing his death in its issue of January 23, 1890, stated:

Jonathan Lenz, the Junior Trustee of the Economite Society, died at Economy on Tuesday night. [Notice is Thursday] He was taken ill two weeks ago and grew worse rapidly until the end came. He was born in Germany [an error, he was born in the Society] and joined the Society when it was located in Butler County. He became a Trustee in 1868, after the death of Romelius Baker. With Jacob Henrici, the Senior Trustee, he managed the affairs of the Society so wisely that the great wealth it now contains was accumulated. Mr. Lenz had charge of the agricultural and other work of the society, while Mr. Henrici looked after the investments and financial interests.

The Society at one time held a controlling interest in the Pittsburgh and Lake Erie Railroad, but sold out to the Vanderbilt interest a few years ago. Since that time the trustees have built large brick works near Leetsdale. Mr. Lenz had charge of these works up until his death. His demise, following as it does close upon that of Miss Getrude Rapp, leaves the Society with less than twenty members.

Mr. Lenz was over 80 years of age, and was about six and one-half feet tall and built proportionately. He was very reticent to strangers, but was a warm friend. Some time ago the two trustees commenced educating George Kirschbaum in business, with a view of making him a trustee upon the death of either one. Kirschbaum took a lantern with him one night a few weeks ago and went searching for a natural-gas leak. He found it and was killed by the explosion. Ernest Woelful was chosen to fill his place. Mr. Woelfel will assume charge of the work heretofore done by Mr. Lenz.

Ernest Wölfel had joined the Society with Kirschbaum on February 15, 1879, but his service to the Society lasted only a few months, for on July 28, 1890, he suffered a stroke and died.

These sudden deaths, especially that of Lenz, speeded on the Economy gold rush that had already been in the making but was blocked by such persons as Gertrude Rapp and Jonathan Lenz.

On January 24, 1890, three days after the last of the Harmonist pioneers had died, the following four persons suddenly became members of the Harmony Society:

Moritz J. Friedrichs
J. Jacob Niclaus
Hermann Fischern
John S. Duss

The admission of these persons to membership is attended by a number of odd circumstances. It had been customary to admit new members on February 15, the anniversary of the founding of the Society, but this time admission was on January 24, unless the date originally was actually February 24, 1890. This might have been the case, since the capital "F" of the originally written "February" is still visible in the original record. Why the February was changed to January I have not been able to determine, unless it was done to fit in chronologically with the next date of admission, February 13, 1890. Yet, it is possible that the writer was so accustomed to write February as a date of admission that he did so before realizing the real date.

The admission of Moritz J. Friedrichs is important evidence for the fact that this admission to membership was without proper form and without honest respect for the real principles of the Society. Friedrichs had joined the Society in 1848 and had then withdrawn. In July 1851, R. L. Baker had written him in response to his application for readmission to the Society that his request had been considered and denied because they had come to know him and were convinced that he did not belong in the Harmony Society. Friedrichs repeated his request for admission soon after, and again R. L. Baker, under date of September 7, 1851, told him very clearly that he would not be admitted. He states that he did not want to make the decision himself and that he placed the matter before the board of elders.

The sense of our board and of the entire congregation is unanimous in *No,* you should not come to us. The reasons cited in my previous letter we consider sufficient: more could be given but we consider this unnecessary. We have learned to know you in such a way, that we firmly believe to have reached a very sound and correct decision for you and ourselves by No, therefore accept it and do not bother us further. September 7, 1851.

It is obvious from the circumstances in which this admission to membership in the Congregation of Saints occurred, that the new members were not interested in searching for the kingdom of God. The Economy gold rush was on, the gold rush which began on February 15, 1887, when Franz Gillman, Gottfried Lauppe, Magdalena Purucker, Caroline Duss, Katharina Nagel, and Karoline Molt had joined the Society. Caroline Duss had been around the Society off and on for many years, and she had long been pleading with Henrici to let her son return to Economy. On February 13, 1890, the Economy gold rush gained momentum with the admission of sixteen members, among them John Duss's wife, Susie C. Duss. This brought the Duss membership in the Society up to four relatives, but this was only a part of the family that lived in the town and without vote constituted a force which might be compared to the picked gallery crowds at our great political conventions. Only four other persons were admitted to the Society after this group had crashed the gates of Holy Zion, and these four were tractable old souls who were brought in for a purpose and also let out when that purpose was fulfilled. As was to be expected, the gold rush was not to run its course without at least some of the spirit of the Yukon. There was not exactly murder, although it came very close to that a number of times, and the violent deaths which occurred so quickly and conveniently were positively embarrassing for a religious society.

Among the large new group of joiners were several old timers:

Benjamin Feucht
Henry Feucht
Margaretha Feucht
Rebecca Feucht

These had already been members of the Society, in fact were descendants of founders of the Society, but they had withdrawn to go on the individual system. Ever since their withdrawal, however, Benjamin and Henry had kept a close eye on the Society and had kept up their contacts with trusted members within the Society. Like the Dusses the Feuchts were waiting, not for the Bridegroom or the march to the Holy Land, but for the fearful guardians of the Harmony Society millions to die, and with two staunch pillars fallen and the Dusses moving in, there was not much time to lose. While Henrici and Wölfel still were trustees the battle did not immediately become acute, but the legal foundations for the battle to come were strengthened. Henrici had never bothered to see to the security of these foundations, so on April 30, 1890, the important legal sins of omission of Jacob Henrici were most carefully corrected and the following renewal of the Harmony Society Articles of Agreement legally and properly recorded at the Beaver County Court House on July 31, 1890, Deed Book 125, page 415, Beaver Co.:

Articles of Agreement, Ratification and Confirmation of and by the Members of the Harmony Society at Economy, Beaver County, Pa., April 30th, 1890.

Whereas, After the death of Geo. Rapp, the founder and leader of the Harmony Society, to wit: On the 12th day of August, A.D. 1847, all the then members of said society by article and a compact in writing of that date duly executed at Economy, in the county of Beaver, state of Pennsylvania, in the presence of Wm. P. Baum, Francis LeGoulan and Andrew Bimber, and subsequently recorded in the office for recording deeds, in and for the county of Beaver, in Deed Book Vol. 25, page 121 etc., adopted and established a system and plan for the regulation and government of the Society, the management of their internal temporal affairs, as also for the management and transaction of their external affairs, and business in and by which articles John Schnabel, Joseph Hoernle, Adam Nachtrieb, John Eberle, Mathaus Scholle, John Stahl, Romelius L. Baker, Jacob Henrici and Jonathan Lenz were appointed and constituted the first Board of Elders therein established; and Romelius L. Baker and Jacob Henrici, two members of the Society and of the Board of Elders, aforesaid, were therein appointed and constituted the members of the Board of Trustees of said Society, provided for and established, which Board of Elders as thus constituted, and their successors, duly appointed, under the authority, and in the manner therein granted and provided, have managed the internal temporal affairs of the Society as therein directed until the present time, the present Board of Elders being constituted and consisting of Jacob Henrici, Ernest Woelfel, Michael Staib, Johannes Scheid, Moritz J. Friedrichs, Gottfried Lauppe, J. Jacob Niclaus, Hermann Fischern and John S. Duss; and Romelius L. Baker and Jacob Henrici the Trustees aforesaid and empowered, jointly and severally in their own names, or that of either of them, to make all contracts, purchase and sell, invest the funds of the Society, collect debts, receive and pay monies, compromise and settle claims and disputes, appoint and discharge attorneys in fact, and at law, institute and conduct legal proceedings and generally to manage and transact all the external business and affairs of the Society, to make donations to withdrawing members and for charitable purposes, etc. . . . Also jointly in their own names, to purchase real estate, and in their joint names to grant, bargain, sell and convey, all or any of the lands, tenements and real estate then or thereafter owned or belonging to the Society, and for this purpose to execute deeds of conveyance in fee simple or otherwise, in their joint names, etc., as by reference to said articles recorded as aforesaid will more fully appear.

And Whereas, Romelius L. Baker and Jacob Henrici accepted said trust, acted as trustees of said Harmony Society, managing and transacting their business and affairs under the authority aforesaid, until the death of the said Romelius L. Baker, on the 11th day of January, 1868, whereupon in pursuance of the authority conferred by, and according to the terms and provisions of said articles recorded as aforesaid, Jonathan Lenz, a member of said Society, and of the Board of Elders, aforesaid, was duly appointed and constituted a member of the Board of Trustees, to fill the vacancy occasioned by the death of said Romelius L. Baker, and thereafter the external business and affairs thereof were managed and conducted and transacted by the said Jacob Henrici and Jonathan Lenz as Trustees, the same being managed, conducted and transacted under and in accordance with the authority given and conferred by the articles aforesaid, until the death of said Jonathan Lenz, on the 21st day of January, 1890, whereupon the Board of Elders, consisting of the members last herein before named and mentioned as constituting said Board, in pursuance of the authority and direction of the articles aforesaid, appointed and constituted Ernst Woelfel (also a member of said Society and of said Board of Elders) a Trustee to fill the vacancy thus occasioned in the said Board of Trustees, and the said Jacob Henrici and Ernst Woelfel have since that time conducted and transacted the business and affairs of the Society according to the terms and provisions of the articles aforesaid.

And Whereas, more than forty years have elapsed since the execution of the articles and compact aforesaid, adopting and establishing the system and plan for the regulation and the government of the internal affairs of the Society, and the management, control and transaction of the external business and affairs thereof, and many changes have taken place in the membership of the Society, most of the then members having since died, and others embracing part of the undersigned, having been admitted, and become members thereof in accordance with the terms and provisions of said articles, all the members of the Board of Elders, except Jacob Henrici, designated and appointed in the said articles, having died, as also their successors in said Board, and all of whom as members of said Board, managed the internal affairs of the Society as above recited, and two of those who have been members of the Board of Trustees and actively engaged in the management and transaction of the external business of the Society under the authority of the articles aforesaid, either severally and in their own names, as trustees, or jointly with their co-trustee, Jacob Henrici, still surviving, and in their joint names as such Trustees, making contracts, purchasing and selling personal property, investing, collecting, receiving and paying monies of the Society, settling claims, purchasing real estate, selling real estate of the Society, executing and delivering deeds, assignments, transfers and release, and generally managing and transacting all the external business and affairs of the Society, have also since died.

And Whereas, Said Society, and the undersigned, the present members thereof, have received and enjoyed and do now enjoy the benefits and advantages resulting from the management and regulation of the internal affairs thereof, by the Board of Elders as aforesaid, as also the benefits and profit of the external business and affairs thereof, managed and transacted by those who constituted the Board of Trustees as aforesaid, and it is deemed right and proper that we, the undersigned, surviving members of the Society, who entered into the articles and compact aforesaid, and the others who have since become members as aforesaid, should recognize, approve, and reaffirm said articles, and approve and confirm what has been done for and on behalf of the Society under and in pursuance thereof.

Now therefore be it known to all whom it may concern that we, the undersigned, the surviving and present members of the Harmony Society, at Economy, aforesaid, and all the present members of said Society, do severally, and each for himself or herself, covenant, grant and agree to and with the others, and each and all the other members aforesaid, and signers hereof, and with those who shall hereafter become and be members, as follows, that is to say:

First: We do hereby solemnly recognize, approve, reaffirm and continue the articles of agreement and compact of our association entered into at Economy, on the 12th day of August, 1847, and recorded in the Recorders office of Beaver County, as set forth in the preamble hereto, and declare the same to be in full force, as a whole, and all parts thereof, including the agreements and compacts mentioned and designated in the first article thereof, as fully and to the same extent as said mentioned agreements were recognized and established by said first article.

Second: We do hereby approve and confirm, any and all acts, matters and things done and transacted by the Board of Elders of the Harmony Society, as the same was from time to time constituted, since the date of the articles aforesaid, establishing said Board, and we hereby ratify and confirm the appointment of the present Board of Elders, to wit: Jacob Henrici, Ernst Woelfel, Michael Staib, Johannes Scheid, Moritz J. Friedrichs, Gottfried Lauppe, J. Jacob Niclaus, Herman Fischern and John S. Duss.

Third: We do also hereby approve ratify and confirm, all acts matters and things done, transacted and performed by the Board of Trustees of the Harmony Society, constituted, first, of Romelius L. Baker and Jacob Henrici until Jan. 11th, 1868, afterwards and from that date until Jan. 21st, 1890 of Jacob Henrici and Jonathan Lenz, and since the last mentioned date, of Jacob Henrici and Ernst Woelfel, hereby ratifying, confirming, holding and declaring as good and effectual in law and in equity, all acts, matters and things done transacted and performed by each and all of said Trustees, in the purchase and sale of personal property, and in the making of contracts, investment of funds, purchase, sale and transfer of stocks, bonds and other securities, loaning or borrowing money, collection and payment of moneys, settlement or compromise of claims or disputes, in the institution and prosecution of legal proceedings, in the employment and discharge of attorneys in fact and at law, in the making of donations, in the purchase of real estate and in the sale thereof, in the execution and delivery of deeds, conveyances, transfers and assignments, whether of and pertaining to real or personal estate, in the execution and delivery of notes or obligations of any kind, and generally all acts heretofore done by said Trustees, in the conducting, managing and transacting of the business of the Society, and whether done by said Trustees, or either of them, severally and in his own name as Trustee, or jointly in the joint names of himself and his co-trustee.

Fourth: We do also hereby ratify, approve and confirm the acts of the Board of Elders in the appointment of Ernst Woelfel, as co-trustee with Jacob Henrici, and declare said Jacob Henrici and Ernst Woelfel, the present Board of Trustees, authorized and empowered to do, perform and transact any and all business of the Society, and to the full extent of the powers, and authorities mentioned and designated in and conferred by the Board of Trustees in and by the articles hereinbefore mentioned, made and entered into August 12th, 1847, and recorded as aforesaid.

In witness whereof we have hereunto set our hands and seals this 30th day of April A.D. 1890.

This English legal document is followed by the German text, and under the German text appear the following signatures:

Jacob Henrici

Ernst Woelfel

John S. Duss

Jacob Niclaus

Moritz J. Friedrichs

Gottfried Lauppe

Johannes Scheid

Michael Staib

H. Fischern

Jacobs X Schellhas

Franz Gillman

Hargo Miller

Conrad Hermannsdoerfer

Thirza Feucht

Rebecka Feicht

Margaret X Feucht
    (her mark)

Christine Haerer

Magdalena Purucker

Susie C. Duss

Lena Fritsch

Bertha Geratsch

Paulina X Stickel (her mark)

Caroline Duss

Julius Stickel

Edward X Kellermann
    (his mark)

Henry Feucht

B. Feicht

Blasius Platz

Sigmund Stiefvater

Regina Lautenschlager

Christine Rall

Caroline Molt

Katharina Nagel

Elizabeth X Beck (her mark)

Lena Rall

Johanna Hermansdoerfer

Sibilla X Hinger (her mark)

Anna X Bauer (her mark)

Marie Diem

Barbara Boesch

Friedericka Munz

Dorothea Hoehr

Barbara X Nix (her mark)

Barbara X Vogt (her mark)

Philipina L. Woelfangel

The above signatures all were made by the several parties in the presence of

A. Gottlieb Riethmueller

John Bailey

Samuel Siber

Gustav A. Schumacher

Christian Kuemmerle

W. H. Breitenstein

Henry Hice

Richard R. Hice

who attested the same as witnesses. The signatures of Jacob Schellhas, Edward Kellermann, Elizabeth Beck, Margaret Feucht, Pauline Stickel, Sibilla Hinger, Anna Bauer, Barbara Nix and Barbara Vogt were written for them at their request, they being unable to write themselves and they each making their mark to their respective signatures. All this was then carefully recorded on July 31, 1890, in the Office for the Recording of Deeds &c. in and for the County of Beaver in Deed Book Vol. 125, page 415.

With this legal document containing the names of all legal members of the Society properly recorded, there was external harmony in the Harmony Society for a while, then quite suddenly the Junior Trustee Woelfel suffered a stroke and a new man had to be elected in his place. The Pittsburgh *Commercial Gazette* of July 31, 1890, published an eyewitness account of Woelfel's[1] burial:

They have a methodical way of doing business down at Economy and in no way was this shown more than at the quiet, decorous and yet odd funeral services of the late Ernst Woelfel. The services were, as is everything else in the gathering, conducted by the venerable Father Henrici, who by the way is the only man in the settlement to whose name the prefix "Mr." is used, and this is done invariably.

On Tuesday evening the friends of the deceased Economite trustee were gathered at the meeting-hall and the senior trustee sang several German hymns, compiled solely for such occasions. This was followed by silent meditation for some moments, when the trained choir of the Economite church chanted a dirge. The remains were then removed to the hearse, and, followed by the women on one side of the street and the men on the other, proceeded to the Old Orchard Cemetery where, as all had cast together everything in a common lot in life, so each would fare no better than his brethren after death. All are placed in nameless graves in the old orchard, which is undotted with a single stone to the memory of the deceased.

When the cortege arrived at the grave the senior trustee kept vigilant watch that the separation of the sexes was strictly enforced, the men occupying one side of the late Ernst Woelfel's final resting place and the women standing on the other. After a hymn by the church choir and a short exhortation from Mr. Henrici the beautiful and touching ceremony of strewing the dead with flowers was observed. Every attendant at the funeral, male and female, had been supplied with a fragrant bouquet, which was cast on the coffin until its outlines were hidden beneath a mass of blossoms. Scarcely, however, had this been done when a transformation scene took place and almost every male person seemed to have a shovel, so quickly was the grave filled up and beaten down, leaving but a brown mound to remind the community that another had gone from its midst.

Trustee Woelfel was 41 years of age at his death, and had been a full member of the community since 1879. His aged mother was still living in Economy, and it was she who picked him up from the door of his room at the time of his death. He left a brother who was in business at Beaver Falls, but neither of his surviving relatives belonged to the Society. He had held the office of trustee only since June 21, when he succeeded Mr. Lenz. The Pittsburgh *Commercial Gazette* also reported the election of John S. Duss as the new Junior Trustee:

J. S. Duss, is comparatively a young member, having only joined the society last February, and is probably one of the youngest in years of the society which is now reduced to about forty in number. No exact statistical information could be obtained, as Mr. Henrici objected. He said to his assistant postmaster and storekeeper in German after being asked for information: "Take him with you to the hotel and give him cakes, and wine and supper, but don't tell him what he wants to know." W. H. Breitenstein received the orders with a twinkle in his eyes which recognized the fact that the venerable chief was understood, and if he withheld information, it would be sought elsewhere. The Sabbath-like stillness of Economy is only broken by the girls as they gather around the pumps to secure the spring-water for evening cooking, and the workmen who gather around the hotel before the bell rings for retiring at 9 P.M. sharp. There is no drinking, no smoking, no loud talk and no train into the city after 7 P.M., unless it is flagged, as it was last night, by the primitive method of an only passenger waving frantically a burning newspaper.

The election of one of the youngest and most recent members of the Society to such an elevated position, which in a short time would make him the successor to such venerable prophets as Rapp, Baker, and Henrici, was not to be without very serious repercussions in the Society and without. For many years Dr. Feucht, a descendant of one of the founders of the Society, had been hoping that he would become Trustee of the Society, but because he had been outside when Lenz died, he missed an opportunity and Wölfel had been elected. Now came another chance to win the coveted prize, but Duss had made too-powerful alliances with the help of his relatives, and as a result Duss, although a member only since January 24, 1890, a few weeks before the Feuchts rejoined, was on July 26 made Junior Trustee. Now things began to get very restless in quiet Economy, so much so that the Pittsburgh *Leader* assigned a reporter to write two long articles analyzing the situation and bringing its readers up to date on the happenings in the famous town nearby. The reporter is not named, but the articles are well written and based on some painstaking personal research. The first article appeared on August 3, 1890, and begins with a brief history of the early days of the Society and shows the close relationship of the Feucht ancestors to George Rapp. The August 10, 1890, article gets into the contemporary situation. Of particular interest here is the realistic evaluation of the situation by Mr. Charles Bentel of Freedom, Pa., grandson of George Bentel, one of the original founders of and donors to the Society. He was asked particularly to comment on a reported move to oust Henrici as Trustee. Although this matter was openly discussed, Bentel did not think anyone would dare make such a move, yet it was made, as we shall see, and it resulted in compelling Henrici to make his first and last financial report to the Society.

The *Leader*'s analysis attracted a great deal of attention and brought replies, inquiries, and suggestions from unexpected quarters. From Stuttgart, Germany, came a letter of August 18 referring to the article and offering the Trustees the aid of the Rapp heirs in their latest battle. This letter was answered by John Duss, stating that the claims made in the article were untrue and based on the actions of an enemy of the Society. He asserted that no attempt had been made to depose Henrici as Trustee, that quite to the contrary, Henrici enjoyed the good will and respect of all members. "Neither Mr. Henrici, our oldest Trustee, nor the members of the Society are in the least upset about these foolish and untrue statements, and while we thank you for your sympathy and good will toward Henrici and others named in your letter, we assure you that we stand in no danger or fear because of ourselves, or because of a lack of Harmony and unity among us." Duss assured Mr. Carl Schmidt, who claimed to be representing the heirs of George Rapp, in this letter of September 10, 1890, that they did not need his help. But the Rapp heirs were to be heard from again through the German Consul at Philadelphia, and under the pressure of their action, even though futile, Henrici was to be forced to make the above-mentioned first and last accounting of the affairs of the Harmony Society under his Trusteeship.

Although the *Leader*'s articles on the Society were the most thoroughgoing and extensive, they were not the first or only new reports about the Harmonists published by the press of this country and Europe at this time. The Harmony Society had always interested the newspapers and their readers throughout the world, both in a positive and negative manner. The tremendous success they made of communism and religion continued to have an inspirational effect upon new prophets with new revelations and more or less new dreams which had not yet been dashed to pieces or modified by the cruel facts of human existence. Reference is here made again to the three new systems brought to Henrici's attention during his closing years in the hope of helping him dispose of the Society's burdensome millions: Koreshanity, Topolobampo in Mexico, and Olombia, that earlier form of today's dream of a one-world federal government. It would be not only highly interesting but also amusing to pursue each one of these movements, particularly in their carefully prepared schemes to get at the millions of the Harmony Society. Cyrus R. Teed, who received his revelation directly from heaven at the Christly age of thirty, came nearest to success, and as a result figured in the lawsuit brought by Dr. Feucht against Duss. With all the new terminology created by psychology, a most readable book could be written on his fascination not only for young women but also for the motherly type of women, such as his associate, Victoria Gratia. Teed started writing to the Society in 1880 and not only did he manage to have one of his angels heard there but there is evidence that he received at least one donation of $100 for his revelation. Teed was looking for a New Jerusalem for his Koreshans and the dying Harmony Society seemed the logical choice for him, although he eventually moved his angels down to Florida, from which place he continued to work on Henrici and Duss. By 1891 the overtures of Cyrus Teed and the replies he received from the Trustees of the Society were so extensively publicized that a friend of the Society, Theo. L. Pitt of Niagara Falls Center, Canada, on November 14, 1891, wrote a letter fully exposing him to the Trustees.

Albert K. Owen, a civil engineer with a poetic soul, thus described his vision of Topolobampo: "What a sight! What a panorama! There was Ohuira—an inland sea! 'If the morning shall discover a deep and safe channel from this inland sea to the Gulf of California, then here,' I said to myself, 'is the site for a great metropolitan city. On that water, now without a sail, will one day come ships of every nation. On this plain will dwell happy families." He wanted only $500,000 from Henrici to make this dream come true, while Dr. Von Swartwout, on the basis of his one-world platform, simply claimed ownership of the entire property of the Society. The Trustees found all of these movements wanting because they had not built on the solid foundation of Christ. They were absolutely right.

10

Henrici's First and Last Accounting, and Death

IT SHOULD BE REMEMBERED THAT SOON AFTER FATHER RAPP'S death the Board of Elders called Henrici to account because of his determination to be independent and above the Society. This had resulted in a stormy session which then caused Henrici to resign from the Board and the Trusteeship. It was not until after several months had passed that he moved back into the "executive mansion" and again resumed his office as junior trustee. With the death of R. L. Baker his inclination to act the autocrat, kindly but yet very firmly, grew, and by the time the Economy gold rush was under way it had become so well established that the Board of Elders drew up and signed the following resolution and presented it to Jacob Henrici.

We the undersigned, members of the Harmony Society at Economy, Beaver County, Pa., have this, the 20th day of August 1891 A.D. unanimously passed the following resolution and herewith request our brother Jacob Henrici, present Trustee of our Society, to kindly examine the same and to please notify us as to his decision in regard to the same. As according to our constitution, the President of the Harmony Society has absolute power, that he may manage our affairs, according to his own personal opinion and judgment and without being compelled to get in any way for that purpose the advice and consent of our brethren, and as that sort of management has been injurious to our interests and so far to a great extent almost caused the entire ruin of our financial standing, we unanimously pass the following resolution:

a. to most kindly request our brother Jacob Henrici, President of the Harmony Society of Economy, Pa., to render us the members of the Harmony Society, within thirty (30) days an accurate, sum-mary statement of all our chattels and immovable property, so that, should it please the Lord to call our brother Jacob Henrici from our midst, that occasion should not be taken advantage of, to defame the name of our brother, which would undoubtedly be the case, considering the unregulated circumstances; if we, the members of the Harmony Society and signers of this document, have not a complete and clear knowledge of everything concerning our own interests.

b. to change the statutes of our community, the Harmony Society of Economy, Pa., in such a way that the Board of Elders in its majority, considers and arranges all affairs and all business of our Society, inside as well as outside, so that the president has the executive power of the Board of Elders, but that the Board of Elders itself forms the resolving power of our internal and external affairs, of the interests of our community.

Thus done, August 20, 1891, A.D. at Economy, Beaver Co., Pa. Johannes Scheid, Gottfried Lauppe, Moritz J. Friedrichs, H. Fischern, Jacob Niclaus, C. Hermansdörfer, Hugo Miller.

This document clearly reveals what a great change had come over the Society since the days of Baker. It proves especially that the newcomers were totally ignorant of the spirit of the old Articles of Agreement and that they had been admitted without the usual probationary and indoctrination period. The very terminology "President of the Harmony Society" betrays the material interests of men who never should have been admitted, and upon whom George Rapp would have pronounced a prophetic curse. Henrici, of course, was not prepared to give an accounting within the time specified, because his accounts were not in that kind of order. Time and circumstances, however, kept pressing upon him, and because there had been considerable agitation in Germany to gather the descendants of George Rapp and others who had founded the Harmony Society into a group which would lay claim to the property of the Society, Henrici on April 1, 1892, was prepared for his statement.[1] As the most accurate statement and inventory of the Society at the time of Henrici's quickly approaching death, it is here given in as complete a form as possible:

Henrici Statement of April 1, 1892

One, Charles Myer, German Consul at Philadelphia, representing and acting for parties, most of whom reside in Germany, and claim to be heirs of George Rapp, the founder of our Society, has applied for letters of administration upon the estate of Mr. Rapp, alledging that he died possessed of large amounts of property, yet unadministered, and which property they alledge is in the hands of the Harmony Society and which should be distributed amongst these parties as his heirs.

In 1885, Mr. Myer made application for letters, but was met by the protest of Gertrude Rapp, who was then living, and after a full hearing, in which Mr. Myer and the parties he represents were represented by attorneys from Philadelphia, the register decided against them and refused to grant him letters.

The matter then rested, without any further action until December last (1891) when Mr. Myer again applied to the register for letters of administration, and was again refused. He has now filed a petition in the Orphans Court asking that Court to grant an appeal from the Register's decision and compel the letters to be granted, and I am compelled to answer this petition and again defend our rights against these unjust demands.

I am now an old man, my health infirm, and this renewed effort to wrong our Society has caused me to make the following statement of facts, which I have caused to be written out, hoping that they may be of use hereafter in defending our rights.

George Rapp was born in the year 1757, in Germany (supposed in Iptingen). He married Christina Benzinger, and had by this marriage two children, and but two; one a daughter Rosena, who never was married, but lived with her father till his death in 1847 and after that continued to live in the family till her death, which occured at Economy about September 7th, 1849.

The other child was John Rapp, a son, also born in Germany.

George Rapp came to the United States in the fall of 1803, bringing with him, his son John Rapp, and was also accompanied by Dr. Christopher Miller. He left his wife and daughter behind in Germany. Having selected a location for the Society at Harmony, Butler County, Pennsylvania, his wife and daughter, with a number of others, under direction of Fredrick Rapp, came over and joined him, and he formed and organized the Harmony Society at Harmony, February 15th, 1805.

The Society continued at Harmony until 1815, when they sold their lands and property at that place and removed to and established the town of New Harmony, on the Wabash, in Posey County, Indiana, where they remained until 1825, when, the location proving unhealthy, they sold their property there also and returned to Pennsylvania, establishing themselves at Economy in the year 1825, where the Society has remained ever since.

George Rapp survived his wife, who died at Economy in 1830 and he died also at Economy August 7th, 1847.

John Rapp, the son, then a young man, became a member of the Society, at its organization. He married about 1807, a Miss Johanna

Diehm, who was also a member of the Society. Of their marriage there was issue one child, and only one, a daughter, Gertrude Rapp, who was born in 1808 (possibly 1807). John Rapp died at Harmony about 1812, leaving to survive him his wife and daughter. His wife lived in the family of George Rapp up to the time of his, George Rapp's, death and thereafter continued at Economy in the family of Mr. Baker and Mr. Henrici till her death in 1873.[2]

Gertrude Rapp joined the Society when she arrived at lawful age and with her Mother lived in the family of Mr. George Rapp until his death, and thereafter in the family of Mr. Baker and Mr. Henrici, until the date of her death in December, 1889, during all her life being an earnest and faithful member of the Society. She was the only grand daughter, and after the death of her aunt Rosena Rapp, the only lineal descendant of George Rapp.

Fredrick Rapp, who for many years was active in the business of the Society was not a son of George Rapp, but an adopted son whose name before adoption was Fredrick Reichart. He was born in Germany and was connected with George Rapp in the business of the association there, so far as it had assumed form and had a distinct business, before its more perfect organization at Harmony, Butler County. When George Rapp came over to the United States, Fredrick remained in Germany and afterwards came over, bringing with him the wife and daughter of George Rapp, and a number of others, who united with the Society, when organized in 1805. Mrs. Merkle, wife of Mr. M. Merkle, now living near Tidioute, Pennsylvania, is a niece of Frederick Rapp, and is now near Eighty years of age. She and her husband came to Economy, from Germany, about 1858 and after remaining a year or more at Economy went to Tidioute.

George Rapp has now been dead about forty-five years. He was the head and leader of the Society from its organization at Harmony until his death, a period of more than forty-two years. He was a firm and consistant believer in the principles of the Society, both in matters spiritual and temporal, and so continued till the day of his death, and of those principles there was none that he advocated more earnestly and zealously than that of entire community of property, which has always been recognized by the members of the Society as the great distinguishing feature of our polity and a fundamental article of our faith and practice, in the management of our temporal affairs. He sought to establish and did establish our Society on the basis of Christian fellowship derived from the Sacred Scriptures, embracing and combining so far as possible the government of the Patriarchal age and the community of property approved by the early apostles of Christ. The membership of the Society fully concurred in and adopted these principles and doctrines and Mr. Rapp became and was the recognized patriarchal head of the Society, till the time of his death.

Thus believing, Mr. Rapp acted according to that belief, and freely gave all that he had in the way of property to the Society, placed it all in the common stock, fully and absolutely, without any reserve, according to the compacts among the members himself being one, and in accordance with the letter and spirit of the compact he earnestly and continuously devoted his time, talents and energies to the promotion of the general good of the Society. He honestly and faithfully practiced what he taught, sharing equally with all his fellow members all he had, and laboring diligently for the good of all, claiming and allowing no distinction or difference, except in so far as his leadership and as the representative of the Society made it necessary to apparently occupy a more prominent position than others, when transacting the business of the Society with the outside world. Not only do the written compacts of the Society, to which he was a party declare the fact that he recognized the community of property in the broadest sense as between all members of the Society and that he regarded every thing that he could claim in the way of property, as part of the common stock which belonged to the Society, absolutely and unconditionally for the use and benefit of all its members, and that he had no individual interest in or title to any part of the property; but he constantly taught and acted upon this principle, and his whole course in life as a member and as the patriarchal head and leader shows his faithfulness and devotion to this fundamental doctrine.

The assertion, therefore, that at his death he had or left any individual estate or property is wholly without truth or foundation to support it. He had the same right in the common property as any other member, the right to have it used for his support, comfort and wellfare, according to the regulations of the Society, so long as he lived. By his own act he vested in the Society all individual property he at any time had and at his death he had no property, nor right or interest of any kind in the property of the Society, as then held, that he could will or dispose of, or that could or did descend or go to any person as his representative because of their relationship to him, whether as lineal descendant, or collateral heirs.

Gertrude Rapp, his grand daughter fully recognized this fact, and that she after the death of her aunt Rosina, was the person that under the law would be entitled to and would inherit anything he might have left at his death. Aware of all these facts and the want of merit and justice in their claims, when she learned of the effort of these alledged collateral heirs to wrongfully obtain a portion of the Society's property and to cause great trouble and annoyance, she objected to and resisted their claims on the ground that if her grand father, George Rapp, left any estate at his death, she alone was his representative and sole heir and entitled to the same, and after they were defeated in their attempt, fearing they might again after her death seek to maintain their unjust claims and frustrate the known wishes and purposes of her grand father, and wrong the Society, she made her last will and testament, therein declaring that she considered and believed that all property her grand father had or could have had or owned, had passed to the Society and become part of its common stock in which neither she nor any other person could have any interest or right as his heir, yet to guard against any possibility that there might have been something at his death, that would not be considered under the law as having passed to the Society, by his own acts, and which might therefore pass to her as his heir, she willed and demised to the Society all estate and interest of any and every kind that she had, held or possessed or had any interest in, whether derived from her Grandfather's estate or otherwise, so that by no possibility, unless through fraud, misrepresentation and falsehood can any person claim anything from the Society on the ground that they are heirs of George Rapp.

I have been a member of the Society since 1826. Soon after uniting with them I became acquainted with its members, taught its school for some years, and was engaged in its store for a time, afterwards was authorized and required to act in a more general way, looking after certain parts of its interests and business, under the direction of Mr. Rapp and as his assistant; in 1834 became a member of, and thereafter until his death, lived in the family of Father Rapp, was thus intimately associated with, and in daily intercourse with him and his family, his wife, his daughter Rosina, his daughter-in-law, widow of John Rapp and her daughter, Gertrude Rapp, all of whom were then members of his family,[2] and this intimate acquaintence with all these persons continued until their respective deaths. My duties, business and residence in the family brought me into close relations with all these and also with R. L. Baker who was then also active in the business of the Society; and with all its leading members at that time, many of whom had been members from its organization at Harmony, Pennsylvania, knew and were well acquainted with John Rapp and his wife, knew of their marriage, knew their daughter Gertrude as a child and as she grew to womanhood. And what I have stated above as occurring before I became a member of the Society is stated on the information received and knowledge acquired from the parties mentioned, in my intercourse with them and was the general repute, understanding and belief of all, not only of the members of the Society, but of these in the neightborhood, the neighbors, who mingled and associated with them and the members of the Society generally and it is in accord with what I saw and observed from day to day in the conduct of the different persons named, in my daily contact and intercourse with them after I became a member of the Society and of Mr. Rapp family; and what I have stated as occuring since I became a member, is stated on my personal knowledge of what occurred; and I may state that I was a close observer of the acts and course of conduct of the parties, conversing with them and hearing their conversation on these and all other subjects, and I am entirely confident of the truthfulness of what I have stated to-wit: That George Rapp was married in Germany, that he had issue of that marriage two children, and but two, John and Rosina; that he came to the United States in 1803, his son John coming with him; that subsequently in 1804 his wife Christina and daughter, also came over from Germany; that the family lived at Harmony, Butler County, Pennsylvania; that George Rapp there founded and organized the Harmony Society of which his wife, son and daughter were members; that his son, John Rapp there married Miss Johanna Diehm, and of that marriage there was issue one child, Gertrude Rapp, who was born in 1807 or 1808; that John Rapp afterward died about 1812 at New Harmony, Indiana, leaving to survive him his wife and daughter; that after I became a member of the Society in 1826, I became acquainted with Father George Rapp and afterward lived in the family; he and his wife lived together in the same house, recognized each other as husband and wife and were so recognized and regarded by all the members of the Society and by their neighbors and acquaintances. They, Mr. Rapp and his wife, recognized Rosina Rapp as their daughter, always so treated her and she was so recognized by all the members of the Society and by the neighbors and acquaintances; Johanna Rapp, widow of John Rapp, lived in the family and was always treated and regarded as their daughter-in-law, and Gertrude as her daughter, and their grand daughter, and was so recognized by all the members of the Society and their neighbors.

The assertions now made by persons wholly unacquainted with the facts, that George Rapp was never married and died without lawful issue, and that Gertrude Rapp is but the pretended and not his real grand daughter, are base misrepresentations and untruths.

Why such falsehoods are now put forth can only be accounted for on the ground of cupidity and a desire to acquire wealth without the toil and frugality usually requisite in obtaining it; a desire sharpened by the monstrous falsehoods so often and so recklessly published in the public press about the enormous wealth, the untold millions of the Society. Why a professedly enlightened and moral public press prints such reckless and foolish falsehoods is difficult to understand. It has been doubtless prompted by unworthy and unreliable persons who hope to profit by stirring up the avarice of some, who have been members of our Society, but who withdrew, or the heirs of such persons; such has been the course of a certain Marckworth, a lawyer, who tried, but unsuccessfully, to establish a claim of Elias Speidel[3] and his heirs, to a portion of our property and estate, the amount of which he most grossly exaggerated. Divers others have besought us for larger or smaller amounts of money under pretext that they represented some, who had been members of the Society but had withdrawn or were dead. The ground usually urged in support of their claims being, that the wealth of the Society was so very great, we could satisfy their claims without feeling it, and in all, or nearly all these cases the parties seem to have been prompted to make the demands because of the wild and extravigant stories published in the News Papers.

Doubtless, too there are some nearer the Society, who without reflection, perhaps, as to the wrong they are doing and certainly without the ordinary feelings of gratitude for kind treatment and generous aid received from the Society, have at least, given countenance and encouragement to such foolish statements, as well as aiding and encouraging other statements that have been published, as to the Society, and the acts, purposes, intentions and motives of those of us charged with the management of its affairs, that are equally unjust, untrue and unwarranted and which, if regarded as true, could only tend to our injury as a Society.

I can only hope that if any member of the Society has so far forgotten his duty to himself, as well as to his brethren in the Society, as to be in any way concerned in, or connected with these publications, whatever may have been the motive, he will see the wrong he is doing the Society, to himself and to those who are laboring for its wellfare, and I cannot but think that if any such person will but stop to think and reflect on his actions, there could be no farther cause of complaint in these directions.

I am now old and my health infirm, but hope it will soon improve. Necessarily, much of the external and financial business of the Society must fall on and be attended to, by my Co-trustee. He of course finds some difficulties, as he has but lately assumed the responsabilities of his position and has necessarily much to learn of the business and its requirements and that takes time, but he has labored and is laboring faithfully to do and manage for the good of the Society. He of course confers with me on all important matters. In view of the fact he is yet new in his position and of the gross exagerations and misrepresentations that have been made and published it is not strange, but rather to be expected, that he finds many things unpleasant, annoying and harrassing in the discharge of his duties, whether within the Society, with its employees, or with those outside.

It never was the spirit, purpose or intent of the Society that its business should be conducted with the single aim of accumulating wealth as some seem to think. Honesty, economy, reasonable industry and proper care of what a kind Providence bestowed, are matters that have always been deemed essential; but the mere accumulating of money or property for its own sake has never been our object.

While in our own way we have sought to aid our fellow men, not so much by lavish gifts in a few instances, as by the reasonable relief, from day to day, of the many who have applied to us in their need, and by what seemed to us the more desirable course, the furnishing of employment to many, both foreigners and natives, though often the value of that labor was to us very little, in comparision with the compensation given. Instances of this have been common, here at Economy and elsewhere.

The aid given to churches, schools, benevolent institutions and individuals all over the land and in Germany and other places has been constant, but such as has been deemed right under the circumstances. But the expectations and demands for aid in all these various ways constantly grows, and there must be a limit to these also, and it is necessary that we exercise greater strictness, and hence we, as trustees, may seem less disposed than formerly, to grant all demands, or to aid every applicant with money, subsistance, or employment.

There has not been and will not be any foolish expenditures of the Society's means to promote the views or aid in the scheme of any party or association outside, and in this as in other matters, there is no reason to doubt the devotion and faithfulness of my co-trustee to our Society, its interests and the trust reposed in him, notwithstanding all that has been published concerning him and myself.

Under these circumstances and to correct any erroneous impressions that may have been made by the numerous wild and exagerated statements, published in the news papers, I deem it proper that I, who have been one of the active trustees since 1847, surviving Mr. Baker, Mr. Lenz and Mr. Woelfel, my co-trustees, in the past, make a statement showing approximately the resources of the Society, not indeed for publication or circulation, for that would be not only useless but unwise; but for the benefit of those, who may have to do with the business of the Society hereafter; the same reason that has prompted me to make the foregoing somewhat lengthy statement as to Mr. Rapp and his family.

The Society being based upon the ideas of entire community of property and patriarchal government as far as applicable to our situation, no complete system, of accounts has been kept, which shows in particular and detail the business transactions of the past nor all the items of property and values owned and held by us, but the whole is substantially as follows:—

Real Estate and Personal Property

About 2500 acres of land, Village etc. Home property.
About 4500 acres of land in Warren and Forest Cos.
of which 2200 acres is in dispute ....

About 2835 acres of land in Michigan ....

Land near Pittsburgh (Mt Washington) ....

Houses and lots (Glenwood) ....

Land at Chartiers ....

Houses and lots at Rochester ....

Brick Yard property (Leet Twp Allegheny Co.) and the
property purchased from the Misses Shields etc. in
all 135 acres or thereabouts ....

Land at Cannelton, 158 acres 82 perches, and lots (See
memorandum "A" hereto attached) ....

Dalrymple farm, Economy Twp 106 acres ....

Beaver Falls Steel Works including stock etc ....

Beaver Falls Cutlery property, water power etc ....

Western File Works, interest in ....

Miscellaneous property (Houses, lots etc) in Beaver
Falls (See memorandum "B" hereto attached) ....

Economy Savings Institution (interest in) see Mem "X"[4]

Stock in Monongahela Water Company, 5127 shares @ $25.00

Stock in Allegheny Nat'l Bank, 70 shares @ $50.00 each.

Stock in Bank of Pittsburgh 193 shares @ $50.00 each.

Stock in Pgh Ft W & C. Ry Co 27 shares @ $100.00 each.

Stock in The Point Bridge, par $25.00 each 600 shares.

Bonds in The Point Bridge, $13,000.00

Stock of Birmingham Bridge Company 483 shares @ $25.00

Stock of Beaver Falls Gas Co. 417 shares @ $100.00 par

Stock of Chartiers Block Coal Company 2271 shares @ $50.00 par

Stock of Beaver Falls Bridge Company 270 shares @ $100.00

Stock of Union Drawn Steel Company 500 shares @ $100.00

Stock of L. S. M. R. R. R. Co., 2802 shares @ $50.00 ....

Bonds of L. S. M. R. R. R. Co. ....

Bonds of P. C & Y Ry Co., ...

Bonds, Judgments, Mortgages etc etc. .... (See memorandum
"C" attached hereto) [4]

Two thirds interest in farm in Nebraska.

Indebtedness

Bank of Pittsburgh (see Memorandum "D" attached) ....

Farmers Deposit Nt'l Bank, (See Memorandum "E" ....
hereto attached) ....

WITNESS MY HAND AND SEAL THIS FIRST DAY OF APRIL
    EIGHTEEN HUNDRED NINETY-TWO,

Witness:

W. H. Breitenstein   JACOB HENRICI, TRUSTEE (SEAL)

K. Rudolf Wagner

      Memorandum A

                                      Cannelton, March 1st, 1892.

Messrs. Henrici & Duss,
Gentlemen:

Yours of the 26th to hand. In reply would say that you have one tract of land containing 158 Acres 83 per., the same that we went over. It can be sold for $20.00 per acre or perhaps $25.00. Then there is the Saw mill lot at Cannelton about ¼ of an acre worth about $50.00. Then there is that lot at Darlington containing about 2½ or 3 acres worth $75.00. per acre. The R. R. Company did claim the lot at one time. I would refer you to Judge Hice in regard to Darlington lot.

Yours truly,
J. B. White.

Memorandum B

Statement of amount of property owned by the Trustees of the Harmony Society at Economy, June 1st. 1891, with Valuation put on the same by the Six Ward Assessors for Tax purposes in Beaver Falls, Beaver County, Pa.

First Ward

House and lots No. 202 & 204, First Ave., from Douglas	$ 900.00
Water Lots No. 56 & 57 on Race	400.00
House Lots No. 206 & 208 First Ave., from Davis	1000.00
House Lots No. 793 & 794 Third Ave., From Murphy	1800.00
House Lots No. 228 E. P., Second Ave., From Risinger	1000.00
House Lots No. Second Street	$1000.00
House Lots No. 787 Second Street	1200.00
Brick House, near Gas Works	2000.00
Vacant Lots No. 277 & 279 Second Street	800.00
Brick Row Main Street	500.00
Casket Works, Lot. No. 55 Water Street)	
Planing Mill & Machinery)	3000.00
House and Lot No. 188 Sixth Ave., from Walsh	1200.00
House and Lot No. 18 & 27 Sixth Ave., from Harrold	1200.00
House and Lot No. 247 Sixth Ave., from Moffott	1000.00
House, and Lot No. 292 Third St., from Minns	1100.00
House and Lot No. 298 Second St.,	1100.00
2 Lots No. 26 & 47, Water St.	400.00
House and Lot Third Ave., of McGown	800.00
Engine Boiler and Lots No. 63 & 64 at Chemical Works.	2000.00

—Second Ward—
Henrici and Lenz,

2 Vacant Lots No. 1488 & 1489, Tenth St., on the Run	$ 800.00
House and Lots No. 347 & 346 8th Ave., Jno. Corbus' House	4500.00

Memorandum B

House and Lot 5th St.,	$ 700.00
House and Lot No. 87 6th St., from McNally	700.00
House and Lot No. 159, E. P., 9th Ave., from Knapp	1200.00

Brick House and Lot No. 12 & 13 7th Ave.,	2000.00
Brick House and Lot No. 157 & 158 10th Ave., M. B.	[missing]
Elliott House	$1000.00
Brick House and Lot No. 84, 7th Ave., from A. C. Thorn	1200.00
House and Lot No. 2 7th Ave., Graham House	1400.00
House and Lot No. 1501 10th St.	850.00
House, 2 Lots No. 311 & 85 9th Ave., from Morlatt	800.00
2 Houses and Lots, No. 370 5th St., from Hillman & Walker	1800.00
Vacant land very small, No. 1518	50.00
55 acres of hillside land	5525.00
House and Lot No. 97 9th Ave., L. G. Townsand House	1500.00
House and Lot No. 97 7th St., Braden House	1000.00
Brick House and Lot 5th St., from Smith	1700.00
House and Lot No. 127, 7th St., Clayton House	1000.00
Brick House and Lot No. 130 to 137 9th Ave.,	7000.00
Lot No. 1506 & 1512 from A. L. McDonald	500.00

Henrici Duss Trustees
—Property in Third Ward—

House and Lot No. 846, E. P. 4th Ave. from Barnish and Bigger	$1400.00
House and Lot No. 847 E. P. 4th Ave., from Jas. Rogers	1200.00
House and Lot No. 832 E. P. from Robert Duncan	1200.00
House and Lot No. 659 977 5th Ave., from Hyde	3700.00
House and Lot 659 & vacant Lot No. 660 from Jno. Kerr	1000.00
House and Lot No. 652 2nd Ave., Jno. Loyd House	800.00
House and Lot No. 641 3d Ave., from Thomas Duncan	1400.00
House and Lot No. 772 3d Ave., from J. P. McGown	1100.00
Two Lots No. 532 & 533 1st Ave., Vacant Lots	$ 600.00
Two Lots No. 530 & 531 1st Ave., Vacant Lot	600.00
House and Lot No. 780 4th Ave., from Everts and Finley	1300.00
Balance of Block No. 11	5000.00
House and Lot No. 640 3d Ave., from McDonald	1400.00
House and Lot No. 661 2nd Ave., from F. Banks	1200.00
Lot No. 529 1st Ave., from Jas. McDowel	300.00
House and Lot No. 953 6th Ave., from C. Hermansdoerfer	2500.00

—Fourth Ward—

7 short lots No. 1529 to 1535	600.00
7 short lots No. 1543 to 1549	600.00
1 Lot No. 1337, 10th Ave.,	300.00
House and Lot No. 1266 9th Ave., from Webster	1300.00
Vacant Lot No. 1336 10th Ave.,	300.00
32 Acres Hillside land	4000.00

—Fifth Ward—

Vacant Lot No. 518, 519 & 520 Lincoln St.,	1000.00
Frame Row Lots No. 515 & 516 1st Ave., from Modes	2000.00
3 Lots No. 22, 23 and 24 Old E. P.	600.00

House and lot 807 4th Ave.,	900.00
3 lots 17th St., Economy plan	800.00

—Sixth Ward—

Lots No. 1211 & 1214 inclusive 9th Ave.,	1600.00
Lots No. 1226 9th Ave.,	400.00
Lots No. 1223 & 1224, 9th Ave.,	800.00
House and Lot (Corner) 8th Ave., and 7th St.,	1000.00
Brick House and Lot No. 1201 8th Ave., from Cunning	2000.00
Farm House 8th Ave.,	$1000.00
3 Lots Brick Yard, No. 1326 & 1327 & 1328	600.00
5 Lots No. 41 to 45 East Ave., W. R. R.	250.00
2 Lots No. 74 and 75 W. R. R.	100.00
10 Lots No. 53 to 63 small Lots W. R. R.	300.00
3 Lots No. 96, 97 and 98 W. R. R.	150.00
1 Lot land No. 260 W. R. R.	75.00
5 Lots No. 63 to 67 2nd Ave., very small W. R. R.	100.00
10 Lots 77 to 86 2nd Ave., W. R. R.	1000.00
4 Lots No. 137, 138 and 145 and 146 W. R. R.	200.00
4 Lots No. 231 to 234, W. R. R.	275.00
9 Lots No. 244 to 252 W. R. R.	675.00
2 Lots No. 273 and 274, West Ave., W. R. R.	200.00
6 Lots No. 311 to 316 West Ave., W. R. R.	300.00
10 Lots No. 301 to 310 West Ave., W. R. R.	500.00
10 Lots No. 291 to 300, 4th Ave., W. R. R.	500.00
1 Lot No. 118 2nd Ave., of Mountford,	75.00
9 Lots No. 292 and 290 West R. R.	450.00
7 Lots No. 275 and 281 West R. R.	350.00
39⅓ acres of land on Hillside	7850.00
4 Lots No. 255 & 258 inclusive West R. R.	300.00
2 Lots No. 103 & 104 inclusive West R. R.	200.00

John Reeves, Agent.

Memorandum D

Liabilities of Henrici and Duss, Trustees at the
Bank of Pittsburgh, April 1st 1892.

Date	Amount	Collateral	When Due
1892.			
Feb. 2	$60,000	(150 Bonds Pgh. Chartiers &) (Youghy R. R.)	Apr. 5th, 1892
Feb. 27	$10,000	($12000 Bonds Little Saw-) (Mill Run R. R.)	June 30, 1892
March 1st	$12,000	($12000 Bonds Little Saw) (Mill Run R. R.)	July 4, 1892

Liabilities Henrici and Duss Trustees as Endorsers.

Jan. 4	$60,000	(240 shares Beaver Falls Bridge)	

<pre>
                    (Co. and 406 shares Beaver Falls) Apr. 7, '92
                    (Gas Co.   )
March 15 $50,000 ($6000 Bonds Union Water Co.)
                    (Beaver Falls.   ) Apr. 17, '92
</pre>

Pittsburgh April 5th 1892. I hereby certify that the above statement is a correct and true exhibit of the liabilities of Henrici & Duss Trustees as drawers and endorsers to the Bank of Pittsburgh as appears by the books on April 1st, 1892.

W. Rosenburg,

Cashier.

Attest.

F. B. MacMillan, Jr.

Memorandum E

Liabilities of Henrici and Duss, Trustees at
The Farmers Deposit National Bank at Pittsburgh, Apr. 1st. '92.

Date	Amount	Collateral	When Due
1891.			
Nov. 6th	$10,000	(178 shares Merchant & Manu-) (facturing National Bank of) (Pittsburgh. Stock 70 shares Al-) (legheny National Bank of) (Pittsburgh Stock.)	On Demand
Dec. 7	$10,000	($12,500 First Mortgage Bonds) (Little Saw Mill Run R. R. Co.)	Apr. 10, 1892
1892.			
March 19	$28,600	($32,500 Second Mortgage Bonds) (Pgh., Chartiers & Y. R. W. C.)	July 22, 1892
March 24	$12,000	($13,000 Second Mortgage Bonds) (Point Bridge Co.)	July 27, 1892

April 5th, 1892.

Whereas.

B. L. Liepott.

T. H. Given,

Cashier.

Memorandum F

Liabilities of Henrici and Duss, Trustees,
to Iron & Glass Dollar Saving Bank.
April 1st. 1892.

Date	Amount	Collateral	When Due
Dec. 26	$10,000	400 shares Monongahela Water Co.	Apr. 26/29
Jan. 12	$26,900	1076 shares Monongahela Water Co.	May 12/15
Feb. 4	$32,058	1284 shares Monongahela Water Co.	June 4/7
Feb. 26	$10,000	400 shares Monongahela Water Co.	June 26/29
March 2.	$10,000	400 shares Monongahela Water Co.	July 3/6
	$88,958	3560 shares Monongahela Water Co.	

I certify that above statement of
liabilities to our Bank is correct.
Witnessed by
F. William Rudel.   Henry Stamm, Cashier.
                                    Iron & Glass Dollar Saving Bank.

After this report had been wrung from the memory of a
dying trustee, who had kept his accounts under his hat, it was
found urgently necessary to borrow one hundred and two
thousand dollars to meet bills of the Society. For this collateral
security had to be given, as shown in the following document
of November 3, 1892:

Pittsburgh, Nov. 3rd, 1892.
Whereas, through the aid of J. T. Brooks, We, Henrici & Duss,
Trustees, have borrowed of Mrs. Rebecca T. McCullough, the sum
of one hundred and two thousand Dollars, and have given therefore
our demand note dated this day, and have also given as collateral
security to said note the following stocks and bonds, viz:
1610 shares stock of the Monongahela Water Co. $25 per share.
  386 shares stock of Tidioute & Economy Bridge Co. $50 pr share.
  178 shares stock of Merchants and Man'frs. Nat. Bank $50 pr share.
  484 shares stock of Birmingham & Pgh. Bridge Co. $25 pr share.
  500 shares stock of Little Sawmill Run Rd. Co. $50 per share.
   27 shares stock of P. Ft. W. & C. Ry. Co. $100 per share.
   70 shares stock of Allegheny Nat'l. Bank $50 per share.
  600 shares stock of Point Bridge Co. $25 per share.
2nd mortgage bonds of Point Bridge Co. to amount of $13,000
2nd mortgage bonds of P.C. & Y.R.R.Co. to amount of $33,000
2nd mortgage bonds of Little Sawmill Run Rd. Co. $12,500
And whereas, the negotiation of said loan was necessary to enable
us, said Henrici and Duss to pay a pre-existing indebtedness of the
Harmony Society to the Farmers Deposit National Bank of Pittsburgh, represented by various time and demand notes to the amount
of $102,000 and the interests of said Society require that the secur-
ities above named be not sacrificed, but nevertheless sold and proceeds applied so far as needed to the liquidation of said debt to Mrs.
McCullough and balance of proceeds or of securities after such payment be given to said Henrici and Duss, Trustees or their successors:
   Therefore it is agreed as follows:
   The said J. T. Brooks hereby agrees that he will personally protect
said Trustees against any unjust or inequitable sale of said securities
whereby the interests of said Society might become sacrificed and on
the other hand said Henrici and Duss, Trustees hereby authorize,
request and direct said Brooks as their Agent and Attorney to proceed

to sell said securities or any of them at the fair and reasonable market value thereof as soon as convenient and apply the proceeds thereof to the payment of said debt to Mrs. McCullough, the balance of cash or securities if any after such payment to be given and paid to said Henrici and Duss, Trustees, or their successors.

J. T. Brooks.
Henrici & Duss, Trustees.

Another important legal act remained to be performed, namely, to record in proper legal form a statement of the membership of the Harmony Society and to define the rights and powers of the trustees. This was especially important because life in Economy had become so confused that it was difficult to say who was and who was not a member, and because many inhabitants of the town who were also employees of the Society had more influence in the affairs of the Society than members themselves. (The number of employees was between three and four hundred.) The important document of December 20, 1892, lists all five Feuchts among the members of the Society, but Henry, Benjamin, Rebecka, and Margaret Feucht did not sign it, only Thirza Feucht. This is mute evidence of the battle which was brewing in the Society between the rival factions and which had not broken out openly out of respect for the dying Father Henrici.

The Feuchts knew very well that signatures to such a document were needed to validate a heavy mortgage which the legal minds now running the Society wanted to legalize the following day because the hand of death already was stretched out for Henrici. The document is produced here as copied from the record in the Beaver County Court House:

December 20, 1892: STATEMENT OF MEMBERSHIP IN THE HARMONY SOCIETY AND DEFINITION OF RIGHTS AND POWERS OF TRUSTEES OF SOCIETY.

Articles of December 20th, 1892.

Whereas, the undersigned, being all members of the Harmony Society, at Economy, Beaver County, State of Pennsylvania, deem it proper and desirable that there should be some suitable and proper and certain evidence of Membership in said Society and that the rights and powers of the Trustees of said Society, should be more clearly defined and understood:

Now therefore, while we do hereby ratify and confirm the Articles of Agreement and Compacts of our association entered at Economy on the 12th day of August 1847, and those of April 30th 1890, confirmatory of the former and ratifying the acts of the Boards of Elders, and the Boards of Trustees, both of which Articles of Agreements are recorded in the Recorder's Office of Beaver County, and are hereby re-affirmed, we and each of us, present members of the said Harmony Society, do hereby state and declare that this declaration, agreement and grant of power, is, and is to be taken and considered, as supplementary to the agreements, compacts and articles above mentioned, to wit:

First: The present members of this Society and Association are Jacob Henrici, John S. Duss, J. Jacob Niclaus, Moritz J. Friedericks, Gottfried Lauppe, Johannes Scheid, Franz Gillmann, Hugo Miller, Conrad Hermansdoerfer, Julius Stickel, Edward Kellermann, Henry Feucht, B. Feucht, Blasius Platz, Sigmund Stiefvater, Regina Lautenschlager, Christina Rall, Karoline Molt, Katharina Nagel, Elizabeth Beck, Lena Rall now Lena Wolfangel, Thirza Feucht, Rebecka Feucht, Margaret Feucht, Christina Haerer, Susie C. Duss, Bertha Geratch, Pauline Stickel, Johanna Hermansdoerfer, Maria Diem, Barbara Boesch, Friedericka Munz, Dorothea Hoehr, Philippine L. Wolfangel, Gottlieb Riethmueller, Samuel Siber, and Elizabeth Siber, and no other person or persons, than those above named, is a member thereof, and that for the future it is agreed, that before any person can become a member of the Harmony Society, he or she shall sign or make his or her mark to his or her name on the roll of membership, which shall always be kept in the Record book of the Society, which book was established by the aforesaid agreement of 1847 and is the same in which are entered copies of said Articles above mentioned and shall also sign a written agreement in said book, binding himself or herself to the observance and performance of all and singular the declarations, stipulations and agreements of the members of the Society, as contained in the several written articles, and the book aforesaid, containing said roll of Membership, shall be the sole exclusive proof of Membership in the Society.

Second: It is hereby declared and agreed that the present Board of Elders of said Society are Jacob Henrici, John S. Duss, Johannes Scheid, Gottfried Lauppe, Moritz J. Friedricks, J. Jacob Niclaus, Conrad Hermansdoerfer, Hugo Miller and Gottlieb Riethmueller: and the present Board of Trustees, of said Society are Jacob Henrici and John S. Duss, and we do hereby grant and assign to said Trustees and their successors and do hereby agree and declare that the legal title to any and all property, real and personal, owned or possessed by said Society, wherever the same is situated or found is, and is to be taken and considered as fully vested in the said Trustees, Jacob Henrici and John S. Duss, above named and held by them in trust

for the Society, but with full and complete power and authority
in said Trustees, their survivors and successors, at such time or times
as they may deem advisable and for the best interests of the Society
to sell and dispose of the same, or any part or parcel of the same,
and for this purpose to make assignments or bills of sale of said property, personal, estate and to execute and deliver deeds in fee simple,
or for any less estate for any or all said real estate thus sold. This
declaration and power to apply to and embrace any and all lands,
wherever situated now, or hereafter belonging to said Harmony
Society, or held in trust for said Society, the title to which may be,
or stand in the name of Frederick Rapp, or George Rapp, or R. L.
Baker and Jacob Henrici Trustees, Jacob Henrici and Jonathan
Lenz Trustees, Jacob Henrici and Ernst Woelfel Trustees, Jacob
Henrici and John S. Duss Trustees, or any or either of them, and
their successors and any Board of Trustees hereafter appointed.

Third: To remove any possible doubt or misunderstanding as to
their right and power in reference thereto, we hereby give and grant
to said Trustees above named, Jacob Henrici and John S. Duss and
to either of them and their survivors and successors, full power
from time to time, and at such times as they, or either of them may
deem for the true interest of the Society to borrow such sum or sums
of money, for such length of time, at such rates of interest and upon
such other terms as the said Trustees, or either of them, or their survivors or successors, may deem advisable; and jointly or severally to
give notes, bills of exchange, bonds, due-bills or other evidences of
debt by pledge or assignment of any stocks, bonds or other personal
property of any kind now belonging, or that may hereafter belong
to said Society, and by mortgage or mortgages upon, or deeds of trust
of all or any part of the real property, which said Society now own
or possess, or hereafter may own or possess, and for this purpose the
said Trustees above named, or either of them, their survivor or successors, shall have full power and authority to make, execute and
deliver any and all such instruments and conveyances as may, in
their judgment, be reasonably necessary to enable them, or either
of them to carry the foregoing powers into full effect.

And in the execution of any instruments or conveyances in writing
or otherwise that may be or so become reasonably necessary in the
exercise or execution of any of the powers herein before granted,
either of said Trustees, their survivor or successors may execute the
same, and for that purpose may sign the joint names of said Trustees,
as in the following form: "Jacob Henrici and John S. Duss Trustees,"
or "Henrici and Duss Trustees," by (by name of Trustee executing)
"Trustee."

In witness whereof, we have hereunto set our hands and seals
this twentieth day of December A. D. 1892.

Jacob Henrici (seal)
John S. Duss (seal)
Johannes Scheid (seal)
Gottfried Lauppe (seal)
J. Jacob Niclaus (seal)
Conrad Hermansdoerfer (seal)
Hugo Miller (seal)
Gottlieb Riethmueller (seal)
Blasius Platz (seal)
Maria Diem (seal)
Friedericke Munz (seal)
Barbara Boesch (seal)
Thirza Feucht (seal)
Dorothea X Hoehr (seal)
    (her mark)
Edward X Kellerman (seal)
    (his mark)
Moritz J. Friedrich (seal)

Sigmund Stiefvater (seal)
Julius Stickel (seal)
Franz Gillman (seal)
Samuel Siber (seal)
Elizabeth X Beck (seal)
    (her mark)
Regina Lautenschlager (seal)
Christina Rall (seal)
Lena Wolfangel (seal)
Karoline Molt (seal)
Christine Haerer (seal)
Bertha Geratsch (seal)
Pauline X Stickel (seal)
    (her mark)
Susie C. Duss (seal)
Elizabeth J. Siber (seal)
Johanna Hermansdoerfer (seal)
Philipina L. Wolfangel (seal)
Catharina Nagel (seal)

State of Pennsylvania
S.S.

This document was then notarized and recorded on the 22nd day of December A.D. 1892 in the office for recording Deeds &c. in the County of Beaver in Deed Book Vol. 139, page 218.

On December 21, 1892, one day after the power of attorney had been signed and a day before it was recorded, the legal minds now running the affairs of the Society obtained Henrici's badly needed signature to a document mortgaging the Society property for $400,000. This document contained two very important changes from such previous documents: 1. both Frederick and George Rapp had been careful to disclaim any personal and individual rights and stressed that their power was only delegated and representative. 2. This gave Duss the right to sign for Henrici, who was *non compos mentis*. Yet, this action was legally binding, but was taken almost too late because Henrici died three days later, on Christmas day. The Pittsburgh *Commercial Gazette of* December 26, 1892, reported:

Last month his condition grew worse and in different times his death was expected. His many pious followers did everything possible to restore their aged leader, and not only secured the best medical attendance, but watched their invalid friend with a loving devotion that has always distinguished the brotherly feeling of the members of the society. Notwithstanding their brave efforts the numbered hours of Father Henrici's life grew fewer until 4 o'clock on Christmas morning, when, with a smile of content upon his aged face, he breathed his last.

Death-Bed Scenes.

The death-bed was surrounded by his many aged brethren, who for years lived in comfort through the excellent judgement and perfect managing powers of the deceased. The termination of his life before their eyes was more than they could stand and many tears dropped from the eyes of the old Economites, although they are all patiently awaiting their turn to die. Father Henrici's useful life of 89 years died out without the shadow of suffering. His illness was not painful, as nothing but old age was considered the immediate cause of his death.

The news of the death of the well-known Economite leader was quickly spread about the quiet little village, all owned by the society. It had an important meaning to the members of the society, in addition to the sorrow communicated. The members have, since the dead leader became the ruling spirit, disregarded business matters entirely and depended solely upon his judgement and the warm interest he took in the transaction of business for the benefit of their enterprise.

Now that his demise has occurred, they will be without the aid of their respected leader and will be compelled to think for themselves until a successor can be appointed. The commanding presence of the deceased, which had been the direct means of keeping the Economites so peaceable together and through dispute and turmoil, for such a long time, will also be absent.

Gloom in the town.

The state of affairs at Economy presented ever a gloomy appearance all day yesterday. The peculiar routine of life as spent in the society since its organization, was carried on as usual, all excepting the spirit of the people. The anxiety and sleepy look on many of their faces indicated the fact, that a few slept that night, owing to the near approach of death to Father Henrici. Otherwise it would be difficult to detect any change out of the ordinary.

There was not even crepe on the door that opened into the house containing the dead. A custom of spending the Sunday morning hours in church was observed as usual, and from 9 until 11:30 A. M., the thoroughfares about the picturesque little village were entirely deserted. The celebration of Christmas was all conducted inside the quaint church, and they praised the Birth of Jesus while lamenting the loss of their faithful old friend and adviser. It was probably the first Christmas they had ever spent without him and that his absence was keenly felt was evident by the listless-attitude of the worshipers. The body lies now in the "great" house of the society, where the

dead trustee lived, on a canvas trundle bed covered by white sheets.
The funeral arranged.
The funeral service will take place on Tuesday afternoon at 1:30
o'clock. The service will be simple, as is customary with the regulations of the society. The elders and a few of the more intimate
friends of the deceased will assemble at the house where the body
lies and after a few services they will follow the hearse in procession
to the orchard where the grave has been prepared. The thin hex-
agonal coffin, which will enclose the remains, will be laid over the
grave as usual. A hymn will be sung, and after a few other remarks,
the body will be interred in the last resting place. Each member of
the society will then throw flowers over it, and then the grave will be
quietly filled and the sad mourners will depart.

As is also customary no monument of any kind will be placed at
the head or foot of the grave to mark the aged Economite's resting
place. There will be to indicate the grave nothing but a little eleva-
tion of the earth above the surface, with either a shrub or flower
planted on it, the affectionate tribute of some near friend. His burial
ground will not be distinguished from the other brethren and sisters
that are now inhumed in the cemetery.
Will lie near Father Rapp.
The resting place of Father Rapp, the Founder of the organization
is in the plot and unmarked in the same manner. Beside him in
different rows beneath the apple trees lie the remains of the original
members of the society.

As in all other cases of death in the ranks of the Economite society
members the name of Father Henrici will be written in the death
register, together with the date of his departure and number an-
nexed, which is to distinguish the grave in the row. A remarkable
feature of the death register shows that the members never die young,
few dying under the age of 70 and many reaching 100 years. As death
is the termination of the member's life none of them learn to dread
the approach of it. They believe that all who have been good and
faithful members of the society and who are not permitted to survive until the Lord's coming, will be raised up to meet Him at His
glorious appearing. Thus they calmly speak of being carried to the
orchard for burial when their work on earth will be done.

A reporter from the *Pittsburgh Dispatch* covered the funeral
and published the following report on December 28, 1892.

The remains of the late Father Jacob Henrici, the leader of the
Harmonites, were buried yesterday afternoon. The interment was
magnificent in its simplicity. No evidence of pomp and no effort at
ceremony attended the burial. As the noted old character had lived
so he died and so he was buried. Among his people he had grown

like a sheltering oak in a forest. He quit the world like a blossom leaves its stem and his tenantless clay was returned to earth as quietly as his whole life had been spent upon it. Regarded and esteemed by his fellows while he lived, he was honored by them in death. Strong men, firm in the affairs of the world, brought flowers to his unadorned casket, and every bud carried to his coffin sparkled with the tears of women who loved him. There was no distinction among his mourners. All were distressed by their loss, and the officers and the servants of the peculiar sect joined in a grief that seemed pathetic. They made no effort to conceal their affliction. They were unable to suppress their sorrow, which was told silently in tears.

The funeral services had been announced to occur at 1:30 in the afternoon, and when the unique German clock in the belfry of the quaint church tolled that hour the three remaining elders who were able to attend lifted their brother from the dead-room in the great hall, and, bearing the remains, marched in melancholy silence to the church across the street.

Mourners follow to the grave.

Immediately following the coffin, dressed in mourning, with her head bowed to her husband's arm, came Mrs. R. M. McCargo, a niece of the dead leader. Then six women dressed in black followed, and the eight persons made up the funeral train. When the coffin and the mourners entered, the sacred edifice was filled with people. Every seat was occupied. On one side were arranged the women. On the other side the men sat. Between the two, on either side the choir stand and pulpit were arranged and between them, and in full view of all, the corpse was placed. The casket was opened and flowers were arranged about the dead man. He was dressed in a black suit. Around him was thrown a shroud, white and pure as the bunch of water lilies held in the nerveless hands that crossed his breast. At his feet a bunch of lilies of the valley hung like tiny bells. On the floor at the head of the coffin was a wreath of roses and lilies and on either side were little bunches of homely posies, all of which had been carried in as tokens of esteem.

Just after the flowers had been arranged Trustee Duss, who succeeds the dead leader, walked up the main entrance to his little pulpit. He was dressed in a neat fitting black suit. His Prince Albert coat was buttoned to the chin. He walked with measured tread. His head was bowed. In one hand he carried a Bible. In the other, with his hat, he carried a small bunch of flowers. He walked to his chair, or the pulpit, and sat for a moment as though meditating.

A funeral sermon in two languages.

Then he nodded his head and the grand old organ just opposite him, in notes that seemed divine, rolled out a sacred melody and the choir in German sang, "How Softly They Rest." Mr. Duss, still sitting in his chair, then delivered the funeral oration, in which he talked glowingly of the deceased. He spoke first in German and then in English. After his first sermon he explained that on account of so many friends being present who could not understand German, he would like to condence his first remarks in English. He asked permission of the elders present and then explained that the English language had never been spoken in the church. He told of the many sterling qualities of the deceased and likened his character to purest crystal. The dead brother, Mr. Duss said, was most noble and always appeared like one from another sphere. He said the dead brother had been frequently misjudged, but he was confident that his everlasting rest was assured. He told of his earnestness and unselfishness and believed that his every act was prompted by a desire to do God's will. He was sometimes too cold and at other times too good, but that under all conditions and circumstances he was a noble, manly man. At the conclusion of his remarks Mr. Duss read several verses from the Bible. He then left the pulpit and walked to the choir stand. He took a seat at the organ and played while the choir sang "Jesus My Trust." After the hymn Mr. Duss returned to the pulpit and announced that all those who desired to take a last look at the dead leader could pass from their seats along where the coffin stood and return to their seats.

A last look at the dead.

Then the organ sounded out a doleful strain, and for 40 minutes the people humbled in the face of death marched by the coffin.

When all had returned to their seats there were few, if any, dry eyes in the gathering. The coffin was then closed up by two of the elders, and by the three pallbearers it was carried to the street, where a little old-fashioned one-horse hearse awaited it. The funeral procession was then formed. It was headed by Mr. Duss and another of the elders. When the hearse moved off the procession followed. A walk had been swept in the snow to the graveyard, just three squares away. The grave had been dug directly at the entrance, and will hereafter stand as the first in a long row of mounds, the resting places of the dead Economites. At the grave after the coffin had been lowered the Männerchor sang "How Shall It Be." Mr. Duss read the Lord's Prayer, each member of the society walked up and threw upon the lowered coffin a small bunch of flowers, and then each turned and walked silently away. After all but two had left the sacred place the grave was filled up. It will be unmarked and will be in no way designated from the rest.

Before Henrici's death, as we have seen, it was found that because of his Santa Claus spirit on the one hand and the II Kings approach to bookkeeping and accounting on the other, the Society's cash reserves were so badly depleted—in

fact, that it had borrowed so heavily to get additional cash—
that its welfare state existence could be continued only by
obtaining a high mortgage on the Society property. After all,
there were hundreds of persons in Economy living off the
dying Society. Yet, this does not mean, as has been claimed,
that the Society faced bankruptcy and that this was avoided
only through the idealism and self-sacrifice of men like J.
Twing Brooks and the genius of the new trustees. That is
nonsense. The Society had been badly managed because of
Henrici's innocent faith in the bridegroom's coming. The same
could have happened to George Rapp if Frederick Rapp and
R. L. Baker had not protected him and if George Rapp, who
also operated on the basis of II Kings and of giving no accounting "because he dealt honestly," had not had the good
hard sense to salt away that half million dollars in cold coin
down in a basement storage vault under his bed for Christ to
claim any time he might knock at the door. Henrici was no
less honest; he was simply less realistic and wise in dealing
with his Bridegroom. He was not a Swabian, which is significant. George Rapp took no chance with the United States
Government or its Treasury, in a sense not even in being left
waiting at the church by a *delayed* bridegroom. As a consequence, Rapp in dying left the Society a half million dollars
in hard money, while Henrici in dying had to sign a document
mortgaging the property of the Harmony Society for $400,000
in order to get the funds needed to meet the bills basically
contracted for those persons, not members of the Society, who
were living by the generosity of Santa Claus. It was a tragic
end to the life of a man who had been a shrewd business man
but who probably had never thought about Keppler's words:
"Fromm soll man sein, aber nicht zu fromm" (One should
be pious, but not too pious) .

The man who engineered the big loans required by the
Society was a hard business man who knew very well what
gold lay buried in the assets of the Society. I bring this chapter
to a close by quoting from his, J. Twing Brooks's, touching
eulogy of Father Henrici.

The strong personality of George Rapp, his fervent piety, his paternal care of his followers, bore to Father Henrici indubitable signs of the Divine presence. It cannot be doubted in later years, when the burden of the society was wholly on his own shoulders, that he was conscious of the same sustaining guidance and power within himself. On no other theory can his prolonged life of self-reliance, dutiful labor and abnegation of self be explained. To the last years of his life Father Henrici cherished the memory of the virtues of Rapp, followed his example, fulfilled his wishes and continued his plans. Rapp's theory of life was simple and sublime. "Christ will soon return to take his place among the children of men," he has said, "we must live as He lived and do as He did in order that we may become companions worthy of Him. Our property shall belong to all in equal parts, that no one may surpass another in wealth. As Christ never married, neither shall our young people marry, and even we who have been married will live in marriage no more." These principles are not declared to be sublime, in order thereby to stamp them with approval, or commend them to universal practice. They are described as they presented themselves to the youthful Henrici; as seeds which took deep root in his soul and which led him to renounce forever every taste, to forego every pleasure, to resist every temptation and deaden every passion, which might impede his spiritual growth or lessen his devotion to the service of Christ and His followers. His continence in every bodily pleasure; his exorcism of every useless habit; his suppression of every mental vice was not a mere spasm of virtue, transiently practiced. His purpose was founded on a high, heroic conception of duty. His purified conscience was the pillar of fire that guided every step of his life and his spirit disdained the weakness of yielding to temptation in any form.

Thus Father Henrici's life, though heroic in purpose and practice, was wholly destitute of pretensions to heroism. For nearly half a century he bore the burdens of leadership among his quaint followers, in entire humility, devoid of ambition, a stranger to vanity, never conscious that he was doing more than he should do; yet unwearied and true to his sense of duty as the needle to the pole. In the discharge of that duty he practised every virtue and made every sacrifice of personal comfort. He thought, toiled and saved for the society. His food was the simplest, his clothes the plainest, his industry the most tiring. Many years ago, in midwinter, he was in a neighboring state on business of the society. A sudden sharp change in the weather had turned muddy roads into a labyrinth of frozen ruts and rough clods. Business next called him to a town twenty-five miles distant. Three or four trains a day were passing between the points of departure and destination, yet he traversed the entire distance on foot. Being asked why he walked so great a distance, over such roads, when a railroad connected the two places, he answered: "My business is not pressing; I have plenty of time to walk and my people expect me to save money when I can do so."

His conscience recognized no distinction between the humbler and more important duties of his station. In early youth he had worked as a vine dresser. It was no uncommon sight in the spring to see him in the vineyard at Economy, binding with skillful hands the drooping vines and lopping the superfluous leaves. Every year at the due season, and until overcome by the debility of extreme old age, attended by a helper and arrayed in garments suited to the work, he explored the marshes in search of thoroughwort; and when an immense crop had been gathered and dried, he would preside over the boiling kettle protected by a coarse apron, and prepared the efficacious remedies so well known in this community—boneset syrup and cider bitters. From these humble labors he would pass to the performance of the important transactions of the society in cities far and near, or preside at the governing boards of corporations in which the society was largely interested, of which he in its interest acted as president.

Thus his daily, yearly round of duties fulfilled the Shaker poet's dream of life:

> Whoever wants to be the highest
> Must first come down to the lowest;
> And then ascend to be the highest
> By staying down to be the lowest.

It must not be supposed that the current of life flowed always in a placid stream, even at quiet Economy. Discord, jealousy and strife are inevitable elements of human life. They may and do exist where property is abundant and owned in common, as among men who contest for the prizes of life in the wider world. Enterprising and enlightened people are not the only ones who are hard to govern. A trespassing cat or chicken may create as great commotion in one place as riot or treason in another. Father Henrici by wise and firm monition subdued trifling jealousies, allayed petty quarrels and silenced local discord. His patriarchal form was abroad unexpected hours from opening dawn till deepening twilight, to see that society discipline was enforced and society rules observed. The Czar of Russia has not more absolute control of his subjects than had Father Henrici over all dwellers at Economy. His name was a talisman; his presence a magic. His stern view of discipline was known to all his associates as well as to the numerous band of employees. Hence whether he was present or absent, still he ruled. It is safe to say that during fifty years of his stewardship, noise, loud talking and laughter were unknown in the streets of Economy, and that no person save the watchman was abroad in the village after nine o'clock.

His habitual mood was earnestness and silence. In the transaction of business he had nothing to say save what related to the matter in hand, and he never indulged in talk about his policy or the general business of the society. Indeed he had no policy but to attend diligently to the subject before him and to walk continually with God. For the general news of the world as conveyed in newspapers and magazines he had no concern whatever. He read and studied the Bible more than all other books combined. Gradually his mind took the cast of this Divine impression. He became less communicative with other men; less inclined to take their advice; more self-reliant and, it must be said, more self-willed. He relied implicitly on his own judgment, believing that in his entire consecration to his Heavenly Father the Divine wisdom and counsel would never be withheld from him. His conduct at times seemed stern and even arbitrary; but the purity of his motive could never be questioned. Even to a venerable associate in his trusteeship, he did not at times spare words of censure. Though a friend to humanity, no individual could claim him as a friend. When his associates, one after another fell before the Grim Reaper, and it became his duty to utter a parting word over the lifeless clay; though the departed had stood longest and nearest to his side, he showed not a trace of emotion or regret. He saw the imprisoned spirit cast off its mortality and take its flight to realms of bliss. He consigned the cast-off mortal remains willingly to the tomb.

It is fit that one whose soul was filled with celestial harmony, should feel rapture in the lovely scenes of nature, and find solace and enchantment in the melody of earth. So it was given to Father Henrici to find delight and repose for his wearied virtue in music. For years after he had passed the limit of four score, he would interrupt the business of the day by an exercise on the piano, the composition of a strain of music adapted to the Lord's prayer, or other sacred homily, and at the close of day he would gather children into the singingroom, give them lessons in music and listen to the melody of their voices. If ever he yielded to the sensation of supreme bliss; if ever he felt transported from the sphere of human existence to the radiance of celestial abodes, it was when in the season of blossoms and flowers, amid the droning of bees and the ravishing song of birds, he walked forth alone in that place of enchantment, among the flowers, the fruit trees and vines of the garden or orchard at Economy. The inspiration he felt in those moments he at least once deigned to reveal.

The story of the tender sentiment which in early youth pervaded his breast toward the gentle Gertrude, and was there reciprocated, survives only in tradition. The imagination can conceive how the young emigrant, in a strange land, graciously received by the monarch Rapp, should be smitten with the charms of the daughter of that house, or how the maiden's quick eye found superior beauty, mind and grace in the ardent young teacher. But the quenchless flame was quenched. Side by side, beneath the same roof, at the same table, they lived in duty, not in love, while youth ripened into prime and prime passed into hoary age, till nature called her first, and he, serene, eulogized virtue over her lifeless form.

It is not known that Father Henrici ever lamented the steadily diminishing number of his followers, for to him every condition of life, every event among men was the will of God. His life-long companion and associate trustee for nearly twenty-four years expressed himself as follows, a short time before his death: "We have been disappointed in the results of our society; that is, we are sorry more people have not embraced our views. When we began there were several hundred of us; we were poor and our anxiety was how we should be able to live and feed and clothe our members. Now at the end of nearly one hundred years, we have more property than we know what to do with, but so few members that the society has become nearly extinct."

A few years ago Father Henrici was asked by one to whom he had kindly given the leading incidents of his life to allow his photograph to be taken, in order that his friend who might survive him could enjoy that precious memorial. He replied soberly and with a shake of his head, "That is against the rules of our society." A moment later a benignant smile spread over his face and he added, "We should live only in our deeds." J. T. B.[5]

PART III

The Duss-Siber-Riethmüller-Duss Trusteeship: 1892-1916

Clear the way for progress on the fly!
Yankee grit, Yankee wit, never shall
say die!
Clear the way, a people proud and
great
Seeks the top, and nought can stop
AMERICA UP TO DATE.

Homage, praise, and admiration due;
These we know we must show
To the WOMAN NEW.
Dressed in Bloomers, My! But she is
great!
Womankind is not behind
But always up to date!

Song Two Step by the last male
trustee of the Harmony Society

11

The Duss-Feucht Battle for the Control
of the Harmony Society

AS WE SHALL SEE IN THE LATER PART OF THIS HISTORY, DUSS VERY
much liked to use the power of the press for his purposes,
and he spent considerable money of the Harmony Society to
win the favor of this important means of communicating with
the public, but in the present conflict within the Society he
and his powerful legal staff did all they could to counteract
the influence of the press. It so happened that in this situation
the Feuchts, because they were fluent in English and German,
were able to communicate with reporters almost as well as
Duss, and the reporters of the Pittsburgh papers were very
capable men who lived and moved in Pittsburgh, Economy,
and Beaver. In the Beaver County Court House they examined
and checked the recorded legal documents bearing on the
transition of power to the new trustee, Duss. I have checked the
newspaper reports against the recorded legal records and have
found that they are generally the most accurate records of the
transactions of this important period that have remained, even
though copies of important newspaper issues for this time have
become rare. The people of the Pittsburgh region and beyond
were highly interested in the events taking place at Economy
because many of them were descendants of members who had
left the Society, because Economy was a popular place for
weekend visits, and because the business enterprises of the
Society had helped develop the Pittsburgh area and had given
extensive employment to persons living there. It was, therefore,
highly interesting to read in the Pittsburgh *Dispatch* of De-

cember 28, 1892, that the property of the Harmony Society had been mortgaged for $400,000. The announcement was exclusive with the *Dispatch,* which was proud of its scoop.

The mortgagee was reported to be Harry Darlington, acting as trustee, presumably for the McCullough estate. The late J. N. McCullough was Vice President of the Pennsylvania Company, of which J. T. Brooks was counsel. Mr. Brooks also was counsel for John S. Duss, and had recently made his home a great part of the time at Economy.

The mortgage was signed by Jacob Henrici and John S. Duss, acting as trustees of the Harmony Society, on December 21, the Wednesday before Mr. Henrici died, and recorded one day later in the Recorder's office in Pittsburgh and at Beaver. The filed instrument set forth that the money borrowed from Henry Darlington, trustee, namely, $400,000, by the trustees of the Harmony Society was for the purpose of paying the debts of the society heretofore legally incurred and contracted. Four notes of $100,000 each, to run five years at 6 percent, were given by the society's trustees. The notes were made payable at the People's National Bank of Pittsburgh. The mortgage was in the usual form and of unusual length only because the society's property at Economy was described in full, which description will be omitted here.

The customary form of attestation by the Justice of the Peace, which was attached to the mortgage, possessed special interest in this case because the instrument was dated December 21, when Mr. Henrici was on his deathbed. The formula ran: "Personally before me a Justice of the Peace in and for Harmony township, etc., came Jacob Henrici and John S. Duss, etc.," and was signed Henry Breitenstein, J. P., but of course the Justice went to Mr. Henrici's bedside.

The *Dispatch* continued:

The object of the loan is stated in the mortgage to be the payment of the debts of the Harmony Society, heretofore legally incurred and contracted. Some members of the Society, as well as the outside public, are in the dark as to the nature and origin of these debts, and wonder that with its supposed resources of cash and negotiable securities the society had been forced to mortgage its old homestead, as it were. The interests of the society outside Economy itself are centralized in Beaver Falls. In that town of over 10,000 inhabitants it is generally supposed that the Harmony Society owns or owned till recently two-thirds of the realty, and Mr. Henrici said four or five years ago that the society had there in one shape and another $3,000,000 worth of property.

It was stated yesterday by a local authority in Beaver Falls that the unencumbered property of the society in the town was of a vast extent still. This gentleman said that the society owned outright the Beaver Falls Steel Works, and a majority interest in the Bicycle Works, the Cold Drawn Steel Company and the Shovel Works. In the File Works, according to the same authority, the society possessed the next to the largest interest, and was negotiating to buy out the preponderant interest owned by the Blake Bros., of New York. The society is also interested in the trunk factory, the brass foundry and two or three other works recently started. The real estate interests of the society in Beaver Falls have been greatly reduced by the hundreds of sales made, mostly in the last decade, but they are still considerable. The amount of money which the society had made by selling building lots in Beaver Falls is not known, but it must have been considerable. The number of householders in Beaver Falls who obtained the title for their land from the Economites must be nearly 1,000, and perhaps more. In addition to these interests the society controls the Economy Savings Institution, a deservedly popular private bank which has always done a very large business.

The well-informed *Pittsburgh-Dispatch* in the same article also called attention to the deed of Confirmation of Association recorded at the Beaver Court House by the majority of the Harmony Society before the mortgage was drawn up, which ratified the articles of agreement and compacts of association entered into at Economy on August 12, 1847, and those of April 30, 1890, confirmatory of the former, and the acts of the Boards of Trustees and Elders. After giving the list of the members in good standing on December 20, it continued:

Absolute control vested in Duss.

The document then went on to say that in order to settle the question of the trustees' authority beyond all doubt, the society, as represented by the subscribers, granted to said trustees, Jacob Henrici and John S. Duss, and to either of them and their survivors and successors, full power from time to time and when they desired for the true interest of the society, to borrow money and give notes, bills, mortgages and deeds of trust in the society's name for the same. This empowering of the trustees, and especially it should be observed of their survivor or successors, was repeated further along, and it meant simply that in the event of the death of one of trustee[s] the survivor could go right along as the representative of the society. Mr. Henrici having died Mr. Duss still alone had the powers he held jointly with the former. The power to borrow money upon mortgage for example. To make this clearer the instrument specifically stated that in the execution of instruments and conveyances one trustee may sign for both, or their successors, or either of them.

This paper made Duss, as the surviving trustee, the sole arbiter for the time being of the society's actions, financial or otherwise. Even after election of another trustee, Duss would have the right, according to this paper, to borrow money, give notes, and sign conveyances for the society, but in his own name. This was an epoch-making change because it gave him more power than either of the Rapps had had. The *Dispatch* cited an attorney, "not prejudiced in Mr. Duss' favor, but who is of high standing," as saying that "the confirmatory articles of association put Mr. Duss absolutely in command of the society, its resources and powers."

The articles bore the signatures of 34 members out of the total 38, or leaving out the dead patriarch, Mr. Henrici, of 33 out of a possible 37. The four members who did not sign and who bluntly refused to sign were Dr. B. Feucht, his brother Henry, whose name was spelled in the document "Fencht," and their wives, Rebecka and Margareth Feucht. Their names appeared in the typewritten document filed at Beaver, but were stricken out, as if it had been hoped they would sign up to the last moment. Of those who did sign, four made their mark. The list was headed by the faltering illegible signature of Jacob Henrici himself. A blot of ink escaped from his pen as he tried to make the capital H, and this divided the whole signature. The first name began below the line and the rest of it straggled up and down in a painfully pathetic way. The bold clear signature of John S. Duss next below was in striking contrast to the feeble effort of Mr. Henrici.

The *Dispatch* thus concluded its report:

John S. Duss was last night practically placed in control of the Harmony Society. His side to the dispute in the organization created the offices of President and Vice President of the society, and at a meeting of the Board of Elders Mr. Duss was not only elected Senior Trustee, the place, vacated by the death of Father Henrici, but he was also chosen President of the entire organization. Samuel Siber, a comparatively new member, was elected Junior Trustee and Vice President of the society. Siber is about 50 years old. He was formerly a policeman in Economy. He can speak both English and German, which it was claimed was his strongest recommendation, as besides Duss he will be the only member who can do that. It is argued in his favor that he will be able to transact business with the business world.

At the meeting of the Board of Elders a resolution was passed expressing confidence in Mr. Duss and highly applauding his management of the affairs of the society.

It was announced after last night's meeting that Mr. Duss had employed an expert bookkeeper, and that a quarterly report of the workings of the society will be made to its members.

John S. Duss is rather striking in appearance. He is admittedly bright and competent. In appearance and actions he much resembles Postmaster General Wanamaker. He is a pleasant talker and has never been known to lose his head.

"Absolute control vested in Duss," "Duss on Top," such were the headlines used not only by the *Pittsburgh Dispatch* but also by other papers reporting on the affairs of the Society. Who was this so-recent member of the Harmony Society, whose name for the next decade was to be so widely publicized throughout the United States?

John S. Duss, the new absolute ruler over the Harmony Society property, was born in Cincinnati on February 22, 1860. He was the son of John Rutz, alias Duss, a man of whom little is known. When young John was somewhat over a year old, his father went to New Orleans, where, so a report has it, he was pressed into the rebel service by the Confederate recruiting officers. Not willing to prove disloyal to the Government, so Duss has reported, he represented himself as being sick during the first few engagements in which he would have been obliged to take part, but at the battle of Bull Run he deserted the Confederate Army, enlisted as private under the name of John Rutz in Company "H" in the 75th Regiment of Pennsylvania Infantry Volunteers, was wounded at the battle of Gettysburg, and died in the U.S. Hospital at Baltimore, Maryland, on July 21, 1863. In an "application of widow" for additional bounty under an act of July 28, 1866, dated September, 1868, Caroline Duss claimed she was the widow of "John Rutz alias Duss," so it is not entirely clear whether his real name was Rutz or Duss. This application was worked out with the help of Dr. Benjamin Feucht, to whom she wrote on June 10, 1868, ". . . because my husband before the war had given himself over to drinking I also did not want to bear his name and later said I will not return to him again when he is discharged." Her letters to Dr. Feucht are full of praise for his kindness and assistance and likewise show the love of the members of the Society for him. The pension for which she applied seems to have been granted, for there is a receipt of October 1, 1869, showing that she had a deposit in the Economy Savings Institute amounting to $1100 which was paying 5% interest, and that on that day she also had a credit of $41.47 in the work book of the Society.

Duss's mother had come to Economy with her small son as early as March 1862, and obtained employment as a nurse, but in the year 1868 they moved to Tuscarawas County, Ohio, for a few months, returning and remaining in the employ of the Society until June 1873. Young Duss during this time attended the common district school at Economy. In June 1873 he moved to the Soldier's Orphan School at Philipsburg (Monaca), to continue his education, remaining there until he completed his 16th year. Upon leaving the Soldier's Orphan School he returned to Economy and lived with his mother, doing some work in the Society's orchard nursery and fruit tree department. In June 1876 Mrs. Duss decided to return to Germany, specifically to move to Kornthal, the pious little town that had been established to stop the heavy emigration of the Harmonists many years before. On June 29 they departed for Germany, where John Duss was to be sent as an apprentice into a business in Stuttgart.

On July 24, 1876, the Director of Kornthal, Johannes Daur, wrote the Trustees of the Harmony Society a friendly letter asking for information about the citizenship of the Dusses because they had applied for membership in that communal society. By fall of that year both were back in Economy, having spent a pleasant summer in Germany visiting friends and relatives. His mother again became a nurse in the Society and young Duss was apprenticed to learn the tailor's trade. In the fall of 1878, he started to teach German in the Economy school and continued until August 1879, when he was admitted as a student at Mount Union College, Ohio.

In March 1882, young Duss left Mount Union with Mr. J. F. Buck, Superintendent of the Stark County Orphan's Home, who had been called to the Superintendency of the Kansas State Reform School at Topeka, Kansas, and who had selected him as a teacher for this school. Because he could not stand the climate, he had to give up his position in July of the same year. It is possible that it was less the climate than the desire to marry that brought this abrupt departure from Kansas, for in that same year he married Susie C. Creese, with whom he had been acquainted at Economy. Soon after, with the help of his mother, who always seemed to have funds available, he bought and ran a farm in Nebraska. At this time he had great dreams of cattle breeding in the great West. Amid all this restless moving around, Santa Claus Henrici and Dr. Benjamin Feucht remained the support of the mother and son. She followed him to Nebraska and provided him with money—Henrici was always generously helpful, but always, whether in Kornthal, Germany, or Red Cloud, Nebraska, piously wept on Henrici's shoulder. From Red Cloud on September 18, 1884, she wrote Henrici among other things: "I was with John 3 days, but I cannot stand it to live in the shanty or hut, for it is only a little room, the wee house is not even as large as your washhouse, for them it will do, and the new house is so unfinished that it will take three months more before one can live in it, and the wind blows so terrifically on the farm that I could not stand it, and nights the wolves howl." So she moved to town and called Henrici's attention to the possibility of making lots of money in Red Cloud by building houses for rent there. The full confession of her woes includes a report of the beneficial results that the "Seiter Bitters" added to Nebraska water had brought to her thirst and health, evidently another name for the famous cure-all remedy of the Harmony Society, later marketed, by Duss as Boneset Cordial. Amid all these complaints is one that, although there are many Germans around—

also a German church—everything around Duss is English "and Sussi (John's wife) will soon not be able to speak a word of German."

Another letter from Red Cloud, dated September 27, 1884, asks Henrici to send her a $1000 bond she had deposited with them because in Nebraska she could get 10% interest and she must look for a new abode because "Mr. Henrici does not want to have me in Economy anymore." In this letter she also makes the significant declaration that she would have joined the Society if Henrici had not told her thrice that she should go to her son John in Nebraska and that Mrs. Ott had told her "I have given my John all the money I have and now the Society is to keep and maintain me with nothing. I always got my pay and now that I cannot work anymore the Society should keep me. To this I should like to remark that I have a mortgage of $1000 from John, and I might have had the last one also, so would you have to keep me for nothing?" Mrs. Ott, of course, had spoken the truth, for John's farm had been subsidized by his mother's money.

To her two long letters, both of which are a strong bid to be permitted to return and join the Society, Henrici writes on October 3, 1884:

Mrs. Caroline Duss, Red Cloud, Webster Co., Nebraska
Dear Friend:
    Your two friendship letters were duly received and contents carefully weighed. According to your wish we herewith send you a draft for $1000 on the Bank of America, New York, for the Bond of same value of the Little Saw Mill Run Rail Road, which we herewith take back from you. Because another's month's interest, namely $5 is due on this we yesterday sent you for it by express a small keg of 5 gallons of our best Cider Bitters, also 5 gallons of our best old Concord wine, as a fare-well present. Soon more.
    Your true friends, Henrici & Lenz.

But Duss's mother would not be brushed off, even though the Society had sent her the bond she wanted cashed for higher interest in Nebraska. She was back in Economy in less than a year working alternately on Henrici and then Lenz, urging them to let her son return, for the farm and cattle breeding were not paying off at all, and life was far more pleasant at Economy. There obviously had been real difficulty, and John Duss was not wanted back. One such instance is covered by a pleading letter to Lenz stating that John had written a dubious letter regarding pay. She feared that Henrici would read it to the Board of Elders and that this might harm him, and pleaded with Lenz to interpret the letter so as not to hurt John, because while Henrici had said that John and his wife "may or should come" and could take over the school, she now believed neither would be necessary because the teacher they had could handle everything. Since the school job was taken, she pleads "And I want to tell you that John can also do other work, you can depend on that. He is not ashamed of anything. He can also tailor. He makes all his own clothes, also theirs and enjoyed it. If only he had been here a while longer in the shop he would also have learned pattern cutting. He is very sorry that the gossip started that time. . . . And John is your God-son, although he of course earlier did not have sense as now, one can often make up for that lost when one is older and has more sense." Most of her letters are in this plaintive tone, working to get her son back to Economy, or complaining about petty annoyances, or longing for death. On July 29, 1888, John Duss, his wife, and two children came to Economy, he as teacher, a short year after his mother had joined the Society. He had—with his mother's and the Society's help—paid for his Nebraska farm in full. On January 24, 1890, he joined the Society, as on February 13 of the same year did his wife Susie—just in time to get a good head start on the Feuchts, whose family history is here recalled as the Feuchts gave it to the Pittsburgh press:

When George Rapp decided to separate from the established church in Württemberg, the great grandparents of Benjamin and Henry Feucht, John Bentel and wife, became his most devoted followers. Mrs. Bentel was a woman of great force of character, who possessed, in addition, what was then regarded as a considerable sum of money and some real estate. All of this she put at Rapp's disposal. There were born to this couple five daughters: Frederika, Johanna, Mary, Katharina, and Wilhelmina, and three sons, George, Arnold, and Israel. These came with their parents to Harmony in the year

1805, and joined their leader Rapp, who had preceded them. Frederika was married the same year to John Mutschler, a follower of Rapp, the latter performing the ceremony. The explanation of this apparently inconsistent act on the part of Father Rapp is found in the fact that it was not until two years after its organization (or in 1807) that the society adopted the idea of celibacy and abjured matrimony, although families "continued to dwell together as before" [actually Father Rapp even in Indiana united couples in sacred matrimony when he became convinced that the way of celibacy was too difficult to follow. (See *Documentary History in the Indiana Decade.*)] On April 29, 1806, their first child, Hildegarde, was born to John Mutschler and wife. Although born into the society and early imbued with the idea of celibacy, Hildegarde could not resist the proposal of young Dr. Conrad Feucht, who had left Württemberg with his father and joined the society at its organization.

The lovers eloped, knowing that their union would never receive the sanction of their parents, let alone that of Father Rapp. Soon after they left, however, their absence was discovered by Father Rapp, with whom Hildegarde was a great favorite. An uncle of Hildegarde, John Reichert, was sent in swift pursuit of the eloping couple who, hearing him coming, hid by the wayside until he had passed, and then continued their journey to Rochester, where they were married by "Squire Sholes," in his day one of the most noted characters of the Beaver Valley. This was not the only instance in which members had left the society on account of celibacy. In 1828–29 Elias Speidel severed his connection with it and went to Marietta, Ohio, as did also soon afterward Israel Lenz, brother of Jonathan Lenz, who later became a trustee of the society. Both married other women who had never been members. Neither Speidel nor Lenz was reinstated.

Doctor and Mrs. Feucht continued their journey to Marietta, where they resided for a short time near Israel Lenz. During the same year, however, they were sent for by Father Rapp, and brought back to the society. The doctor at first refused to return, but finally consented to do so through the persuasive influence of John Reichert, whom Rapp sent as his representative. When they returned, however, in 1829, they insisted on living together as man and wife. This aroused a storm of opposition on the part of the other members and compelled the couple to separate, he living at his father's and she going to her own people. Thus matters continued until after the birth of a daughter, Tirza. This led to fresh complications, which were at length settled by Rapp, declaring that the Doctor and his wife must remain in the society as husband and wife, even though all the other members were opposed to it.

More children soon made their appearance, namely Henry and Benjamin. Their father, Dr. Feucht, became physician to the society when Dr. Miller seceded with Count Leon, and he continued as such until his death in 1847. In 1845 Hildegarde became ill. She realized that her end was near and sent her boys for Father Rapp, then in his 88th year and quite feeble. Accompanied by Jacob Henrici he drove over to the house of Mrs. Feucht, where the dying woman asked Father Rapp to take care of her orphan children. Father Rapp conferred the obligation on Henrici because of his age. The mother died the following spring. After her burial, so the Feucht record has it, Rapp took the boys out driving in his carriage, and told them that when he first started to separate from the church in the old country, their grandparents were neighbors of his who became his followers. One day when the authorities came after him to put him in the Asberg (prison), he went to their grandmother, who hid him in a garret and spread flax or tow over him. When he organized the Society in America they gave the common treasury a considerable sum, which she and her husband kept about their persons.

Eight or ten months later Dr. Feucht died, and Henrici became father and guardian of the young orphans. The doctor in his will had declared a wish that one of his sons should be a physician. Soon after his father's death, Henry became ill of typhoid fever. Dr. Linnenbrink was called to attend him and was soon afterward made physician to the Society. With him both brothers studied medicine, but only Benjamin graduated. In due time he became the Society's physician and continued such until 1865, when his marriage led to his separation from the Society. In 1855 he was appointed postmaster, physician, and storekeeper under Baker and Henrici. Soon after his marriage, he removed to Beaver and practiced with Dr. David McKinney, later of New Brighton. In the fall of 1865, his brother Henry and Margaret Ross left the society in order to marry. While Henry was in business in Massillon, Ohio, in the year 1889, Chas. Kauffman, Superintendent of the Society's brick works, was sent out by Father Henrici to ask Henry to return, which he did the same year, with his brother Benjamin and both their wives, and engaged in work for the Society. On February 13, 1890, the Feuchts rejoined the Society as members. An earlier attempt to rejoin, one report has it, failed because Henrici lacked the strength to get them elected.

The trouble between the Duss and Feucht factions began in earnest on April 25, 1892, when Henry Feucht was expelled from the Society. An illuminating source of information during this period is the revived book of record. Upon Father Rapp's death the new Articles of Agreement had stipulated that a book of record was to be kept in which all important acts of the Society were to be entered. This book of record had never been properly kept and had been permitted to lapse entirely after a short beginning. On April 25, 1892, it was resumed, and for a deadly legal purpose which at once becomes clear. The book opens thus:

Verhandelt Economy Montag April 25 1892 im Rathe der Aeltesten der Harmony Gesellschaft, im Hause der beiden Trustees wo [Duss here scratched out several words and wrote the "wo" over it in red] die Rathsversammlungen von jetzt ab stattfinden sollen. Die Sitzung wurde von den Vorstehern Henrici & Duss um 7 Uhr Abends eröffnet. [Acted at Economy Monday April 25, 1892 in the Council of Elders of the Harmony Society in the house of the two trustees where the councils from now on are to take place. The meeting was opened by the Trustees Henrici and Duss at 7 in the evening.]

The first item of business was the vote that the book of record be reestablished as record of all official and binding acts of the Board of Elders. As soon as this business had been settled a motion was made to deprive Heinrich Feicht (Feucht) of all his business assignments in the Society and to confine him to his house. This motion was not supported, so another

was made to exclude him entirely from the Society, and this
passed by a vote of eight to one. All members of the board
except Henrici signed, Duss last. This record is of special interest because Duss had often asserted that he was against
Feucht's exclusion. Puzzling also is the opening statement in
the record that the meeting was opened by the Trustees Henrici
and Duss. The impression is left in the record that this action
was taken in a meeting over which Henrici presided, which
was not the case because he did not sign the minutes, which all
the rest did. The recorded vote was eight to one; the eight
who voted for expulsion signed the record which states that
this vote makes the exclusion legal by "our Constitution," but
it does not state that the one vote against exclusion was that
of Jacob Henrici. We here have clear evidence that the Duss
clique was in opposition to Henrici. The information missing
in the official book of record is found in the *Pittsburgh Times*
report of May 2, 1892:

Henry Feicht[1] expelled.
The troubles of the Economites reach a climax.
An old and prominent member hustled out—He takes the case into
the Beaver County Courts by means of a Bill in Equity—Another
sensation sprung in the shape of an audit of Trustee John S. Duss's
Books—President Henrici refuses to sanction the expulsion. "Koresh"
Teed's intrusion started the trouble.
The internal troubles that have agitated the Harmony Society, of
Economy, for many months past, have reached a long-anticipated
climax in the shape of court proceedings. Henry Feicht, a born
Economite and one of the most prominent men in the celibate
community, has been unconditionally expelled from the organization
by the Board of Elders. Mr. Feicht immediately consulted his lawyers,
and among other steps which have been taken, a bill in equity was
prepared and filed in the Beaver county courts at Beaver, Pa. The
bill calls for an investigation of the case through the appointment
of a master.
How the storm broke.
The trouble has been precipitated through much discontent in
the society. The affiliation of Trustee John Duss to Dr. C. R. Teed,
the Chicago "Koresh" has been the main cause. Since Dr. Teed first
appeared among the Harmonites their quiet community has ceased.
The expulsion of Mr. Feicht will drag into the courts a long list
of stories that have been the gossip of the Economites for many

days. A salient feature of the expulsion is the fact that old Father Jacob Henrici, the patriarch of the society, is strongly opposed to the expulsion and openly told this to the Board of Elders.

Right on the heels of the expulsion of Henry Feicht comes an investigation of the accounts of Trustee John S. Duss. It is a regular audit and an expert accountant has been employed by the Board of Elders. Mr. Duss says it is merely a straightening out of the affairs of the society.

The expulsion of Mr. Feicht occurred at a special meeting of the Board of Elders held on last Monday. It was called for the purpose of acting on this case. Mr. Feicht has been frank in the expression of his opinions about the relations of Mr. Duss with Mr. Teed. This has made Mr. Duss and his contingent exceedingly angry. They have been boiling with suppressed wrath. On one occasion Mr. Duss made several stinging remarks publicly after church services on a Sunday morning. On Monday, when the Board of Elders met, one of those present made a motion to relieve Mr. Feicht from the supervision of the society's orchards, conservatories and gardens, a responsible position which he held. The motion found no seconder. Then another and more sweeping motion was made to the effect that Mr. Feicht be expelled from the society unconditionally. The motion was seconded and the eight members of the Board of Elders voted for it. The secretary of the meeting drew up the notice to Mr. Feicht of his expulsion on the spot, and it was signed by all present. Trustee John A. Duss withheld his name until all the others had signed the paper.

Henrici refuses to sign.

A dead silence ensued when Mr. Duss had signed. Mr. Henrici had not been consulted and the elders were anxious. It was finally decided to call him in and ask for his signature. The patriarch of the society, bent with the load of nearly 90 years, was led in.

"What does this mean?" he demanded, in his still sturdy accents, "this meeting at such an unusual time?"

Mr. Duss made an explanation.

"What!" thundered Mr. Henrici, sweeping the room with his stern glance, "you would expel this old Economite, who knows more of the society than all of you? Shame on you. He is better than any of you, and I will have nothing to do with this business. It is not right! It is not right!" and Mr. Henrici walked out of the room, leaning on his cane and refusing all offers of assistance.

Then Mr. Duss broke the silence, saying that Mr. Henrici was getting old, and that allowance would have to be made for this.

The paper was thereupon sent to Dr. Benjamin Feicht, a leading Economite. He sent it to his expelled brother. The latter took the paper to his attorneys. The first step to be taken upon mature consideration was the drawing up of the following petition:

"We, the undersigned members of the Harmony Society, do hereby protest against the action of the members of the council of Monday, April 25, 1892, having for its object the expulsion of our fellow member Henry Feicht." Many prominent and time-honored names have been attached to this petition, for Mr. Feicht is popular and respected among the members of the society. The matter has been kept exceedingly quiet by both sides. The bill in equity was drawn up several days ago, and filed in a manner not to attract attention. It asks for the appoinment of a master, who shall hear both sides of the case.

In taking the matter into the courts Mr. Feicht will probably introduce a number of the society's family skeletons to the public. His attorneys have suppressed the case as much as possible in order to work it up, and the end of the suit may be of much more serious import to the society than many of its members have ever dreamed.

This may swamp the Economites.

It is the opinion of expert legal talent that should Mr. Feicht desire to retaliate for his apparently uncalled for expulsion, he could make it extremely sultry for the entire society. In 1849 Joshua Nachtrieb, a member of the society, had a quarrel with the management and left the society. Although he was not even expelled or suspended from membership he brought an action for damages in the Pittsburg courts. He was adjudged heavy damages. The society was placed in a quandary and appealed to the State Supreme Court. Had it agreed to pay Nachtrieb his damages, dozens of others who had left the community under similar circumstances, could have successfully pushed similar claims. The State Court sustained Nachtrieb, who was represented by Attorney Edwin M. Stanton, who became Secretary of War during the Rebellion. The case was again appealed in the United States Supreme Court and all but one of the Justices sided with Nachtrieb.[2] This Justice won the case against his colleagues on the ground that the society held a receipt from Nachtrieb for $2,000 "in full." This money had been received for a special service and the term "in full" saved the society. Since then changes have taken place in the laws which greatly increase the chances of the plaintiff in such a case.

Mr. Feicht will not talk.

Mr. Feicht, when seen by a representative of *The Times* last night, refused to talk for publication.

The auditing of the accounts is the result of a movement which originated some weeks ago by one of the elders. He at first circulated a petition for an audit among the members of the society. The petition did not suit and was changed to one requesting the audit of the accounts of Mr. Duss himself. In this shape the petition was adopted by the Board of Elders including Mr. Duss. An expert accountant was put to work and he has made partial reports at special meetings held by the elders.

Duss is silent also.

Mr. Duss when seen last night by a representative of *The Times* said: "I have nothing to say about Mr. Feicht's expulsion. I have decided to quit talking to the newspapers, as it has done me more harm than good. With regard to that audit, it is only a perfection of the society's accounts. They will be made as perfect as possible and will be kept that way in the future."

Mr. Feicht, the expelled member, has an honorable lineage. His great-grandparents became members of the society when it was formed in 1804. His mother was a member and reared him and his brother as Economites. For years the two were members. About 20 years ago they left the society, but came back about one year ago, convinced that their place was in the community. Dr. Feicht, the brother, left a lucrative practice in Allegheny, while Henry left a fortune which he made in raising trees in Ohio. Both are favorites with Mr. Henrici, and the latter's refusal to sanction the expulsion is regarded as significant. Henry Feicht's daughter is engaged to be married in a few weeks to Assistant General Passenger Agent Woods, of the Allegheny Valley railroad.

When Duss later embarked on his career in music, he loved to give press interviews and proved himself to be a master of this means of public communication, but at this time he was strangely sensitive about statements in the press and could never say enough to question the accuracy of press reports in matters dealing with the Harmony Society. My own research has convinced me that the reporters of Pittsburgh were unusually well informed and that their reports were surprisingly accurate.

The press report just quoted is almost identical with another report in another Pittsburgh paper which I have not quoted because both date and name of the paper have been lost, making accurate reference impossible. This report, however, does show that Henrici had lost to the Duss clique. It also explains why the entire Feucht faction never gained a voice on the Board of Elders and was never represented there. At the next session Feucht's office was turned over to Riethmüller and soon after the Board voted to assign him an able-bodied assistant in case he should run into resistance from Feucht. When Feucht refused to turn over his keys they simply changed the locks on the doors and locked him out of his places of work. Feucht, of course, decided to sue the "hergelaufene Lumpen" (itinerant bums) who had usurped the power of the Harmony Society. Continuing on its course to get full control of the assets of the Society, the Duss faction made an attempt in the meeting of June 13, 1892, to depose Henrici because he was "already too old" and to "give Duss a second Trustee as representative for Henrici." Now things were moving too fast even for Junior Duss, especially because the threat by Feucht of legal action for illegal exclusion had reached Judge Hice, the legal counsel of the Society. Word was sent to the Board that Judge Hice would meet with them, and after such meeting the Board on July 28, 1892, reversed itself and reinstated Heinrich Feucht, thus preventing a lawsuit then. But the affair had gone far enough to reveal just what the Duss clique was after, and the entire scene showed who was really running the Society. While the Board could not exclude Feucht out of fear of unpleasant legal effects, it used other means short of exclusion to make life miserable for him within the Society.

Duss so far had beaten the Feuchts to the draw by the following moves:

1. by his mother's advance work and membership in the Society,
2. by becoming a member of the Society before the Feuchts returned,
3. by making friends and influencing votes for his election as Junior Trustee,
4. by following the expert counsel of interested, shrewd lawyers,
5. by using Society assets to employ an expert accountant and more legal talent,
6. by preventing any Feucht from obtaining a voice on the Board of Elders or as Trustee. To keep the Feuchts out, he later brought an old friend, Siber, into the Society and got him elected Junior Trustee when Henrici died. Anything to keep the Feuchts out of power.

Henry Feucht's expulsion on April 25, 1892, had almost brought on a lawsuit. That was prevented when the Board at the insistence of their lawyer Hice reversed itself and canceled the expulsion. Things seemed to quiet down then until, again under pressure of attorneys, Duss, without taking the

Feuchts into his confidence about the state of the Society, used unfair means to obtain signatures to those two documents which gave him such frightening powers that the Feuchts were convinced he had conspired with others to take over the entire property of the Harmony Society.

The move to get the badly needed signatures of members before Henrici died was made on advice of expert legal talent, and it took the Feuchts completely by surprise, as the following report in the December 28, 1892, issue of the *Pittsburgh Commercial Gazette,* announcing that Duss is "supreme," clearly proves:

There is one person at least in the society who does not agree with Mr. Duss in all things. He is Dr. Frederic Feicht, [*sic*] one of the original Economites. He gave his objections in plain terms yesterday, beginning with the statement:

"I never do things by halves, and I never act without thinking, therefore, my refusal to comply with Duss' request in signing that ridiculous document giving him full control of everything, was duly considered. My brother and his wife, beside myself and my wife, were all well acquainted with Mr. Duss, and although we are friendly, as far as acquaintanceship is concerned, yet I cannot understand how a young man, only two years in the society, can expect to be guardian to aged brethren on the brink of the grave, after spending a whole life time peaceably in the society.

"Further than that, the whole piece of business was a deep-laid scheme, and was carried out in a manner that was exceedingly clever, yet could readily be detected. You will agree with me after the method is explained. To begin with, Father Henrici was a much-loved leader, as the many tears at to-day's services showed. He was a man of remarkable energy and great wit, and the perfect manner in which he conducted our society shows that he entertained but one action, and that was for our welfare. He never discriminated, but treated everyone alike, in fact he was above reproof. He even made a will in which all personal belongings were to be turned over to the society.

"Now, on the face of his many years of labor and tender devotion for our sake, the very members of the society who professed to love him commit an act that was extremely cowardly and devoid of all principle. I refer to the signing of that damaging document which contains entirely the future of our formerly peaceable organization. It was circulated in a rather novel manner and was in itself the most cheeky request ever heard of. The substance of the document was that each individual connected with the society should turn over all their claims to Mr. Duss, who would thereafter be privileged to spend it for his own convenience or else foolishly speculate with it. The document was written in such language that might prove deceiving to the ordinary reader. I interpreted the true sense of it.

I think it was a most grievous offense to Father Henrici, who was at the time of its circulation lying on his death-bed, ignorant of the thing and dying with the happy thought that his good work would continue until every member had passed away. Worse than that, Mr. Duss was his own champion and made his own canvass. He went to each member's house and secured the signature of thirty-two, all except me and my family connections. I allowed him to read it and then flatly refused to sign, and he didn't press very hard for an explanation."

"Did you make any effort to advise the members before all the signatures were attached?"

"Not much. Duss was entirely too shrewd for me. He didn't even notify the members of his intention but sprang into their midst and before they half understood the importance of the document had complied with his request. My knowledge of his history and family connections made me suspicious, and upon learning the full value of the document readily understood the importance. There is no reason whatever why anything like that should be in [line missing] well-known fact that the estate belongs equally as much to the one as to the other, and it has always been the custom of the members to abide by the management of the superior trustee. Now, if Mr. Duss knew this and intended to work hard for the society in general, why did he want to empower himself with such an unlimited amount of authority?

"Another peculiar feature of the affair is that it happened several days before the death of Father Henrici. Suppose our dead leader would have recovered from his illness, who do you suppose would have the most authority? Mr. Henrici would not have had anything at all to say, because his former assistant held a paper that authorized him to distribute the wealth of the society. Another feature never before heard of in the history of our society was that Mr. Duss didn't ask Father Henrici to attach his signature to the document and at the same time he should have been only acting under his sick leader's orders. If Father Henrici heard of the affair before his death I believe that he would have recovered long enough to express his opinion on the matter."

The *Commercial Gazette* article here cited also shows the deep suspicion the Feuchts held toward Duss and Teed. Dr. Feucht brought it up:

Suppose any person in our midst was an accomplice of Teed's, don't you think it would be a good opportunity to bring that fellow into the society? Teed remarked some time ago that he would yet have control of our organization and who knows but what he has been quietly working for some time past.[3]

When Dr. Feucht was asked if the members would then appeal to the court for justice he said he would and maybe something would be done before the time of Teed's arrival. When he was asked if he anticipated his coming, he replied: "I anticipate everything and a disaster to our society will occur." When pressed for further information Dr. Feucht concluded:

I haven't considered the matter at all, but I will certainly take some action if everything doesn't go right. I can't stand idle and see the society go to ruin, and I think Mr. Duss is acting very queer which fact confirms my many suspicions. I can prove that my anticipations of trouble are true and that the members, owing to their old age, are not responsible for their action. I can see a strange discontent among them that I have never noticed before. It was only yesterday that an old man, dying from dropsy, and who is a friend, called upon me and showed his dissatisfaction. He was one of the parties who signed the document, and it was the previous confidence and harmony of the society that led him to do so. He told me that he did not understand the meaning of the paper, as the former leaders never made such a request. He is much agitated over the matter now, as is likewise many of the other members who signed. Every person knows that old men become weak in mind and that a strong will has great influence over a weaker one which accounts for them consenting so readily. In the time they will all come to realize their mistake, therefore I can safely predict the result of the occurrence.

Another incident that partly shows the future course of our organization, happened this afternoon when Duss delivered the funeral address. For the benefit of the English-speaking people present he repeated his sermon in English, a thing that has not occurred inside our church for twenty-five years. I could notice the look of disappointment on many of the dear old faces and I felt very bad myself. It was not only on account of the sermon, but the fact that Father Henrici's dead body was lying in the church made it more repulsive to us. Many times during his lifetime our dead leader has preached over the remains of dead brethren, and although the church was crowded with outsiders he never changed his language. Our society is entirely independent of the world and our suffering and exclusive lives is our own selection. Therefore Duss has no right to

Friederika Munz, old surviving member when Duss became Trustee.

Sara Forstner (Zundel), wife of Jacob Zundel. Original Utah pioneer, born in Old Harmony, Butler County, Pa. Buried in Willard, Box Elder County, Utah, cemetery.

Regina Lautenschlager, old surviving member when Duss became Trustee.

Sketch of the street "Am Roten Gaessele," Economy, 1889.

Father Henrici, from Kodak picture taken at Economy, July 1888, by Franklin T. Nevin.

Economy, Pennsylvania, looking across the fields and town to the Ohio River.

The community laundry and cider and wine press building of Old Economy.

Ousted Harmonists and descendants of leading Harmonist pioneers. From right to left: Dr. Benjamin Feucht; his niece (Henry Feucht's daughter), Anna Feucht; his wife, Rebecca Ott Feucht; and his daughter, Stella.

The ouster and pretender to Rapp's mantle and millions: John S. Duss, schoolmaster, tailor, bronco buster in Nebraska, heir to Harmonist millions, litigious bandmaster, and once heir apparent to Maurice Grau's Metropolitan Opera Company.

Ousted Harmonists and descendants of leading Harmonist pioneers:

*Margaret Ross Feucht,
Henry Feucht's wife.*

*Henry Feucht, brother of
Dr. Benjamin Feucht.*

*Beaver Falls, Pennsylvania. The Harmony Society owned this land
and developed the city by easy term loans, long before FHA.*

A product of the Harmony Society. (Duss signs himself President!)

AT THE ST. NICHOLAS, COLUMBUS AVENUE AND SIXTY-SIXTH STREET, MAY 26 TO SEPT. 14.

Office of
R. E. Johnston
Manager

Telephone call:
2746
Madison Square.
Cable Address:
Melonero
New York.

INCOMPARABLE

Duss AND HIS *Band*

ST. JAMES BUILDING,
BROADWAY AND TWENTY-SIXTH STREET.

New York City, July 29 190

Short Autumn Tour
DUSS
126 Consecutive Nights
in New York.

DIRECTION:

R. E JOHNSTON

St. James Building,
Broadway & 26th Street,

Telephone:
2746 Madison Square.

CITY OF NEW YORK, Sept. 28,

What happened to Harmonists' millions: some Duss letterheads.

add to our suffering by adopting a course that he knew would prove objectionable to us.

Another astonishing feature of the service was the unnecessary apology that he made in English to the onlooker. Don't you remember when he acknowledged that English had not been heard in the church for over twenty years, and that he had old-fashioned ideas about what was right, the modern way of being courteous might prove offensive? The coolness that he showed while undergoing the remarkable confession was surprising indeed, and I know exactly how the others felt. It all goes to show that Mr. Duss intends making a new organization out of the society entirely. His modern ways and ideas were plain in his remarks, and I am sure that I understand them properly.

Dr. Feucht charged that many damaging stories of a rather serious kind were in circulation about Mr. Duss and his history before becoming a member of the society. They had been hushed previously, but Dr. Feucht now thought that Duss's opponents would use them against him in connection with the leadership of the society.

Since Duss, entirely against their will, had used unfair but cleverly legal means to make himself supreme, the Feuchts could only take recourse to the press and the courts. Both moves could have been prevented if Duss had taken them into his confidence about the state of the Society and if he had enlisted their support by giving them at least one voice on the Board of Elders or as Junior Trustee. Instead, his will to power filled the vacancy created by Henrici's death by electing a complete outsider, a friend of Duss named Siber, to the Board and the Junior Trusteeship. No insult added to the injury of the two documents enthroning Duss, prepared in time to use the still powerful influence of a senile and practically dead Henrici to do what was not really his will, could have caused more bitterness. It was all part of a plan to oust the Feuchts completely, a plan cleverly devised with the help of shrewd Pennsylvania lawyers who knew how much gold lay buried in the hills of Economy. Legal action combined with an appeal to public conscience was the only path left for the Feuchts.

On February 10, 1893, the Feucht faction of the Harmony Society filed a bill in equity in the Court of Common Pleas in and for the County of Beaver against the Duss faction of the Society, asking that a receiver be appointed for the Harmony Society. Now Mr. Duss really was worried, but as always, he had the comforting hand of J. T. Brooks to guide him. Here is an example of the kind of advice Duss received. On February 9, 1893, the day before the bill was filed against him, J. T. Brooks wrote him:

I have just read your letter of yesterday—and must first express the pleasure I feel in knowing that you are again well—at least able to be out and attending to business.

First. I have no fear whatever of a Receivership. A Receiver would be appointed only on a showing that the company (Society) is insolvent and its property in danger of Sacrifice—or that its present management is weak or corrupt—Neither of these facts can be shown—for the good reason that they do not exist. The consequences following an *application* for a receivership are all that is to be feared. Such application if made, will doubtless precipitate a panic at the Bank and throw everything into confusion. In such a state a receivership may become a necessity to protect everybody—

I would not seek in any way to anticipate this trouble—except to sell securities as fast as possible—get money and pay off depositors as fast as possible. Get your funds together as you can—take from Thompson & Co. what they have and get it into currency and take it to the Bank—Keep the amount of cash there, large as you can. I made special arrangements with Thompson & Co to *hurry* along the sale of what you have—This is all we can do now, unless the judge or Mr. Wilson can move a little faster than heretofore and convert those judgments and mortgages—I advise you to try to sell the Tidioute Bridge Stock—I will give it to you for this purpose next Monday. As to the preparation of any paper such as you suggest—or asking members to say or do anything in view of the approaching festival I earnestly advise you against anything of the kind—Do nothing whatever to excite further irritation or discussion—In your sermon next Sunday, dwell on the harmony and brotherly feeling that once existed in the Society and urge members to have the same spirit now—avoid every word of criticism or reproach toward any member—Single out no man or no deed for even indirect allusion—and simply plead for unity and harmony. Having done your full duty in this respect, be content and the future will be well. Silence is your very best guide at this critical moment. I will be glad to confer further with you next Monday. Sincerely yours, J. T. Brooks.

This advice was more easily given than followed, for there

was another faction attending meetings of the Society which had questions to ask which Duss did not want to answer. It is, of course, always easy to be generous when one has all the power and financial assets that were at the disposal of Duss and his lawyers, but this generosity was not real because it did not go to the heart of the trouble, namely, the exclusion of the Feuchts from all participation and information about the affairs of the Society which their ancestors had help found and build. That becomes clear when we read the accounts of the meeting Duss called on February 13, 1893, to obtain signatures to the following resolution:

WHEREAS, it has become known to us that Benjamin Feucht and Rebecca his wife and Henry Feicht and Margaret his wife, Tirza Feicht, Dorothea Hoehr, Regina Lautenschlager, Edward Kellerman and Christina Rall have caused to be filed a Bill in Equity in the Common Pleas Court of Beaver County, Pennsylvania, against the other members of the Harmony Society asking among other things for the appointment of a Receiver, the winding up of the Society and a sale or division of the property of the Society in which Bill false and scandalous charges are made against our Trustees and Elders and ourselves,

Now be it resolved:

(I) That we sincerely depreciate the filing of such a Bill and announce our determination to sternly oppose and defeat it by every honorable means. That it is directly contrary to the fundamental law of our Society and seems to have sprung from selfish and unchristian motives.

(II) That we denounce as untrue the charges made in said Bill against our Trustees and Elders and ourselves and we now take this opportunity of expressing our entire confidence in our present Trustees and Elders.

(III) That we request our Trustees to employ Counsel and take all steps they may deem wise to defeat said Bill.

Duss followed the advice of his lawyer and used his sermon and the religious appeal to gain his purpose, but there were members of the Society who saw through his methods and the result was quite a display of disharmony. Here is a firsthand account of the meeting on February 13, 1893, to gather signatures for the statement carefully prepared by his attorneys:

The senior trustee then made a brief address before allowing any person to sign. He said that he held no ill will toward those who had openly avowed themselves to be his enemies, and hoped they would attend the annual festival Wednesday and break bread as was the custom. He believed that his prosecutors believed that they were right in their course, and he had nothing but the most charitable feelings for them. Here Mrs. Margaretta Feicht broke in with a laugh and sneer and said: "You can afford to be charitable; you have robbed us of everything we ever had." "That's right," said Henry Feicht, and Benjamin Feicht cried "hear, hear." A general ripple ran over the audience and Trustee Duss saw that there was trouble ahead. He started to allow the women to sign the bill when Julius Stickel, who had allied himself on neither side, jumped to his feet and cried out: "This is no place to discuss this matter, before our farm hands and children, and make us the laughing stock of the community." Trustee Duss tried to quiet him in vain and the Feichts and their supports cried "good," while other hissed, and the room was in an uproar, amid which Duss stood immovable as an oak. Stickel took his hat and started for the door. He kept up his fiery tirade and said: "I have been wronged, robbed, cheated, deceived. The meat I get is bad. There are bad practices being carried on in this community, you are guilty of adultery, and these crimes were not preached against last Sunday. I am ashamed of the entire business, and I shall never enter this church again." By this time he had reached the door and passed out, shutting the door with a bang.

All this time the room was a scene of disorder. The Feichts and their adherents shouted "Hear," "hear," "good," etc., while hisses could be heard from the other side. When Stickel passed out of the room Trustee Duss succeeded in getting the people quieted again and the signing of the bill went on. When all who occupied seats in the front had signed Duss looked around the room and called on several by name, but all refused to affix their names until he called on Regina Lautenschlager, one of the plaintiffs in the bill in equity, and to every person's surprise, she said she wished to sign the bill. Benjamin Feucht jumped to his feet and objected but Trustee Duss told him to remain quiet, and once more asked the woman if she wished to sign. She replied by coming forward. When she started down the aisle, Henry Feucht ran and met her and caught her by the arm and said: "Do you know what you are doing? You are committing perjury." "No, I am not," the woman said. "I took no oath."

Feucht tried to push her back in her seat. The woman was hurt by his violence and cried out with the pain. Several started to her aid and it looked threatening for a moment, but she pushed past him, seated herself at the table and signed the bill amid a great deal of applause. [She later withdrew her signature saying she did not hear well and did not know what Duss wanted.]

She was the last one to sign, and the names that appeared on the papers are as follows: Katherine Nagel, Maria Diem, Frederika Munz, Caroline Molt, Barbara Boesch, Johanna Hermansdoerfer, Elizabeth Siber, Susie C. Duss, Siegmund Stiefwater, Regina Lautenschlager, Franz Gillman, Gottlieb Riethmueller, Moritz J. Friederichs, J. Jacob Niclaus, Conrad Hermansdoerfer, Hugo Miller, Blasius Platz, and of course the signature of John S. Duss, senior trustee of the society, will be affixed.

After the signatures had all been affixed and order restored, Trustee Duss lead in a hymn and then dismissed the meeting. It is hinted that the other side will take proceedings to make the Feuchts explain how they induced Anna Lautenschlager to sign the bill in equity, and many interesting developments are expected.

That Duss, who had *not* been educated for the ministry and surely never had the call that Father Rapp or Father Henrici had, was coached by his *legal* advisers in the use of his ecclesiastical office is clearly illustrated by the letter of his highly paid legal adviser, already quoted.

On the morning of March 3, 1893, the Court convened shortly after 10 o'clock. There was plenty of room for the two contending battalions of attorneys, for the best that Beaver County could do in the way of a crowd, as the *Pittsburgh Dispatch* reported the next day, did not exceed a score of very placid gentlemen of bucolic aspect, who chewed tobacco and were not the least disturbed by the almost inaudible chanting of affidavit after affidavit. The lawyers on both sides yawned a great deal when they were not reading affidavits, and even the Court seemed rather disposed to slumber at times, though toward the close of the day a handy paperweight served to alleviate Judge Wickham's ennui for a while.

There was a strong array of legal talent present, the strongest, of course, on the side of the Harmony Society Duss faction. The attorneys for the plaintiffs were George Shiras III, C. C. Dickey, J. R. Buchanan, and District Attorney M. F. Mecklen. Opposed to them were Judge Henry Hice, Judge Fettermann, J. Irvin Brooks, W. H. S. Thompson, and D. T. Watson. Duss sat behind Mr. Brooks at the counsel table, and Henry Feucht and Mr. Stickel were the only other Harmonists present. Several Pennsylvania Company clerks, as well as Second Vice President J. T. Brooks, represented the railroad's interest in the case, which was practically dominant. It was a hopeless battle from the start.

The long Bill in Equity was first read, naming

BENJAMIN FEUCHT and REBECCA, his wife, HENRY FEUCHT and MARGARET, his wife, TIRZA FEUCHT, DORO- THEA HOEHR, REGINA LAUTENSCHLAGER, EDWARD KELLERMAN and CHRISTINA RALL.

VERSUS

THE HARMONY SOCIETY, JOHN S. DUSS, SAMUEL SIBER, Trustees, JACOB NICKLAUS, MORITZ J. FRIEDERICHS, JO- HANNES SCHEID, FRANZ GILLMAN, HUGO MILLER, CON- RAD HERMANSDOERFER, JULIUS STICKEL, BLASIUS PLATZ, SIGMUND STIEFVATER, KAROLINE MOLT, KAT- RINA NAGEL, ELIZABETH BECK, LENA WOLFANGEL, CHRISTINA HOERER, JOHN S. DUSS, SUSIE C. DUSS, BERTHA GERATCH, PAULINE STICKEL, JOHANNA HER- MANSDOERFER, MARIA DIEM, BARBARA BOESCH, FRIED- ERICKE MUNZ, PHILIPINA WOLFANGEL, GOTTLIEB RIETHMUELLER, SAMUEL SIBER, and ELIZABETH SIBER.

The bill charged that under Duss the Society was being mismanaged financially and spiritually, that the Society as a religious organization had ceased to exist, that Duss preached the doctrines of Cyrus Teed, that he had avowed a sympathy with Michael K. Mills, commonly known as "Prince Michael" of Detroit, that the Society had lost its religious purpose, and that the majority of the Board of Elders now consisted of "con- firmed and common drunkards," that Duss, in violation of a long-established usage and law of the Society, on the 27th day of December, 1892, made one Sieber a member of the Board of Elders and at the same time placed him in the position of Trustee, said Samuel Sieber having been a member only a few months and being illiterate and incompetent to manage the affairs of the society, that the principle of equality had been abolished, and that Duss and family were living in luxury, that through coercion and misrepresentation Duss on Decem- ber 21, 1892, obtained the signatures to the document giving him the power to sell or mortgage the property of the Society, that when the power of attorney naming Henrici and Duss as Trustees was signed, Henrici was mentally incapable of com-

prehending any business, that Duss refused to render account
to the elders or members of the Society, that Duss had sold,
assigned, and disposed of dividend paying stocks to the amount
of nearly two million dollars, that members of the Society were
ignorant of the true state of the accounts of the Society and
had no means of ascertaining the same except through the
court, that all bringing the lawsuit as defendants were surviving
members of the Society. For these reasons they requested that
a receiver be appointed, that an injunction be issued restraining
Duss and Sieber from selling or mortgaging the property of the
Society or otherwise interfering with its affairs, that Duss and
Sieber be ordered to give a full account of their trust, that a
Master be appointed to investigate the losses sustained through
the fraud and mismanagement of Duss and Sieber, and that
they be ordered to pay over the balance to a receiver for the
use of the Society and its members, that the court decree a
dissolution of the Harmony Society, a winding up of its affairs,
and a distribution of its assets to the parties legally and equitably entitled thereto.

This bill had been served on Duss and his faction of the
Harmony Society on February 15, 1893. After the bill in
equity had been read, the affidavits supporting it were introduced. The reading of these consumed the entire morning
session. They included the sworn statements of Benjamin and
Henry Feucht, Rebecca and Margaret Feucht, Charles Kaufmann, Julius Stickel, M. J. Friederichs, William Roseburg,
Charles Norcross, and Dorothea Hoehr.

Julius Stickel's affidavit said that he and his wife, Pauline,
were members of the society in good standing since March,
1888. Until recently he had been a friend of John Duss, and
sufficiently intimate with him to know his incapacity and
general unfitness to be trustee. Mr. Stickel gave a vivid description of the visit of Miss Emertz, one of Teed's so-called
angels, to Economy. A great deal was made of Duss's connections with Teed and the fact that Teed had come to Economy,
stayed with Duss, and got $750 of the Society's money before
leaving. Duss was particularly vulnerable on this point because
it agreed with the general impression of those loyal to the
Society that Duss was out to make this stronghold of German

culture in America into something "Irish" or "English," and to German-Americans of that time this sort of activity ranked about equally with blasphemy and the sin against the Holy Ghost. Only a few years later, in 1898, Carl Weil, with this in mind, sent Duss a long article he had published on the right and duty of German-Americans to use and preserve the German language in America. Teed's revelations could live only in the English language and Rapp's mysticism only in German.

Stickel alleged gross misconduct by Duss and the council in providing food and care for the members of the Society. He complained that only three members of the council could speak English and that they were ignorant, inexperienced, and mostly drunkards. Items of Duss's extravagance and bad judgment were cited, such as: Building a chicken house containing 40 chickens, at a cost of $600; a pig pen, which was fatal to the pigs, at $1,000; music stands, conservatories, etc., costing $3,000; a useless sawmill at $50,000, and other works of no value. He was sure that Duss was a man of bad habits, that Duss had told him all Society property would be sold, that he meant to use the assets and credit of the Society for embarking in manufacturing. He felt that neither Duss nor Siber was in any way qualified to handle the remaining dollars of the Society. He concluded that Mr. Henrici did not understand what he was doing when he signed the power of attorney, and that for six months prior to his death knew little of the Society's affairs.

Another man to appear against Duss was Charles Kaufmann, who from 1884 till 1890 was employed to attend to the general business of the Society, buying goods for the store, contracting for the labor and materials, and superintending building operations, who was consequently competent to judge of the Society's financial condition. Mr. Kaufmann swore in his affidavit that in 1886 he discovered the Society was losing a great deal of money. He called Henrici's and Lenz's attention to it, but without results. Kaufmann left the Society because he foresaw its ruin. When Duss was made trustee the reckless expenditures continued. The saw and planing mills were both run at a loss. They could not be operated profitably. Nobody with an ounce of business sense, claimed Kaufmann, would have located them at Economy as Duss did. Mr. Kaufmann declared very

positively that he knew Duss well and knew that he was without
any business knowledge whatever. Kaufmann's more startling
charge was that Duss in 1891 took his cousin, Frederika Kroll,
to Chicago and placed her with Teed in his angel house, which
he called a disreputable place. Here again much is made of the
Teed connection, which is another dark spot that caused the
Feucht faction to be extremely suspicious of Duss. Kaufmann
expected nothing but bankruptcy and disgrace as the results
of Duss's administration.

Dr. Benjamin Feucht's affidavit did not vary a great deal
from that which he had previously published through the
newspapers in the hope of breaking Duss's dictatorship in that
manner. These reports have already been presented. Showing
what extremely poor contact Trustee Duss was maintaining
with all the members of the Society and what utter disregard
he had for the older members, Mr. Feucht alleged that Duss
mortgaged the Economy property 24 hours before he attempted
to get the authority to do so by getting the power of attorney
from the Society. Henrici, Feucht alleged, was entirely incapable of comprehending any act when he signed the mortgage.
Dr. Feucht, as a physician, was certainly better qualified to
judge the condition of a dying man than young farmer and
schoolteacher Duss. Feucht charged Duss and Siber and the
council of nine with utter incompetency and ignorance of
ordinary business methods. He asserted that Siber was a basket
maker and constable, and Duss entirely ignorant of manufacturing, his life having been spent in the West, farming and
teaching school.

Henry Feucht's affidavit constituted a substantial outline of
the entire case against Duss and the other defendants. It contained a great deal of material that had also previously been
presented to the public through the medium of the press. Some
of his charges were more specified and more detailed. In 1889,
Henry Feucht said, he learned from Henrici and other sources
that the Society was in debt from $100,000 to $150,000. Since
then he claimed that over $1,000,000 had been lost through
the ignorance and incompetence of Duss and his associates.
Among the losing ventures he listed: a glass works at Beaver
Falls, $22,000 lost out of $30,000 invested; the file works and

cutlery works in Beaver Falls, total loss; the saw and planing mills, $56,000; the temple which he claimed was built for Teed, $12,000. Feucht claimed Duss refused the council's request to furnish them a statement of the Society's accounts, and that the Economy Savings Institution was practically insolvent, owing its depositors $300,000 and with only $20,000 cash on hand.

William Roseburg, the Pittsburgh banker, in his affidavit declared that he discovered the shaky financial condition of the Society the previous spring and that a very careful examination of their affairs showed that their liabilities exceeded their assets. Other affidavits presented were in line with those just mentioned. All reflected the distrust of Duss, for which Duss alone was responsible, for the orderly and fatherly management of a Trustee in his position should have taken these members and descendants of founders of the Society into his confidence in the interest of the remaining group. Constantly the image becomes clearer that Duss was the willing tool of a powerful group of capitalists who had plotted to liquidate this tremendous property to enrich themselves, as they ultimately did. This was shown clearly in the afternoon session, for the morning session was taken up with the affidavits mentioned so far.

A recess was taken at 12 o'clock until 1:40. Duss and his attorneys accepted Judge Hice's invitation to dinner, and the attorneys had an amusing if not very filling experience with the palatial restaurants of Beaver. Then they all came back to the nearly empty courtroom and set about reading the long-winded affidavits again with all their might. This time all the swearing was done in Mr. Duss's behalf.

The affidavits of the members of the Society's council, of Mr. Duss himself, and of a number of his friends and acquaintances were read. Many hundreds of typewritten pages testifying to the worth, the honesty, the prudence and the business ability of Mr. Duss were read by Messrs. Thompson and Fetternman in turn. A better character was never given a human being. Even from the grave there came an endorsement of Mr. Duss, for a statement made by Mr. Henrici before he died to J. T. Brooks, and sworn to by the latter as an exact report of the patriarch's words, was offered in evidence. In this singular document Mr. Henrici was reported to have expressed his approval of Mr. Duss's management of the Society's affairs, and conduct generally as trustee. Mr. Henrici pointed out the difficulties his colleague and successor was bound to meet, and deprecated the tendency of some to throw additional obstacles in his path. A passage upon which Mr. Watson, who read the Henrici testament, laughingly laid considerable emphasis, referred caustically to the willingness of some newspapers to print sensational stories about anything.

The most important affidavit was the tremendously bulky one furnished by James Dickson, the accountant who had been studying the books of the Harmony Society during the past year. This affidavit claimed to contain a full, and reportedly reliable, schedule of all the Society's assets and liabilities, together with much testimony of an important nature as to the handling of the funds by Duss since April, 1892, and it will therefore be given in full in the Documentary History. In this hearing the affidavit apparently was given only in abstract, Dickson asserting that the Society had no books until he undertook to strike a balance and to begin a set in April, 1892. Dickson did not state the assets exactly, but the Society still owed $419,000, of which $400,000 was the Darlington mortgage. The Society was also liable for $320,000 which the Economy Bank still owed, but he asserted that the Society was able to pay out of its own assets this entire amount. Dickson summarized the financial status of the Society as follows: Debts, including the Darlington mortgage, $609,000; assets, after the payment of all debts if the present management of the Society were not interfered with: $700,000 or $800,000. This figure, of course, did not include the vast holdings in tremendously valuable real estate, including the extensive lands in and around Economy, the most desirable real estate in the entire Pittsburgh area.

Dickson's affidavit revealed the fact that the floating debts of the Society had been quite large for many years. Nearly all the affiants suggested that the late Father Henrici was really responsible for the financial embarrassment of the Society. Henrici, it was pointed out, did not conduct the affairs of the

Society with the usual human purpose of making and accumulating money, but of giving work to the Society's employees and benefiting the community of which the Society was a party.

Duss in his affidavit denied every one of the charges made in the bill of equity, and furnished a sketch of his life. The most interesting statement in it referred to the financial status of the Society when Duss assumed charge. He said that he found the Society owed for borrowed money and for debts about $1,400,000. Of this $300,000 was owed to Pittsburgh banks, secured by the Society's stocks and bonds. Since that date Duss claimed he had paid off $1,000,000 by selling the Society's property, real and personal, and by borrowing $400,000 from Darlington. Today, Duss claimed, exclusive of the Darlington mortgage, the Society owed $200,000, to meet which the Society owned stocks and bonds and personal property amounting to $372,586.52. He did not believe, he testified, that the Society was bankrupt, or that it needed to be wound up and have a receiver appointed. He denied having misappropriated a penny or misconducted the affairs of the Society in any particular. He disclaimed responsibility for the unfortunate business ventures of the Society mentioned in the bill. He asserted that he did not have the house built which he was charged with preparing for Teed, and that of all the structures he was alleged to have erected, he had directed only the building of a pig pen, hen coop, and other small matters aggregating in value less than $2,000. A significant part of Duss's testimony stated:

Realizing the peculiar position of affairs at Economy and the fact that I was yet a young man, I felt that I should conduct myself with deference to Mr. Henrici, and at first I took scarcely any part in the management of the business affairs of the Society. In April 1891 my mother departed this life and Mr. Henrici and the Board of Elders decided that Mrs. Duss and myself should take up our abode in the Big House where Mr. Henrici lived. This we did leaving our children under the care of my mother-in-law Mrs. Creese.

After numerous modest and quiet attempts at trying to get any information from Mr. Henrici, each one of which was anything but successful, I came to the conclusion that in order to become conversant with the Society's affairs, investments and general financial condition, I must myself go to work and discover them, a proceeding that was surrounded with many difficulties. In the first place, with the exception of the Economy hired help account, there was no system of books or accounts kept by the Society.

Besides that I was hampered by reason of several parties without and within Economy, including the Feuchts doing all they could to influence Mr. Henrici against me and make him think my desire was to oust him or supersede him as Trustee. My first discovery of any note was some kind of a land deal which had taken place between Trustee Lenz, deceased, and the heirs of one Davidson's lands situated in or about Warren County Pa., [which] were sold at Sheriff's sale, the Harmony Society, through its trustees being the purchaser. Mr. Davidson prior to the time of his insolvency was interested with the Society in a Glass factory in Beaver Valley. Mr. Davidson's insolvency came about through the workings of this Glass factory. The Davidson lands which Baker and Henrici had bought at Sheriffs sale shortly after turned out to be oil territory and became quite valuable, a fact which caused the Trustees to remember their former friend and associate in the business, Davidson. They accordingly employed him and his sons as managers of the Society's oil wells: said Davidson, his wife and children receiving such sums of money, which in the aggregate amounted to something like $100,000. After all the Society had done for Davidson he was not satisfied and having sometime before published a history of his connection with the Society in pamphlet form; the Society having also published one in answer thereto, he threatened to publish another pamphlet unless some more money were given him and as a result Baker and Henrici in December 1867, for the sake of establishing the former friendly relations existing between the Society and the said Davidsons made him a donation of $10,000, upon payment of such sum he and his wife executed a formal release to the Society which recites that they had no claim against the Society, but that for the sake of establishing the former feeling of friendship etc., which had existed between them and the Society they accept this present of $10,000. It appears that along in 1887 or 1888 Samuel Davidson, the leading spirit of the Davidson family began to talk to Mr. Lenz about the injustice meted out to (the Davidsons) by the Society. After meeting Mr. Lenz at various times Mr. Davidson succeeded in getting him interested to such an extent, that as William Merkle, the Superintendent of our property at or near Tidioute says, Mr. Lenz came to his house one evening and appeared to be greatly worried. He began to talk about the Davidson matter and stated as follows: "I am going up to Warren in the morning and if I do not find that paper this thing must be made right with the Davidsons." The paper he referred to was the receipt of December 27th 1867. He went to Warren, found it not, returned to Tidioute and either at that time or later on agreed that the Davidsons should receive 2200 acres the best part of the

Society's property and that the Society and the Davidsons should each execute quit claim deeds to the other. The survey was made and the deed was in course of preparation when Mr. Lenz died.

Mr. Henrici when the facts became known to him refused to carry out the plan of Mr. Lenz and litigation began.

This Davidson matter necessitated a search for whatever contracts, correspondence or other writings pertaining to the former relations between the Davidsons and the Society that might still be in existence.

The Society's various documents were not filed away in one place, but were poked away, some in the safe or other places at the store, some in the vault at the Big House, some in Mr. Henrici's desks, bureau drawers, chests and in fact throughout various wardrobes, chests and boxes from cellar to garret throughout the house. Mr. Henrici was cautious in this search, not allowing me to examine any papers contained in the vault or any of his various desks or chests, unless he was present and first personally examined them. By dint of considerable effort and perseverance I succeeded in getting him now and then to devote a half day to this search.

In the course of several months we concluded our investigation. This investigation proved valuable to me, in as much as we had come across various papers which were either in themselves valuable or led me to investigate on certain lines, whereby I gradually became in a general way somewhat conversant with the Society's interests and investments.

One thing that struck me as peculiar, in the course of time, was the appearance now and then, in the mail, of slips of paper, which read something like this, "Henrici and Duss, Trustees, your note of $20,000 is due at this bank the day of ...." These notices became more and more frequent and ranged in the amounts from $5,000, to $60,000. Mr. Henrici was accustomed to sign the names of both Trustees to such notes and other papers without consulting me, and without my knowledge.

After I had been in the position of trustee for over one year I became possessed of sufficient data to enable me to form some kind of an idea of the financial condition of the Society, and I then recognized the necessity of employing some skilled accountant, who could not only assist me in discovering the exact condition of the Society, but also could formulate and prepare proper books of account for the Society and for its different businesses and industries.

After inquiry I was recommended to Mr. James Dickson as the person who could assist me in my undertaking, and accordingly I employed him for the Harmony Society from April 1st, 1892, and he has from that time and until now been employed as our accountant and auditor.

Mr. Duss's testimony finally referred to the accounts which

Dickson had kept and that they would show how the cash obtained from sales of Society property was applied, and what balance of cash was still on hand. Duss continued:

To give in detail, the difficulties and dangers since 1891 in the reduction of the indebtedness of the Harmony Society would make a very long affidavit, and I am advised is unnecessary, but I again repeat here that I have examined the affidavit of Mr. Dickson and I aver his statement of facts is true, and that the different assets therein mentioned were sold for the sum therein stated, and that all these moneys were applied to the payment of the debts and maintenance of Economy and were not sold any property except as stated in this affidavit and that of Mr. Dickson.

The manner in which the Harmony Society had incurred such an enormous debt is not personally known to me, for all of it was contracted before the time when I became trustee. I am not responsible for any of it. Very much of the indebtedness runs back many years in its origin, and I think when the accounts of the Harmony Society are fully written up it will be found that a large sum of money has been paid out in the last, say, fifteen years, for the interest on borrowed money.

Then, again, I believe that large sums of money were expended at Economy in the support and pay of a large number of hands which the trustees employed in and around Economy. I think it is within bounds to say that the trustees, at one time, had in the employ of the Society, and supported and maintained, say, three hundred men and women, many of whom had their families, and families and working men both were fed by the Harmony Society, besides the labor being paid from $10.00 to $15.00 per month. The product of the farms and the dairy was not nearly sufficient to meet the necessary expenditures in the support and maintenance of the members of the Society, and these working men and their families.

I agree with Mr. Dickson that while we have no actual figures to show, the probabilities are that for several years last past, prior to Mr. Henrici's death, it cost from fifty to one hundred thousand dollars more to maintain Economy and the working people than the value of the entire agricultural and dairy products.

Besides these things large sums of money were lost in two concerns, one known as the Beaver Falls Cutlery Works, and the other as the Western File Works, the losses in these two institutions aggregating, say, over $1,000,000.00.

The total results up to date, are that since I took charge I have paid off the entire indebtedness of the Company the sum of over $1,000,000.00, and that I did this by the sale of assets, real and personal, and the borrowing of the money from Mr. Darlington on a mortgage, the items of which are given in the affidavit of Mr. Dickson.

The Harmony Society exclusive of the mortgage, now owes about $200,000.00, and it has to meet this indebtedness the following assets:

The Harmony Society now has assets as follows:

PERSONAL PROPERTY

		Par	Par
600	Shares Stock Bridge Co.	$ 25	$ 15000.
386	Shares Stock Tidioute Bridge Co.	50	19000.
2271	Shares Stock Chartiers Block Coal Co.	50	113550.
2200½	Shares Stock Little Saw Mill Run R. R. Co.	50	105025.
383	Shares Stock Birmingham Bridge Co.	25	9575.
225	Shares Stock Eclipse Bycicle Co.	100	22500.
	Bonds Saw Mill Run R. R. Co.		20500.
	Bills Receivable,		4283.07
	Meyrs Mortgage,		30657.57
	Union Drawn Steel Co. Mortgage,		19875.
	Bank Balance		12320.88
			372586.52

REAL ESTATE AND IMPROVEMENTS THEREON.

The Harmony Society holds, through its Trustees, the following real estate:

What is known as the home tract in Economy Township, Beaver County Pa., containing about 2900 acres. On this are erected a large number of buildings and the town of Economy.

Property at Leetsdale Allegheny County Pa., consisting of about 188 acres, on which there are erected about 30 houses. The Harmony Brick Work is also situated on this tract.

Property in Warren County Pa., consisting of about 5,000 acres, on which oil was formerly developed, but which is now covered with timber, from which most of the pine timber has been cut, and on which the Harmony Society for many years has been cutting hemlock and such other timber as there is there.

Property at Chartiers Rocks, in Allegheny County Pa., containing about eight acres.

Land in Michigan containing about 2000 acres.

A lot in the 32nd Ward of the City of Pittsburgh, being worth about $4,000.

Certain Real estate at Glenwood, in Allegheny County, worth about $4,000.

Real estate in Rochester, Pa., consisting of four lots on which two houses are erected.

Real estate and contracts for the sale of lots, purchase money mortgages, &c., at Beaver Falls, Mr. John Reeves being the agent of the Harmony Society for such property.

The real estate and improvements belonging to the Beaver Falls Cutlery Company, which consists in the buildings in which the Cutlery business was carried on. The Harmony Society has in this Corporation the 8/10ths interest. The Beaver Falls Cutlery Company is indebted to the Economy Saving Institution in a sum exceeding $500,000.00 for money borrowed from the same. No work has been carried on at said establishment for many years.

The town of Economy consists of a number of brick and frame dwelling houses, hotels, stores, meeting houses and other buildings, and is located in Harmony Township on the bank of the Ohio River.

The home real estate alone consisting of 2991 odd acres, with the improvements thereon is fairly worth say $750,000.00.

I have no doubt whatever of the solvency of the Harmony Society, and the only thing in my judgment that could cause its insolvency would be to interfere with the present management by the appointment of a receiver, or the issuing of an injunction. This, of course, would utterly prevent the continuance in the plan of the payment of the debts, which plan I adopted under the advice of the gentlemen I have named, and it might result in the total ruin of the Society, and its property. If the present management is not interfered with, and we are allowed to continue, as we heretofore have done, I feel confident that within ninety days we will be able to pay all of the floating debts of the Society, and at maturity promptly meet the mortgage debt to Harry Darlington, Trustee, and, after paying all of our debts, that we will have Economy and a large tract of land, besides other property left, and that though with diminished means the Society will still continue, and a large number of aged men and women who are entirely dependent upon it for support will pass the balance of their days in comfort.

Duss made the first and last report of Henrici on the state of the Society, which has been given above, a part of his affidavit as evidence given by Henrici in his favor, and concluded his statement with the resolutions of his faction of the Society for which he had obtained signatures under such turbulent circumstances in the church at Economy.

Of great importance was the lengthy affidavit of Judge Henry Hice, covering twelve typewritten pages. Judge Hice's business connections with the Society went back to the year 1858, when Baker was still chief trustee. The Society was then engaged in farming at Economy, having a large amount of land under cultivation. As the old Baker records showed, they were then also much occupied in raising stock, but they had then just become involved in the Darlington Cannel Coal Railroad, and at that time or soon after became interested in the manufacture of oil from Cannel Coal and shale in the neighborhood of Darlington, Beaver County, Pa. They had investments and mortgages but Hice was not informed about the extent of these. N. P. Fetterman had been the general counsel of the Society then, and from 1863 Hice became their attorney in their matters in Beaver County, as also in some matters outside of that County, until the month of May 1874, when Hice accepted the position of Judge of the Courts of Beaver County. He then ceased to be their attorney, but continued to be more or less conversant with the business operations of the Society, and from January 1, 1885, he again acted as their legal counsel. Because he was one of the most informed legal minds involved, it is worth following the essence of what he had to report.

The Society having acquired a large tract of land, being the site of the present Borough of Beaver Falls, the Trustees determined to lay it out in lots and sell the same. For this purpose, about the year 1865, they employed H. T. and J. Reeves as their agents to make sale of these for them. As their agents these men took charge of the business, had the land laid out into lots under the direction of the Trustees, sold a very large number of lots, and continued to act as their agents in this matter until the death of H. T. Reeves in 1889, since which time John Reeves alone acted as their agent, and continued to act as such at the time of the trial. The Trustees then also adopted the policy of loaning money monthly, on easy terms, to the purchasers of lots, to enable such purchasers as needed such aid to erect dwellings on their lots, a predecessor to present-day FHA loans. This was done in many cases and quite a large amount of money thus was invested. In the course of time many of these parties failed to meet their payments, and the Trustees were compelled to make amicable arrangements with them, buying back the lots with the improvements, or where this could not be done, selling the same at Sheriff's sale, and in many instances having to purchase the properties at such sales. In this way and by having erected a number of dwellings, quite a number of the improved properties were acquired by the Trustees, which had to be looked after, kept in repair, and rented or again sold. The care of these, the renting thereof, the collecting of rents, and the like were also placed in the charge of the Reeveses.

Mr. Henrici encouraged manufacturing enterprises in Beaver Falls, declaring that the growth and success of the place depended very largely upon the establishment and successful operation of manufacturing industries therein. With this view the Trustees acquired interests, and in some cases controlling interests, in various manufacturing establishments; among them was the Beaver Falls Cutlery Company, in which they invested directly some $285,000 and which was operated for many years, but was not successful financially and resulted in great loss. There were also:

The Beaver Falls Car Works, in which they invested about $47,000 and which was carried on for several years, was fairly remunerative, but it burned down, with destruction of the machinery and the material on hand, causing a large loss.

The Beaver Falls Steel Works, in which they invested about $125,000, which was (and at the time of the trial still was) owned wholly by the Society, and had been and then was operated by the Society, and with reasonable profit.

The Shovel Works, operated by a limited partnership association in which the Society had an interest to the extent of $27,500, which interest they disposed of some years ago at about cost.

The Western File Works, also owned and operated by a limited partnership association, their direct investment therein being about $75,000, an investment which they were still holding at the time of the trial.

The Pottery Works, which they acquired in payment of a debt for money advanced, and which they operated for some time and subsequently sold to Mayer Brothers.

The Valley Glass Works, owned by a corporation, The Valley Glass Company, a considerable portion of the stock of which at the time of the trial was held by them; the amount, however, Hice could not state with accuracy. The works had burned down by the time of the trial.

There were other manufacturing concerns in Beaver Falls, in which they had considerable interests, such as The Pittsburgh Hinge Works, The Coffin and Casket Works, etc., etc.

They also took an active part in the establishing and carrying on of the Beaver Falls Water Company's Works, investing in that project something like $125,000, or perhaps more, but they disposed of this late in the year 1889 or early in 1890.

They also subscribed largely to the capital stock of the Beaver Falls Gas Company and aided in the establishment of that enterprise, but disposed of their interests therein during the year preceding the trial.

The investment in all the above-mentioned enterprises was made from ten to twenty years before Hice gave his testimony, while Henrici and Lenz were trustees of the Society, except for the Valley Glass Company, in which investment was made during the trusteeship of Henrici and Woelfel.

In addition to all these direct investments in the various concerns mentioned, large amounts of money were loaned to many of them by the Economy Savings Institution, a banking firm of which the Society Trustees were the principal owners, which loans were made at the instance of Mr. Henrici.

Besides their various building enterprises in Beaver Falls, the Society was active in the building of the Pittsburgh and Lake Erie Railroad, investing therein $400,000, which they disposed of in 1883 at large premiums.

When the building of the Pittsburgh, Chartiers and Youghiougheny Railroad was projected, Mr. Henrici took a deep interest in the enterprise and the Trustees took a large amount of the capital stock, their entire holdings therein aggregating nearly 8000 shares of $50 each at par, circumstances having arisen that depreciated the value of the property, as they held and operated and making it impossible for the company successfully to maintain and operate the same. About the same time they also invested about $100,000 in the stock of the Chartiers Block Coal Company, which stock they held at the time of the trial and which then was valuable stock. About this time they also invested considerable amounts of money in the Phoenix Ferry Company, the Anchor Transportation Company, The Chartiers and Youghiougheny Railroad Company, but what amounts Hice could not state, only that none of these enterprises proved successful.

Hice spoke of a number of oil wells which the Society had on their lands in Warren County, Pennsylvania, which were operated by them during a period commencing about 1860 and continuing for some years. This business had proved quite profitable and large sums were realized therefrom, but Hice had no knowledge or means of knowledge of the amounts they made. Quite a large business was done by the Society in the way of lumbering on portions of their lands in Warren County, principally under the direction of Mr. Lenz. Hice did not know the results of this business except by statements of Mr. Lenz, who in a complaining way, not long before his death, stated to Hice that the expenses attending the business were very great and that in the way in which they had been managed it was a losing business.

As for the agricultural business—the farming and dairy business carried on at Economy, both Henrici and Lenz informed Hice that it was not satisfactory financially, that the wages and support of their employees on and about the farms and the expensive way in which it had been conducted much exceeded all the income or profit arising therefrom, but that it seemed impossible for them to change their course and discharge employees, who were helpless and dependent on the Society. Hice stated that from what he had learned and seen of these operations he was satisfied that for years the operations at Economy taken as a whole had resulted in very large annual loss.

About Henrici in particular, Hice stated that from the time of Baker's death in 1868 he took the lead in all matters of business outside of Economy. He described him as a man of great force in his views and opinions, but honest and honorable in all his motives. He was not given to consult his fellow members or even his co-trustee, at least in the more ordinary matters of business, having great confidence in his own judgment in all matters pertaining to the business of the Society, and, having once determined and entered upon a line of policy as to any branch of their industries or business, he was most persistent and persevering therein, pursuing it to the end, even though, as was sometimes the case, such policy seemed to others unwise and dangerous. As an illustration of how difficult it was to swerve Henrici from his purpose, Hice cited the example of the Cutlery Works. During the operation of the Cutlery Works some of those concerned pointed out the fact that the business was a losing one, very largely so, and that the market would not take the goods produced at prices that justified their manufacture, and urged on him the propriety of closing the works, at least for a time. But Henrici replied: "No, the Works must run, many of the employees are entirely dependent upon the work here for a living, and the Works must not stop."—"But the goods cannot be sold, and what shall we do with them?"— "We have room to pile them up, we must wait for a market," he replied.—"But too many goods are being made, the trade does not demand them, and to store them up is taking great risk from fire, rust, and depreciation generally"; to which he replied: "We must make goods, I say the Works must run even if we do lose." Henrici, according to Hice, kept the Works running until goods accumulated to an amount so great that of many kinds, sale could not be made for several years. Many rusted and had to be refinished, and the whole resulted in a very great loss. Hice was ready to give other illustrations of this trait of Henrici's character showing similar results.

As to all their business matters, Hice found Henrici somewhat exclusive in the manner in which he conducted them, relying upon himself as the head of the Society and, as far as Hice could observe, he seldom communicated his actions to others. Hice stated that he did not seem disposed even to keep accounts and records of their business and affairs because he thought it was sufficient if he himself knew and understood them. When Hice became aware of this he urged him to have accounts kept by employing some good German as an accountant, because he thought a German would be more satisfactory to him and to the Society, but his reply was that it was not necessary because they did not need it.

Belief in the community of property was the one great test and condition of the membership in the Society, Hice asserted. Henrici had very strong convictions as to the merits of this doctrine, and seemed to extend it even beyond the members of the Society to embrace in a sense their employees in and about Economy, at least so far as providing them with food, housing, rent, fuel, and the like were concerned, for as a rule all were provided with these things, and he did not think it necessary or proper to keep an account with these people, except only as to money paid them as wages, and as to transactions with others outside. Within, he felt his knowledge of them was sufficient, without any accounts.

After the death of Mr. Lenz, who was, to some extent at least, conversant with their affairs, there was no one except Mr. Henrici who really knew the condition of their affairs or business, and owing to the want of proper records, it was difficult for any one to ascertain that condition, except so far as Mr. Henrici might see proper to communicate it, asserted Judge Hice. Such was the situation when Duss became trustee. They had not sufficient records to furnish information. Duss had informed Hice that he could not get definite and satisfactory information from Henrici, and Duss made inquiry of Hice as to different matters. Duss then employed Dickson as an expert accountant to assist him in his investigations, and to establish a proper system of accounts of the Society's business. Hice declared that he had found Duss to be an "intelligent man *much above the average,* well informed in business matters, quick of comprehension, but conservative, prudent, and careful." Hice found that the Society was by no means insolvent, spoke of its many assets, and asked that Duss be allowed to continue on the course he had begun. Such testimony from a respected former judge and a man long associated with the Society naturally carried a great deal of weight.

The testimony of John Reeves of Beaver Falls, Pa., real estate agent of the Society, substantiated what Judge Hice had said, asserting that the accounts they kept with the Society also were rather mixed up, but that the "total amounts of purchase money would much exceed $1,500,000." After all, he was speaking about the development of the entire borough of Beaver Falls, Pennsylvania. The Reeves testimony was not so well organized, and he excused himself by saying that it would take much time and study of his books, "as the account and reports embrace rents received, interest received, and the different items would have to be separated to give exact figures, which would require much time as the number of written reports exceed 300."

Very effective, of course, was the comparatively short affidavit of J. T. Brooks. Brooks asserted that during the past five months he had become intimately acquainted with the financial condition of the Harmony Society and with the measures which had been taken during that period to get its affairs into good condition. He had been in almost daily consultation and co-operation with one or more of the Trustees, especially Duss. Brooks said that about the last day of October 1892 the Harmony Society was directly indebted, upon its own obligations, which were held mainly by various banks in the City of Pittsburgh, to the extent of about $350,000. These obligations were for the most part in a form which might result in great loss, if not disaster, to the Society in that they consisted of promissory notes of the Society, some payable on demand, some payable on time, the latter frequently maturing and in large amounts requiring constant renewals, and payments of discount. In certain cases distinct demand was made that the debt should be partly or wholly paid. A portion of these notes was secured by the deposit of stock or bond collaterals; in some cases the collateral was insufficient to protect the debt; in other cases the collateral was largely in excess of the amount necessary to insure full payment of the debt. Some of these stocks and bonds which were thus held as collaterals had a ready market value, but were not marketable because of conditions which affected unfavorably their salability, while still others were entirely, at least for the present, worthless. In respect to some of the more valuable of these collaterals, certain parties who knew of the disordered condition of the Society's finances and who at the same time were directly or indirectly connected with the management of the banks that held the Society's notes, which were secured by these collaterals, were awaiting favorable opportunity to buy these collaterals at forced sales, which they believed would inevitably and in a short time occur.

Brooks also testified that about October 1, 1892, the Harmony Society was the principal owner of the Economy Savings Institution at Beaver Falls, a private partnership, having at that time a very large indebtedness, partly to a bank in New York City, but mainly to a large number of depositors. A considerable portion of the assets of this savings bank was at that time not easily convertible into ready cash, and it was feared that, unless immediate steps were taken to put the Harmony Society into condition to be able fully to protect its creditors, its stocks and bonds held by banks as collateral would be sold at a sacrifice and the depositors of the Economy Savings Bank at Beaver Falls, becoming unduly alarmed, would likewise compel a needless sacrifice of the assets of that bank as well as the other "vast properties" of the Harmony Society.

Brooks further testified that about October 1, 1892, when the financial condition was as he had described it, the then Senior Trustee of the Society, Jacob Henrici, by reason of advanced age and growing infirmities, which soon after ended in death, ceased to participate actively in the management of the Society's affairs, and that the same devolved almost entirely upon the then Junior Trustee, John S. Duss. Brooks asserted that it was then, for the first time, that a fixed and certain plan for the settlement of the Society's affairs was adopted by Mr. Duss and that the same plan had been pursued steadily and successfully to the time of the trial. The plan he stated briefly to be this: First, to borrow a considerable sum of money at a reasonable rate of interest and on time long enough to enable the Society leisurely and without sacrifice to convert its doubtful securities into cash. Second, with the proceeds of this loan pay the most pressing obligation in the Pittsburgh Banks and at the same time strengthen the Savings Bank at Beaver Falls with a large reserve of cash. Third, to sell as rapidly as possible, but without sacrifice and without attracting public attention, the marketable stocks and bonds which had been held by the Pittsburgh banks as collaterals, and apply the proceeds of such sales as fast as received to the payment of other bank debts, and to the further support of the Economy Savings Bank at Beaver Falls, Pa. Brooks asserted that this plan had been carried steadily forward and that it had proved a complete success. Every debt in every bank in Pittsburgh and New York had been paid in full; every individual creditor of the Harmony Society had been paid when his debt became due; every depositor of the Economy Savings Bank at Beaver Falls had received payment in full of his deposit on demand.

Nearly, or quite three-fourths of, all those depositors had been paid in full and the Economy Savings Bank had a cash reserve on hand now larger than its liabilities to depositors, even if they were three times as many as they then were. The bonds and stocks of the Society had been sold from time to time in lots so as to avoid sacrifice, and portions of its property consisting of lots improved and unimproved were in the hands of experienced men for sale, with sales being made almost daily, and the money therefrom received was being applied daily to the further reduction of the direct and indirect liabilities of the Society.

Brooks further asserted that he had personal knowledge of the fact that the present Trustees of the Harmony Society were pursuing a wise and prudent policy in respect to the Society's affairs; that they were acting wisely in disposing of interests in manufacturing enterprises, in selling undeveloped and unproductive properties, and in applying the proceeds to the payment of debts, thereby reducing interest payments and expense of superintendence. He explained that they were also reducing the number of hired men who for years had been employed at the Economy farm at a great waste and loss, and in other respects were carefully and judiciously administering the affairs of the Society and reducing the expenses in every possible direction.

Brooks climaxed his affidavit with the assurance that, from his personal knowledge and participation in the affairs of the Harmony Society and from the intimate relation he had borne to the Trustees during the past five months, he had no hesitation in declaring under oath that the conduct of the said Trustees in managing the affairs of the Harmony Society "is and has been" characterized by prudence, energy, intelligence, and entire integrity, and that, if not interfered with or obstructed by persons who were not familiar with the affairs of the said Society or who from mistaken ideas of duty were seeking to place the properties of the Society under the control of strangers, the present Trustees would in a reasonable time be able to discharge all direct and indirect liabilities of the Society and have property undisposed of amply sufficient to support in comfort and plenty all members of said Society throughout their lives.

More, of course was not needed. While the mass of figures presented in the affidavits defied analysis offhand, the impression they made was that the Society had been for a long time in a perilous condition financially, and could only be brought out of danger by most delicately careful management. Judge Wickham seemed to voice the feeling of all those who on March 3, 1893, saw the Society's assets and liabilities laid bare for the first time in its history when he called it an astounding revelation. After Messrs. Dickey and Shiras had briefly addressed the Court for the plaintiffs, and Mr. Watson had replied for the defense, Judge Wickham rendered his decision without a moment's delay:

Everyone who has heard the revelations contained in the affidavits read in this court today must be astonished. It is clear that when John Duss became a trustee of the society he found that it was hanging on the brink of an abyss. He went to work to save it. To me he seems to have been the society's savior at a most critical time. If he is allowed to remain he will apparently bring the society out of its trouble. I do not know Mr. Duss at all but he seems to me to be the only man who in the last 20 years brought modern business ability to the management of the society's affairs. Mr. Duss must be judged by his associates and advisers. When he found himself as trustee confronted with the responsibility of guiding the society through a stormy sea he did not call Mr. Teed, however he may have felt toward that notorious impostor some time before, to his assistance, nor did he consult clairvoyants, but he went to men of high standing, like Mr. Brooks, Mr. Watson, Judge Fetterman, and Mr. Thompson. They advised him well, if the result of their advice is shown in his handling of the society's affairs during the last year. Judged by his conduct in the past, when he saved the property of the society and protected the plaintiffs in this suit as well as the other members, and also saved his community from a financial panic, Mr. Duss is the best receiver the society could have. I do not think a receiver is needed. I therefore refuse to grant the petition for a receiver, and deny the motion for a preliminary injunction.

The affidavits in the case were then ordered filed and the court adjourned. The bill was allowed to stand for further proceedings. On March 10, 1893, a rule was issued on the defendants to file their plea, demurrer, or answer to the bill, within thirty days after service of notice of rule, or have an order entered, that the bill be taken *pro confesso,* and a decree issued against them in their absence. On March 21, 1893, the service was accepted for the Harmony Society by W. H. S. Thomson, attorney for the defendants. On April 19, 1893, the answer of the defendants was filed.

On June 30, 1893, by direction of the plaintiffs the attorneys for the plaintiffs discontinued the bill and all proceedings thereon. What had happened? Duss had settled out of court by buying off the Feuchts at a comparatively cheap price by using his weapon of an expert accountant's report combined with an unbeatable array of legal talent that controlled the courts of Pennsylvania. This expert accountant's report of the society's economic condition will be published in full in the forthcoming *Documentary History* of the Harmony Society.

Historians and economists interested in the financial standing of the Harmony Society will always be grateful to Nachtrieb and the Feuchts for compelling the Trustees of the Society by law to render an accounting of the condition of the Society, particularly at the end of the Henrici era, for Henrici had been living in the times as it were, of Abraham, Isaac, and Jacob, while the money he spent was being reckoned according to the system and time of Carnegie and Vanderbilt. Without the Nachtrieb and Feucht lawsuits we would never have been able to get a relatively reliable picture of the economic empire of the Society. In Baker's time the records had still been kept, so that one could tell where the Society stood, although even then there was that special buried fund of half a million in hard money of the British Empire and the United States which would never have been accounted for without the Nachtrieb lawsuit, and the Huber funds never were accounted for. Nothing did more to prevent the appointment of the receiver for the Society, as requested by the Feuchts, than the affidavit of the expert accountant, James Dickson. The very fact that Duss did not make this information available to the Feuchts until compelled to do so, and also the fact that his faction would not tolerate a man of such education as Benjamin Feucht, M.D., on the Board or as fellow trustee, made his management of the

Society's affairs suspect. Dr. Feucht was the most experienced and best educated man in the Society. By ability and in terms of service to the Society over three generations, one of the Feuchts deserved to be on the Board of Elders. There can be only one explanation, namely, that Duss and his attorneys from the beginning had planned to get rid of the Feuchts and gradually the rest of the members, and liquidate the Society's property to the greatest personal enrichment possible. This they ultimately did. They were in agreement with the basic request made in Feucht's lawsuit, namely to dissolve the Society and distribute its property to all members, but they did not want all the present members to share in the gains because they could afford to wait until more had died or had "voluntarily" withdrawn. They did not have to wait very long before their clever plans were realized. One thing is certain; the Feuchts would not have sued if Duss had dealt openly with them and rendered this account without being under compulsion of law and public opinion to do so.

12

Lawsuits, Payoffs, and Conflicting
Supreme Court Opinions

THE FEUCHTS AND DUSSES WERE NOT THE ONLY ONES INTERESTED in the Harmony Society millions. In Germany, lawyers were busy organizing 109 alleged heirs to the estate of George Rapp. The matter aroused considerable interest in the papers over there, and as early as 1885—as we have seen—the German Consul at Philadelphia had applied for letters of administration on the estate of George Rapp. This had resulted in Henrici's first report on the Society and caused Gertrude Rapp to make a will in which she left all to the Society. The German Consul, however, was not to be discouraged from other attempts to get at the Rapp millions for his clients. Because the Register of Wills of said county had refused to grant him letters of administration on the Rapp estate, this German Consul, Charles H. Meyer, again appealed to the Court of Beaver County. Judge P. J. Wickham, on March 2, 1893, dismissed the appeal from the decision of the Registrar of Wills at the cost of the appellants, with the following strong and emphatic words:

Mr. Meyer, in his petition, states that in case letters are granted him, "tedious actions at law" will be required to enable him to get hold of any assets. It is perhaps a duty the Court owes to those he represents to say plainly and emphatically, that under the admitted facts, no litigation however "tedious" could benefit them. They never had and never can have any interest in George Rapp's estate. When it descended to and vested in his grand daughter, it became her's solely and absolutely, and the possibility of their heirship ceased. They are now chasing a Will o' the Wisp. Their claim is a

254

dream born of a dream. Their prospective fortunes are as unreal as the mythical millions awaiting deluded Americans in "Chancery," or the Bank of England, fattening on accumulating interest as the centuries go by. It would be as profitable for these claimants to take out letters of administration on the estate of Adam, as on the estate of George Rapp. The sooner they are made to realize the futility and absurdity of their pretentions, the better it will be for their purses and peace of mind.

This decision, it will be observed, is based entirely on what may be termed the primary merits of the case. I have not deemed it necessary to consider the question of laches or *res adjudicata,* or the alleged want of proof of relationship.

The main point of the Feucht Bill in Equity had been that the Court should order and decree a dissolution of the Harmony Society and a division of its property "amongst the parties legally and equitably entitled thereto." Duss and the masterminds directing him had been at work on this very plan ever since Duss became a member of the Society, but they knew that it would be to their great advantage to move carefully and slowly toward that end because time and human temperament were working for them. There was absolutely no danger that the Society would not be able to meet its obligations, even a run on their bank. The assets were so vast, as the affidavits of Brooks and Dixon had shown, that there would be plenty for all, especially if some of the more impatient gold seekers could be bought off reasonably, while death from old age would very soon and inevitably thin the ranks of the members. This master plan of dissolution included admission of new members who would be sure to cause no trouble and would still provide the legal evidence needed that the Society was legally alive. It was the impatience of the Feuchts, somewhat natural because they were older than the Dusses, that caused them to accept a payoff sum for withdrawal from the Society and to sell their birthright for a bag of peanuts.

As already mentioned, the bill in equity was permitted to stand, and the trial went on, often bitter and dirty in its accusations, but a settlement was sought and found by paying the Feuchts off with the total sum of $28,000 plus a seven-acre piece of real estate in Stowe Township, Allegheny County, Pennsylvania. Duss at this time was paying about $5,000 for withdrawal. Ten years later this went up to $75,000, and when Duss himself "withdrew," leaving his wife in charge as "Trustee," he was paid $500,000 in bonds.

Even before the Feucht settlement on June 5, 1893, the membership of the Society had declined and continued to do so during the year 1893. On January 4, 1893, Elder Gottfried Lauppe died. On February 21, 1893, Johannes Scheid, who had been born twelve years before Henrici came to the Society, died in membership. With the death of these old members there was another opportunity to make one of the Feuchts a member of the Board and thus make a move toward reconciliation and establishment of confidence. Instead, the master plan called for admission of a new member on March 14, 1893, Leonhard Härer, who six days later was elevated to the Board of Elders, disregarding the established principle of serving a time of probation for membership and service in that high office. This, however, provided legal evidence of life in the Society. Between March 6 and 13 of the same year, Hugo Miller, who had helped Duss secure the necessary signatures to the new articles, withdrew with his $5,000. He also had joined the Society with Mrs. Duss, and in effect was paid $5,000 for the three years he had served in the Society at no expense whatever to himself. On March 27, 1893, the Board of Elders, i.e., Duss, Siber, Friedrichs, Hermannsdörfer, Niclaus, Riethmüller, Platz, and Härer, discussed the desire of the Stickels to withdraw from the Society and decided that "the Trustees should settle this matter as soon and as cheaply as possible." The payoff in this case was dirt cheap and the terms anything but harmonious: Julius Stickel, his wife, and daughter were given the total sum of $3,620 and given until May 1 to get out of Economy. They also had joined the Society with Mrs. Duss, three years before. The minutes of the Board for May 8, 1893, report that J. Jacob Niclaus had left the Society. He had come into the Society with Duss and was now paid off with the higher sum of $5,000. Sigmund Stiefvater, who had come into the Society with Mrs. Duss, was the next to depart, with a donation of $5,000. The exact date of the settlement is not recorded in the minutes. On June 8, 1893, the minutes of the Board report the departure of Moritz J. Friedrichs, who also received the standard rate of

$5,000. He had come back to the Society with Duss, and in his case the papers plainly stated that he had been bought off for $5,000.

The payoffs continued on June 9, 1893, when Blasius Platz, who had joined with Mrs. Duss, withdrew with his $5,000. On June 22, 1893, Christina Haerer (also Härer, Hoerer) and son Leonhard, the last one to join the Society (on March 14, 1893), withdrew with $5,000 for the two of them, Christina Haerer also having come in with Mrs. Duss on February 13, 1890. On June 26, 1893, Mrs. Elizabeth Siber withdrew with $4,000. She had joined with her husband on February 15, 1892, and he had soon after become Junior Trustee. He then withdrew soon after with $1,000, making a cheap settlement again at $5,000 for the couple.

When members formerly withdrew from the Society, they signed a simple receipt written out by one of the Trustees and consisting of about one sentence running to a few lines. Such a receipt had won the Nachtrieb case for the Society before the United States Supreme Court. Now that lawyers were directing the affairs of the Society, such withdrawal receipts became intensely legal and left no legal loopholes. Members withdrawing from the Society now signed this form which was prepared in the year 1893:

I, _____, a Member of the Harmony Society at Economy, Beaver County, Pa., being desirous of terminating said membership and withdrawing from said Society, do declare that I do hereby of my own wish and purpose surrender and renounce forever my membership in and connection with said Society, likewise all my rights, interests, and privileges as a Member thereof: And further in consideration of the sum of Five Thousand Dollars ($5,000) in cash paid to me out of the funds of said Society, by John S. Duss and Samuel Siber, Trustees, receipt whereof is hereby acknowledged, I do hereby release, cancel and discharge any and all claims whatsoever which I, my heirs, assigns or lawful representatives may or could ever have against said Society or its Trustees, its property or assets, or any part thereof, I hereby declaring all such claims to be fully compensated, settled, released and discharged. And I do further declare that I have received said sum of Five Thousand Dollars and have surrendered, compromised, settled, released and discharged all claims I or my heirs, assigns or lawful representatives have or could have against said Society, its Trustees, its property or assets or any part thereof, entirely at my own solicitation, and without any invitation, request or solicitation so to do, by said Trustees or either of them, and in full knowledge of the fact that said Society owns, in addition to its property at Economy and Leetsdale, several thousand acres of land in Michigan and in Warren County, Pa.; also certain tracts of land in Allegheny County, Pa.; also stocks and bonds in various railroad, mining, manufacturing and bridge companies to the nominal amount of several hundred thousand dollars; also various judgments, mortgages and unsold lots in Beaver Falls and New Brighton of the nominal value of several hundred thousand dollars; also that while it may be possible that said Society may have a large amount of property after payment of its debts, I am entirely satisfied to accept as my full share and interest therein said Five Thousand Dollars and I will never hereafter make any claim for other or further payment of any sum whatever, nor for the delivery of any other property of said Society to me, no matter what may be the value of the property and assets of said Society after payment of its debts; all such claims thereto being by me hereby expressly barred and discharged.

Witness my hand and seal this   day of   1893.

With the "loss" of so many members, the Society now faced a shortage of males to serve on the Board of Elders, so the proposal was made to fill the vacancies with women. As a result Fridericka Muntz, 71 years old, Susie C. Duss, 33, and Regina Lautenschlager, 76, were elected to the Board on June 8, 1893. There were now two Dusses on the Board, and from this point on it becomes amusing how young Duss charmingly sways his Board according to his wishes. The move to elect women to the Board was, of course, made on the basis of good legal advice. For such legal advice in the matter of titles to lands in mortgage to Harry Darlington, Duss had paid D. T. Watson $2296.77. J. T. Brooks wrote Duss that this bill was half of what he expected. His own fees at this time were higher. Thus on January 13, 1893, he received $10,000 payment in full of services and expenses to December 31, 1892, in respect to reorganization of the finances of the Society and of "various corporations and institutions in which said Society is interested, especially the Economy Savings Institution at Beaver Falls, also for legal and professional services and for negotiating loans for the Society to the amount of between five and six hundred thousand dollars, assisting in selling securities etc." From this point on J. T. Brooks was paid a basic salary of $500 a month by one contract of May 26, 1893. There was another previous contract made in January 1893 by which he had received $2500 in June, 1893, but these amounts were minor in comparison to what he was to get as share from the total liquidation of the Society property toward which they were working, namely, one-fourth of all. Thus, even after his death, his estate was paid the sum of $95,000 on May 23, 1903.

The Feucht affair had scarcely been settled by compromise and proceedings on the Bill discontinued as of June 30, 1893, when Shiras and Dickey, the same attorneys who had fought for the Feuchts, under date of September 15, 1893, wrote Duss and Riethmüller, the Trustees of the Society:

Take notice that the undersigned parties, comprising certain heirs, and former members of the Harmony Society, intend beginning proceedings to prevent, among other things, the further sale or donation of the personal property of said Society by its Trustees, and to demand a detailed report of such personal assets as have been sold hitherto and the application of the proceeds thereof.

Also, take notice that the right to sell or mortgage all or any part of the land comprising the town of Economy and its adjacent farms is further denied by the undersigned and it is our intention to seek to enjoin such sales and to bring suit in ejectment against any and all persons who may take possession under any alleged deed from you. Christian Schwartz, Charleston, W. Va; Allen Shale, New Springfield, Ohio,; Anthony Koterba, New Middletown, Ohio; B. C. Henning, Beaver County, Pennsylvania; Bentle Heirs; Hahn-Scheid, Heirs; John Bender, Allegheny County, Pennsylvania,; Michael Steib-Heirs, by

Shiras & Dickey
their attorneys.

The *Schwartz et al.* case was brought in the Circuit Court of the United States for the Western District of Pennsylvania, because those bringing the suit lived in various states. It was in a sense the product of the research into the Feucht case which Shiras III had done. Dixon's extensive report had, of course, further opened the eyes of this attorney to the vast assets of the Society, and the Feuchts had also passed on the word to friends about the gold in the Economy hills. Economy at this time was frequently in the press of the nation as a top news item. Although a settlement had been made with the Feuchts, there were other descendants of members of the Society who had withdrawn who had a strong claim to the property of a Society, which obviously was making good progress toward liquidation, as is seen from the Bill of Complaint brought by Christian Schwartz, a Citizen of the State of West Virginia; Anthony Koterba, David Strohaker, and Allen Shale, Citizens of the State of Ohio, and G. L. Shale, a Citizen of South Dakota. The relation of these persons to the Society was as follows.

Among the original members of the Harmony Society were Christopher Schwartz, Joseph Koterba, Christina Strohecker, Maria Lorenze, and Jacob Scheel (Shale), and John Bamesberger. All names varied in spelling. Christopher Schwartz and his wife, Barbara, came from Germany in 1817, and when the Society settled in Beaver County in 1825 this Schwartz, and his wife and six children, went to Economy and were admitted to the Society. Christian Schwartz was born in Pittsburgh in 1823, went into the Society when three years old and remained therein for a period of twenty years, during which time he worked faithfully in behalf of the Society, when, falling in love with Dora Schneider, a niece of a Mrs. Kriter, a member of the Society, he left the Society and was married, and of late has been living at Charleston, West Virginia. The father of Christian Schwartz died in Economy on July 5, 1858, his mother on February 11, 1857, his sister Fredericka on January 11, 1857, his sister Maria on May 26, 1878, his sister Louisa on March 29, 1889, his brother Joel, who was born in the Society, died therein in 1858, and his brother Joseph died at Economy on June 25, 1889. The parents of Christian Schwartz and his brothers and sisters remained continuously in the Society from the date of their admission until their death. Each of the said parents, brothers, and sisters died intestate, leaving surviving them, as their sole heir and legal representative, Christian Schwartz. Christian Schwartz claimed that his ancestors and relatives, in addition to giving the Society large sums of money when they joined the Society, contributed also very largely in after years to the growth and prosperity of the Society by a life of labor and devotion to its best interests. Christian

Schwartz left the Society only because he wanted to marry and could therefore not remain in it. All the members of his family were buried in the cemetery of the Society at Economy.

Joseph Koterba, the father of Anthony Koterba, was one of the founders of the Harmony Society, having come from Germany in company with Father Rapp and assisted in the organization of the Society in Butler County in the year 1805. Two years later Andrew Koterba, the half-brother of the plaintiff, was born in the Society and remained therein twenty-three years, until his death in 1880, dying intestate and leaving Anthony Koterba as his heir.

The Bill of complaint asserted that in the year 1805, the paternal and maternal grandparents and parents of plaintiff David Strohaker [also Strohecker] joined the Harmony Society, contributing thereto many thousand dollars. And his grandparents remained members until their decease and died intestate, and the father of the plaintiff continued a member until his marriage to Mary Reif, a member of the Society and mother of the plaintiff, whose parents likewise were members of the Society. David Strohecker asserted that his parents were compelled to leave the Society in order to marry because the doctrine of celibacy was then enforced. Also Catharine Strohecker, the aunt of the plaintiff, was a member of the Society and died therein intestate, and David Strohaker claimed to be heir of these relatives.

Next it was asserted that Maria Shale (Scheel) and her two sons, Jacob and Lawrence, came from Germany in the year 1804 and were among the first to join the Harmony Society, the sons assisting in the building of the three towns of the Society and continuing largely by their labors to the founding and maintenance of the Society. It was claimed that these parties also died intestate, leaving as their heirs plaintiff G. L. Shale, the son of Lawrence Shale and nephew of Jacob, a citizen of the State of South Dakota, and plaintiff Allen Shale, the grandson of Lawrence Shale (or Scheel), a citizen of the State of Ohio.

The *Schwartz et al.* Bill of Complaint submitted for the November 1894 term of the Circuit Court of the United States for Western Pennsylvania, was not well drawn up and in many points looked more like an appeal to public conscience and opinion than a rational presentation of a carefully built up legal case. This was true of all cases brought against the Society by former members, or descendants of members, because their attorneys never had access to the all-important records of the Society to prepare their cases properly. Whatever was charged in a Bill of Complaint throughout the history of the Society had to be based on oral testimony, the few legal documents that had become public knowledge, and former trials. It never occurred to any of the attorneys opposed to the Society to demand and obtain access to the records and books of the Society. In fact, the Society trustees always managed to spread the report that all records of original donations to the Society had been destroyed, in order to make the feeling of communism more effective. My research has convinced me that not even that statement is completely true, for I have found early records of original contributions, and the records of original contributions made which were really destroyed must have been a special set of formal records. The failure to produce such records for the attorneys of the plaintiffs seems even more fantastic when we consider that Duss took special pride in the claim that he was the first to establish order in the records of the Society. That would certainly mean that all important records could have been produced with a reasonable amount of search. Surely his expert accountant would have been able to produce records then claimed to be nonexistent, records which my own research has uncovered, but the fact remains that vigorous attorney Shiras of Pittsburgh and his father, Shiras II, then an Associate Justice of the Supreme Court in Washington, did not present a Bill of Complaint which could easily have been extremely well documented and probably have won his case. Of the twenty-six complaints brought in the Bill, I quote numbers 20, 25, and 26 as being the most significant.

20th. That on the 12th day of April, 1894, the said Duss, without any authority from the members of the Harmony Society, and in the utmost disregard to his trust secretly entered into an arrangement with said Hice, Reeves and one James Dickson, whereby he, the said Duss, agreed to convey the town of Economy, the surrounding properties and certain other lands of the Harmony Society, situate in Allegheny County, to the Union Company, an alleged corporation created under the laws of the State of Pennsylvania. And your orators allege that a conveyance has been made by said Duss for the lands as aforesaid and that the same was made without the knowledge of your orators or any members of the said Society, excepting possibly Susie C., wife of said Duss and Gottlieb Reithmueller. That by the said pretended conveyance and sale of the home of the Harmony Society and its other properties the said Duss has attempted to wholly terminate the existence of said Society, not only as to the government thereof by the Board of Elders, and by the members, but also as to the ownership of any property. That the said Union Company, in addition to said Duss and Riethmueller is composed of said Hice and Reeves, debtors of the said Harmony Society as hereinbefore stated and one James Dickson, the private bookkeeper and confidential agent of said Duss whose interest in said corporation was acquired by gift from said Duss.

That your orators are advised that it was not competent for the said trustees to convey said properties to the said Union Company, but such transfer was a breach of trust and wholly invalid. Your orators therefore demand a full answer and disclosure as to said pretended sale and transfer to whom the several shares therein have been issued and on what consideration.

25th. That recently said Harmony Society has become dissolved as aforesaid, that all of its purposes and practices established as aforesaid by the founder of said Society and by the ancestors of your orators have been abandoned, that the pursuit of agriculture no longer exists in said Society, that its chief assets consisting of bonds, stocks, and other securities and the town of Economy with its buildings and the adjacent lands of said Society, consisting of some 3,000 acres, and which constituted the basis of organization and business of said Society have been sold and conveyed away by the said Duss as aforesaid in fraud, however, of the rights of your orators and their co-tenants, and that by reason of the facts hereinbefore set forth your orators and the said last members, except the said Duss and wife, are now tenants in common of all of said lands and tenements and entitled to partition thereof, in proportion to their respective interests.

26th. That for some time past the members of said Harmony Society have been retiring therefrom and have received the amount of their interest in said association in the land or money, or both, the land being set apart in severalty to them and have released all of their rights and interests in said association in consideration for such payment or conveyance to them and that by said retirement and withdrawal the membership of said association has been reduced to the persons hereinbefore named members, that by common consent this association has ceased to exist as an association and that if the property thereof has ever been impressed with a trust (which your orators deny, as being contrary to public policy and void in law or equity) such trust has wholly ceased and the assets of such dissolved association have reverted to the donors thereof among whom were the ancestors and intestates of your orators as hereinbefore fully set forth.

On the basis of the twenty-six complaints brought forth, Schwartz et al. asked the Circuit Court to do as follows:

FIRST. That a receiver may be appointed by your Honorable Court, to take charge of the property and assets, real and personal which were of this said Society including the land fraudulently conveyed away as aforesaid to the said Union Company, until the final decree in this cause.

SECOND. That now by a preliminary injunction and hereafter by a perpetual injunction under the seal of your Honorable Court, the said Duss may be restrained and enjoined from encumbering, selling, assigning or in any way intermeddling with any of the property and assets which were of said Harmony Society and from creating any debt, obligation or liability of said Society, and from in any way interfering with its affairs.

THIRD. That your Honors will decree that said Duss shall make full discovery of the accounts, liabilities, debts assets which were of said Harmony Society, and that said Duss may in a like manner account for his management thereof since he became a trustee of said Society.

FOURTH. That the Union Company and the said Duss, Reithmueller, Hice, Reeves and Dickson, its members, agents, and officers be restrained and enjoined by preliminary injunction, to be perpetual or final hearing [sic] from in any manner granting, conveying, charging or encumbering the said land or any part thereof so as aforesaid conveyed by said Duss and Reithmueller.

FIFTH. That the said deed and conveyance made by the said Duss and Reithmueller to the said Union Company be decreed fraudulent and void and without effect as against your orators and that the Union Company and its said members, agents and officers be ordered and decreed to surrender the said deed of conveyance to the clerk of your Honorable Court, for cancellation by him.

SIXTH. That an account may be stated by your Honorable Court against the said Duss of the losses which the said Society has sustained through his fraud and mismanagement and that he be decreed to pay over to the Receiver so appointed by your Honorable Court for the use of your orators and the other parties entitled the balance so ascertained against him.

SEVENTH. That your Honors will order a decree a marshalling of the assets which were of the Harmony Society and a winding up of its affairs, and a division and distribution of its assets, real and personal, either by means of a sale under order of your Honorable Court, or in such other manner as your Honors may deem most expedient, to and amongst the parties legally and equitably entitled thereto, including your orators, and that your orators may receive their just share and proportion of said assets, real and personal, in severalty.

EIGHTH. That your Honors will grant unto your orators such other and further relief as to your Honors may seem meet and as the exigencies of the case may require.

NINTH. And may it please your Honors to grant unto your orators a writ Subpoena under the seal of your Honorable Court, commanding the defendants to appear upon a day certain in your Honorable Court and answer the Bill of Complaint and an answer under oath is hereby waived and stand and abide what your Honorable Court shall decree in the premises, and your orators will ever pray, &c.

SHIRAS & DICKEY,
Counsel for Plaintiffs.

In the November 1894 term of the Western Pennsylvania United States Circuit Court, the attorneys of the opposing parties agreed to request the Court to appoint W. W. Thompson, Esq. as Examiner and Master in the case. This then was done and soon after a Pittsburgh paper reported that the troubles of the Economites, like Tennyson's brook, run on forever, and that at times it is difficult to determine, right off hand without posting up on ancient history, whether Mr. Thompson is sitting as coroner or judge. George Shiras III was positive that the Society was dead, that it just disintegrated and fell to pieces without knowing it or leaving a will. He was quoted as saying:

Either the retiring members have no right to take large sums of money, and Trustee Duss has no right to give it to them, or if he and they have such rights, no trust exists. That is plain. If there is a trust they cannot divide up, and if there is no trust then the property should be divided up among all those living who were members of the trust, and all the heirs of the dead members.

Much of the testimony taken was for the purpose of proving that the members and trustees voluntarily abandoned the original purposes of the trust, or Society, and that as an organization it had drifted so far away from the original plans upon which it was formed that it could no longer be recognized as the Harmony Society, and that, therefore, a receiver ought to be appointed for it. To strengthen these arguments Shiras brought in Moritz Friedrichs, who told how J. Twing Brooks came to him and asked him if he would not like to go back to his relatives in Germany. He replied that he had no money and then told of the efforts made by Fred Verick, another attorney of the Pennsylvania Company, and Charles Kaufman, also claimed to be in the employ of Brooks, to get him to release his claim. They finally got him to sign the documents "quit-claiming" everything for the withdrawal sum of $5,000. At this time the view was still strongly held that the Pennsylvania Company was operating with Trustee Duss to get rid of the members, in order that that big corporation might foreclose mortgages on the Economy property and then erect their shops on the beautiful Economy tract of land.

The testimony and the Master's Report were not completed and filed until April 11, 1898. Errors in fact, which could have been prevented by more careful research, weakened an otherwise sound case. Although the plaintiffs' attorneys vigorously attacked the report, which dismissed the case at the cost of the plaintiffs, Judge Acheson upheld it in February 1899. In August 1899 the case was entered in the United States Circuit Court of Appeals at Philadelphia, where the lower court was again upheld. All the while, not one lawyer demanded to see the full, available records and books of the Society. In January 1901, the plaintiffs petitioned the United States Supreme Court for a writ of certiorari, which petition was granted by Chief Justice Melville W. Fuller, February 11, 1901.

The case was argued April 22 and 23, 1902, and decided October 27, 1902, in Duss's favor, with Mr. Justice Gray and Mr. Justice Shiras taking no part in the consideration and disposition of the case because the latter was the father of the main attorney of the plaintiffs.

The slim majority opinion of the court reasoned as follows, showing the basic fact that those who were most influential in the Pennsylvania courts could not be shaken. The Supreme

Court's majority held that the facts did not show that there was any dissolution of the Society; that the relations of the members and the Society were fixed by contract; that the plaintiffs could not have other rights than their ancestors had; that no trust was created by the agreement of 1836, and that under its terms, when the plaintiffs' ancestors died or withdrew from the Society, their rights were fixed by the terms of that agreement; that the members who died left no rights to their representatives, and had no rights which they could transmit to the plaintiffs. Because the master, the Circuit Court and the Circuit Court of Appeals, had found that the Society had not been dissolved, either by consent of its members or by the abandonment of the purposes for which it was founded, the Supreme Court refused to review the disputed facts involved in the finding of the master. Chief Justice Fuller and Mr. Justice Brewer dissented and wanted to reverse the lower court decisions, so although Duss and his attorneys had won another victory, it was a close one. The involved legal statements by Mr. Justice McKenna combined with the dissent of Chief Justice Fuller and Mr. Justice Brewer on this most important case cover thirty-seven pages and cannot be given here, but they are readily available under the citation: *Schwartz* v. *Duss,* 187 US 8, 47 L. Ed. 53, 23 S. Ct. 4 (1902).[1] Goethe caught the sense of this in his *Faust*:

Es erben sich Gesetz' und Rechte	Law and Justice eternally descend,
Wie eine ew'ge Krankheit fort,	Direful as a disease which has no end;
Sie schleppen von Geschlecht sich zum Geschlechte	They drag themselves from race to race,
Und rücken sacht von Ort zu Ort.	And move insidiously from place to place.
Vernunft wird Unsinn, Wohltat Plage;	Reason becomes nonsense, benevolence a pest,
Weh dir, dass du ein Enkel bist!	Till you, the descendant, are sorely oppressed!
Vom Rechte, das mit uns geboren ist,	Yet of the law which is our inborn right,
Von dem ist leider! nie die Frage.	Alas, that question never comes to light!
	(Alice Raphael translation)

Since April 11, 1894, when the case started, nine of the seventeen subscribers had died, leaving eight, consisting of Duss and his wife, one Gillman, seventy-seven years of age and unable to read or speak English; and five women of the ages of eighty, seventy-seven, fifty-eight, fifty-four, and forty-seven respectively. Among those who had died since the year the first legal move was made in this legal battle were Gottfried Lauppe, Thirza Feucht, Johannes Scheid in 1893; Elizabeth Beck and Dorothea Hoehr in 1894; Lena Rall Wolfangel in 1895; Conrad Hermansdoerfer, Philippina Wolfangel, Maria Diem, and Regina Lautenschlager in 1896; Gottlieb Riethmueller and Eduard Kellerman in 1897; Benjamin Feucht in 1898, and Friedericke Muntz in 1901. "The service of one of these families is said to aggregate three hundred years of unrequited toil. They are entitled to invoke the aid of the court in the winding up of this concern, and these decrees ought to be reversed," said the Chief Justice of the United States Supreme Court. If Shiras III had had full access to the records of the Society and had been able to study them fully to prepare his case on a sounder basis, the decrees probably would have been reversed.

Duss had not bothered to wait in Economy for the decision. When it came, it reached him in Boston, where the vast resources of the Harmony Society were helping him gain national attention as a newly discovered millionaire and band director— a truly unique combination in the history of music. To this musical phenomenon we must now devote our attention.

13

Broadway Potpourri: Harmonist Millions, Duss, and Barnum

ON JUNE 8, 1902, THE *New York Sunday Telegraph* GAVE HALF-inch headlines and the better part of a page to an amusing little opera celebrating a new star composer and conductor in the New York, and even in the entire American, musical world: Duss, the sole Trustee of George Rapp's Harmony Society. The words of the opera were by Owen Donavan, and M. De Lipman illustrated the text with five sketches of Trustee Duss striking the following poses, baton always in evidence: Ready, Dolce Con Amore, Scherzando, Sforzando, Pianissimo Religioso.

The text of this amusing opera contained more truth than poetry or music, and reveals clearly the results of a tremendous publicity drive which had spared no expense of Harmony Society funds to bring fame to Trustee Duss and a real novelty to the bored citizens of New York City. I refer to this amusing and amazing evidence of the conquest of Broadway by one of the heirs of the Harmony Society millions, and will explain further how this and other musical triumphs were achieved, because they are a part of the history of the Harmony Society. The *Sunday Telegraph* sketch highlights all that was characteristic of Duss's conquest of Broadway: his great egotism and vanity, his tremendous wealth, his impatience with anyone who tried to share the top spot with him, his use of Society history to make himself more interesting, his showmanship, and his love for making speeches between numbers of the program to cover for his lack of musical ability.

269

Duss had already been severely criticized by the music critic of the Rochester, N.Y., *Herald* for talking during concerts given there on May 22 and 23, before his opening in New York City. The critic reported that what he had said was neither interesting nor amusing, that in his evening concert he had undertaken to roast the musical critics of an afternoon paper for having said a few things not quite to the director's liking.

It seems necessary to inform Mr. Duss that the papers of Rochester have treated him with extreme consideration, in view of the fact that he appeared here under the auspices of and supposedly in aid of one of the quasi-charitable institutions of the city. Had the band come to Rochester solely on its merits as a musical organization, it would have been considered solely on that basis; but charity covers a multitude of sins—and other things.

Rochester has had its fair share of band concerts; it has a band or two of its own, but not one of the local directors has any pretension to shine as a buffoon. So when Mr. Duss began his chatter about this, that and the other thing last Thursday evening it came as a surprise. Rochester music lovers are not accustomed to have the leader of a band or orchestra come on the stage after the intermission and remark: "It's raining outside." That is not what they paid a dollar at the box office to have him do. But the man who has paid his money to listen to a concert is more or less at the mercy of the man who gives the concert. Mr. Duss should remember that when he feels that he is about to have a fit of talking.

It is understood that the Duss Band is to give a series of concerts in New York City this summer. If Mr. Duss undertakes to occupy his programme time with replies to all his New York critics the chances are that he won't have time to play any music at all—that is, if the New York press condescends to take him seriously. Last evening, with only one critic to engage his irate attention, Mr. Duss talked at such a rate that he omitted the final number on the programme. Eccentricity is sometime pardonable, but rarely when it is studied.

The Harmony Society had always loved music and had always had a band. When the members went out to gather in their harvest, their band would lead the procession out into the fields, and often their band played concerts for persons outside the Society. When Duss took over in Economy he devoted considerable time and much money to building up an Economy band which now no longer consisted of members but of nonmembers living in the vacated houses of the Society. To improve his band he imported talent from other cities and gave them magnificent uniforms. Duss was a born showman and he combined his love for showmanship with his love for music. At first he took his band on trips into the neighboring cities, and in September 1895 they went to Louisville to participate in the G.A.R. national encampment. In the Fall of 1896 he took them to St. Paul and the year following to Buffalo. Early in 1900 he merged his band with the Great Western Band of Pittsburgh and after this it became known as the best band of the Pittsburgh area. This move, combined with the constant publicity given Economy through its many legal battles, brought Mr. R. E. Johnston, the New York impresario, who had heard of Duss and his accomplishments from a mutual friend, to Economy early in 1902 to listen to Duss and his band. As a result Duss and his band were offered an engagement for the summer season in New York City, to begin May 26 and close September 28.

There were several factors responsible for Duss's quick rise to national fame, but basic to all was the almost unlimited amount of capital which he could spend without ever being required to give an accounting. When the Junior Trustee Gottlieb Riethmueller died on February 10, 1897, the few remaining members of the Harmony Society millionaire's club voted to make him sole trustee, so he was in unquestioned command of all funds and actually became the millionaire bandmaster described in the Donavan-Lipman opera. With this money he not only bought his band but also the services of Mr. C. B. Bradford, who became his general agent, with offices in the St. James Building, Broadway and 26th Street, New York City. Mr. Bradford and Mr. Johnston saturated New York City with Duss publicity before he arrived and helped convince the people that Duss unquestionably was a musical wonder, but in an interview which Bradford gave to *Printers Ink*[1] he was frank enough to state "the splendid advertising that has been done for him is almost as much responsible for filling that vast auditorium nightly as the talent of Duss and his assistants." Mr. C. B. Bradford was selected to run Duss's advertising campaign, so he claimed, because he was a practical printer, brought up at the case, and a man fed on advertising when he was a baby. "It was not contemplated," Bradford said, "to make this advertising anything like what is done for ordinary shows, but something better, and, so far as I know, I am the first practical printer ever chosen for a position of this kind. There is lots of money behind the show and it was decided to run the advertising on a high plane. No expense whatever has been spared to exploit Duss thoroughly, nevertheless I am not wasting money."

Bradford showed the reporter of *Printers' Ink* a 36-page booklet illustrative of the style and character of the literature they were distributing to advertise Duss and his incomparable band. It was printed on the best paper, filled with halftone pictures, elegantly gotten up throughout. They were putting out 300,000 copies of the book, although it was an expensive piece of auxiliary advertising. The book had style and character, which ensured favorable comment at once. It was a better booklet than had ever been issued by any other enterprise of that kind. From cover to cover it showed care in every detail. It was designed not to be thrown away even after it had been read. It was almost exclusively made up of press notices taken from metropolitan and other papers during the previous three months. These press notices, of course, had likewise been induced by carefully prepared advertising methods. The book was an epitome of what the press and public had said about Duss. These booklets were distributed by Duss's two uniformed giants, who in themselves were a great attraction. Walking between them they had a midget, the name of "Duss" on the front of all their caps, so that even those who could not get near enough to receive a booklet on Duss could see whom the men were advertising.

The triumvirate of Duss, Johnston, and Bradford became to the world of music what Barnum and Bailey were to the circus world.

Barnum had been the first to enliven his offerings by freak shows, and to popularize his show by a kind of extravagant advertising and publicity, then new in American life but which has remained characteristic of American show advertising ever

since, though no one, except perhaps Duss, excelled Barnum.
Barnum made his dwarf, Charles Stratton, famous under the
name of "General Tom Thumb," and this dwarf was one of
his leading attractions. From Barnum and Bailey Duss took over
not only his dwarf, George Liable, but also the two giants,
who circulated around New York City and at St. Nicholas
Gardens advertising Duss's incomparable band. Duss's giants
and his dwarf were as famous in New York and did as much
to boost his show for him as Barnum's own dwarf. When
attention was lagging he managed to have one of his giants
hale the dwarf into court, from which the following report
would then reach the press with photographs of the giant and
the dwarf no higher than his belt.

A giant was the complainant and a midget the defendant in an as-
sault case today before Magistrate Barlow, in the West Side Police
Court.... All the principals are employed at the St. Nicholas Gardens.
... "I know what this case is," said Magistrate Barlow, "I can see that
the complainant needs protection. You must not bother this man,"
to the midget. "Keep out of his way." "He's always in my way," said
the Midget, rebelliously. Magistrate Barlow dismissed the defendant
and the giant told his woes to an *Evening Journal* reporter. "That
midget used to be in love with the snake charmer when we were all
with Barnum & Bailey's circus," he said. "I didn't care about the
snake charmer, but I used to talk to her and he got jealous. Since
then he's been annoying me. He puts placards on my back and
does other silly tricks. He's like a flea that annoys you and you can't
do anything. I couldn't hit him, so I had to have him brought to
court." The midget told a different story. "That big giraffe is dream-
ing if he says I was in love with the snake charmer," he declared.
"He's the cause of all the trouble. I couldn't punch his face, 'cause
I couldn't reach it, but I did kick his shins. I'll punch his ribs in if he
bothers me again."

Duss and his promoters thought so much of their giants as
an advertisement that they used a picture of them on most
of the literature that they sent out, besides the portrait of
Duss, which was on every scrap of advertising matter they
used.

When Bradford was asked what advertising they were doing
outside of New York, he explained that New York papers
cover a very large territory and, because they were in them

all, they certainly got their money's worth out of them. But Bradford was also planning ahead for the tour which Duss and his band expected to take after finishing the series in New York. Bradford handed out a list of the towns in which they would play and explained that although there were a lot of towns on the list, "every newspaper in every town receives every day a notice about 'Duss'—not forgetting mention of the date when he will appear at that particular place." This was a system that had never been so carefully and thoroughly worked before, by any agent. In speaking to the reporter of *Printers' Ink,* the newspaper's advertising trade paper, Bradford asserted:

I am satisfied that even now curiosity has been aroused about Duss in every place where he will play in the coming Fall and Winter. People may say that it is an easy matter to advertise a show when you have plenty of money behind you. But it does not follow that because you have it you can waste it. I am doing my best to secure effective and lasting advertising at a reasonable cost. We don't spare the dollars but neither do we squander them. Not how cheaply, but how efficiently we can secure the desired publicity is our motto. Of course you understand that, in this line of business, much valuable advertising is secured without any cost. Duss is a public performer, and, as such, is seen by the newspaper critics and frequently written about. Under the head of musical and theatrical news he is often mentioned. That is advertising, and it has often led the advertising men in other lines to think that—these free notices being taken into consideration—we fellows had little or nothing to do. Two or three days of my routine work here would soon convince them to the contrary.

Bradford was working for Duss all the time he was awake, ever planning, ever devising and evolving new advertising ideas, to be succeeded the next day by newer ones. Bradford and Johnston were of the school of Barnum and Bailey but with much more money to spend. The public loved what they handed them, because fully a hundred thousand dollars had been invested in the New York Duss enterprise, without expectation of making money but only fame for Duss.

To give Duss a good start in New York City, Johnston arranged to have him give his first concert at the Metropolitan Opera House, which had been dark since the opera season ended. After one night at the "Met" Duss and his band opened at the St. Nicholas Gardens at 66th Street and Columbus Avenue, staying there for the rest of the summer. To make everything more attractive to the public Johnston stated that thousands had been spent on the decorations alone and that a cold air system had been built which guaranteed to keep the temperature fifteen degrees cooler than the atmosphere outside. Characteristic of all the opening press comments is the stress placed upon Duss's background as Trustee from Economy, Pa., and Duss loved to exploit this background of the Harmony Society, which interested everyone. *The New York Herald* headlined the event with: "MILLIONAIRE MAKES HIS DEBUT WITH BAND. DUSS, OWNER OF THE TOWN OF ECONOMY, IS ORIGINAL, AND HIS MUSICIANS MAKE LOTS OF NOISE." The military band was called badly balanced, the bass instruments being too numerous, and "the result was more noise than music." Duss was called original, having marked mannerisms in his gestures, "and he has a bad habit of talking to the audience without rhyme or reason." There were frequent references in the papers to Duss's "expensive band" and to the "former socialist," who gives promise of rivaling Sousa as a poseur and advertiser, if in no other way." In this first evening Duss also offered one of his own creations, a tonal description of the battle of Manila, of which it was said: "It will do—for its kind."

The *New York American* on May 26, in writing about "Mr. Duss, of Economy," reported that some few years ago Innes and his band formed the star attraction at the Pittsburgh Exposition and that Duss, who was well acquainted with the directors of the exposition, requested that Innes play a march he, Duss, had composed. Innes demurred at first, but finally consented, providing Duss would buy several hundred tickets for the night his composition was to be played. Duss agreed, and Innes then suggested that the composer lead the band himself. A special train then brought almost the entire town of Economy to Pittsburgh for the affair, and Duss led a band for the first time in his life. According to this report his march was, of course, wildly applauded by the Economites, and the intoxication of the applause led Duss to make up his mind to have a band of his own. Within a week he had hired musicians from Chicago, New York, and other cities to come to Economy. He paid them from thirty-five to forty-five dollars a week, and all they had to do in return was to play with his band twice a week.

Added attractions at the St. Nicholas were the flower girls, the perfume fountains, refrigerated air, the two giants in uniform, the midget, and an automaton in the form of an overdressed woman, which offered flowers to feminine visitors. The *New York Telegraph* of May 28 said that Duss leads the audience as well as the orchestra and that the cyclonic methods of the millionaire bandmaster and Economite pleased New York and filled the St. Nicholas Rink every night. The *Telegraph* again stressed Duss's background more than his music and explained: "The orchestra is a fad with Duss, now that he has millions to spend and only a few old people, survivors of Father Henrici's band, with any strong claim on the wealth." "A millionaire several times over, is attracting more attention than any other musician that has come to New York in a decade."

The atmosphere of the "Met" obviously had still overawed Duss on his opening night, but after his first night in the redecorated St. Nicholas he really let himself loose. From now on he quickly earned a reputation for eccentricity as great as that which it took Sousa years to acquire. *The Dispatch* of May 28, 1902 reported on his St. Nicholas Garden performance:

There he plays waltzes with a swinging of the body which inspires his large audience with an evident desire to get up and dance. Last night after an intentional imitation of Sousa in conducting a march, which caused a great laugh, Mr. Duss showed how he himself would rouse enthusiasm. With his arms working like a Pennsylvania Dutch windmill he had his audience so excited that when he got to "The Grand Hurrah" he was waving his baton around his head like a successful candidate watching returns on election night. If last night's mannerisms on the part of the new bandmaster are a fair sample of his peculiarities in conducting it will not be long before the vaudevillians and others will have him on the rack as they have Sousa.

Such antics were supported by many other daily events. He had the money and he was eager to spend it, so he would give his sixty bandmen an excursion to the then-famous bathing resort, Long Branch, or his press agent would announce that by Mr. Duss's orders 300 bottles containing prizes were thrown into the sea a few days ago, from launches that cruised off Manhattan, Brighton, Rockaway, and Long Branch. The first prize, of course, was a season ticket to hear Duss and his famous band. Because this publicity stunt was so successful, he immediately announced that on the following Saturday five hundred more prize bottles would be cast into the sea.

Next, the agents Johnston and Bradford began to supply the papers with Duss anecdotes, many under the heading of "Duss Does Things." "Duss is musical and sentimental: Duss is gentle and tender; Duss is rural and humane and forgiving, but Duss is a demon if imposed upon. No one can deceive Duss and escape. Duss forgives and forgets errors and mistakes; Duss overlooks neglect and tardiness, but Duss never leaves the trail of a sham. Duss won't be swindled. Duss pays high prices and adores luxuries; Duss is a liberal dealer and a broad spendthrift, but Duss won't be overcharged. Who knows all this besides Duss? Lots of firms and the United States Government itself." This is then followed by instances and anecdotes of his dealing with express companies in New York and the Government in Washington.

Another news item that served Duss's purpose well was the purchase of the $40,000 Innes band library. Since Mrs. Innes and Conductor Innes were getting a divorce, she tried to attach the property on its arrival in New York in a special car, but Duss had already dispatched Mr. Johnston to Washington, followed by a trio of detectives and Mrs. Innes's lawyer, and Duss managed to protect his interests by arranging a special telegram sent by Innes from Cincinnati to his New York attorney.

That long, hot summer, New York was dependent for its concert music on two men of opposing quality: Franz Kaltenborn, poetic, romantic, sentimental, idealistic, graceful, scholarly, intellectual, musical, truly beautiful; and Duss, who was described by the *New York Press* as "materialistic, sensational, practical, forceful, ingenious, aggressive, and not so truly beautiful." Kaltenborn was blond, tall, slender, with what women termed a darling of a moustache, and tender blue eyes. The ladies loved him because he embodied a union of the graces of art with the charms of nature. Duss was of a different type.

No poetry in Duss. Duss means business. Duss is a practical man. Duss's motto is "I strive to please," which he lives up to admirably. Duss has no sentiment in himself, but this does not prevent him from recognizing the sentiment of others. . . . Kaltenborn inculcates a reverential calm; Duss develops a lively vivacity. Consequently the old and middle aged whose fires of romance have burned low admire the young conductor mightily, while their juniors, being full of sentiment, hold by his rival who allows it expression.

Kaltenborn's Circle was described as a sort of melodic Quaker meeting, while St. Nicholas was a kind of Lover's Lane. Marriages were made by Duss, courtship was conducted under his auspices, and true love blossomed at the wave of his baton. At St. Nicholas the young people went a-wooing, holding hands, exchanging admiring glances, whispering tenderly. Duss press agents claimed that he could put as much sentiment into ice cream soda as other and baser men can distill in champagne. For the special refreshment of modest Phyllis in her wooing by Corydon, Duss invented a libation which cheered but did not inebriate, the Duss Lemonade, costing a quarter but worth a dollar. It was claimed to be as colorful as Duss.

Here is an example of a Duss press agent release which was then distributed to reporters for background material and further Duss publicity:

Although it is not generally known, Duss has a front name—John, John Duss. Here is republican simplicity. Though he discourses many airs, Duss puts on none. With the argument that great men need no prefix, he calls himself Duss—directly and without circumlocution—as Shakespeare, Milton, Homer, Dante, Verdi, Wagner. Therefore also Duss. It is an honest word, rolling neatly in sibilants off the tongue, striking an impressionistic picture on the memory and like good wine, needing no bush. The John is superfluous, irrelevant, unnecessary. Pan the great god himself, had no Christian name, but played his pipe as plain Pan. Apollo, the patron and founder of music, was not known as Andrew, though to his melodic ear alliteration was sweet. Duss has proper precedents for his lack of ostentation. Other geniuses have lost their baptismal names after long continued effort; Duss begins without one. Successive ages have forgotten the familiar appelations of Socrates and Eschylus; even his own generation cannot be familiar with Duss. He was born Duss, he lives Duss, he will pass down the corridors of time Duss. Perhaps Ralph Waldo Emerson, as all wits do occasionally, dropped into punning when he wrote—"So nigh is grandeur to our Dust," and Shakespeare himself, in a like humor, undoubtedly referred to the St. Nicholas when he cried in "Cymbeline"

> Golden girls and lads all must
> As chimney sweeps, come to Dust.

Thereby arguing the universality of our musician's influence. In the generic, primitive, basic and original "Duss" is an ill word for poetry, rhyming only with such abhorrent matters as muss, fuss, and cuss. Hence authors of all ages have taken poetic license with the bandmaster's name, clapt a "t" on the end of him and set him to the time of must, trust and just. Or, as Hamlet would say—

> O that the Duss which fills the world with awe
> Fits to a T within the poet's maw!

While Duss had spent $100,000 to advertise himself and his band for this summer season, he did get results, and since he believed that any kind of publicity was good publicity, he was pleased. His private office of propaganda was functioning so efficiently that he began to make the mistake of believing that he really was what his propagandists made of him. He began to speak as a great authority on controversial musical questions of the day and with the help of his press agents also got these interviews into the newspapers of the nation. Thus the *New York News* was induced to print a sensational article in the issue of June 13, 1902, with Bandmaster John S. Duss holding forth pontifically on the question: "Wagner and Rag-time—Their Claims to be Considered Classical," in which he defended both Wagner and ragtime as classical and religious. Typical of the man was this statement in the article: "Possibly I am particularly and peculiarly sensitive to Wagner's music because I was born a Wagnerian. I dreamed of Wagner's music before I had heard a strain of it, and when a lad of nine I for the first time had its glorious harmonies burst upon me, I exclaimed: 'This is my music. This is the realization of my dream.'"

It was behavior such as this which caused the New York

correspondent to report as follows in the *Pittsburgh Dispatch* of June 21, 1902, on the local boy who had conquered Broadway:

Bandmaster Duss and Gotham Critics.

It seems that the spectacular Mr. Duss from Economy is taking himself too seriously. Good-natured New York goes to listen to his concerts in an old skating rink, and enjoys the music to the accompaniment of the opening of beer barrels and the shrill solicitations of Mr. Duss' flower girls to buy a "buttonin." The New York papers treated the new bandmaster extremely liberally, taking him on his face value, which he generously displayed on the street corners in flaring colors and supported by an army of adjectives that would have brought the flush of envy to the cheek of a circus agent. New York, therefore, does not take Mr. Duss seriously, and, in the vernacular of the day, "she lets him down easy."

Now he bobs up with some rather ungracious evidences of "I told you so's," and gives out the impression that he forced a surrender from the critics of New York. My Dear Mr. Duss, in New York, you are not judged from the standpoint of high art. No beer garden entertainment is. The New York papers made no satirical references to the band from "the wild and woolly west" that came to conquer, as you like the people of Pittsburgh to believe.

On June 25, 1902, some one replied to this in the *New York Musical Courier,* defending Duss as a careful worker "with a splendid grasp of the musical proposition before him," but the defense could never be made to stick because of Duss's pathological need to be popular and advertise himself. The *Dispatch's* New York correspondent knew what he was talking about, because on June 10, 1902, the *New York Telegraph* had headlined one of its news articles with

DUSS BANDMEN IN ROW WITH BEER MEN

stating that the musicians had been deprived of refreshment supplied by the leader. Duss refused to interfere in the argument because he said it was the carelessness of the bandmen that permitted the waiters to sell their free beer to the audience. The Duss Bandmen, sixty in number, and the St. Nicholas Garden waiters, thirty in number, were at swords' points. The clash was on every night during intermission.

Said Duss: "I said I'd furnish refreshments for the band."
Responded the giant hornblower: "Well, the beer has flown."

Replied the bandmaster: "I know it, it has flown too freely."

Bewailed the trombone man: "But we mean the flow has been cut off. The keg is absent and clams are no longer in evidence. Why?"

Said Duss: "Because I agreed to furnish the repast for my men, not for the waiters, the ushers, the floor cleaners, the janitor's friends, and, in fact, the vast audience."

In further confirmation of the New York correspondent's report of the "beery" atmosphere of Bandmaster Duss's *Nicholas Garden* or *Rink,* the *New York Daily American* on July 23, 1902, headlined:

MANTELLI WOULDN'T SING IN BEER GARDEN.

The paper then explained that those who wondered at the sudden illness of Mme. Eugenia Mantelli, the well-known Italian contralto, which prevented her from singing with the Duss band at St. Nicholas Garden and resulted in the cancelation of her engagement there, would be interested to know what precipitated her indisposition.

The reasons were: Mantelli heard at the last moment that if she sang at the St. Nicholas she would lose the opportunity of being the leading contralto in the Mascagni Italian Grand Opera Company during the sixteen weeks that organization was to be in America the following winter. The fact simply was that Mantelli had been told by the managers for Mascagni that if she sang with Duss she could not be a member of the Italian composer's company. She faced the possibility of losing four months with a big operatic organization for one week with a brass band. "They drink there—and smoke, maybe?" inquired the contralto, astonishment and horror overspreading her face. Being assured they did, she turned pale, and by the time she had reached her hotel, the Empire, she was so ill she could hardly stand. A physician was summoned hastily, and was not long in reaching a diagnosis of nervousness approaching the prostration point. A few minutes before the beginning of the concert Johnston got the news and had to announce that Mantelli could not appear. The thought of beer and cigarettes made her ill again later and her Duss contract was canceled. Immediately after that she signed a contract for the Mascagni engagement and left for Oak Hill in the Catskills.

These two beery items also were publicity, and more people

drank beer than champagne! There were many other news releases, like the story that Duss would build his own theatre in New York City, like the continued folksy, intimate anecdotes about the great millionaire conductor who was just one of the people, even though he was a musical and all-around genius. Barnum with much less money to back him up had been successful with his ideas, and so was Duss. By August 9, 1902, Duss could tell the press that he had played the longest New York engagement ever played by a musical organization, although he had come out of the West an unknown quality a few months before and gained fame in a single night. By August 15 he would complete his 84th concert, he would continue his New York season until October 1, ending the season with a record of 126 nights. The *East Orange Record* reported on August 9, 1902: "No bandmaster—no musical organization —ever played this length of time in New York, or any city in the United States, and when we consider the magnitude of the Duss organization—sixty artists whose salaries are the highest ever paid to supporting musicians—Duss's New York accomplishment is something for him to be proud of."

The day after this publicity Duss again brought his giants in the headlines by having them arrested for trying to force their way into Oscar Hammerstein's Paradise Roof Garden at forty-second and Seventh. They were dressed in very gaudy costumes, bearing the Duss advertisement on their backs, and they bore a note from Duss asking that they be permitted to enter. Although they bought tickets, William Hammerstein, nephew of the proprietor, refused to admit them in such clothes, and when they tried to force an entrance Hammerstein called a policeman to arrest them. The policeman was two feet shorter than Duss's giant twins, and the spectators at Hammerstein's Paradise said it was the most amusing attraction of the evening when the policemen took the two away and charged them with disorderly conduct. Duss's Johnston then bailed them out.

At the conclusion of his all-summer engagement at the St. Nicholas Garden, Duss's two hundred employees presented the popular bandmaster with a well-advertised thousand-dollar diamond medal, and over six hundred floral pieces were sent to him from friends in New York, Pittsburgh, and other cities. The papers reported that he chivalrously thanked his admirers in a characteristic speech from the stage. It was estimated that over eight thousand heard his last concert in the St. Nicholas. For the night after that he had rented Madison Square Garden for the Duss Musical Jubilee, which was to be his farewell summer concert in New York. It was called by his press releases quite the largest musical offering ever seen in New York. Five hundred artists took part in the program and it was estimated that no less than twenty-two thousand people were in attendance.

After completing his long New York engagement Duss took his band on a tour which included Utica, Syracuse, Toronto, Buffalo, Jamestown, New York, Pittsburgh, Cumberland, Baltimore, Newark, New York, Boston, and Worcester. They then disbanded for the season. Noteworthy is the reception in these various cities, where not all comments could be influenced and controlled by his press agents. Although he had given two final concerts in New York, he could not refrain from giving a last final concert of the season at the Metropolitan. The *New York World* of October 27, 1902, reported as follows:

DUSS LETS US HAVE A REAL GOOD LOOK.
ECONOMITE BANDMASTER FAR OVERSHADOWS BAND AND HE'S ALWAYS IN THE LIMELIGHT.

Ego was the chief characteristic of the Duss concert at the Metropolitan Opera-House last night. First was this silently manifest in the lettered legend "Duss," which bespoke the simple vanity of the man, from the top of a rack of metal strips which served the purpose of church chimes.

Presently Duss began to exhibit himself. He came forward most consciously, then proceeded to direct with an evident desire to attract the attention of the audience to himself. To this end he indulged in various tricks which it might not be too severe to call "faky."

One thing he seemed to dearly love to do was to face the audience with his back to his band and manipulate his baton in a way to suggest the drum major.

When a horseshoe of flowers was ostentatiously handed over the footlights to him he squirmed and smiled and cast his eyes in a "Oh,-how-could-you-be-so-kind?" sort of way which reminded the spectator of an old maid receiving an unexpected proposal.

Later on he made a little speech to the audience with a few home-made gestures and two or three below-the-belt punches at the Queen's English. He was attempting to say that one of his singers had failed to put in appearance and to beg that her absence be condoned.

In this connection he took occasion to add that his other "lady singer," who had just sung, was not feeling very well herself; in fact, "she was hardly able to stand up!"

When the cornet soloist took a long blow at his horn, Duss pulled his watch to "time" the player on the Hold-Her-Bill! note.

Throughout the evening Mr. Duss seemed bent on showing how capricious and amusing he could be.

At Utica fewer than 500 came to hear him and found that his success was founded not alone on advertising, though he had made "liberal use of printer's ink. They found he was not "handicapped by any false modesty or retiring disposition," and that in conducting he employed a variety of movements that could scarcely be exceeded by a professor of gymnastics. They felt he was conducting a band not because he has to but because "he sighs for fame"—"which he values more than money."

In Syracuse, where the reporters found his musicians "gaily decked in gold braid," they, as usual, found Duss very ready to talk to them.

"When I get up in front of my band, I know that it's the greatest band that I ever stood before. . . . My motions breathe something even as the gestures of an orator. What do the old up and down movements of the baton signify? Nothing at all, mine mean something."

The *Toronto Mail* found "Although the amount of 'circus booming' that has been bestowed on Mr. J. S. Duss might leave the impression that he is a charlatan, the concert he gave last night showed him to be anything but that." They praised his band and enjoyed his concert, but that, of course, was the work of artists, as more observant critics had noted, who ignored him when possible and performed from pre-Dussian training and memory.

The *Buffalo Evening Times* reported that "the many who came to the concert divided their time between listening to the sweet music of Duss' Band and watching Duss himself." The reporter claimed, as others also had, that Duss directed with his hands, his arms, his head, his hair, his ears, and that his varied and strenuous, his subdued and gentle movements, seemed to mean more to his band than the contortions of most directors.

One of Duss's favorite pieces on this tour was his own "Battle of Manila in a Nut Shell." Duss was a very patriotic man and he loved to play patriotic airs and bring the audience to its feet in a loud and thrilling rendering of the national anthem. People loved it, and he would then make a speech complimenting them on their unabashed patriotism.

After his final farewell concert in New York, Duss brought his band to Boston, where he was kindly received. To be sure, the reports of the critics did not measure up to the newspaper reports his press agents had managed to get into all the Boston papers before his arrival, but in general he got a surprisingly good press in Boston, so much so that he himself was surprised. The *Boston Herald* of October 28, 1902, headlined him in half inch letters: DUSS AS AN ACTOR AND AS BANDMASTER. HE IS A GREAT SUCCESS IN BOTH ROLES, AND HIS BAND DISPLAYS WONDERFUL TEAM WORK. The *Boston Evening Transcript,* commenting the same day on his concert in Symphony Hall, said that Sousa and other bands had done better in point of actual sonority and musical playing, but a more remarkable conductor than Duss had never been seen in Boston.

We have had Mr. Arthur Nikisch, of the languourously graceful motions. We have had the sprightly Eduard Strauss, who led a waltz with such abandon that he was inspired to do a pas seul himself, there on the podium. Sousa, too, with his dignity and military precision, is not strange to us. The salient qualities of all these conductors, with the addition of a dash of easy non-chalance and also of a hearty, cordial way of taking the audience into his confidence, are combined in Duss. He is, consequently, an absorbingly interesting leader to watch, a man naturally graceful, so graceful that he frequently fell, quite unconsciously, into attitudes that suggested the statue of the Marble Faun in the niche in the wall to Duss's right, high above his head.

There were two especially impressive moments in the evening concert. One was when, during the playing of his own composition, "The Trolley," at a signal from Duss five trombone players and two cornetists swept to the front of the stage and there, seven abreast, blared forth a triumphant melody. The other moment came when he played a medley of patriotic airs and when it came to the turn of the "Star-Spangled Banner," all the players stood up, and the audience too, obeying a magnetic signal from Duss. The *Boston Post* was more reserved about it all and remarked: "These tricks take well with the average audience, though they would manifestly be out of place in a high class concert." The *Boston Herald* cartoonist used the occasion to draw Duss in his various gymnastic contortions, so Duss got a lot of publicity also in that way. Even more publicity came, however, through the Washington, D. C., press release that Bandmaster Duss had won the $4,000,000 suit in the Supreme Court of the United States and that he therefore kept control of the Harmony Society funds. Duss received the telegram informing him of his legal victory during the intermission of the concert, and in capitalist-minded Boston this certainly did not serve to diminish Duss's fame as the millionaire bandmaster. The next day he took his band to Worcester, Massachusetts, where both the *Evening Gazette* and the *Spy* had prepared the way for him and where he was well received. In Worcester, as everywhere, he was ready and eager to take the reporters into his confidence: "What they say of my manners, my studied poses and all that affects me not at all. It is the music, poetry of motion. I cannot conduct any other way. I try to interpret the idea, the musical idea."

Duss and his band soon after disbanded and he returned to Economy, to a hero's welcome. He had previously, as early as June 23, in fact, confidentially publicized his reason for not playing a fall season. As the published story ran, with proper headlines in the *New York Telegraph* on June 23, while Mrs. Duss and the noted bandmaster were at breakfast the previous morning, she had picked up a copy of the newspaper saying that the beauty contingent of "The Show Girl" would occupy boxes at the concert in St. Nicholas Garden that night.[2] Besides this, the paper intimated that, in the various cities to be visited in a tour after the New York run, this sort of thing would be a regular feature of Mr. Duss's performance.

"Whose idea is this?" said Mrs. Duss to her husband, who

was busy dashing off a symphony on the back of the menu card. "Johnson's," was the mumbled reply.

By this time, the paper stated, Duss had finished the musical composition and was writing the oratorical remarks that would accompany each number of his program. Mrs. Duss then expressed the wish that he would promise to give up his public career after he fulfilled the St. Nicholas Garden engagement. Duss went to see manager Johnson who then claimed he would be forced to give up $140,000 if he released him for the balance of his contract. Duss then, the report went on, noted the amount on his cuff and closed off with: "Just as soon as I finish the new costumes for the band I'll write you a check for the amount. Call at my hotel tomorrow morning between 9.10 ¾ and I'll dash off the little obligation. I appreciate your leniency, Johnson, and were it not that I am raising my own salary this week, I'd see that you were substantially rewarded for your kindness in acquiescing so readily to Mrs. Duss's wishes." Another Duss inspired anecdote? Before Duss had gone to New York for his concert series he had covered himself by telling the remaining members of the Society in a session of the "Board" that their case was coming up in the Supreme Court and that, while he was not interested in adding to his burdens by accepting the offer of Mr. Johnston, his acceptance would assure the Society of a living if the decision of the Court should go against them!

As one compares the advance reports of Duss's coming concerts in various cities and the following actual reports on them, these points stand out: there is an astounding similarity even down to entire sentences and paragraphs in all advance reports, due, of course, to the advance copy sent out by Bradford and Johnston and fed by them into the newspapers; there is generally the same agreement in the first part of the reports on the actual concert, again taken from mimeographed sheets prepared in advance and handed to the reporters to help them write their reports. Originality is generally found only in the comments speaking on the actual performance, and here there is usually a great divergence between the advance copy and the final report. Duss's publicity relations were extremely well handled, although every now and then a reporter would let it be known that he had been amply supplied with prepared Duss material. In the concert tour to come, this technique was to be improved and Duss was using the winter in Economy to prepare for it. Summing up the season, then, these were the results: Duss had made himself one of the most publicized bandmasters in America, and Duss was now the undisputed master, under his legal masterminds, of the Harmony Society millions through the Supreme Court Decision in the Schwartz case. The Society's funds had paved the way for the great New York summer season but there was even more money left where the other money had come from, and Duss was determined to use these funds even more lavishly.

> Clear the way for progress on the fly!
> Yankee grit, Yankee wit, never shall say die!
> Clear the way, a John Duss proud and great—
> Seeks the top,
> and nought can stop
> John Samuel, up to date.
> (Adapted from Duss's two-step, "America Up To Date.")

14

Harmony Society Millions and the Metropolitan Opera House Orchestra

JOHN S. DUSS, SOLE TRUSTEE OF THE HARMONY SOCIETY, COULD not forget the fame of his 1902 summer season and the pleasure of touring various cities of America as the head of the "Peerless, pre-eminently popular, peculiarly progressive, predominantly powerful, and practically perfect" DUSS BAND—always combined with the fascinating Harmony Society background—and his impresario could not forget that the United States Supreme Court had made Duss master, under his attorneys, who were working for their tremendous share of the Society's wealth, of all the vast property of the Society. Having become more established in his control of Society funds by virtue of the decision of the highest tribunal in the land, Duss more than ever longed for the highest recognition that America could provide.

Duss's mother in 1887 had prepared the way to his present power by joining the Society and pleading with the then-Trustee, Henrici, to give him a chance to work for them. At that hime he was busting broncos, so he claimed, out west in Nebraska. In that very same year one Jonas Clark, who had made a fortune by his own hard work instead of by legal machinations, announced the founding of Clark University as an educational institution for the economically less privileged. On the excellent site the pioneers of the Harmony Society had provided for just such a plan, Duss could have done even better than Jonas Clark in Worcester, Mass., or than R. H. Conwell, who with his own hard-earned money in 1884 (1891) founded Temple University and himself provided funds for the educa-

289

tion of 10,000 young men. In doing so he would have carried out the suggestions of the economist Friedrich List to Frederick Rapp, and he would have built a fitting monument to some of the greatest idealists who ever came to the shores of this nation. But Duss was a supreme egotist whose heart was set on becoming the greatest conductor of his age, a man who believed in his heart that money could buy even the Metropolitan Opera House Orchestra as a backdrop and instrument for his ambition and to satisfy his pathological *Geltungsdrang* (megalomania). All this was entirely agreeable to the legal masterminds working behind his well-tailored stuffed shirt, for it kept him busy and allowed them to mine the Harmony Society millions as quickly as possible without his interference. They needed his camouflage and he needed their brains more than he knew, and it was also agreeable to the Metropolitan Opera House Orchestra, for Duss offered the highest salaries that had ever been paid, and money was absolutely no consideration in his ruthless ambition to establish himself as the greatest conductor of the age, if not of all time. Erdmann Tichert, writing in the *Indianapolis Sentinel* on October 7, 1903, after watching Duss "conduct" the Metropolitan Opera House Orchestra, saw through it all and presented the picture beautifully in these words: "At this moment his success as an orchestra conductor is probably due to the fact that he finds his way through an orchestra score instinctively, in the same way a carrier pigeon finds its destination. It reaches its home without difficulty, provided no one takes a deadly shot at the pigeon. This deadly shot for Duss would be the loss of his millions and that would practically mean the end of his phenomenal success as an orchestra leader. But whether or not it would end his aspirations and his ambition to accomplish great things for himself, so that the public and the critics would take him seriously—that is a thing for the future and for himself to decide. At present his efforts are the result of a combination of magnetism, millions and nerve."

In spite of his successful season in New York during the preceding summer, one thing irked the great bandmaster, namely, the comments about the beery atmosphere in which he won his laurels and the fact that the great singer Mantelli had cleverly

bowed out of her contract with him and refused to sing in a
beer garden. Duss decided to go high hat. He took off the
braided uniform and put on the Prince Albert and the cut-
away, and bought the Metropolitan Opera House Orchestra.
How was that possible?

An unhappy circumstance happened to favor Duss's driving
ambition. Maurice Grau, in February of 1903, had definitely
retired from the important post of purveyor of opera to New
York—and therefore to the United States, and the musical world
found itself in a state very closely bordering upon chaos. Duss,
backed by the Harmony Society millions, appeared as the
favorite son of this chaos, as all the world knew through the
international publicity given to the decision of the United
States Supreme Court in behalf of John S. Duss. The musical
chaos was all the greater because Mr. Grau had filled his role
so completely. It was no exaggeration to say that, in the higher
walks of music, Grau was to New York, if not also to London
and Paris, very nearly the whole thing. He was trusted implicitly by rich men and women who gave of their millions to
make grand opera possible in America. Duss's first New York
appearance had been carefully scheduled in the Metropolitan
Opera House on May 25, 1902, and although millionaire bandmaster Duss was not listed with Cornelius Vanderbilt, John
Jacob Astor, J. Pierpont Morgan, W. K. Vanderbilt, E. H.
Harriman, and the like among the boxholders for the opera
season, these names were listed in the elegant Metropolitan
Opera House program which still bore the name of Maurice
Grau Opera Co. as lessee for the 1901–1902 season, and which
proclaimed the fame and face of the newly rich Duss and His
Incomparable Band on practically every page of the booklet,
with four pictures of Duss in uniform on the back cover to
make up for the pages missed. The Metropolitan Opera House
had just lost its great leader, and, although Grau's place was
hard to fill, there were many musicians who felt qualified. As
one critic wisely observed, "I have observed modesty has never
been the besetting sin of the musician"—true especially of John
Duss. And so it was that, while Andrew Carnegie and Frick
were reported to be boosting Mr. George H. Wilson as Grau's
successor, Duss, now a millionaire by grace of the United States

Supreme Court, and "red-handed from a great artistic success," the longest in New York city, was pushing himself as a serious contender for the crown that Maurice Grau had laid aside. Duss's position was unique in an impressive way: he was the only millionaire who wielded a baton professionally. Duss did not manage to take over Grau's crown, but he came rather close to it in his struggle; he did get the Metropolitan Opera House Orchestra and some of its best singers, at least for a time, and he was so pleased with his conquest that he decided to bring Venice to New York for them as a special home for his newly won bride. But he was still sole trustee of the Harmony Society; before he could put over the "Met" deal there were a few legal and business affairs to attend to in Economy, especially the basic matter of even more capital for his ambitious plans.

During Duss's absence as bandmaster in New York and elsewhere, it was, of course, not necessary to hold the regular meetings of the Board of Elders at Economy. The lawyers were working. At the first resumption of his meetings on November 18, 1902, Duss scared his "Board" again, as he had done before leaving, by saying that the Schwartzes were still trying to get another hearing before the Supreme Court and that matters were still not final. Having thus properly preached the law to his remaining Society of six women and two men, he informed them of the sweet gospel message that the American Bridge Company had purchased over one hundred acres of their land. At the end of these minutes of December 29, 1902, recorded by K. Rudolf Wagner—not a member of the Society but a man with more influence in it than any member other than the Dusses—and his lawyers, Duss later wrote that someone must have "purloined the report of Duss" which belonged here. Such "purloining" seems to have been quite frequent under either the John or Susie Duss Trusteeship, for in spite of the expensive business organization, fundamental records were lacking even when the WPA began its work on the archives.

On April 16, 1903, an important meeting of all members of the Society was called in his executive mansion, a meeting which also included the following nonmembers but real directors of the business affairs of the Society: Henry Hice,

Charles A. Dickson, K. Rudolf Wagner, Agnew Hice, and Charles Reeves May.

After several introductory words, so nonmember Karl Wagner records as secretary of the Society, an agreement of ratification and confirmation was presented for consideration and approval. This was written in English with a German translation and the latter was loudly read to all present and "made completely clear to them." The concluding accounts of John S. Duss as Trustee, also for the Union Company, were read over in German and "completely explained and the questions regarding same made by various members explained and answered." The reports of the various affairs arranged with John Reeves and Henry Hice and the different matters which these had together with the Society and in which they for many years were associated with the Society were then explained to the members by the Trustee. All members of the Society then ratified and signed the articles as presented to them and made them legal by signing the English and the German articles. The English version reads as follows:

Whereas, on the 30th day of April A.D. 1890 the then members of the Harmony Society executed a certain article of agreement of ratification and confirmation, whereby they re-affirmed and re-adopted the contracts of membership theretofore existing between said members, and which fixed the rights and duties and obligations of the several members of the said Society and also ratifying and confirming each and every act, matter and thing which had been done and transacted for and on behalf of the said Society by its Board of Elders and by its Board of Trustees, as the said several Boards had from time to time been constituted prior to the said 30th day of April 1890, which said article of agreement is recorded in the office for recording deeds in and for the County of Beaver in Deed Book Vol. 125 page 415 and

Whereas, subsequently, to-wit, on the 13th day of February A.D. 1897 by reason of diverse changes in membership and the deaths of diverse members, it became advisable to modify said articles of agreement so that the powers, rights and duties, theretofore rested in and exercised and performed by the Board of Trustees should be vested in a sole Trustee and John S. Duss was duly declared that sole Trustee; and whereas, since the execution of the said articles of ratification and confirmation on the 30th day of April A.D. 1890 the said Harmony Society has been involved in long and serious litigation which has terminated under a decree of the Supreme Court of the United States in a manner favorable to and upholding the rights of the said Society, and during that period, by reason of said litigation and otherwise, it has been necessary for the Trustees and Trustee to negotiate diverse sales of property, real and personal, and purchases thereof, and to borrow diverse sums of money and make payment thereof and to make settlements with diverse parties sustaining business relations with said Society and whereas, by reason of death, the membership of said Society has been reduced to eight members, viz: Karoline Molt, Katharine Nagel, Johanna Hermansdoerfer, Christine S. Rall, Barbara Boesch, Franz Gillmann, John S. Duss and Susie C. Duss, wherefore, it has become advisable to further alter and add to the said articles of agreement and whereas, there has been read over and fully explained to the Harmony Society and each of its members, the accounts of the said John S. Duss as Trustee, from the time of his appointment to this date, said accounts showing on their face all the money and property, acquired by said Duss, as Trustee, and all the moneys and property by him paid out, sold or conveyed, and the purposes for which, in each instance, the same were sold, paid out and conveyed and there has also been explained and made fully known to us the present financial condition of the said Society and what its assets and property consist of, and what its debts and liabilities are. Now, therefore, Be it known to whom it may concern that we, the undersigned and surviving, and present members of the Harmony Society, do severally, and each for himself or herself, covenant, grant and agree to and with the others, and each and all of the others as aforesaid and signers hereof, and with those who shall become members hereafter as follows:

First: We hereby expressly affirm and declare the existence of the Harmony Society as a society.

Second: We do hereby approve, ratify and confirm each and all of the several articles of agreement and compacts heretofore executed by the members of the Harmony Society, including that executed on the 13th day of February 1897, excepting the sixth clause of the article of agreement executed on the 9th day of March A.D. 1827 (the said sixth clause having been annulled and abrogated by an agreement executed on the 31st day of October 1836), and we do declare that the said several agreements (excepting the said sixth clause) are in full force and effect, and constitute the contract of membership by which the several rights, duties and obligations of the members of our Society are to be determined, except in so far as the said articles are hereinafter modified.

Third: We do hereby approve, ratify and confirm any and all acts, matters and things done and transacted by the Board of Elders, as the same has been constituted prior to the date hereof, whether the said Board has at any time consisted of the entire number of members fixed by the several articles of agreement hereinabove ratified and confirmed, or of a less number.

Fourth: We do hereby approve, ratify, and confirm each and all of the acts, matters and things done, transacted and performed by the Board of Trustees, as the same was constituted prior to the 13th day of February 1897 and as the same has been constituted since that date, consisting of John S. Duss, as sole Trustee, and including herein all matters directly or indirectly connected with the litigation of the Society; the settlement of claims against the Society; the adjustment and settlement of its several liabilities growing out of any business transaction or business enterprises in which the said Society has, at any time, been interested. And we further ratify, approve and confirm in every respect, all the items and the whole of the said accounts of the said John S. Duss, Trustee and each and every act of his in reference to the assets, property and business of the Society.

Fifth: From and after the execution hereof, the Board of Elders of the Harmony Society shall consist of two members and their successors, chosen in the manner provided by the articles of agreement hereinbefor ratified and approved and from and after the date hereof the said Board of Elders shall be John S. Duss and Franz Gillmann. In witness whereof, we have hereunto set our hands and seals this sixteenth day of April A.D. 1903 as members of and constituting said Harmony Society and also as the members of and constituting the Board of Elders of said Society.

Witness:		
C. A. Dickson	Franz Gillmann	seal
Agnew Hice	Katharine Nagel	seal
Chas. Reeves May	Karoline Molt	seal
	Susie C. Duss	seal
	Johanna Hermansdoerfer	seal
	Christine Schoenemann-Rall	seal
	Barbara Boesch	seal
	John S. Duss	seal

The original German wording of these minutes is vague and the entire legal hypocrisy of this transaction becomes entirely clear when we consider that all the reports which were claimed to have been submitted to the members were never made part of the record and could not possibly have been explained to the members fully and completely in the time available for the meeting. One need but read the report of the expert accountant as presented at court when the Feuchts sued Duss to convince oneself, for matters had become even more involved since that time. Yet it was all completely legal, with each step carefully prepared by the best legal talent then to be employed in the U.S.A. Also, Duss was in a hurry to get his "career" as Conductor of the Metropolitan House Opera Orchestra going, and for this he needed more capital, and for the Venice in New York which he planned to build he needed even more capital. Basic to all this was the document for which he needed all signatures. Let us consider the ages of those remaining members who signed: Gillman, 74; Katharina Nagel, 62; Karoline Molt, 59; Susie C. Duss, 44; Johanna Hermansdoerfer, 50; Christina Schönemann-Rall, 81; Barbara Boesch, 87; and John S. Duss, 43.

As soon as this document had been signed, the following quite legally handed in their resignation from the Society and requested the customary donation upon withdrawal: Karoline Molt, Johanna Hermansdoerfer, and Katharine Molt. According to the official minutes recorded by nonmember K. Rudolf Wagner, Franz Gillman then made the motion, and it was seconded by Christine Schöenemann-Rall, that the resignations be accepted, and that Johanna Hermansdoerfer, Karoline Molt, and Katharine Nagel be permitted to withdraw from the society, and that the Trustee give each a donation as he would see fit, and that the sum of $75,000 is suggested to each as proper, and that each give a proper receipt and agreement of withdrawal. This motion was then unanimously carried. Gillman, of course, was mentally entirely incapable of making such a motion, but let us not forget that Dickson, Hice, and May were present with John and Susie Duss to give him moral support. The Harmony Society then consisted of these members: the two Dusses, Gillman, Christina Schöenemann-Rall, and Barbara Boesch.

On the following day, April 17, 1903, just to provide for any legal eventuality, the following document was executed between Trustee Duss and Franz Gillmann, Christine Rall, and Susie C. Duss:

Since we have been requested by J. S. Duss to give him permission to use as much money of the Harmony Society as he finds necessary to carry through his musical enterprizes this summer, so be it known to all whom it concerns that we the undersigned members of the Harmony Society herewith entitle our Trustee J. S. Duss as follows:

namely that said Trustee according to his judgment may use the sums of $5,000, $10,000, $15,000, or $20,000—just according to what he finds necessary, of the funds of the Harmony Society, but that he should give certificates for each amount used, with his personal signature. These certificates to be payable in six months at 4% interest per year. [Neither these certificates nor a record of these "loans" by Duss have ever been found.]

On April 25 J. S. Duss, then acting as Secretary of the Board, which according to the articles of April 16 now consisted of Franz Gillmann and John S. Duss, recorded the minutes of the meeting he held with Gillmann, in which it was decided that Barbara Boesch and Franz Gillmann were to move into the Great House and that Mrs. Duss was to engage the necessary housekeeping help. Trustee Duss then properly and legally informed the Board, consisting of Gillmann and himself, that he would leave for New York the next day to begin his musical undertakings for the summer. "Close of the meeting. J. S. Duss, Secy." Legally everything was now clear and safe for Duss's departure.

On April 29, four days after this important Board meeting, Conductor J. S. Duss, elegantly dressed in Prince Albert and wing collar, made his debut as Conductor of the Metropolitan Opera House Orchestra of sixty pieces at the Armory, Scranton, Pennsylvania. An expensive Souvenir program, profusely illustrated and on slick paper with photographs of Duss, M. Edouard De Reszke, and the great MME. Nordica, Soloists, on the front cover, was ready for the occasion. The program informed the audience as follows about the erstwhile bandmaster and now genius conductor of the Metropolitan Opera House Orchestra:

John S. Duss has gained in one season that which many conductors have striven for years to attain—fame, success and serious recognition in the musical world. No one in these times can gain such consideration unless he possess the marvelous attributes necessary to fill every requirement the world demands from the orchestral conductor of to-day. Duss has every attribute; a thorough knowledge of music, temperament, authority, accuracy of conception, magnetism and grace. It has been the good fortune of but a few of the world's great conductors to be the happy possessors of both the last named qualities. Perhaps the fact that Duss is one of these few is answerable in a great measure for the unqualified success he has achieved. Suffice to say, that whatever the secret of his popularity may have been, no other conductor has ever before woven himself into the hearts of, or obtained such a firm hold upon, the so-called "fickle" New York public, as to retain their admiration and support for so long a season as it was his privilege to play last summer—one hundred and twenty-eight consecutive nights—a record unparalleled and never known before in the history of music in America. His genius is unquestioned; his ambition unbounded. He has become a factor in the musical world and is there to stay. Duss is the conductor of the century.

But Duss's nerve did not stop with this autobiography. On page 11 of this program he wanted to make sure that his audience would not overlook his important contribution in improving the Metropolitan Opera House Orchestra, so he lined himself alongside his predecessors. Since this great contribution might be overlooked by future historians of the Metropolitan— programs even if expensively printed are so easily lost as years go by—this part of the "Met's" musical history is hereby recorded for posterity.

The orchestra of the Metropolitan Opera House, of New York, is one of the most evenly balanced instrumental bodies in the world. Some years ago, when Anton Seidl was at its head, he insisted upon improvement in the brasses, and as a result the orchestra became famous for the richness and sonority of its horns and tubas. Later, Emil Paur overhauled the woodwinds and more recently still Signor Mancinelli, with his Italian love for the beautiful in music, improved the strings. And now comes Duss, who readjusts each department, balancing the one with the others, weeding out here, adding there, and, with his keen musical insight, strengthening the entire body and making of it a rounded and perfectly balanced orchestra. There is but one other orchestra in the country that has the sina qua non of possible perfection—daily rehearsals—and that is the Boston Symphony. The Metropolitan Orchestra has had this advantage over all of its competitors—it has been drilled in operatic as well as symphonic and other purely classic music. Its repertoire is tremendous. In its personnel it is as nearly suited to the requirements demanded as it is possible to make an organization of its kind. There are no orchestral players in the world who receive the salaries that are paid its members. Each of its men is a solo artist.

The reference to the high salaries paid the members of the orchestra was repeated throughout the land in the course of the tours on which Duss now took the orchestra, but never was any mention made of the fact that these high salaries were paid out of the sweat and toil of the hard-working honest members of the Harmony Society. Inevitably there would be the statement in the press release that Duss had found the Society heavily indebted and he had saved it from financial ruin. When the Works Projects Administration began its extensive "clean-up work" in the Great House at Ambridge during the Depression, it still found great stores of Duss publicity material that had been prepared and used on this and other tours. Here is a partial list of mimeographed material which Duss's staff sent out ahead of his arrival and then handed out again to each reporter who came to his generous and talkative interviews:

HOW TO PRONOUNCE THE GREAT BAND LEADER'S NAME.
WHO THE DEUCE IS DUSS?
DUSS, THE GREAT CONDUCTOR PRAISES WOMEN.
PEN PICTURES OF A FAMOUS BAND MASTER.
DUSS AND A FEW DUSSISMS.
DUSS ON MUSIC.
DUSS DIDN'T KNOW IOWA WAS "EAST."
DUSS, NORDICA AND THE SCRIBE.
DUSS VERSUS AFFECTATION AND COMPLIMENT.

By bombarding reporters with such material, he often managed to get into print exactly what he wanted the papers to say about him, and as a result many of the newspaper reports, particularly those from the Southern States, where the newspapers either had less capable or lazier reporters, printed reviews of his concerts which are almost identical. The original parts of these reports are often limited to sweet and friendly Southernisms returning Duss's compliments made to the audience in the course of his speeches, "sugah for sugah." Here is the text of "Duss, Nordica and the Scribe," which Duss's agents prepared to counteract the general skepticism about his ability as conductor. Many reporters in the various places visited found it easy to fill their columns quickly by making it part of their report:

Mme. Nordica, while touring as soloist with J. S. Duss and his Orchestra, became acquainted with the editor and owner of one of the leading daily papers in one of the cities visited. Not taking part in the afternoon concert, Mme. Nordica attended the same, sitting beside the newspaper man.

The gentleman was versed in the knowledge of music to enable him to be somewhat above the average music critic. As the people came streaming into the auditorium, he turned to Mme. Nordica and said: "I must confess that I am prejudiced against this man Duss." "Why so?" asked the genial diva. "From what I heard of him," replied the editor, "he is a born business man." "Well," said the singer, "now is your opportunity to see him as the artist."

As the concert progressed—and with each number increasing enthusiasm, the most prejudiced was forced to acknowledge a Duss ovation, pure and simple; the man's magnetic strength and artistic insight compelled one to take his finished interpretation as authoritative. Inquiringly, Mme. Nordica turned to the scribe, but before she could more than look her question, he remarked, "Duss is a great conductor." This conversation, at least the editor's part of it, was repeated in his paper the next day. As Duss and his associates were about to leave the city, the editor with a party of friends called to bid farewell to the talented company. Duss greeted the newspaper men cordially and referring to his novel article in that morning's issue said: "I am surprised that you could have been prejudiced by what you read in the newspapers, for my observation has led me to think that it is the exception rather than the rule for editors or critics to agree. It is the accepted theory that this characteristic is possessed only by the musicians, but now that you confess 'seeing, hearing, is believing' I shall be glad to propose your name and advocate your admission to our fraternity."

Amid the general laughter that followed, as the car moved out of the depot—the converted editor called—"Mr. Duss, if ever you get tired of conducting I'll be glad to make room for you on my staff."

Duss's Metropolitan Opera House Orchestra tour with Nahan Franko, Concert Master, and Madame Nordica and M. De Reszke as soloists, included also Miss Electra Gifford, Soprano, and Romayne Simmons at the piano, and had a business staff which included a treasurer, a press representative, a special booking and advance agent, an advertising agent, an advance representative, a stenographer, and a baggage man.

The tour, which began in Scranton on April 29 and ended with Duss's opening at his reconstructed Venice in Madison Square Garden on May 31, included these cities: Reading, Washington, Baltimore, Wilmington, Columbia, Charlotte, Asheville, Knoxville, Atlanta, Nashville, Memphis, St. Louis, Kansas City, Topeka, Lincoln, Omaha, Des Moines, Davenport, Milwaukee, Detroit, Cleveland, Utica, Syracuse, Buffalo, Toronto, Ottawa, Montreal, Troy, and Hartford.

Conductor Duss was directing the Metropolitan House Orchestra in Convention Hall at Kansas City, Missouri, on May 12 when his wife, Susie, called a meeting of all members of the Harmony Society to consider important business. Without the backing of the Supreme Court's decision they would not have dared to venture on such business. Attending the meeting were: Franz Gillmann, age 74, Christina Schöenemann-Rall, age 81, Susie C. Duss, age 44, and Barbara Boesch, age 87. The minutes of the meeting were recorded as usual by Wagner, Duss's faithful servant. At their request the following were also present: Henry Hice, Charles A. Dickson, Louisa Schumacher, and Agnew Hice. At the request of Mrs. Duss, Mr. Wagner explained to the members in German that John S. Duss had asked to be permitted to resign from the Society, likewise from the Council of Elders, and at the same time lay down his office of Trustee. This request was presented in writing and reads as follows:

To the Council of Elders of the Harmony Society: The undersigned, a member of the Council of Elders and Trustee of the said Society herewith submits his resignation as member of the said Council of Elders and as Sole Trustee of said Society, and requests that it be accepted and approved. Economy, Pa., May 12, 1903. John S. Duss. [See Harmony Society Minutes, 1899–1903]

Franz Gillmann, the other member of the said Council of Elders, hereupon elected Susie C. Duss as member of the Council of Elders of the Harmony Society, by virtue of the powers of the same. Further, Wagner, at the request of Susie C. Duss, explained that as Christine Schoenemann-Rall was being cared for by her daughter, Mrs. Louisa Schumacher, also that it was the wish of Mrs. Rall in future to enjoy the same personal care and attention of Mrs. Schumacher, and that in view of the circumstances it seemed advisable to give Mrs. Schumacher a present, consisting of seventy-five bonds of the Liberty

Land Co., which are property of the Harmony Society, and that this present should be made after the death of Mrs. Rall, provided she dies as member of the Society, and also under the condition that Mrs. Schumacher gives her mother, Mrs. Rall, the desired care and attention.

Hereupon a request of John S. Duss to withdraw from the membership of the Harmony Society was read, as follows: "The undersigned, member of the Harmony Society, submits herewith his wish to withdraw from membership in the Harmony Society herewith declaring that it is his wish and intention to move away from Economy, and to receive a present from the Trustee of the Society, according to the custom of the Society. Economy, Pa. May 12, 1903. John S. Duss." And it is considered advisable, that, all circumstances being considered, it be advisable to give said John S. Duss a present of five hundred (500) bonds of the Liberty Land Company. After all this and the preceding had been discussed and fully understood, Christine Schoenemann Rall made the following proposal:

That the resignation of John S. Duss as member of the Council of Elders as well as Trustee and the election of Susie C. Duss as member of the Council of Elders and as Trustee of the Harmony Society, and the request of John S. Duss to withdraw from the Society and the intended purpose of the present new Trustee to give Mrs. Louisa Schumacher a present consisting of seventy-five (75) bonds of the Liberty Land Company, and the said John S. Duss at his separation from said Society a present of five hundred (500) bonds of the Liberty Land Company, individually and together are herewith accepted, confirmed, and approved, and the Trustee is instructed to execute all this; also to take care that the necessary legal documents are set up, executed and signed for said purposes. This proposal was supported by Franz Gillmann and all members were in agreement with it. A document was then presented containing the nomination and election of Susie C. Duss as Sole Trustee of the Harmony Society through the Council of Elders, and containing the confirmation of this by all members of said Society; the same was then signed by all members. Close of the session. K. R. Wagner.

This is the last entry in the book of minutes of the Society. A clever legal gimmick had been used, thanks to the U. S. Supreme Court's decision, whereby Duss got five hundred thousand dollars for withdrawing and moving away while he was already enjoying himself as "Conductor" of one of the world's greatest orchestras. But he actually continued to live at Economy and enjoyed the wealth of the Society in addition to his "present" whenever he desired. All this was transacted while he was on tour.

Most of the music critics who reported on the Duss tour saw through the entire show and recognized that the first concert master of the Metropolitan Opera House Orchestra was in fact directing the concerts, quietly and without a smile, permitting Duss to go through his gymnastics and pose as their head. It took Atlanta, Georgia, to provide the social scandal of the tour. It occurred to several leaders of Atlanta Society that it would be a nice thing to entertain the singers on the Duss tour, so Mme. Nordica and M. de Reszke were invited and they accepted the invitation. Elaborate preparations were made for the affair. Society folk were on hand to meet the artists, but they did not appear. Nor did they send excuses, because they had discovered that their bread-and-butter man John S. Duss had not been invited.

The climax of the tour had been planned as the New York summer season at Madison Square Garden with its rebuilt Venice. Here is the way the New York *Daily News* of May 31, 1903, heralded the event:

NEW YORK'S VENICE UNDER DUSS' REIGN

Metropolitan Orchestra and Grand Opera Stars at the Garden tonight. There is a new constellation in the heavens. It needs no telescope to see it. It is of the first magnitude. It shines like a crown of glory over the Northeast corner of Madison Square. At the feet of Miss Minerva, and to those who can translate the language of the stars it reads as DUSS. It will be a gala night tonight. Madame Nordica will be there, and M. Edouard de Reszke, and a chorus of 1,000 voices. These 2 artists will make it the occasion of bidding New York Au revoir, and they will sing, of course, the songs for which 9 out of 10 of their hearers would clamor. The Orchestra fresh from a tour of conquest of the West and North, are in fine fettle and the concert will be a great one. Duss will hold the Garden for the Summer with a unique idea of "Venice in New York."

The *New York Herald* of June 1, 1903, reported the opening night in greater detail:

Mme Nordica was the heroine of the opening of Mr. J. S. Duss' "Venice in New York" at Madison Square Garden last night. She made her entrance in a startlingly dramatic fashion in a gondola and after a superb rendition of the "Inflammatus" from Rossini's "Stabat Mater" thrilled the thousand auditors in the Garden by singing as an encore "The Star Spangled Banner." As the first notes of the national anthem rang out clear and true the great audience rose to its feet and joined with the trained voices of the Metropolitan Opera House chorus in the chorus of the song. At its conclusion the enthusiasm was intensified when Mme Nordica made her exit through the Canal on a gondola. Her admirers on "The Island" and in the promenade section bombarded her with bouquets and the whole audience cheered as she stepped from the boat and disappeared behind the scenes. De Reszke entered over the "Bridge of Sighs." It was a great night for Mr. J. S. Duss, the bandmaster from Economy, Pa. for he wielded his baton over the superb Metropolitan Orchestra and you could see by the easy manner in which he accomplished the feat that he could do it with his eyes blindfolded. Of course, Mr. Nahan Franko was there, and Mr. Duss graciously allowed the concert master one chance to publicly direct the musicians. The Metropolitan Opera chorus gave a superb rendition of Handel's "Hallelujah Chorus" from the "Messiah" and other numbers on the programme were handled as only the Metropolitan Opera Orchestra can handle them. At the end of the programme the audience joined enthusiastically with Mr. Duss in singing "America." As to "Venice in New York"—well, there is a "Grand Canal," not as deep as a well and just about as wide as a church door, but it will do. Then there are real gondolas, with gondoliers from Dever's district. The scenery is very blue sky, with moving clouds and twinkling little stars. There is a bridge over the canal that leads to an island in the center of the Garden and stationed upon it are 2 gendarmes. The houses in this scenic Venice are sadly mixed. True, there is a so-called Palace of the Doges and 1 or 2 other palaces, but there are also some buildings that might have sprung from the brains of Tammany's prize architect. However, there are electric fans to keep you cool, electric lights in subdued hues and good music by the Metropolitan Orchestra under its new conductor, Mr. J. S. Duss of Economy, Pa. It was a great night for Mr. Duss, as his audience was truly representative of New York. It came from 5th Avenue and from the fashionable hotels and from every section of the city. Tonight the Metropolitan Orchestra will play, Mr. Duss will conduct, Mme Macond will sing, Mr. Franko will give a violin solo, and refreshments will be sold to those who wish them. Venice will then become Coney transferred to Manhattan.

Venice brought Duss a great deal of publicity, but it was the last summer that the Metropolitan Orchestra played for him under that coveted name.

The *Pittsburgh Leader* on July 26, 1903, published an extensive illustrated account of "Venice which the genius of a Pittsburger has fashioned out of Madison Square Garden." Here is the text of the report. It represented Duss at the zenith of his musical career:

I have just come from Venice. The blue waters of the Adriatic carried me around and around, past the palace of the doges, before the majestic Campanile, beyond the San Giorgio church, in front of the Palazzo de Vendramin, where the world's greatest master of the music drama, Wagner, passed his last hours on earth; the home of fair Desdemona, who married the Moor, Othello, and died by his jealous hand; in short I have feasted my eyes upon the matchless beauties of old Venetian architecture, fraught with the songs and stories that have had so much to do with the world's history.

I happened to be passing down Broadway in the city of New York the other night when my eyes were attracted by a myriad of incandescent lights which flashed out the name of "Duss" and the one word "Venice." So I just stepped in out of modern New York into ancient Venice.

It was a revelation of scenic beauty, a masterpiece of spectacular cunning, the very acme of stagecraft, was this reproduction of the famed city of the doges. Madison Square Garden has been more than transformed; it has been rewrought into a replica in miniature of the poetic city by the Adriatic. I had heard about this Venice which John Duss, of Pittsburg and Economy, had contrived as a unique setting for his engagement with the orchestra of the Metropolitan opera, and had conceived a cheap, tawdry, tinseled picture drawn to please the eye, but with no regard for historical fact or the truth of nature and art. But I was mistaken. Before I heard a note from the instruments of the orchestra or the throats of the soloists, before even the versatile Duss had stepped into the halo of incandescents that throws its sheet of light from ten columns of genuine Venetian marble, I had taken off my hat to the genius whose unique idea was here exploited, whether Duss himself, his manager Johnston, or the scenic artist Voegtlin, I did not know or care. I stood in old Venice and that sufficed.

Entering the garden my eyes fell upon the splashing waters of a real lagoon in which moved genuine gondolas propelled by the sturdy oar strokes of a Venetian. Stepping forward I was ushered up the gradual ascent of a bridge whose architecture was the classic style of old Venice. From this bridge, which forms the entrance to the island, the beholder gets his best view of the miniature city of Venice. At the extreme end of the garden the artist has painted a realistic view of the Adriatic with characteristic bits of Venetian scenery. Three or four fishing boats, with idly flapping sails, lay at anchor in the harbor; a portion of the public gardens are shown, and two narrow streets wind in and out between the buildings and are entered by ivy-clad gates leading in from the promenade. This promenade follows the outer edge of the real canal in its oval course around the immense auditorium. Two bridges cross the canal, one at the entrance already described, and the other in front of the scenic picture. The latter is used by Mr. Duss and his players to reach their raised platform. . . .

Duss's Madison Square Garden season was a great popular success. Although Duss had spent between $75,000 and $100,000 on the transformation of Madison Square Garden, and although he was paying the Metropolitan Orchestra the highest wages paid anywhere, prices were kept to a popular minimum, because the project was heavily subsidized by Harmony Society funds. With the help of Duss's high-pressure publicity manager, attendance was kept up satisfactorily through the hot summer. An early form of air conditioning and the sale of beverages helped keep the temperature well below the level of heat outside, and that added to the attraction. On page 382 of his *The Harmonists, A Personal History,* Duss gives the following example of the kind of publicity stunts used to keep himself and his project in the news:

One lovely summer evening I was conducting the orchestra in Saint-Saëns' *Danse Macabre.* Under the influence of this deeply melancholy "Dance of Death," the audience sat very still. Suddenly I heard a commotion behind me, and the orchestra, almost to a man, stretched necks and gaped toward one point in the arena, neglecting to perform. Continuing to conduct and to sing until I brought the men back into line, we finished the selection; whereupon I turned to my illustrious concertmeister, Nahan Franko, with the question-mark in my eye, to which he replied: "Somebody fell into the canal, or tried to commit suicide."

The whole thing had been prearranged by the press again, and the stunt worked to Duss's satisfaction, for the next day the press carried a romantic story, also arranged and "embellished with all sorts of trimmings," of a young and lonely Iowa girl who leaned too far over the side of the gondola and fell head-long into the canal, and how a gallant gentleman arrayed in full dress plunged to her rescue (the water was only three feet deep). Duss concludes: "A clever publicity hoax, engineered for fifty dollars by our efficacious press agent. . . . But it worked."

After his "Venice in New York" Duss took the Metropolitan Opera House Orchestra on a tour to the West, visiting such cities as Indianapolis, Omaha, Denver, Salt Lake City, Tacoma, Seattle, Portland, Sacramento, and San Francisco.

The great star and top attraction of this tour was Mme. Nordica. She was a gracious lady who well knew how to let a little of her glory reflect upon the glory-famished Conductor Duss, who was always so eagerly trying to share her limelight. The following episode may illustrate this. The press agent had managed to get some publicity for Duss by press notices about a quarrel between "Professor J. S. Duss, the famous orchestral conductor" and Mme. Nordica. Both Duss and Nordica played their parts well, as the *Baltimore American* report of October 6, 1903, shows:

Mme. Nordica was seated in one of the dressing-rooms fanning herself when approached. After learning the nature of the visit, she denied the story in toto.

"Where do such stories originate?" she remarked, inquiringly, and then, without waiting for an answer, said, with a smile, but in a tone that carried enough of sarcasm to make it doubly interesting, "Mr. Duss, we will have to investigate and find out what our troubles are."

Madame was plainly in a charitable frame of mind as well as a good humor, and in speaking of the rather small attendance and in reply to a remark that many well-known people were still out of town, remarked: "Yes, it is early in the season, and it is still quite warm, too."

In addition to her other jewels, Mme. Nordica wore three magnificent jewel and gold decorations pinned to her bodice, and Mr. Duss spoke of these, remarking that one, a gold medallion hanging on a ribbon from a diamond pendant, had been presented to Mme. Nordica during her visit this summer to Munich by the Prince Regent of Bavaria, with the stipulation that the decoration must be returned to the government at the death of the great singer.

One other decoration worn was conferred upon Madame Nordica while in Germany by the Duke of Edinburgh, and a third was presented by the Crown Prince of Wales from the Royal Society of Music of Great Britain.

Madame Nordica interrupted Mr. Duss to remark: "The Professor wears a handsome decoration given to him by his orchestra today." She explained, with a smile toward Mr. Duss that conveyed only the most friendly impressions, that the conductor had received the gift, as a mark of esteem on the part of those whom he has so successfully directed. The gift is in the shape of a medal, worn about the neck by a red, white and black ribbon. It consisted of a gold and enamel lyre, set in the middle with a splendid specimen of the white diamond, on the four sides of the pendant protruding the ends of gold trumpets.

On October 7, 1903, the Indianapolis *Morning Star* highlighted "NORDICA IN HER DRESSING ROOM. Great Singer Closely Guarded by Maid, Valet and her 'General Factotum.' HER WHITE SATIN GOWN ABLAZE WITH JEWELS. Conductor Duss Gives Her $1,500 a Night, but Says She Wanted $2,000." Again the medal given her by the Prince Regent of Bavaria was pointed out to the reporters, and again Duss was there to share her glory:

Conductor Duss, the most unique musical figure in America, and the most democratic of men in his position, stood at the door chatting with The Star as genially as if he were not already worth $4,000,000 and certain heir to $10,000,000 more.

The newspaper man, not being certain of his identity, inquired whom he had the honor of addressing.

"I am the whole thing."

"You are Mr. Duss?" (Giving the "u" the sound of the letter in "us.")

"No, I am Duss" (using the "u" as in "you").

"Does Nordica really get $2,000 a night?"

"She gets $1,500. I know, for I pay her." She wanted $2,000.

"Weren't you afraid to come to Indianapolis? You know it has the name of being—"

"A bad city musically," said Mr. Duss, completing the sentence. "I said we would visit some towns like that and make the people want to come. I carry the finest orchestra on tour. Of course it is more expensive travelling by special train as I do."

The *Indianapolis News* of the same date called Nordica's

singing "great" and described it as "The Really Serious Part" of the program. It commented on Duss "as a speaker." "The extra numbers were some of them two-steps (by Duss) and some of them speeches by Mr. Duss. The two-steps were interesting, but the speeches more so. Mr. Duss seized every available opportunity to address his audience, and was plainly disappointed that only three opportunities came. 'In half a minute I'll become a comedian,' he remarked, not realizing apparently that with his patriotic neck ornament, his funny conducting and his style of bowing with the baton across his knees, jockeywise, he had already stepped well into the comedian's role."

The Indianapolis Journal of the same date reported "BIG CROWD SAW DUSS. MILLIONAIRE MUSICIAN AMPLY REPAID THEIR CURIOSITY.—Duss Makes Two or Three Speeches." The most perspicacious review, however, has already been mentioned, namely, the one by Paul Erdmann Teichert in the *Indianapolis Sentinel* of October 7, 1903. This paper summarized the event in these headlines above two articles which elaborated on them: DUSS CAME, SAW, AND HIS ORCHESTRA CONQUERED. Noted Conductor Has Money, Brains and Love of Music, Says Teichert, But His Musicians Direct Themselves.—Mme. Nordica Pleases Audience. The other headline: MME. NORDICA WEARS A WEALTH OF JEWELS. Noted Prima Donna Presents a Dazzling Appearance at Duss Concert Tuesday Night—Retinue of were times in the concert when undoubted confusion reigned Servants Attends Her in Her Palatial Private Car.

The Milwaukee Sentinel commented that "Duss is not satisfying in scholarship or his style of conducting," that the orchestra "lacked authority," for which Duss "evidently was not blameless," and pointed out that Nahan Franko speedily redeemed the Wagner number (Parsifal Vorspiel). The *Milwaukee Evening Wisconsin,* remarking on the late arrival of Mr. Duss, offered the explanation that "he was trying, probably, to arrange the red, white and blue ribbon supporting the decorations, about his neck—but Mr. Franko, the concert meister, took the band through the opening number, and he did it well—in a quiet musicianly manner." This paper also commented that Duss lacked scholarship and that if he were a conscientious musician he would think more of the work of the composer and less of the arts of Duss.

On October 9, the *St. Paul Pioneer Press* reported that there and the orchestra swung along on its own responsibility, or again rushed to a climax ahead, or took its time and came in behind its leader. "Mr. Duss is theatrical in manner, and the stagey whirls of his baton are disconcerting and bewildering, and have a peculiar syncopated method of marking the time peculiar to themselves." The *St. Paul Daily News* again spoke of the millionaire and business man who retained the alertness of the counting room, a man "you might judge, as could corner the wheat market as easily as he could direct a symphony or write a sonnet." It called for stricter discipline in the orchestra to enable it move with more certainty through various compositions, and it wanted more careful selection of music, more classics rather than the popular in an orchestral concert. In Milwaukee Duss had actually been hissed for offering so many popular numbers.

Newspaper reports of performances in Denver, Butte, Salt Lake City, and Seattle were less critical of Duss, but always Nordica is the featured performer. In Salt Lake City again, Duss's press agents managed to get him a lot of personal publicity in connection with the Harmony Society, but in general, when the critics got down to serious musical reporting, they headlined NORDICA as the most gifted and the most genuine artist of all.

In San Francisco it was Ashton Stevens of the *San Francisco Examiner* and caricaturist Igoe who were most fascinated by Duss as a new phenomenon on the stage. Igoe has left us with vivid illustrations of Duss in San Francisco and Ashton Stevens reports so accurately and yet so generously that his account with headlines must follow here:

NORDICA, THE DIVA, IN COMPANY OF THAT MILLIONAIRE CONDUCTOR—HOW DUSS PLAYED METROPOLITAN ORCHESTRA—A Musical Function of Unusual Merit Introduced by a Moderate Disaster That Elicited Some Stray Eloquence.— by Ashton Stevens.

In the Alhambra last night the great Nordica sang as she always sings, and Duss played the Metropolitan Opera House orchestra—

that is, when it was not playing him. And almost as many people as the theatre could hold made an enthusiastic night of what had promised to be a fizzle; for the opening note was not sounded till ten minutes after 9 o'clock.

The organization had played a matinee at Stanford University, and the already belated baggage, which included the orchestra scores, and possibly the fraternal decoration that Mr. Duss wears at his chest, had miscarried. While the baggage was being recovered, Max Hirsch, the young but veteran treasurer of the Metropolitan Opera House, entertained the crowd with a small speech descriptive of the disaster, the effect of which was soothing and amiable. Society, which came in at least forty carriages and was brightly if not operatically attired (who would dare write a notice of this kind that contained no mention of Society and the clothes?), filled in the waiting with the customary mots and epigrams. Oaklanders put up their watches and politely tried to appear to be something else. The eager "last-boat" face was nowhere to be seen. Mr. Hirsch's speech was a great success.

At 9:10 to the minute Mr. Duss appeared in the leader's stand. Tall, darkish, smooth-shaven, eye-glassed and of a wonderful serious-ness of manner, he was from the start something entirely new and different in the way of a leader. He looked more like a lawyer than a leader, and if I may continue the figure, there was something legal-like in his handling of his hands, and something of the old-school lawyer's courtesy in the elaborateness and pride of his bow. And of a sudden he limbered; high went the stick at the end of his right arm, forward shrugged his shoulders, and then his whole body swayed like a long tree, and his two arms swung and raised and lowered and twisted to the rhythm of *Elgar*'s "With Pomp and Cir-cumstance."

I dare say that Mr. *Elgar*'s march, written in celebration of the latest of the English kings, is a good one; but in the first sight I all but forgot the incidental music. Mr. Duss was such an absorbing drama that for the time being nothing else mattered. I could not have been more enthralled visually had Mr. J. Pierpont Morgan been holding the baton. Mr. Duss, you know is a millionaire. Some millionaires fancy yachts, others automobiles, still others racing stables and such; but this one fancies a fine big orchestra made up of some of the best bandsmen in the country. Talk about delight-ful toys!

Attached to Mr. Duss' organization is a literary bureau, largely biographical and critical of himself. I was full of the product of this bureau. I had the official estimate of Mr. Duss—authorized by him-self—in my head and in my pocket, and being just a little bit of a musical one myself I found no difficulty in transposing it from the key of "He" to that of "Me." This is the result: "I (J. P. Duss) have

lived for the most part in a small Pennsylvania town, where I rapidly became a leading figure in the business life and carried to
success gigantic enterprises aggregating millions of dollars. The same
qualities that made my fortune have won me notable triumphs in
the field of music, always working toward realizing my chief ambition—that of orchestral conductor. I have studied music since I was
six years old, played in turn every string and wind instrument, and
heard all the world's best music. It is not strange, therefore, with
such an equipment, material and artistic, that I have scored success
from the first that has been little less than phenomenal."

With Mr. Duss' acting in my eyes and his autobiography filling
the rest of my head, was it a wonder I was slow in settling down to
the business of the night?

Even now I approach the matter in anything but the right calm,
authoritative, infallible judgment. I know that musically I do not
hold the aggregator of millions in the same esteem as he holds himself. I think some of the stock is watered. Businessman to businessman,
he will pardon me if I knock off say fifty per cent. That still leaves
him a leader that is only quite as good as Mascagni or the late Anton
Seidl, and a very likable one at that.

For in spite of his seriousness and his gestures and the lodge-token
on his chest, Mr. Duss is likable. In such a big undertaking as the
Vorspiel to "Parsifal" he is wise enough to keep his gestures from
interfering with the real work of Seidl's old band. Every movement
is a picture, but not an imperative command. The bandsmen smile,
but just the same they attend to business, as a business man would
have them do. And in the lighter pieces they give the boss full swing,
and he sounds a brisk, popular personality. So long as you do not
take him as seriously as he would appear to take himself, praising
Mr. Duss is not the hardest thing in the world to do. And in his
makeup there is just enough of the freakish to tempt the whole
town to see him. The band is a wonder, and Nordica—there is only
one Nordica.

Stevens returned to Duss's concert the next day, which was
attended by a small audience, but now Duss aroused his admiration because while he may have "carried to success gigantic
enterprises aggregating millions of dollars," yet he did not find
him mercenary as a leader. For a large audience or for a small
one he waved his baton with equal zeal. He found his gestures
quite as large as before and of an even greater variety than
those of the opening concert. "Mr. Duss," he wrote,

fits the action to the piece; there is never an instant of monotony in his posing. I cannot overestimate when I say that he has command over a thousand signals. I do not say that these signals have absolute command over the members of the Metropolitan Opera House Orchestra, but obviously they mean a great deal to the new leader, and no amount of indifference, or even smiles, on the part of his bandsmen would seem to discourage his wig-wagging. For the time being the organization belongs to Mr. Duss, he pays the salaries and plays the band. It is his privilege to be the pianola attachment on the Metropolitan orchestra. And he loves it. Sometimes I fancy him singing as he swings:

> I love to be the leader of the band,
> I love to have the baton in my hand,
> I love to make the fiddles wail and moan—

But not to deface the facts for a bit of pleasantry, I hasten to add that Mr. Duss is a pianola only in such big pieces as are beyond the scope of his personal technique, so to say. His Wagner performances, for instance, are stenciled. Into them he does not introduce any of his own eccentric virtuosity, and 'tis better so.

The Rochester, N. Y. *Post Express,* in writing about Duss's San Francisco performance, thought that his gift of humor had never been adequately recognized, for when the audience there vigorously applauded Strauss's "Don Juan," Duss was so pleased that he responded with the polka from Delibes' "Sylvia."

Although with less humor, the above well represents the consensus of all the critics hearing Duss in the San Francisco area. The *San Francisco Call* gave the orchestra credit for playing compositions well but hastened to add that it lacked leadership. From San Francisco Duss took his tour to Los Angeles, Dallas, Galveston, Houston, Little Rock, and Chicago, where one critic wrote: "To watch him conduct is to become impressed, semi-occasionally, that he does not know exactly what he is doing, but the players get through all right, and therefore we should not quarrel with the leader, even though he may make all sorts of unnecessary motions."

When Duss returned to New York City a lot of trouble was awaiting him. One of Maurice Grau's famous singers, Edouard de Reszke,[1] figured in an action for $20,000 damages against Duss, and the incident stirred up no end of talk in New York's musical circles. The process servers were unable to find Duss, for although he had stated in his request for a departing present from the Harmony Society that he planned to move away from Economy, he was now "back home in Economy." The suit brought against Duss was for alleged breach of contract with De Reszke, who charged that he was engaged by the Duss interests for a series of at least 20 concerts. He was to be paid $1,000 a concert. He claimed he was not allowed to sing and was not taken on the tour just concluded. Included in the suit was Mr. Johnston as the manager for Duss.

Duss and Johnston had embarked in the theatrical business as partners that fall, the papers reported. They put out a number of attractions. Among others, Carrie Nation (1846–1911) figured as one of the star features then touring the one-night stands in the poetic drama "Ten Nights in a Barroom." Nordica and De Reszke were under the same management but the latter was scratched because Duss felt he did not "take" with the audience. Johnston was cornered by the reporters and advanced the cause of their publicity by refusing to talk on this issue and about reported losses connected with their ventures. He claimed he did not know where Duss was. Soon after, the reporters caught up with Duss in Economy, where he said: "Yes. It's De Reszke's move and not mine. I am right here in Economy, at home, and anybody can find me at any time. Of course, I have been about my own business—not in New York, not in Pittsburgh, not in Economy—but I have been traveling under the broad light of the sun and am here and at home to all who have errands with me. If the process-server, who is said to have been on my trail, failed to find me—well, that isn't my fault." Duss then refused to talk about the suit beyond stating that he was guarantor for Johnston. The case was probably settled out of court by an assignment of some Harmony Society bonds to De Reszke, because even years later such bonds can be traced bearing his name.[1]

Another lawsuit involving Duss was brought by his manager in behalf of Duss against the new manager of the Metropolitan Opera House. The Pittsburgh *Post* of November 14, 1903, gave this interesting report:

Conried must settle with Duss.

Added to his litigation over "Parsifal" and his troubles with his various operatic stars, Manager Heinrich Conried, of the Metropolitan Opera House has now locked horns with John S. Duss, who promises to make things lively for the new impresario before the season is over. Mr. Duss says he will play at the Metropolitan Opera House, Mr. Conried says he shall not, and there you are. While the argument is progressing, R. E. Johnston, manager for Duss, has started a suit against the German manager, and is already buying new clothes on the verdict he expects to get. Conried made a contract with Johnston to have Duss and his orchestra play at the Metropolitan for a series of 16 Sunday night concerts during the opera season. According to the terms of the contract, Conried was to receive a rental and a certain percentage of the receipts. Altogether when first viewed the contract certainly looked distinctly in favor of the theater manager, for Duss at Madison Square garden had proved that he could draw bigger crowds with an orchestra than he could with his band of brass. Johnston's shrewdness, however, was in making an early contract. Conried in perfecting his arrangements for the season, went at the task with a lavish hand. He executed a number of contracts with foreign orchestra leaders, and before he knew where he was he found himself with a lot of practically unnecessary material on his hands. He had more imported leaders than he knew what to do with. The only way out of the difficulty was to utilize some of them to fill in on Sundays. Of course it was not expected that they would be able to give the finished program of an orchestra kept specially for this purpose, but whatever the reasoning, Herr Conried notified Mr. Johnston that he would not be able to fulfill the contract he had made for Duss. The result was a few curt notes, a little argument, a failure to compromise, and the institution of a suit by Johnston. The Duss people demand big damages. They hold that on the strength of the contract with Conried they have engaged some of the biggest stars in the country to appear at these concerts in connection with the Duss orchestra, that they have already gone to considerable expense, and that they will be held to the contracts they have made. There is no doubt that the suit will be pressed to an issue. Duss, it is known, has paid large salaries for artists to appear at his concerts here, and he is prepared to exhibit the contracts he has made this time. Whether he will hold himself ready to fill the Metropolitan dates on Sunday nights and not appear anywhere else on these dates is not known. The musical people of New York take the Pittsburgh man quite seriously since he substituted his orchestra for his band. At first they were inclined to think he was rather eccentric, but later he became quite popular. At one time there was an agitation on foot to have him take the leadership of the Philharmonic orchestra, and again advances have been made for Duss to establish a permanent orchestra here.

As one looks back over the years of toil and sweat and priva-
tion which the Harmonists endured while the wealth was
amassed that made it possible for Duss to purchase one of the
world's most expensive toys for the gratification of his personal
vanity, one must say that there is a positive side to his eccentricity. Other millionaires built colleges, universities, and libraries with the money they controlled, yet others squandered
it on a dissolute life. Duss at least gave some excellent musicians
an opportunity to see the United States and to offer classical
and popular music to many cities which otherwise would not
have heard such a great voice as that of Mme Nordica, with her
royal jewels, or have heard the great Metropolitan Opera
Orchestra. Nor would the thousands sweltering in the heat of
New York City have found such an amusing and cooling refuge
from the heat of the sidewalks of New York as in Duss's Venice
in New York. Although effervescent and tragic as expender of
the Society's wealth, he could have softened the judgment of
history on his actions had he had the decency and humility to
state on each program from coast to coast:

These Metropolitan Opera House concerts and the heavenly voice
of Mme Nordica are brought to you by the courtesy of the Harmony
Society.

Even today the Metropolitan Opera takes time at each opera
broadcast to remind its audience, through a voice that has become symbolic of opera in the United States, that they are
hearing these great works by courtesy of a great oil company
whose products are at their disposal. Did the Harmony Society
deserve less recognition?

But Duss was too vainglorious to reflect on anything but himself, and this is most graphically illustrated by the following
revealing report:

DUSS' PRESS AGENT AT WORK

An edition de luxe of "Band Leader Duss," the crowning achieve-
ment of a wonderful press agent, has made its appearance. The book
is bound in a sort of snuff-yellow wall paper, with a hole cut in the
front cover to let the countenance of the bandmaster beam through.
Within, scattered through a score of pages of press notices, are 23
pictures of Duss, leading one to the inevitable conclusion that he

has a kodak concealed in every horn in his band. There is Duss in
repose, in action, in contemplation, in joy, as in Mendelssohn's
"Spring Song," riding with the Valkyries, in what Sentimental
Tommy called "the attitude of all geniuses about to have their
photographs taken," and as "the hatred killer." But the picture of
Duss seraphic is easily the best. It shows a two-thirds figure in profile,
the left hand holding the baton and the score of "Palm Branches,"
the right hand supporting the raised chin. The eyes have a look as
far away as Economy. On the rear cover is an Economized doric
pillar, adorned with a wreath of laurel and bearing the one word
"Duss."

Duss's astronomical fame as a great bandmaster and conductor did not last even as long as the money he got out of the
Harmony Society. He had another season in New York with his
Venice, but his orchestra was not again called the Metropolitan
Opera House Orchestra. Some of the newspaper reports I have
cited from critics from coast to coast shout that Barnum &
Bailey might have taken over the classics for a while during a
strange interlude, but the classical standard of quiet and serene
beauty (*Stille Einfalt und edle Grösse*) soon reestablished itself
and Duss returned to the level from which his sudden wealth
had thrust him. The Metropolitan regained its sense of dignity and decorum under solid German musical scholarship
and taste, and Duss went back to his uniform and band.

15

Dissolution and Desecration of Rapp's Divine Economy

AS EARLY AS 1893 DUSS AND RIETHMÜLLER HAD MOVED TO DIVIDE up and sell the home lands of the Harmony Society. They had advertised these lands for sale as follows:

ECONOMY LANDS FOR SALE

The Harmony Society offered for sale, in tracts to suit purchasers, its farm of three thousand acres adjoining Economy. These lands are situated sixteen miles from Pittsburgh. They have a front on the Ohio river of about three miles, and are intersected their entire length by the Pittsburgh, Ft. Wayne & Chicago railway. The Pittsburgh & Lake Erie railroad is on the opposite side of the river, and when the government locks on the upper Ohio are completed these lands will have transportation facilities afforded by two leading railways and a river navigable at all seasons of the year.

Twelve hundred acres of this land form a level, unbroken plateau, eighty feet above the river, which is flanked by a range of high hills covered by native forests and intersected by cool and shady ravines. This plateau is designed for suburban homes for citizens of Pittsburgh. It is thirty minutes' ride from the Union Passenger Station and has been surveyed and divided into spacious lots, which will be offered at reasonable prices and on easy terms for home and business purposes. The superb scenery of the Ohio valley at this point, the opportunities for fresh air, natural gas, pure water, shady recesses among the hills, good drainage and entire freedom from smoke and dirt, present attractions for a suburban city which are without a rival in the state. The best of brick, stone and other building material can be had in inexhaustible quantities at country prices on this farm.

Correspondence and personal interviews with real estate dealers and persons desiring to locate charitable and other public institutions, and especially those wishing a delightful country home at low cost and within easy distance of Pittsburgh, are respectfully invited. DUSS & RIETHMUELLER, Trustees, Economy, Beaver County, Pa.

Litigation and threat of the same delayed this method of liquidation for some time because it provided too clear evidence of the fact that the Society was being dissolved, or rather that it no longer existed as the Society which Rapp had founded as the Divine Economy, and such obvious moves toward dissolution made the "Society" vulnerable to attacks from descendants of members who had either voluntarily or against their will departed from the Society. This situation also brought worries about a clear title to the land, if purchased. In spite of lawsuits and threats of these, the legal masterminds kept working at the liquidation until on May 24, 1902, the Pittsburgh *Gazette* was able to publish the great news: that the American Bridge Company would construct a monster new structural bridge works in Beaver County, near Economy, on the Pittsburgh, Fort Wayne & Chicago railroad. Four works of the company were to be abandoned in Pittsburgh and McKees Rocks and possibly the Walker works at Homestead. Skirting the new works on the Pittsburgh side of Economy, a new town was planned which would provide homes for the 4,000 men to be employed there. The Pennsylvania Company would erect a new station on the Fort Wayne railroad. The American Bridge Company planned to build a modern hospital and hotel, and a new community would spring up. There was to be an office building erected by the bridge company, which alone would cost $150,000. Contiguous to the new works extensive yards were to be built for steel barge construction. The investment in works and town was to aggregate $3,500,000. The new plants near Economy were planned to handle 20,000 tons of material monthly, making them the greatest works of the kind in the world. The next greatest then was Pencoyd, near Philadelphia, which fabricated about 8,000 tons a month.

The site of these improvements was the 105 acres for the purchase of which the American Bridge Company began to negotiate with the Harmony Society in March of 1902. Purchase of this land would probably have been completed earlier but the United States Supreme Court had not yet given its decision in the Schwartz case and when that decision came it was by such a narrow margin that the Schwartz group made great efforts to bring about a second hearing before the Supreme Court. When these efforts failed, the deal was completed, although construction had started.

The American Bridge Company had already purchased the Berlin Bridge Works, which were built on 39 acres of land previously sold to that Company by the Harmony Society. That the deal with American Bridge was not completed until later is shown from the fact that Duss did not announce the completed purchase to the Society until the meeting of December 29, 1902.[1]

One of the new departures at the American Bridge Company plant to be built on this Harmony Society land was to be a great yard for construction of steel barges. There were to be seven large buildings, forge, machine, template, eyebar, assembling and riveting, receiving, and shipping buildings. Besides these there was to be a large group of smaller buildings, including power plant, paint shops and a number of others.[2]

With this American Bridge Company deal firmly settled, the process of buying out members of the Society and "accepting their resignation" with large departing gifts—so large that they gave every appearance of bribes—began in earnest, as already reported. Let us review the documents, beginning with the all-important Schwartz case decision.

October 27, 1902: The decision of the Supreme Court of the United States, in *Schwartz* v. *Duss*, 187 U.S. 8, wiped out any right in the heirs of deceased members, and in effect found that the primary object of all Harmony Society agreements was: "the complete and final consummation of communal ownership." One justice abstained; Chief Justice Fuller and Justice Brewer dissented and would have found for a resulting trust for the benefit of the heirs of deceased members and survivors.

December 29, 1902: Duss announced to the Harmony Society that the American Bridge Company had completed purchase of the 105 acres in which they were interested.

April 16, 1903: Previous articles of agreement confirmed in a legal document signed by the remaining members of the Society: Franz Gillman, Kathrina Nagel, Karoline Molt, Susie

C. Duss, Johanna Hermansdoerfer, Christina Schoenemann Rall, Barbara Boesch, and John S. Duss. This same document reduces the Board of Elders to two and declares them to be: John S. Duss and Franz Gillman.

April 16, 1903: As soon as the above document had been signed, the following offered their request to withdraw from the Society and "to receive from the Trustee of the Society a donation, in accordance with the usage of the Society":
Katharina Nagel, Karoline Molt, Johanna Hermansdoerfer The withdrawals were immediately accepted and each was granted a donation of $75,000.

April 17, 1903: Franz Gillmann, Christina Schoenemann Rall, and Susie C. Duss sign a document allowing Trustee J. S. Duss the right "according to his judgment" to use "the sums of $5,000, $10,000, $15,000 or $20,000, according to what he considers necessary, of the monies of the Harmony Society" for his musical undertakings.

May 12, 1903: Duss submits his resignation as member of the Board of Elders and as Sole Trustee of said Society, and requests the approval or acceptance of the same. Witnessed by Henry Hice, Charles A. Dickson, Agnew Hice, and K. R. Wagner, the remaining members of the Society, Franz Gillmann, Christina Schoenemann Rall, Susie C. Duss, and Barbara Boesch, accept this resignation. Duss was not present but was conducting the Metropolitan Opera House Orchestra at Convention Hall in Kansas City, Mo. As soon as this resignation had been accepted, Franz Gillmann (whom Harbison in his book on D. T. Watson, Duss's chief lawyer, called "a nearly imbecile old man"),[3] because he was the only remaining member of the Board of Elders, elected by his one vote Susie C. Duss as second member of the Board of Elders, "and both then elected Susie C. Duss Trustee of the Harmony Society, by virtue of the powers they had." Next Frau Schoenemann Rall was given a present of $75,000 with the understanding that this donation was to go to her daughter Mrs. Schumacher upon Mrs. Rall's death. Next, John S. Duss's request to withdraw from the Society and to receive a donation was presented and immediately approved with a present of $500,000.

The business of this momentous day was concluded with the

signing by the four remaining members of the following legal document:

WHEREAS, on the 12th day of May, A.D. 1903, John S. Duss, sole trustee of the Harmony Society at Economy, did resign his trust, which resignation was duly accepted, he having on the same day withdrawn from fellowship in said Society, whereupon upon due consideration, and in pursuance of the power in them vested, the Board of Elders did constitute and appoint Susie C. Duss the successor in trust of the said John S. Duss, as sole trustee of the said, The Harmony Society at Economy, and it is proper that sufficient evidence of such appointment, and of the acceptance of the trust thereunder, be entered of record in the Office of the Recorder of Deeds in and for the County of Beaver, in which County most of the lands of the said Society are situate, and in which other places as the business of said Society may require.

N O W THEREFORE, it is hereby witnessed, That Franz Gillman and Susie C. Duss, the now members of the Board of Elders of the Harmony Society, in pursuance of the power in them vested by and under the several agreements and contracts existing between the members of the said Society, do hereby make, constitute and appoint Susie C. Duss, a member of the said Society, and of its Board of Elders, sole Trustee of the said Society.

To have, hold, and exercise all the rights and powers conferred, and to discharge and perform all and singular the duties imposed upon and required of such sole trustee, in and by the several Articles of Association, and compacts of the members of said Society, as executed and adopted by them, and recorded in the Recorder's Office of Beaver County.

And Christina Schoeneman Rall, and Barbara Boesch, who with the said Franz Gillman and Susie C. Duss, are all the now members of said Society, and constitute the same, do hereby unite herein for the purpose of signifying their approval of the appointment of the said Susie C. Duss as hereinabove set forth.

IN WITNESS WHEREOF, we have hereunto set our hands and seals this 12th day of May, A.D. 1903.

Witness:	Franz Gillmann	(SEAL)
Charles Reeves May	Susie C. Duss	(SEAL)
K. R. Wagner	Members of, and constituting Board of Elders.
Agnew Hice	Franz Gillman	(SEAL)
	Susie C. Duss	(SEAL)
	Christina Schönemann Rall	(SEAL)
	Barbara Boesch	(SEAL)

STATE OF PENNSYLVANIA

SS.

County of Beaver.

Before the subscriber, a Notary Public in and for said County and State, came Franz Gillmann and Susie C. Duss, members of the Board of Elders of The Harmony Society, and the said Franz Gillman and Susie C. Duss, and Christina Schoeneman Rall and Barbara Boesch, the parties subscribing the foregoing instrument, and acknowledged the same to be their act and deed, and desired the same to be recorded as such.

Charles Reeves May
Notary Public

My Commission expires Febr. 12, 1905.

I, Susie C. Duss, a member of The Harmony Society, and a member of its Board of Elders, do hereby declare my acceptance of the appointment of myself as sole trustee of The Harmony Society, as made by its Board of Elders and approved by the members of the Society as set forth in the foregoing instrument.

IN WITNESS WHEREOF, I have hereunto set my hand and seal this 12th day of May, A.D. 1903.

Susie C. Duss   (SEAL)

Witness:
Charles Reeves May
Agnew Hice
K. R. Wagner
STATE OF PENNSYLVANIA

SS.

COUNTY OF BEAVER.

Before the subscriber, a Notary Public in and for said County, came Susie C. Duss, and acknowledged the foregoing Acceptance to be her act and deed and desired that the same might be recorded as such.

WITNESS my hand and Notarial seal this 12th day of May, A.D. 1903.

Charles Reeves May
Notary Public

My Commission expires Feb. 12, 1905.

Susie was now wearing Father Rapp's pants, and that she was determined to take care of her own interests while she had this power is attested to by two very interesting documents which seem to have been kept from the knowledge of former Trustee Duss. The great legal engineer of the Harmony Society dissolution, J. T. Brooks, had died in the meantime and $95,000 were still due his estate from the Harmony Society, which Susie conscientiously paid on May 23, 1903, as shown by the documents quoted below:

Pittsburgh, Pa., May 23, 1903.

RECEIVED from S. C. DUSS, Trustee of the Harmony Society, ninety-five thousand ($95,000) dollars in bonds of the Liberty Land Company, said bonds being numbered 1331 to 1425, inclusive, being balance in full due the estate of J. T. BROOKS, for special and extraordinary legal and other services rendered the Harmony Society for the period beginning about the month of December, 1892, and ending in October, 1901.

Witness   Annie M. Brooks
Charles T. Brooks   C. A. Dickson

Pittsburgh, Pa., May 23, 1903.

WHEREAS S. C. DUSS, Trustee of the Harmony Society, this day delivered C. T. BROOKS for Annie M. BROOKS Executrix of the Estate of J. T. BROOKS, dec'd, Ninety-Five (95) Bonds of the Liberty Land Company, said bonds being numbered 1331 to 1425 inclusive, being balance of Ninety-Five Thousand Dollars (95,000.00) in full of agreement and settlement for special and extraordinary services, legal or otherwise rendered by said J. T. BROOKS from about December 1892 to October 1901 to the Harmony Society, and

WHEREAS said ANNIE M. BROOKS, Executrix as aforesaid, desires that SUSIE C. DUSS shall have thirty (30) of said bonds for her own personal use and benefit, the same being part of the same settlement this day made,

NOW THEREFORE, in consideration of the delivery to Susie S. Duss of said Thirty (30) bonds of the Liberty Land Company, being numbered 1396 to 1425 inclusive, I hereby agree to save said ANNIE M. BROOKS AND her heirs harmless from any loss or expense that may hereafter fall upon said ANNIE M. BROOKS or her heirs by reason of the delivery to me of said Thirty (30) bonds. And I further agree to save said ANNIE M. BROOKS and her heirs harmless from any claim or claims that may be made by John S. Duss, late Trustee of the Harmony Society upon said ANNIE M. BROOKS OR HER HEIRS, by reason of the settlement above mentioned or the delivery to me of said Thirty (30) bonds.

S. C. DUSS, TRUSTEE.
(signed)

When I later showed former Trustee Duss a copy of the latter document and asked for some clarification, he wrote the following note on my copy: "This seems to be a suggestion typed. I know nothing of its being carried out. J.S.D." The document was by no means a suggestion but a record of a completed transaction. I did not press the point further so as not to endanger the safety of the records that remained.

On August 19, 1903, John S. Duss then made the Beaver County Trust Company trustee of all his property received from the Harmony Society in order that he might devote all his time to his musical interests. This document follows:

WHEREAS, I, John S. Duss, of Economy, Beaver County, State of Pennsylvania, am engaged in various musical undertakings, and expect to pursue the same as a musical director or otherwise, and for this reason have not the time in which to look after my business affairs, and am desirous of being relieved of the attention required thereby; and

WHEREAS, I also desire to make a provision for my wife and children in the event of my death.

NOW THEREFORE, Know All Men By These Presents, that I, JOHN S. DUSS, in consideration of the premises, and also of the natural love and affection which I bear to my wife and children, and to provide for their future needs and comfort, as also in consideration of the sum of one dollar to me paid, the receipt whereof is hereby acknowledged, do hereby sell, transfer, and set over (the delivery thereof being simultaneous with the delivery of this instrument) unto Beaver County Trust Company, Trustee, for the uses and purposes hereinafter mentioned, four hundred (400) bonds of the Liberty Land Company, a corporation of Pennsylvania, having its principal office in the City of Pittsburgh, in the State of Pennsylvania, each of said bonds being for the sum of one thousand ($1,000) dollars, and which are numbered from sixteen hundred one (1601) to two thousand (2000) both inclusive.

The purposes, uses and terms of the trust hereby created are as follows:

1. For the period of three years from the date hereof, to collect the interest and income of said bonds, and to pay the same to me, semi-annually.

2. In case of my death during the said term of three years, to deliver said bonds in equal parts to my wife, SUSIE C. DUSS, and my children, JOHN S. DUSS, Jr., and VERA DUSS; or, in case of the prior death of any of them, then to the survivor or survivors of them, in equal parts.

3. At the termination of said three years, at which time the trust hereby created shall terminate, to deliver said bonds to me (if I be then living), and upon delivery of my receipt for the same to the said Trustee, all and every duty and liability of the said Trustee shall cease and determine.

4. In case any of said bonds shall be paid off, the said Trustee shall invest the proceeds in good and safe securities, and my approval in writing of any investment selected by said Trustee shall be a full and

absolute protection to said Trustee against any claim for damage by reason of any loss that may be suffered because of such investment.

5. The delivery of the securities in which the trust estate may at the time of its termination be invested to the party or parties entitled thereto, shall be a full, absolute and complete discharge of the said Trustee; and the Trustee shall not be required to convert any of said investments.

6. The compensation of the Trustee shall be five per centum of the net annual income of the trust estate.

IN WITNESS WHEREOF, I have hereunto set my hand and seal this 19th day of August, A.D. 1903.

Witness:

MILO K. LIKE.   JOHN S. DUSS,   (SEAL)

August 21, 1903, By virtue of a Resolution of the Board of Directors of Beaver County Trust Company, this day adopted, the trust hereby created is hereby accepted, and the delivery of this instrument together with bonds of Liberty Land Company #1501 to 1900, in lieu of #1601 to #2000 is hereby acknowledged.

Attest: BEAVER COUNTY TRUST COMPANY,

AGNEW HICE, Secretary   By   F. G. BARKER, President

Less than a year after John S. Duss had thus freed himself completely of mundane affairs in order to devote himself fully to the enjoyment of his publicity and fame as conductor and bandmaster, Christina Schoenemann Rall died on April 15, 1904, thus assuring her daughter Mrs. Schumacher of the $75,000 inheritance which the Society on May 12, 1903, had so generously provided for her. On December 6, 1905, Barbara Boesch, who had been in bad health for a long time, also died, leaving the comparatively young Susie Duss alone with the "nearly imbecile" Franz Gillmann as the two surviving members of the Harmony Society. The decision then was made to dissolve George Rapp's divinely established Harmony Society. Those who reached this decision, of course, did not have the least conception of the divine purpose which had inspired Father Rapp and his Associates in the great work they had undertaken with such strong faith. That faith no longer lived in these material, and, by grace of the U.S. Supreme Court, legal heirs of George Rapp. And Susie C. Duss showed this changed character by her actions. First, the property of the Harmony Society was divided between the two survivors, quite harmoniously and legally, and then, quite legally, Franz Gillmann gave his half of the Harmony Society property back to Susie, making her the chief heir to the Harmony Society millions. To keep the historical record of this legal dissolution straight I herewith present these documents dissolving the century-old Harmony Society:

In view of the determination of the undersigned this day arrived at to dissolve the Harmony Society, of which they are the only members, they have on this 13th day of December, A.D. 1905, met together and have canvassed, counted and considered the property owned by said Society, and its several liabilities, and after a full consideration and examination of all their assets and accounts do make, and do hereby agree that said assets and liabilities are correctly and accurately set forth in the schedule marked Schedule "A," hereto attached and made part hereof.

They, and each of them, do likewise hereby express that they have severally received into their possession one full share and moiety of said assets, after making a due allowance for the liabilities, which said assets are set forth in two schedules, being Schedule "B," and Schedule "C," hereto attached, and all and every of the several assets mentioned and described in Schedule "B" have been received into severalty by me, Franz Gillman, and each and every of the assets mentioned and described in Schedule "C" have been received by me, Susie C. Duss, and we and each of us do severally acknowledge that we have taken the same into our several and separate possession.

WITNESS our hands and seals this 13th day of December, A.D. 1905.
WITNESSES:

s/ W. S. Dickson	s/ Susie C. Duss	(SEAL)
s/ Fred Knoedler	s/ Franz Gillman	(SEAL)
s/ John Stoffel		
s/ Charles Reeves May		

SCHEDULE "A".
ASSETS.
(Economy, Pa., December 13, 1905)

CASH ON HAND.

Deposit, Pittsburgh Trust Company,	3,287.58	
Deposit, Colonial Trust Company, New York	2,111.86	
Deposit, Beaver County Trust Company, New Brighton	9,533.34	
Deposit, John T. Reeves & Co., Beaver Falls, Pa.,	5,317.05	
Deposit, Real Estate Trust Co. of Pittsburgh	1,128.70	$ 21,378.53

BILLS RECEIVABLE.

C. A. Dickson	14,179.40	
Beaver County Land Company	5,599.74	
Agnew Hice	5,000.00	
Duss-Phinney Company Registered	43,000.00	
Gottlieb Kroll	84.00	
Joseph C. Bruff	134.03	$ 67,997.17

OPEN ACCOUNTS RECEIVABLE

Duss-Phinney Co., Registered (Interest)	775.00	
Mrs. Mary E. Spitzer	849.30	1,624.30

STOCKS.

Beaver County Land Co., 250 Shares	25,000.00

BONDS.

Liberty Land Company, 1,177 bonds,	1,177,000.00
HOUSEHOLD GOODS AND PERSONAL PROP- ERTY AT ECONOMY	
	$1,293,000.00

LIABILITIES.

BILLS PAYABLE.

Notes at Beaver County Trust Co.,	50,000.00	
Notes at John T. Reeves & Company,	25,000.00	
Note at Real Estate Trust Co. of Pitts- burgh,	18,000.00	93,000.00

NET WORTH	1,200,000.00

SCHEDULE "B".
(F.G.)
(Economy, Pa., December 13, 1905.)

Stocks. 13,000.00	
Bonds. 587,000.00	
ONE-HALF HOUSEHOLD GOODS AND PERSONAL PROPERTY AT ECONOMY	600,000.00

The above Schedule "B", is the Schedule "B" mentioned in the foregoing instrument signed by me.

Franz Gillmann
Dec. 13, 1905.

Witnesses:
W. S. Dickson
Fred Knoedler
John Stoffel
Charles Reeves May.

SCHEDULE "C".
(S.C.D.)
(Economy, Pa., December 13, 1905.)

Stocks	12,000.00	
Bonds	590,000.00	
Bills Receivable, See Schedule A,	67,997.17	
Cash, See Schedule A,	21,378.53	
Open Accts., Schedule A,	1,624.30	91,000.00
ONE HALF HOUSEHOLD GOODS AND ALL PERSONAL PROPERTY AT ECONOMY,		$ 693,000.00

The above Schedule "C" is the Schedule "C" mentioned in the foregoing instrument signed by me, and in accepting same I agree to pay the liabilities mentioned in Schedule "A".

                                        Susie C. Duss.
W. S. Dickson   Dec. 13, 1905
Fred Knoedler
John Stoffel
Charles Reeves May.

December 13, 1905: FRANZ GILLMANN GIVES HIS HALF OF THE HARMONY SOCIETY TO MRS. SUSIE C. DUSS.

WHEREAS, I, FRANZ GILLMAN, of Economy, Beaver County, Pennsylvania, having been for many years a member of the Harmony Society, which Society was by the mutual consent of the members thereof, namely Susie C. Duss and Franz Gillman, dissolved on this 13th. day of December, A.D. 1905, whereupon I received the full and equal one-half of the property of said Society, as shown by the Schedules and Receipts therefor signed by myself and Susie S. Duss, and

WHEREAS, I am now about seventy-six years of age, and have no kindred from whom I ever expect or desire to receive any attention or care, while on the other hand I have experienced during my declining years great kindness, consideration and care from Susie C. Duss, and she has expressed her intention of continuing the same consideration in the future which she has given me in the past, and I feel that to me there would be neither use nor advantage, but annoyance and care, in the ownership of so much property, and believe that under the circumstances I cannot better dispose of it than to give the same to the said Susie C. Duss, and I have determined so to do, and have, indeed, already given to her all of the property receipted for by me and mentioned in said Schedule, together with my interest in all the household goods and furnishings and other personal property which are retained in the Great House at Economy, in the Church, in the Town Hall, and in other places at Economy, except Seventy-five thousand ($75,000) dollars of bonds of the Liberty Land Company, which I retained, and I believe that it is wise, should at any time a question be raised by any intermeddler as to the fact of my having made such a gift by the delivery of the property, that such gift should be evidenced by a writing signed by myself.

NOW THEREFORE, I do hereby declare that I have this day given to SUSIE C. DUSS, and executed such gift by the actual delivery of possession thereof unto her of all the property mentioned in the schedule marked "A" hereto attached and made a part hereof, and signed by me in the presence of the same witnesses who witness my signature hereto.

IN WITNESS WHEREOF, I have hereunto set my hand and seal this 13th. day of December, A.D. 1905.

WITNESSES: Franz Gillmann.   (SEAL)
W. S. Dickson
Fred Knoedler
John Stoffel
Charles Reeves May

SCHEDULE "A".
(Spcl F.G.)
(Economy, Pa., December 13, 1905)

130 Shares Beaver County Land Company Stock	$ 13,000.00
512 Bonds of Liberty Land Company,	512,000.00
ONE HALF HOUSEHOLD GOODS AND ALL PERSONAL PROPERTY AT ECONOMY,	$525,000.00

Witnesses:
W. S. Dickson   Franz Gillmann.
Fred Knoedler
John Stoffel
Charles Reeves May.

The above inventory of the Harmony Society property does not tell the full story of the property for much of it had been conveyed out of sight and reach.

With the pay-off of members in 1903, the real estate development of the lands of the Society went into high gear. The Society lands sold to the American Bridge Company soon housed the extensive plant already described. With it housing was built for the workers employed and this entire area was given the name of Ambridge; the very name that Rapp and his believers had given the town they built was wiped out. Similar real estate boom plans were then developed for Economy by the Real Estate Trust Company, 311 Fourth Avenue, Real Estate Trust Building, Pittsburgh, Pa. At first this was advertised as a plan for an expanded town of Economy, which was to be based upon three divisions: French Point and Village lots which included the old houses of Economy up to 14th Street, The Village Plan which included the old core of Economy, and then the choice new development called "The Orchard of Economy Plan." No lots in the Orchard were to be sold until the widely advertised opening day of sale. Large and expensive maps of building-sites were printed representing "The Great New City of E C O N O M Y."

People were informed that with the 7,000 to 8,000 workmen that the American Bridge Works would be sure to have employed, the 500 to 800 that the Pittsburgh Steel Construction Company will have employed in its

present building and the two other immense structures that it will soon have under construction, together with the 3,500 to 4,000 workmen that will find work in the great steel barge building industry contemplated; in the immense boiler works that may be brought into existence to meet the increasing demands of the United States Steel Corporation, which has steam going out of more boilers than there are houses in Pittsburg; and in the metal tie and metal telegraph pole industry that is more than probable, a population of 71,000 may be considered a careful forecast.

This figure was considered conservative and it was claimed that an optimist would forecast 100,000 population within ten to fifteen years for Economy. "Already, while we have been making preparations to establish this grand City of Economy, the large town of Ambridge has sprung up at the side of it. Apartment houses will be erected on an elaborate scale; residences are going up in all directions; stores are being built in numbers and mighty appeals have been pouring in to us ever since last February, beseeching us to open this vast tract which now goes on the market for the first time." The great attraction about the new tract of land was that it was so near the colossal works of the American Bridge Company, which were being made larger and larger by the construction of additions which exceeded the magnitude of the present or original plan. The terms were ten percent down and three percent monthly for balance, with no taxes or interest until delivery of deed. Fifteen percent discount was to be allowed when all cash was paid within thirty days, and ten percent discount when a third was paid in cash and a purchase-money mortgage given for balance. To make prompt payment on installments attractive, a rate of four percent annual interest was to be given on each payment made promptly, so purchasers of lots would draw an equivalent of what their money would earn from money on deposit in the bank. A new water works system was to be built at once, all modern conveniences provided, including a complete sanitary sewerage system. "Pittsburghers accustomed to very small portions of level land, when it is possible to get level land at all between the mountainous hills which make Western Pennsylvania famous, will be astonished to see miles of it here at Economy. Just as level as the prairie lands of Illinois and Kansas. Not only level, but picturesque. A marvel scene of nature. You will not wonder why the good old Economites settled on this perfect spot." The three blocks bounded by Church Street and Ohio View Avenue on the sides parallel to the Ohio River, and 12th and 15th Streets running from the Ohio, were marked "Harmony Society Gardens."

While this real estate development was going on, Duss was enjoying his musical career and Susie Duss became interested in Florida real estate. She had spent the winters of 1903 and 1904 in Florida and found the climate so pleasant that she purchased a tract of land on the Atlantic beach near the town of New Smyrna. Later Duss also moved down there and both found it a convenient place to be, helpful for other causes in the making.

Although the Supreme Court decision had discouraged the heirs of deceased members who sought to claim an inheritance as heirs, that decision left open the effect of the agreements of 1890 and 1892, and the conveyance of the Society's land to the Union Company, upon the question of the dissolution of the Society. Many Germans who claimed relation to Rapp and members of the Society had right along been interested in the Harmony Society millions; now two collateral kinsmen of George Rapp living in Bayonne, New Jersey, produced evidence that they were descendants of Johann Michael Rapp, the uncle of Father Rapp, and they proved that they were the next of kin living. These two descendants, Ada Everitt and Louisa R. Tryon, through their attorneys, John Cadwalader, Jr., Franklin L. Nevin, and Charles E. Simpson filed an equity suit in the United States Court at Pittsburgh in February 1907, asking that the court find that a resulting trust had arisen in their favor as heirs at law of the original donor by reason of the dissolution of the Society and the perversion of the property from the uses intended by its contributor.

In discussing this lawsuit in his *The Harmonists,* Duss (on pages 388–89 of his book) states that one of the most pestiferous and trying incidents of the case was the rule served on them to produce the deposition of Dr. Smith, in the case of *Schreiber* vs. *Rapp.* This gave them no end of vexation and expense. The trouble was caused by a reference to testimony in this case in John Archibald Bole's *The Harmony Society* (Philadelphia, 1904) asserting that Peter Schreiber brought an estimated $8,000 into the Society and was considered one of the financial founders of the Society's wealth, which he was. Duss states that Bole had obtained permission from him to consult the documents of the Society but that this permission was granted on the sole provision that the manuscript of his book be submitted to him for approval before it went to press. This condition in itself is perplexing, but even more so is his comment that the manuscript did not reach him. Duss does not say why, but in view of Bole's expression of gratitude to the Dusses in the preface to his book for "permission to use freely the material at Economy," it is very doubtful whether the fault lay with Bole. Duss at that time was interested in things other than examining a scholarly history of the Harmony Society. As he explains:

It seems that the opposing attorneys imagined that through this footnote, which referred to a contribution by Peter Schreiber to the Society, they could find a clue advantageous to their case. Failing to find any trace of Dr. Smith's deposition, we filed a reply declaring that we had neither knowledge nor possession of the deposition—in fact, we did not believe that it existed. The court ordering a continuation of the search, other parties examined all the documents extant—all to no avail. After [*sic*] Mr. Bole testified that he had no idea where he got hold of the Smith deposition, and it also appeared that the testimony in the Schreiber-Rapp case was taken orally. After more than six months of worry and work on the Smith testimony Judge Lanning discharged the rule. (pp. 388–89)

Because, in my own research on this history of the Harmony Society, I studied the case of *Schreiber* vs. *Rapp,* the above statement by Mr. Duss is baffling, to say the least. John Archibald Bole did this study under Marion Dexter Learned, one of the greatest and most exacting Germanists of this country, and he approved Bole's study for publication in the new series of the *Americana Germanica,* published in Philadelphia in 1904. The footnote appears on page 9 of Bole's monograph, and the text which it documents is so clearly stated that one cannot wonder at the court's insistence that the document be produced. It was an important document and with Bole's reference it should have been found without any trouble, especially because Duss took such pride in having introduced such excellent bookkeeping methods and order in the records of the Harmony Society. But it is with this case as it had been in previous lawsuits: the trustees of the Society held the records and controlled access to the archives. That this record existed is shown by the fact that Bole cited it, and his citation of the record is substantiated by my own research because I found the record and herewith produce that part of the first page to which Bole referred as a late addition to the evidence in this case, just to prove that a thorough search was never made for this 7½ x 12¼ inch document consisting of twelve legal-size pages, carefully sewed together and marked carefully as pertaining to the Schreiber case.

Peter Schreiber admr.
vs. George Rapp R. L. Baker
John Schreiber & others

Action of Account render tried at
December Term 1835
Mssr Agnew Shannon Fetterman &
Roberts for Plf Wm Allison for defts

Testimony on part of Plf. Dr. Smith—affd—I was acquainted with Peter Schreiber. I cant tell when he joined the Society, but think it was in 1806. When he joined, Rapp told me he had 1800 acres of land in Ohio, and had also a great deal of personal property, many horses 6 or 8 of them, 8 or 10 head of Cattle, a great number of hogs, and a good deal of other property, 2 waggons, and I rather think he had sheep—After being in the Society some time, applications were made to him to buy his Ohio lands, and Peter went out into the State of Ohio. Rapp said he has got the money, and afterwards spoke of the wealth of Peter Schreiber, and said that Peter S. & John Neff were the foundation of the wealth of the Society, and told the people, that it was their wealth that enabled them (the Society) to build manufactories, and commence mercantile business on a large Scale. Rapp said this repeatedly in the Society, and at Economy—Mr. Rapp told me that P.S. had sold his lands for from 4 ½ to 5 $ per acre. When he and his wife went out to receive the money, I was in the Store, and when they came back they stopped at the Store, and brought the saddle bags in the Store, and they were heavy—from thence they were carried into Rapp's house. The proceeds of the sale amounted to 8000 $ & the personal property to $ 2000.

The taking of testimony in this case lasted about three years and caused the Dusses considerable worry and expense, but it also gave Duss a convenient explanation for the fact that his name suddenly vanished from the headlines of the musical world. On page 389 of his book he expresses it in these words: "the necessary attention to the legal proceedings brought to a sudden termination my meteoric career in the world of music."

The Dusses need really not have worried about this case, because of the decision of the Supreme Court in the Schwartz case, and because George Rapp's granddaughter, Gertrude Rapp, before her death had made a will under expert legal direction, which was probated, and which stated that she believed all property rights that might have belonged to her father, John Rapp, her mother, Johanna Rapp, her aunt, Rosina Rapp, and her grandfather, George Rapp, of all of whom she was sole heir under the laws of Pennsylvania, were the property of the Society, but that it being rumored that persons claiming to be the heirs of George Rapp were contemplating making claims against the Society, she devised any property rights she might have to the Society.

Judge McPherson, in 206 *Federal Reporter* (590–610), stated the opinion of the Circuit Court from which I quote the following climax (page 610):

But there is another reason why the plaintiffs cannot prevail; they have never had a title of any kind. If George Rapp ever owned anything to which they might have succeeded, this something could hardly be described as property at all if it had not been capable of transmission. How indeed do the plaintiffs themselves claim to have acquired it? They have been at pains to prove that they are among George Rapp's next of kin, and this must be because they are compelled to stand upon the proposition that they succeeded to something at his death. And this means that if George Rapp were alive to-day he could successfully make the claim put forward by their bill. If he could do this, he would be obliged to put his case on the ground that he had always owned a contingent interest of some kind, and that this had now ripened into a vested right. But certainly, if he ever had such an interest, the plaintiffs' theory requires us to suppose that it disappeared mysteriously at his death, because it was not capable of being handed on to another person. But unless this interest were capable of being transmitted by the usual methods, it would offer us the spectacle of a peculiar estate indeed—one that is not unfairly described in the defendants' brief as a metaphysical conception, something that the plaintiffs somehow received in 1905 and not before, obtaining it then because of George Rapp's merits, but contending nevertheless that it was something George Rapp in his lifetime never had. We do not find it necessary to decide precisely what kind of a valuable interest George Rapp may have had in the society's property when he died in 1847. If he had any interest at all, we need not discriminate between a resulting trust and a base fee, nor do we need to explore other regions in the law of real property; this much at least seems clear: The interest could only have been contingent, but (if it existed at all) it was real enough to be capable of transfer. Call it what we will—a contingent right, a somnolent capacity, a budding estate, or any other fanciful name—it must at least have been alive at his death if it has developed since into a full-grown right, and if it were alive then we may safely conclude that it did not evade the intestate laws of Pennsylvania. Scheetz v. Fitzwater, 5 Pa. 126, Harris v. McElroy, 45 Pa. 216, Slegel v. Lauer, 148 Pa. 236, 23 Atl. 996, 15 L. R. A. 547. These statutes act upon every property right of every name, nature, and description, and, if this particular possibility was then a part of George Rapp's possessions, it passed at his death to his daughter and his granddaughter as his next of kin, and afterwards to his granddaughter alone; and, as she disposed of it by a last will and testament in which the plaintiffs have no beneficial interest, they cannot maintain the present bill. They must themselves claim under the intestate laws of Pennsylvania as George Rapp's next of kin, but the claim must fail, because they were not his next of kin at the time of his death. It was then that his property rights passed—if he had any—and not 60 years afterward. The decree is affirmed, with costs.

Gertrude Rapp's will then left any right or property she might have had to the Harmony Society. She had never married, and her will was drafted by some of the cleverest lawyers in the United States. Those who managed the funds and property of the Society always could afford to buy the world's best legal talent, and they did so.

While the great legal mind, D. T. Watson, was busily occupied with the Everitt-Tryon case, an attack came from the Commonwealth of Pennsylvania, which should have entered the situation long before, especially since, before the Economy gold rush by those who should never have become members of the Society began, old and genuine Harmonists had stated that if Christ should not come to claim the property they had accumulated for Him, they wanted their possessions to become the property of the Commonwealth of Pennsylvania to help reduce its taxes. That solution would have been equitable and pleasing to the Harmonists, who had always loved Pennsylvania. Here for the first time was a sound and serious challenge to the Dusses as the then principal owners of the Harmony Society property. The *Pittsburgh Chronicle* of March 1, 1907, thus reported the action:

STATE IS TRYING TO SEIZE HARMONY SOCIETY PROPERTY—Attorney Albert P. Meyer is Appointed Escheator by the Auditor General and Proceedings will begin at once. TWO CITIZENS WILL SHARE ITS PROCEEDS. Property Worth Six Million Dollars is Involved on the Basis that Heirs are Lacking—MANY SAY THEY ARE HEIRS—The Commonwealth of Pennsylvania is endeavoring to seize the property of the Harmony Society at Economy and in Warren county. Auditor General William P. Snyder has appointed Attorney Albert P. Meyer, of Pittsburgh, escheator. He will endeavor to take possession of and secure all the property, real, personal and mixed, which belongs to the society, of which John S. Duss, the famous bandmaster and his wife, Mrs. Susie Duss, are the surviving members, Mrs. Duss being the sole trustee of the society. The ground on which the state is working is that there are no heirs to the property and it should, therefore, escheat to the state. The property is valued at $6,000,000.

The appointment was made on the information of George C. Buell, of Allegheny, and Charles F. Straube, of Beaver, who petitioned the attorney general to appoint an escheator for the property. The petition is based on the fact that the society has served its purpose, that there are no heirs and that under the law the property and assets should escheat to the state.

Buell and Straube, the informants, were seen this afternoon at the home of Br. Buell, in Allegheny, Mr. Buell said that he and Straube were actuated in the first place by personal motives, as the law of the state of Pennsylvania provides that the informants should receive one-third of any escheated property.

C. F. Straube himself was in the business of real estate, insurance, and collections in Economy and for some time had been watching the developments taking place with regard to the Harmony Society property. Contrary to Duss's statement on page 395 of his *The Harmonists,* it was not Buell but Straube who started the escheat move. On September 18, 1906, he addressed the following letter, which marks the beginning of this move, to the State Treasury Department, Harrisburg, Pa.:

Gentlemen: On behalf of O. P. Straube, assessor 4th ward, Ambridge Borough, Beaver Co. I would thank you for information regarding his duties in the following case, to wit—:

Since the decision of the U.S. Supreme Court in 1901 giving J. S. Duss, as Trustee, the right to sell lands for the Harmony Society, he at once formed new Land Co-s and sold all of their Estate including the town of Economy with 3200 acres of land for the figure, as reported, of $3,200,000.00 receiving therefor $1,000,000 in cash, balance bonds & mortgage. These bonds & mortgages to the present assessors best information, have never been taxed and on presentation to them of the legal blanks they have again returned them unsigned and unsworn to, thus avoiding the Ends of justice and equity. As a legal process would likely involve expenditures much in excess of the remuneration received by the assessor, he would thank you for any information as to his next step and duties. This evasion of taxes has been practiced it is alleged, since the aforementioned time, apparently with the help of the assessor being in their employ, and the following persons and corporations participating in it: Union Land Co., J. S. Duss, S. C. Duss, Harmony Society, Beaver Land Co., Liberty Land Co. As the law makes the negligence of the assessor a misdemeanor and he desires to fulfill his duties conscientiously, he desires the instruction of the State Department on this matter. Yours truly   Chas. F. Straube

On September 21, 1906, George C. Buell then wrote C. F. Straube as follows:

Dear Sir:

The letter you have forwarded to me, in reassessments of Economy Estate properties, is received, and it seems to be in trend with the Assessor's evident duties in that regard, both as a matter of public right and for his own official protection. It seems to me now that this present circumstance may form the basis for an information in chancery against the parties you mention for an accounting etc., and the circumstances may justify the Attorney General of the State in filing such an information in order to obtain proper data for the Treasurer and the Assessor, upon which suitable taxation may be had. If this were done, it would open the doors of access to the parties who are claiming to be next of kin and parties in interest under revertionary rights. This access could be obtained by cross-bill. If claimants proceeded direct, it will be well to ask the use of the name of the Attorney General anyway in such proceedings, and should he refuse, it would be quite essential to make him a party defendant, in order that suitable decrees upon findings could be entered and thus cut off any right of escheatment to the State.

I do not understand that the Supreme Court of the United States gave Duss the right to sell lands for the Harmony Society, either directly or indirectly; that suit was dismissed out of Court for want of proper parties, and, as I understand it, carried no affirmative decrees except that of dismissal, and I therefore deem it advisable to make no such admission in your letter. State the facts only, so far as you know and so far as it may seem appropriate to recite them for your present specific purpose. Otherwise I think it might be well to include a suggestion to the Attorney General that he file an information in chancery, such as I have suggested above, as being the only thoroughly available means of acquiring the necessary information.

I am responding to your communication immediately upon its receipt, but I believe that I have covered the grounds you wanted. If not, you can communicate again. If any general doubt exists in your mind as to the propriety of addressing the State Treasurer by letter, it might be advisable for us to present the matter in person to him at Harrisburg. Certainly the importance of the assessment would justify such a course, and perhaps produce better results than by correspondence.

With best wishes, I remain, Yours truly, George C. Buell.

These two letters are the beginning of the Escheat Case of the Commonwealth of Pennsylvania against the Duss party. George C. Buell of Allegheny City and Charles F. Straube of Economy became informants to the Department of the Auditor General at Harrisburg, Pennsylvania, of Escheatment of the Estates of and properties of the Harmony Society at Economy, but Buell died before the case was settled and Straube got nothing. Bitter experience later made them realize what powers were holding back action in this matter. Correspondence with various offices in Harrisburg shows that Duss's attorneys used many technical delays to hold back this trial. This tactic is also admitted on page 202 of Francis R. Harbison's *D. T. Watson of Counsel,* Pittsburgh, 1945. These delays were helped along by the Attorney General, who excused his failure to act to attorney H. G. Wasson in a strange manner, explained to Straube in a letter from Wasson of October 29, 1909:

> I saw the Attorney General when I was in Philadelphia this week, and he told me that the Suggestion for Quo Warranto which I had filed last Spring had been mislaid or put away so safely that notwithstanding a diligent search for the past week or ten days they were unable to locate it, but that if I would send him another one he would take the matter up and act at once. I am having a new Suggestion made and will get it to him this week. When I came home I found a letter on my desk from his office to the same effect.

This explanation came after a delay of three years during which Straube had constantly sought action.

On May 26, 1910, the *Beaver Falls Review* headlined the news that Sheriff Hartzell had returned home to Beaver after a delightful trip to Florida, where he had gone to serve papers on Mrs. John S. Duss, Mr. Duss not being there. The paper explained that the suit against Mrs. Duss and her husband was instituted in the Beaver County court by Hampton Todd, attorney general of the state, for the purpose of recovering all the property which was or might be in the possession of the trustees at the time of the actual dissolution of the Harmony Society.

The suit was entered on the grounds that the Harmony Society was a religious organization dedicated to religious or charitable work; that as such a society it had ceased to exist and under and by virtue of the laws of the commonwealth, such property as remained at its dissolution accrued to the public treasury for public use. Because the entire plots of ground covered by Ambridge and Economy were conveyed to the purchasers by the last trustees, now the defendants, some question of the validity of the title had arisen. "It is believed that the title, however, is sound. An attorney for the state says that inasmuch as the trustees had the power to convey, all such property has a good and sufficient title. The legal point is: To whom does the money thus acquired by the trustee, belong?"

In the neighborhood of 2,500 reconveyances of land and houses by the owners or former owners of the Harmony Society or their agents had reportedly been made by this time, so the publication of the suit brought at last by the Commonwealth through Attorney General M. Hampton Todd in Beaver County naturally caused considerable worry among the parties who had their money invested. Because many persons called upon Attorney H. G. Wasson to learn how they stood, he gave out the following statement through the press:

There should be no uneasiness on the part of bona-fide purchasers in the old Economy tract. The State is not seeking to disturb such titles.

The Harmony Society in times past has made hundreds of conveyances which are perfectly good. The same is true of the titles which come through the Union Company and the Liberty Land Company, exploiters of the town of Ambridge. All the State of Pennsylvania is after is to compel an accounting of what the society and its officers received and still own.

At this time the papers expressed the opinion that many other attorneys than D. T. Watson would finally be brought into the case and that it would be a hard-fought battle. The original informants in escheat proceedings who had filed notice with the Auditor General three years before, would be entitled to one third of the assets or money that the State would recover, so that the successful termination of the action on the part of the Commonwealth would make Buell and Straube wealthy men. Their portion was expected to amount to more than $1,000,000.

In spite of constant urging on the part of Mr. Straube, the office of Attorney General continued to delay and it was not until the June Term, 1910, that the suggestion for Quo Warranto was entered in the Court of Common Pleas of Beaver County, Pennsylvania: The Commonwealth of Pennsylvania, Ex Relatione M. Hampton Todd, Attorney General, vs. The late Religious Society, known as the Harmony Society, Susie C. Duss, last elected Trustee of the said society; John S. Duss, De Facto Trustee of the said Society and Susie C. Duss and Franz Gillmann, sole surviving members of said society. After further delay the Court fixed November 10, 1910, for the hearing of the pending motions in the Harmony Society litigation, and on December 4, 1911, Judge P. J. Holt gave this opinion, which reflects how complicated the legal situation had now become:

In this case a suggestion was filed averring the dissolution of the Harmony Society, an alleged religious organization, and that by reason of such dissolution the property of the said society escheated to the Commonwealth. The relator suggests that the court award a writ of quo warranto directed to the sheriff of Beaver County commanding him to summon the said Susie C. Duss, individually, and as trustee of the late Harmony Society, the said Franz Gillman and the said John S. Duss individually, and as de facto trustee of the late Harmony Society, to appear before the court on a day certain to show cause by what authority they hold the property of the late religious society known as the Harmony Society, and why the same should not be adjudged to have escheated to the said Commonwealth, and to direct the Liberty Land Company, the Beaver County Land Company and the Commonwealth Trust Company, of Pittsburgh, to appear and show cause why the property of the said late Harmony Society in the possession of them, or any of them, should not be by them severally assigned and conveyed to the said Commonwealth. Upon filing the suggestion in open court the court awarded the writ as suggested; and it then appearing to the court that the rights of the different persons might be properly determined by one writ, it was ordered that the late religious society known as the Harmony Society, by Susie C. Duss, its last elected trustee, John S. Duss, individually and as de facto trustee of the late society known as the Harmony Society, Susie C. Duss, individually, Franz Gillman, individually, the Liberty Land Company, a corporation, Beaver Land

Company, a corporation, and the Commonwealth Trust Company of Pittsburgh, a corporation, should be introduced into the writ, and the names of the said parties other than those representing the said late religious society known as the Harmony Society should be added to it and notice to them given to appear and take defense, and that the introduction or addition of such parties into the writ is reasonable and just; and it thus further appearing to the court that the said John S. Duss, Susie C. Duss and Franz Gillman were nonresidents of the State of Pennsylvania, the sheriff was directed to make service upon them agreeably to the provisions of the Act of Assembly of July 9, 1901, where ever found. At the time of the filing of the suggestion Susie C. Duss, John S. Duss and Franz Gillman were, and still are, residents of the State of Florida.

The writ was duly served on John S. Duss, Susie C. Duss and Franz Gillman, as directed, in the State of Florida, by the sheriff of Beaver County, and by the sheriff of Allegheny County on the Commonwealth Trust Company and the Liberty Land Company.

John S. Duss, Susie C. Duss, and Franz Gillman have appeared specially, and each has made a motion to set aside the service, for the reason that said order and service were illegal and invalid, the court being without jurisdiction to make the same, and having no jurisdiction over the said John S. Duss, Susie C. Duss and Franz Gillman, they being citizens and residents of the State of Florida and not being citizens or residents of the State or Pennsylvania or within the County of Beaver.

Counsel for the relator take the position the service made outside the Commonwealth of Pennsylvania was authorized by the Act of July 9, 1901, P.L. 614, relating to the service of process, the 13th section of which reads as follows: "Service of the writ of quo warranto and the writ of mandamus may be made upon the defendant wherever found, as in the case of a summons." Similar language is contained in the Act of 13th March, 1815, 6Sm. 287, relative to the service of subpoena in divorce; and the Supreme Court in construing that act, held that the expression "wherever found" meant, wherever found in the State of Pennsylvania, and that service upon a respondent beyond the limits of the Commonwealth was not authorized. Ralston's Appeal, 93 Pa. 133.

We are therefore unable to sustain the position of counsel for the relator that service beyond the limits of the Commonwealth is authorized by the Act of 1901.

We must therefore, examine the legislation which existed prior to the passage of the Act of 1901 relative to the service of writs of quo warranto in order to determine whether or not the service of the writ should be set aside. The service upon the Beaver County Land Company and the Commonwealth Trust Company, of Pittsburgh, was authorized by the statute of 1901.

The Eighth Section of the Act of June 14, 1836, P.L. 624, authorizes service in certain cases upon parties residing beyond the limits of this State. This section reads as follows: "If it shall appear to the court or judge as aforesaid, that the several rights of different persons may be properly determined by one writ, it shall be lawful for such court or such judge to make such order or orders for the introduction or addition of such persons into the writ, or for notice to such persons to appear and take defense, as shall be reasonable and just."

In the case of Commonwealth v. Dillon, 61 Pa. 488, it was held that under this section the court may make an order for service on persons residing in another state. Counsel for John S. Duss, Susie C. Duss and Franz Gillman maintain inasmuch as it does not appear in the suggestion that any of the property of the late Harmony Society is within the jurisdiction of this court, property in their hands in the State of Florida cannot be reached in this proceeding, and that, therefore the court is without jurisdiction or authority to direct the writ to be served on them in another state, even under the authority of the case of the Commonwealth v. Dillon, supra. In delivering the opinion of the Supreme Court in the case last cited, Mr. Chief Justice Thompson said: "It will be observed that the power to make the order provided for in the section quoted, is not limited by the bounds of jurisdiction in ordinary common law actions; nor does the mode of bringing in parties at all resemble the course of proceeding in such actions. It is a proceeding sui juris, and applicable to the case mentioned in the act, namely, to the unlawful intrusion into municipal or corporate offices or the attempt to exercise corporate franchises where they have not been granted, tryable on a writ of quo warranto. We are, therefore, not bound to test the power which may be exercised in such a process by proceedings in cases which are dissimilar, following common law forms in a common law jurisdiction. The remedy by quo warranto is by statute, and is special, and as the statute is remedial it is to be so construed and administered as to advance, that is to render effective, the remedy. This is the rule of all remedial statutes."

Counsel for the motion to set aside the service of the writ also take the position that the case of Commonwealth v. Dillon is not decisive of the question now under consideration, for the reason that the rights of Dillon and others in that case were those of stockholders or officers in a Pennsylvania corporation, and on that account they were such parties in interest as are contemplated by the statute. We do not understand that the decision was based upon that ground, alone. Mr. Chief Justice Thompson further said: "In framing the section we have quoted, the revisors no doubt anticipated just what has occurred here—non-residence of corporators and officers, or a portion of them, within the jurisdiction in which the corporation itself may be located, and the consequent impossibility of trying their title to a corporate office or their right to exercise a franchise elsewhere than within the jurisdiction of the situs of the corporation. They therefore provided for notice to parties beyond the reach of judicial process. And there is no hardship in this. Notice is all that the service of a writ gives even to residents, and the liability to notice in case of non-residents is the condition under which a non-resident becomes a corporator or an officer in a corporation. This is what the law provides, and what a party so situated must be presumed to have known, since the Act of 1836, when he becomes such officer or corporator. No question of state rights arises in the case, so far at least, as the state of the residence of the corporator is concerned. The notice is not compulsory process, nor is it to be served by virtue of any commission; there is therefore no invasion of the rights and sovereignty of the state of the resident. Should the party choose to appear he encounters no difficulty in making his defense, or trying his case. On the other hand it is of consequence to the Commonwealth to retain the right of judicial action in regard to the corporations created by her laws, no matter where the parties may be found. . . .

"That the legislature may provide for serving notice on parties interested in the subjects of litigation in the State, who are out of it, is familiar to the profession at least in equity proceedings. The nineteenth section of the Act of April 6th, 1855, authorizes the service on persons whom the court may adjudge or deem to be proper and necessary parties in equity, anywhere in or out of the United States, and on default of appearance after such notice, to adjudicate upon such interest."

The primary question in this case will be whether or not the property of the late Harmony Society escheated to the Commonwealth upon its dissolution. At the time of the dissolution, if it was dissolved, if the position of the relator should be sustained, the property of the society became that of the Commonwealth of Pennsylvania by escheat. If it be true as contended for by counsel for the motion that the effects of the late Harmony Society, whatever they are, are in the hands of John S. Duss, Susie C. Duss and Franz Gillman, in the State of Florida, their removal by these parties, if the property escheated, was unlawful; hence, John S. Duss, Susie C. Duss and Franz Gillman are vitally interested in two questions that must be determined before any of the property of the late Harmony Society, wherever situate, can be seized by the Commonwealth, and these are: (a) Whether or not the Harmony Society was dissolved, or ceased to exist, and if the society was dissolved or ceased to exist, (b) whether its property escheated to the Commonwealth. In both of these primary questions John S. Duss, Susie C. Guss and Franz Gillman are surely interested, and were entitled to notice of the proceedings instituted primarily for such purpose and ultimately to reach the property of the society. The notice to them, in the language of the chief justice, is not compulsory process. Should they choose to appear they encounter no difficulty in making their defense or trying their case. If the property of the Harmony Society has escheated to the Commonwealth, would the Commonwealth be powerless to have the matter adjudicated merely because the persons who may have taken possession of the property were beyond the limits of the Commonwealth? We think not.

Should John S. Duss, Susie C. Duss and Franz Gillman decline to appear, it may be that they would not be precluded by this proceeding from showing in another jurisdiction, if the Commonwealth should institute proceedings there to recover any of the property of the Harmony Society in their hands, that the Harmony Society was not dissolved, or that its property had not escheated to the Commonwealth. Before the Commonwealth can recover any of the property of the Harmony Society, if there was an escheat, there must be an adjudication of the fact. The only place where such proceedings can be instituted by the Commonwealth is within the State of Pennsylvania. The Commonwealth might not have authority, and, indeed, it should not be required, to institute proceedings beyond the territorial limits of the State for the purpose of having an adjudication or finding in escheat. Besides it is alleged in the suggestion that there are certain bonds, the property of the Harmony Society, in the hands of the Liberty Land Company and in the possession of the Commonwealth Trust Company of Pittsburgh. Susie C. Duss and Franz Gillman are interested in these bonds if the Harmony Society has not been dissolved; or if dissolved, and its property has not escheated to the Commonwealth; and for such reason it was proper to give them notice of this proceeding. In passing upon these motions we are not concerned in the writs of the case, one way or the other.

From what we have already said, the motions to set aside the service of the writ should be overruled.

The Liberty Land Company and the Commonwealth Trust Company have also made motions to set aside the service of the writ, alleging in support of the motions that the court was without jurisdiction to make the same, having no jurisdiction over them, the said companies having their proper places of business in and being residents of the County of Allegheny and not of the County of Beaver. As we have already said, we think the service on these companies was good, under the Act of 1901 as well as under the Act of 1836. Their Motions should therefore, be overruled.

The writ was also served on the Beaver County Land Company, to which a part of the land of the Harmony Society had been conveyed, which company has filed a demurrer to the suggestion of the Commonwealth. Having overruled the motions to set aside the service of the writ we will not, until a later date, file an opinion on the demurrer.

The court then ordered that each of the motions to set aside the service of the writ was overruled.

In spite of this victory for Straube it was in effect but another delay in favor of Duss and his group. When Buell died in 1912 Straube turned to the press for help to force progress in the case, but he was informed that two of the papers which he tried belonged to one of the men he was fighting in his suit, while two others were the property of his financial ally. So he turned to the New York *Journal and American,* which had already given the matter some publicity. On May 13, 1912, Straube finally got a letter from William M. Hargest, Assistant Deputy Attorney General, in which he quoted the following explanation of delay given by H. G. Wasson, who had presented the suggestion for a writ of quo warranto to the Court of Common Pleas of Beaver County:

More in the nature of a move to delay than otherwise, on January 1st last a plea of abatement was filed. To this plea we have demurred, and argument on the demurrer has been fixed for Wednesday. We are not at all disturbed by this proceeding and believe that ultimately, with more expedition than in the past, the quo warranto proceeding will be sufficient to determine all the rights of the interested parties.

The Dusses, meanwhile, were in Florida, beyond the reach of the Commonwealth of Pennsylvania, but Watson knew that the Pennsylvania Court had *jurisdiction of the property in dispute,* and could dispose of it without the Dusses' appearance. Judging by Duss's discussion of the case in his *The Harmonists,* it seems that he never quite realized this dangerous implication, or was it that he had great confidence in the power of those with whom he was involved? Probably so. If the Commonwealth of Pennsylvania were to win this case, Duss's lawyers, who had been fighting this legal battle for twenty years, would also be heavy losers because much of their pay was in bonds of the Liberty Land Company, which were secured by the property of the Harmony Society. Watson became sick of the case because it worried him and because, of the many legal battles he had fought for the Harmony Society, the Escheat case was the most difficult and the one which threatened to annihilate all his previous victories. For if the Commonwealth could prove that the Harmony Society was a religious organization, it could take all the property, while if it could prove that the Harmony Society was a charitable society over which courts of equity had jurisdiction, then the Commonwealth could see to it that the charitable purposes would be carried out or again take over the property for public use. The long history of the Harmony Society, if presented for the Commonwealth of Pennsylvania by as capable and sensitive a man as D. T. Watson, would have convinced any intelligent and honest jury that the Harmony Society was not only a religious society but also a charitable society. That D. T. Watson himself was honestly convinced of this before he adjusted his legal mind to another way of thinking so that he could win this case is proved by his letter written to Agnew Hice on February 28, 1912, enclosing a letter from Frederick Rapp, whom he erroneously calls Father Rapp. The latter is reprinted in my *Georg Rapp's Harmony Society*. Watson writes:

I am in a fighting humor just now, having insulted a Bishop this morning, undergone torments myself for four hours, and am now leaving in an hour for my train. I want to make you as miserable as I am and therefore I enclose you a translation of a letter that was written by Father Rapp in 1822. I have marked different portions of it which will give you great consolation, and especially that where he demonstrates that the Harmony Society is a religious society and therefore has no business whatever to have any property. You need not telegraph your thanks for this, although I know that you will duly appreciate it. I will be back about the 28th of March, and if, in the meanwhile, anybody attempts to excite the judges in your county to activity as to the Harmony Society, you just go to the judge quietly and tell him that we want no foolishness; that he has waited long enough and he can wait until I get home, even if it takes all summer.

Francis R. Harbison in *D. T. Watson of Counsel*[3] (pp. 198–209) relates in considerable detail how this case troubled Watson and how thoroughly he prepared for it, but he does not quote these letters. There were many other letters from Frederick Rapp, Father Rapp, and others, which would have been even more convincing, but no one seemed interested in bringing these all-important and decisive letters into any court. If D. T.

Watson had been fighting for the Commonwealth instead of for Duss and himself, he would not have had to do the research on communism and religion that Harbison tells about; hundreds, even thousand of letters in the Harmony Society files would have spoken so eloquently and convincingly for the Commonwealth of Pennsylvania that the Commonwealth would have won. The Dusses knew this and therefore stayed away under the legal protection of the State of Florida, and D. T. Watson knew this, so he found one delay after another to give him time to study such completely irrelevant works as Petrie on Asceticism and the Encyclopaedia Britannica. He had to do this to cloud the issue and find legal loopholes to win his case, even against attorneys who did not have the intelligence to call for the letters and full record of the Harmony Society and fight the case on the basis of this internal and pertinent evidence. That Duss and D. T. Watson realized that the Commonwealth had a sound case—even though its attorneys might not have had the determination, ability, or interest to fight it to victory—is shown by the fact that they agreed to a compromise solution. This solution did not endanger the earnings of the lawyers or the property then in the hands of the Dusses, but it did give the Commonwealth a part of the property, a sort of token escheat. Because the matter had become so involved and because the compromise required concessions which officials of the Commonwealth of Pennsylvania were not authorized to make, the proposed compromise was placed before the General Assembly. On June 17, 1915, Governor Martin G. Brumbaugh approved the following joint resolution of the Pennsylvania General Assembly, which as No. 55 had first been approved in the House of Representatives on April 28, 1915:

Whereas, At number two hundred seventy-five of June Term, one thousand nine hundred ten, the court of common pleas of Beaver County, in the Commonwealth of Pennsylvania, did, on the suggestion of the Commonwealth at the relation of the then Attorney General, Honorable M. Hampton Todd, issue its writ of quo warranto, directed to the late religious society known as the Harmony Society, Susie C. Duss, its last elected trustee. John S. Duss, de facto trustee, and the said Susie C. Duss, John S. Duss, and Franz Gillman, individually, and did cause said writ to be served on the Beaver County Land Company, the Liberty Land Company, and the Commonwealth Trust Company of Pittsburgh, trustee;

And Whereas, Answers have been filed by several of the said defendants, and a replication has been filed by the Commonwealth;

And Whereas, By the said pleadings, it appears that it is alleged by the Commonwealth that the said Harmony Society was a religious society, organized in the year one thousand eight hundred and five, and which acquired property in Beaver County in the years one thousand eight hundred and twenty four and one thousand eight hundred and twenty five, and at other times thereafter, which property was held for religious uses; and that said society at different times conveyed its real property to The Union Company, the Beaver County Land Company, and thousands of different persons, and that said real property was situate not only in Beaver County but in Allegheny County, Butler County, and Warren County, and other counties of this Commonwealth; that the said The Union Company had conveyed some twenty five hundred acres of land formerly occupied by said society to the Liberty Land Company, in consideration of the delivery of twenty five hundred Liberty Land Company's purchase money mortgage bonds of the par value of one thousand dollars ($1,000.00) each; that the said society had been dissolved and ceased to exist, and that its assets had been, in fact, illegally distributed among the members of said society and others, and that of right all the property of said society, real or personal, on its dissolution or ceasing to exist, had vested in the Commonwealth of Pennsylvania;

And Whereas, It was alleged by certain of the defendants that said society was not a religious society, but a trading or business association, and did not hold any of its property, real or personal, for religious or charitable uses or purposes, and that its members had at any time the right to dissolve the said society and divide its effects among themselves, and that they had so done;

And Whereas. It appears that the pendency of the said litigation directly or indirectly affects or has a tendency to cast a cloud on many titles to real estate in Beaver County and other counties of this Commonwealth, wherever said society, at any time since one thousand eight hundred and five, owned and conveyed real property, and said litigation has tendency to embarrass thousands of owners of small homes in mortgaging or conveying the same;

And Whereas, It appears that of the purchase money bonds of said Liberty Land Company, issued as aforesaid, only ten hundred and seventy six (1076) remain outstanding, the residue having been cancelled or retired; and that of the said outstanding bonds one hundred and ninety two (192) are owned by innocent third parties, at no time members of said society, and that, except as to sixty seven (67) of said bonds, former members of said society have pledged all of said bonds owned by them to secure certain indebtedness of themselves or of said society, aggregating two hundred and fifty thousand ($250,000.00) dollars, and that the interest coupons on said bonds have not been paid for the past six years;

And Whereas, It appears that the stock of said Beaver County Land Company is owned by former members of said society, except as to some two (2) shares thereof, and that said stock has been pledged to secure said indebtedness of two hundred and fifty thousand ($250,000.00) dollars, or a portion thereof; and that said Beaver County Land Company is seized in fee, as appears by the recorded instruments, of about five (5) acres more or less of land situate in the former village of Economy, Pennsylvania, now the borough of Ambridge, Beaver County, Pennsylvania, and also of certain scattered lots located in the city of Beaver Falls and the adjacent territory, in Beaver County, Pennsylvania, the whole of which is real estate of said Beaver County Land Company, and assessed in nineteen fifteen for the purpose of local taxation at an amount not exceeding ninety seven thousand two hundred forty-four ($97,244.00) dollars, and that said corporation owes debts exceeding one hundred seventy thousand ($170,000.00) dollars;

And Whereas, Counsel representing the Commonwealth and the defendants, after many conferences and consideration of the matter involved, have agreed upon terms of settlement and compromise of said litigation in nowise prejudicing the positions assumed by the defendants in said pleading, and not intended by them to recognize or admit any right of the Commonwealth, but only to put an end to protracted litigation and quiet title to real and personal property, wherever situate, that was at any time held by or for said society. By said agreement it is proposed to convey in fee simple absolutely to the Commonwealth of Pennsylvania those two certain parcels of land, both situate in the Fourth Ward of the borough of Ambridge, county of Beaver, and Commonwealth aforesaid, bounded and described as follows, to wit:—

(1) All that certain parcel, commonly known as the Great House Block, bounded and described as follows, to wit:

Beginning at the northeast corner of the within described parcel (said corner being a point formed by the intersection of the south line of Fourteenth street with the west line of Church street, S., 0° 29′ East, three hundred and ninety-seven hundredths (300.97) feet to a point at the corner of Church and Thirteenth streets; thence along the north line of Thirteenth street, S., 88° 54′ West, three hundred ninety-eight and eighty-five hundredths (398.85) feet to a point at the corner of Thirteenth street and Ohioview avenue; thence along the east line of Ohioview avenue, N., 0° 41′ 38″ W., three hundred one and ninety-three hundredths (301.93) feet to a point at the corner of Ohioview avenue; thence along the south line of Fourteenth street, N., 89° 2' 30" E., three hundred ninety-nine and ninety-six hundredths (399.96) feet to a point at the place of beginning.

(2) All that certain parcel, being part of the block commonly known as the Music Hall Block, bounded and described as follows, to wit:

Beginning at the southwest corner of said block, being the corner formed by the intersection of the northerly line of Fourteenth street with the eastern line of Ohioview avenue; thence by said northerly line of Fourteenth street, N., 89° 2' 30". E., four hundred and eighteen hundredths (400.18) feet to a point at corner of Church and Fourteenth streets; thence by Church street, N., 0° 29' West, one hundred eighty-three and seventy-one hundredths (183.71) feet to a point; thence S., 89° 6' 30" W., four-hundred and eighty-eight hundredths (400.88) feet to a point on east line of Ohioview avenue; and thence by Ohioview avenue S., 0° 41' 38" E., one hundred eighty-four and nineteen hundredths (184.19) feet to the place of beginning.

And by said agreement it is further proposed to pay to the Commonwealth of Pennsylvania the sum of fifteen thousand ($15,000) dollars cash forthwith, upon the conclusion of the proposed settlement and the entry of the judgment and the order or decree hereinafter mentioned, and to pay the record costs of said proceeding.

And Whereas, In the opinion of the Attorney General, the Auditor General, the State Treasurer, and of counsel for the Commonwealth in said litigation, it is for the best interests of the Commonwealth, both in its corporate capacity and as custodian of the welfare of its citizens, that said settlement should be made, and that the title to all said real and personal property that was of said society should be quieted and settled in so far as relates to the said claim of the Commonwealth.

Resolved (if the Senate concur), That the Attorney General, the Auditor General, and the State Treasurer be, and they are hereby, authorized and empowered to make said settlement and compromise in the name and on behalf of the Commonwealth, and to receive for the Commonwealth the deed for said described real property, with the reservation of possession, as aforesaid, as to a portion thereof, and to receive for the Commonwealth the said sum of money; and thereupon there is hereby released to the said defendants or parties upon which said writ was served, and to each and every of them, their heirs, grantees, and assigns, all the real and personal property that was of the Harmony Society at any time, and not included in the property to be conveyed to the Commonwealth under the terms of such settlement; and the said Attorney General, Auditor General, and State Treasurer are authorized to apply to the court of common pleas of Beaver County to have entered in said litigation such judg-

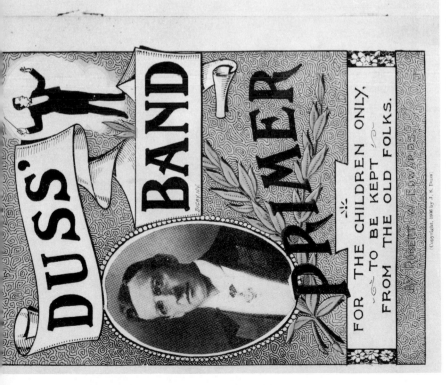

I IS FOR INSTRUMENTS ALL OF GREAT FAME.

J IS FOR JOHN. MAESTRO DUSS' FIRST NAME

DUSS IS PRONOUNCED TO RHYME WITH PUSS.

DUSS' BAND

PRIMER

FOR THE CHILDREN ONLY, TO BE KEPT FROM THE OLD FOLKS.

BY ROBERT W. EDWARDS.

(Copyright, 1900 by J. S. Duss)

What happened to Harmonists' millions: colored Primer to advertise Duss's Band

The main heir to the Harmony Society millions. By lavish expenditure of vast sums obtained from the Society, he made himself famous throughout the United States, first as a bandmaster and then as a conductor of the Metropolitan Opera House Orchestra, *which he took on a coast-to-coast tour costing him a minimum of $100,000 for transportation alone.*

The Fuss About Duss.

Spending the Harmony Society millions.

DUSS IS TRANSFORMING MADISON SQUARE GARDEN FOR HIS ORCHESTRA AND

CONDUCTOR DUSS.

What happened to the Harmony Society millions: Madison Square Garden transformed into an idealized Venice, with gondolas manned by "genuine" gondoliers as background for Duss.

WHEN MAESTRO J. S. DUSS FITS
HIS ACTIONS TO THE PIECE

CONDUCTOR DUSS IN A VARIETY OF CONTORTIONS AS REGISTERED BY CARICATURIST IGOE

What happened to Harmonists' millions: Conductor Duss as seen by Igoe of the San Francisco Examiner, October 29, 1903.

Oak under which the vanguard of the Harmonists camped the first night, June 6, 1824.

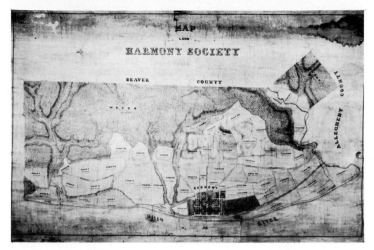

Map of the Harmony Society home tract. Under the Duss Trusteeship a large part of the Society's land was sold to the American Bridge Company, and the rest divided up and sold in small lots. Under the Duss Trusteeship the very name of Economy, which George Rapp and his pioneers had built, was wiped out and replaced by Ambridge.

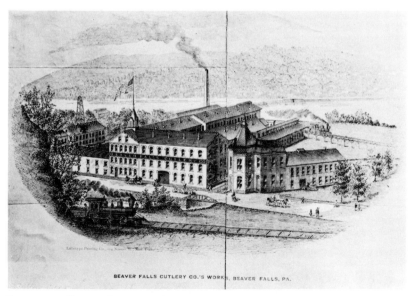

Beaver Falls Cutlery Works, Beaver Falls, Pa., showing sleeping quarters of the Chinese on the left. (about 1875–1878)

The Ambridge plant of the American Bridge Company today, built on the former land of George Rapp's Harmony Society. Courtesy American Bridge Company

Barbara Boesch and Franz Gilman, members of the Harmony Society. Boesch died in 1905 and Gilman in 1921.

Digging in Rapp's cellar for the half million dollars in British and American silver and gold coins.

Bandmaster John S. Duss and wife, main heirs to the Harmony Society millions.

Father George Rapp, founder of the Harmony Socie

First Trustee George Rapp and last Trustee Susie Duss.

ment, order and decree as will effectually conclude all litigation and forever extinguish any and all title or claim which might or could be asserted by or through the Commonwealth, except tax claims, if any, against all the property, real or personal, of said society, held by the parties to said suit or served with said writ, or by any person holding through or under them or said society.

Provided, however, That the settlement hereinabove approved shall not be an expression of legislative intention in any way binding upon the officers of the Commonwealth, except as to indicate the minimum amount which, in the judgment of the Members of the General Assembly, should be taken, accepted, or received on behalf of the Commonwealth. The minimum amount believed to be substantially, in total, the equivalent of the sum of one hundred thousand dollars ($100,000) in cash; and

Provided further, That no settlement shall be agreed upon or become effective until the same has been approved by the Governor of the Commonwealth.

APPROVED—The 17th day of June, A. D. 1915.

                     MARTIN G. BRUMBAUGH.

It should be noted that the General Assembly in this resolution holds to the important point that the Harmony Society was a religious society. This makes the jury verdict which settled Quo Warranto proceedings in the Court of Common Pleas of Beaver County appear incredible. As part of the final record of dissolution of George Rapp's "divinely established religious Harmony Society," however, the incredible and desecrating verdict of the jury terminating the Quo Warranto proceedings begun in the June 1910 term and ending on February 3, 1916, is reprinted here. These two documents put an end to all legal controversy, as far as the real estate, stocks, bonds, and money were concerned, but not with regard to the unique archives and library of the Harmony Society.

February 3, 1916: DIRECTED JURY VERDICT IN ESCHEAT
     CASE V. DUSS et al.
     COMMONWEALTH OF PENNA. vs HARMONY SOCIETY.
In the Court of Common Pleas of Beaver County, Pennsylvania.
No. 275 June Term, 1910. Docket Book #92, Page #564.
                     Verdict.
"And now to-wit, February 3, 1916, we, the jury em-panelled in the above entitled case find for the Plaintiff (the Commonwealth of Pennsylvania) as to all that certain tract of land described in Schedule A (said schedule refers to Deed Beaver County Land Co.

to Commonwealth of Pennsylvania, for Music Hall and Great House Blocks, 4th Ward, Ambridge, Deed dated Feb. 4, 1916, Beaver County Deed Book #253, Page #32) —attached hereto and made part hereof— the said to be conveyed to the Commonwealth.

And we further find for the Commonwealth of Pennsylvania the sum of $15,000 cash, to be paid by the defendants or some of them, to the said Commonwealth of Pennsylvania, to be and to become the property of the Commonwealth absolutely.

And as to all other lands, goods, chattels, real and personal, that are or were of the said Harmony Society or any of the members thereof, or any property held in trust for the said Society, now or at any time held by the Liberty Land Company the Beaver County Land Company or the Commonwealth Trust Company of Pittsburgh, or by any person upon whom the Writ of Quo Warranto in the above entitled case was served, we find for the defendants.

And we further find that none of the said property ever was or is held by any religious society or for any religious or charitable uses, and that the defendants, their heirs, grantees, successors and assigns have a good and indefeasible title thereto.

And further we find that all conveyances made by the said Harmony Society, by the said Beaver County Land Company or by the Liberty Land Company, are so far as relates to any claim on behalf of the Commonwealth of Pennsylvania at issue in the above entitled case, good and valid."

(Signed)   ROBERT BLYTHE, Foreman.
Schedule A attached to Record.

Under date of February 14, 1916, there appears on the Record the receipt for $15,000 cash and for the deed conveying property described in Schedule A, said receipt signed by Harry G. Wasson, J. Frank Reed, and Harry K. Siebeneck, Attorneys for the Commonwealth of Pennsylvania.

Even though this jury found, let us say, that black is not black but white, any person who will take the trouble to examine the letters of Father Rapp and his Associates will be amazed that a jury could be so blinded in a verdict terminating the affairs of this religious Society and Church. The original Articles of Agreement had called the Harmony Society a congregation and church, and numerous letters of members had testified to it as a religious society, holding property in common, as in the days of the first church, for *religious and charitable purposes*. The jury verdict is a legally stated untruth and an insult to the Harmony Society, which always considered itself the Bride of Christ and was anxiously, eagerly, and prayerfully awaiting the coming of her bridegroom, Jesus Christ, the Son of God, in order to place all the property it had acquired by His Grace at His disposal. The charitable purpose for which the property of the Harmony Society was being held was even spelled out clearly in so many words in the Articles of Agreement of 1823, which include this statement covering the contigency of withdrawal from the Society:

And if the case should happen that said persons all or individually in a few or several years should leave the congregation [Gemeine or Gemeinde], be it for whatever reasons it may, they each, together and individually bind themselves especially that they never and in no case will make a bill or demand for their work and services rendered, neither of the Society nor of any individual member of the same, also that they never will make, demand or urge any other kind of pay under whatever name or terminology it might be, *but will have done it all out of Christian love for the welfare and use of the congregation [Gemeine or Gemeinde] namely to be used for widows, orphans, sick, and persons unable to work (gebrechlichen),* or they will receive it as a present if George Rapp and his Society should freely want to give them something.

But what became of the survivors, and Rapp's materialistic heirs? Franz Gillmann died on a Sunday night at 11:45 P.M., December 11th, 1921 at New Smyrna, Florida, aged 93 years and 10 months. He was buried on a Thursday afternoon, December 15, 1921, at Old Economy Cemetery, Church Street, 4th Ward, Ambridge, Pennsylvania.

Mrs. Susie Duss died on June 13, 1946, and was cremated June 17th at the Crematorium at Orlando, Florida. As she was the first woman trustee, so she was unique in that, as last trustee of the Harmony Society, she was the first and only legal Harmonist to have religious funds of the Society spent on the pagan rite of cremation.

John S. Duss died at 5:53 A.M. on December 14, 1951, of myocardial failure and was buried December 17 in the Harmony Society Cemetery at Church and Ambridge Street, in Ambridge—i.e., Economy—Pennsylvania.

His death came only after a terrific struggle with the angel of darkness, as if to impress upon him the importance of the powerful individual for whom he was calling, for in death he remained the strong-willed egotist he had been in life. According to the report of the man who attended him in his last hours, there was something Faustian about his passing and the room was filled with feathers torn from the wings of the messenger who had come for him. The urn containing Mrs. Duss's ashes was placed at John Duss's feet in his casket. The funeral service was Lutheran and his grave was not marked. Although he followed Harmonist custom in not having his grave marked, he made sure while in the flesh that the main road now passing through former Economy would be named D u s s, while the names of the real Harmonist pioneers of Economy-Ambridge were forgotten.

16

What Became of the Harmony Society Millions?

FIRST LET ME EMPHASIZE THE FACT THAT THERE WERE MILLIONS of dollars, which means billions in terms of our current devaluated currency, in spite of all the denials made. That they cannot be traced exactly to all receivers is due to the strange attitude toward bookkeeping even in the Duss era, where an expert accountant was employed by Duss and his costly lawyers but where the decisive accounts were kept outside of Economy under the direction of lawyers not members of the Society. These accounts are not found in what is left of the Harmony Society Archives, probably because they would reveal too much to research. To further complicate such research, one highly important point was not covered in the materialistic compromise settlement of the escheat proceedings: the Commonwealth of Pennsylvania made no claim to the furnishings of the historic buildings awarded to it, and it disregarded the unique and priceless Harmony Society Library and Archives still housed in those buildings. Either by default or plan, these became the personal property of the Dusses. As the published archives of Duss's great lawyer, D. T. Watson, reveal an almost abysmal ignorance about the history of the Harmony Society, with the exception of its material possessions, so the compromise settlement shows a complete disinterest on the part of the Commonwealth of Pennsylvania in the Harmony Society's archives and records, an attitude that has not essentially changed to this day. Legally, all these treasures then housed in the Harmony Society buildings deeded to the Commonwealth were by this compromise acknowledged to be the personal property of the Dusses and for this reason they quite legally moved freight-car loads of Harmony Society property to Florida. They also sold or gave away furniture, works of art, valuable household goods, books, and Harmony Society records, because these had legally become their personal property. This explains the fact of the dispersion of a considerable part of the library and archives. Books and documents continue to be offered for sale through dealers in rare books and documents, and through others, as I well know from offers that have been made to me.

Duss's personal interest in the history of the Harmony Society did not really develop until quite late in his life; indeed it first became important only when the WPA was set up to ease the economic problems of the depression. This brought a large work force to the Harmony Society buildings to clean up and order what was left of the library and archives of the Harmony Society. Although, generally speaking, this WPA project did a great deal of good for the Harmony Society archives and library, much valuable material was lost in the cleanup because the persons employed were not schooled for such scholarly work. During this time Duss was working on his memoirs and as a person having the ability to read old German script he was frequently called upon to decipher and interpret old documents and letters. In his vigorous manner he would then scrawl his comments on the original documents without any feeling for the original text or its condition, because, after all, he felt that this was his personal property and the Commonwealth should feel happy to have this "Duss collection" with the comments of the donor. At this time he was spending his winters in Florida, but during the summer, by arrangement with the Commonwealth, he continued to be the master of the "Great House."

By discovery and purchase of many documents and papers of Count Leon and Dr. Goentgen in Louisiana at this time, shortly before the outbreak of World War II, I became acquainted with the Harmony Society Archives and the extensive WPA project at Economy. This then led to my acquaintance with Duss. We spent many hours together discussing the history of the Harmony Society and in many ways had much in common, especially our great admiration for the pioneer work of the Harmonists. As long as I did not insist upon the religious character of the Harmony Society and as long as I did not challenge his fundamental thesis about the leadership of the Harmony Society, namely that he was "the greatest Roman of them all," everything went along smoothly. But in any way to question his trusteeship or his handling of the Harmony Society archives and the dissolution of the Society brought temperamental outbursts that often caused me to think that he was protesting too much. He was pathological about his point of view and would fly into a rage and temper tantrum when confronted with documentary evidence. No manuscript then was safe from destruction in such a confrontation. He came to love the history of the society very much at the end of his days, but only with himself as the climax of that history. He accepted and incorporated into his memoirs without acknowledgment results of my research during this period, so long as these did not challenge his part in this history or his interpretation of it. In his last years the history of the Harmony Society became his very life and he did much to keep the history of the Society alive in the Pittsburgh area because he considered himself the reincarnation of that history.

But what became of the Harmony Society millions?

1) They enabled Henrici to keep thousands of Americans from becoming unemployed, although he lost money in the operation.

2) They helped other religious communities here and abroad.

3) They made Duss famous as a bandmaster and gave him the illusion that he was the greatest conductor of the age.

4) They gave a luxurious free trip, and subsidized income, to the Metropolitan Opera House Orchestra from coast to coast.

5) They provided the funds to give a taste of luxury to thousands in New York City through Duss's Venice in New York, with the Metropolitan Opera House Orchestra providing the music.

6) They made it possible for the Dusses to live a life of leisure and luxury.

7) They provided the financial backing for Carrie Nation

in "Ten Nights on a Barroom Floor," thus showing many the dangers of liquor.

8) They made Henry Hice, the Reeves family, and other agents of the society wealthy.

9) They added greatly to the wealth of J. T. Brooks.

10) They helped D. T. Watson found his Home for Crippled Children in Sewickly, Pa.

11) They gave a millionaire's education to the Dusses' children.

12) They helped build railroads.

13) They fed and sheltered thousands of unnamed knights of the road.

14) They paid out in the course of the Society's history well over half a million in lawyers' fees and property shares, first, to establish and maintain the Harmony Society property as eternally indivisible and nonpersonal—set aside for religious and charitable purposes, and later, when Rapp's materialistic successors and heirs took over control, to buy legal talent to nullify and void this legal and doctrinal status established by approximately a century's costly legal battles, in order to convert the nonpersonal and indivisible property of the Society into private and divisible property, thus exactly reversing the doctrinal and legal status upon which the Society had been founded and by which it lived until the death of Henrici.

15) They gave the State of Pennsylvania, as the result of quo warranto proceedings, approximately two city squares of buildings and park as a museum and memorial of the Harmony Society. In the session of 1919 the General Assembly of the Commonwealth of Pennsylvania passed an act dedicating to public use as a historical memorial and public park these lands and buildings, and providing for the custody, maintenance, and use thereof. This act was approved by Governor William C. Sproul on July 22, 1919. This museum now contains a large collection of tools, furniture, and paintings which belonged to the Society, but which Duss insisted on calling the "Duss collection," for it had been Duss's personal property. Most valuable of all, however, is what remains of the library and archives of the Society located in the "Vaterhaus," the former residence

of George Rapp and his family, later inhabited by the various Trustees of the Society. The appendixes to this volume give surveys of this library and the archives for the benefit of those interested in special research in this extremely valuable and rich collection of source material covering the history of our country from the beginning to the end of the Harmony Society. Because of the extensive social, religious, and business contacts of the Society, both nationally and internationally, its Archives constitute one of the most valuable collections of the United States.

At the conclusion of this chapter, I present three tables to show, as accurately and graphically as the available record permits, how the property of the Harmony Society was divided and how members of the Society fared in comparison to the attorneys who presided over the liquidation of Rapp's divine Economy.

The first table shows the fate and fortune of members of the Society from the critical year of 1890 to the legal dissolution of the Harmony Society in 1905.

The second table lists the Liberty Land Company bonds paid to attorneys for legal services, which these attorneys or their heirs still held on February 21, 1927, each bond valued at $1,000 par. These bonds were part of an issue of $2,500,000 par value of 5.4 percent purchase money bonds on "certain lands of Harmony Township and Economy Township in Beaver County." Liberty Land Company bonds actually is just another name for that part of the Harmony Society land described more fully in the record found in the Recorder's office of Beaver County, Pennsylvania, in mortgage book, vol. 94, page 26, hence these bonds are only part of the total property of the Society. This table does not include all the money paid to attorneys in cash but lists only what they still held on February 21, 1927, as *preferred* bonds. Other figures were not available, but this table shows that in 1927 attorneys still owned 240 bonds, or $240,000 of Harmony Society assets.

The third table compares gifts granted departing members at three periods of the Society's history, with fees paid for legal services in these times, insofar as they are available.

TABLE I

Settlements Made With Harmony Society Members from 1890 (Start of Gold Rush) to Legal Dissolution

The first date is year of first membership. Line shows duration.

First year	Name	Membership span / event (1890 1891 1892 1893 1894 1895 1896 1897 1898 1899 1900 1901 1902 1903 1904 1905 1921)	Departing gift
1828	Beck, Elizabeth	——Died (1894)	Free burial
1857	Boesch, Barbara	————Died (1905)	Free burial
1835	Diem, Maria	———Died (1896)	Free burial
1890	Duss, John S.	————Resigned (1903)	$500,000
1890	Duss, Susie C.	—————Resigned (1905)	$1,293,000
1856	Feucht, Benjamin	—Resigned (1893)	
1858	Feucht, Henry	—Resigned	} The Feuchts together received $28,000 and Stowe Township property — $28,000
1890	Feucht, Margaret	—Resigned	
1890	Feucht, Rebecka	—Resigned	
1848	Feucht, Thirza	—Died (1893)	
1890	Friederichs, Moritz J.	—Resigned (1893)	
1887	Gillmann, Franz	———————————Died (1921)	$5,000 / $525,000 willed to Susie C. Duss
1890	Haerer, Christina	—Resigned (1893) Leonard was Christina Haerer's son. Together they received	$5,000
1893	Haerer, Leonard	—Resigned (1893)	
1827	Henrici, Jacob	—Died (1892)	
1890	Hermannsdoerfer, Conrad	———Died (1896)	Free burial

1890 1891 1892 1893 1894 1895 1896 1897 1898 1899 1900 1901 1902 1903 1904 1905 1921

Departing gift

Year	Name	Event	Departing gift
1890	Hermannsdoerfer, Johanna	Resigned (1903)	$75,000
1827	Hoehr, Dorothea	Died (1894)	Free burial
1890	Kellermann, Edward	Died (1897)	Free burial
1887	Lauppe, Gottfried	Died (1893)	Free burial
1835	Lautenschlager, Regina	Died (1896)	Free burial
1890	Miller, Hugo	Resigned (1893)	$5,000
1887	Molt, Karolina	Resigned (1903)	$75,000
1841	Munz, Friedericka	Died (1901)	Free burial
1887	Nagel, Katharina	Resigned (1903)	$75,000
1890	Niclaus, J. Jacob	Resigned (1893)	$5,000
1890	Platz, Blasius	Resigned (1893)	$5,000
1841	Rall, Christina	Died (1904)	$75,000
1848	Rall, Lena	Died (1895)	Free burial
1892	Riethmueller, Gottlieb	Died (1897)	Free burial
1836	Scheid, Johannes	Died (1893)	Free burial
1892	Siber, Elizabeth	Resigned (1893)	$4,000
1892	Siber, Samuel	Resigned (1893)	$4,000
1890	Stickel, Julius	Resigned (1893)	$3,620
1890	Stickel, Paulina	Resigned	
1890	(Stickel) Geratch, Bertha,	Resigned	
1890	Stiefvater, Sigmund	Resigned (1893)	$5,000
1879	Wolfangel, Philippine L.	Died (1896)	Free burial

Bertha Geratch was a daughter of the Stickels. The three together received $3,620 as departing gift.

TABLE II

1927 List of Bonds of Liberty Land Company Given in Payment for Legal Services and Entitled to Preference

No. of Bonds

Annie W. Sutton, Bonds formerly owned by Estate of Robert Woods Sutton, Deceased:
Bonds Nos. 283 284, 285, 286, 287, 1369, 1370, 1388, 1389, with interest coupon due May 1, 1911, and all subsequent coupons,   **9**
(¼ of one of these bonds belongs to H. F. Stambaugh).

D. T. Watson Home for Crippled Children:
Bonds Nos. 326, 327, 328, 329, 347, 348, 349, with interest coupon due May 1, 1911, and all subsequent coupons, (These bonds purchased from Estate of Ernest C. Irwin, Deceased).   **7**

H. F. Stambaugh:
Bonds Nos. 299, 300, 364, 400, 1390, with interest coupon due May 1, 1911, and all subsequent coupons.   **5**

John M. Freeman:
Bonds Nos. 918, 917, 916, 915, 1314, 1313, with interest coupon due Nov. 1 1911, and all subsequent coupons.   **6**

John M. Freeman:
Bonds Nos. 316, 317, 330, 331, 332, 218, 219, 220, 221, 222, 224, 236, 237, 238 239, 240, 241, 242, 243, 244, 245, 246, 247, 277, 279, 280, 281, 282, 288, 289 290, 278, with interest coupon due May 1, 1911, and all subsequent coupons.   **32**
(½ of one of these bonds belongs to Fidelity Title and Trust Company, Trustee for the D. T. Watson Home for Crippled Children).

Fidelity Title and Trust Company Trustee for D. T. Watson Home for Crippled Children:
Bonds Nos. 901, 902, 903, 904, 905, 906, 907, 908, 909, 910, 911, 912, 913, 914, 1291, 1292, 1293, 1294, 1295, 1296, 1297, 1315, 1316, 1317, 1318, 1319, 1320, 1321, 1322, 1323, 1324, 1325, 1326 1327, 1328, 1329, 1330, 2269, 2270, 2271, 2272, with interest coupon due Nov. 1, 1911, and all subsequent coupons,   **41**

Fidelity Title and Trust Company, Trustee for D. T. Watson Home for Crippled Children:
Bonds Nos. 301, 302, 303, 304, 305, 306, 307, 308, 309, 310, 311, 312, 313, 314, 315, 318, 319, 320, 321,

322, 323, 324, 325, 333, 334, 335, 338, 339, 340, 341,
342, 343, 344, 345, 346, 350, 351, 352, 353, 354, 355,
852, 853, 854, 855, 856, 857, 1028, 1029, 1030, 1031,
1304, with interest coupon due May 1, 1911, and all
subsequent coupons,   52

*Agnes McG. Hice, Executor of Estate of Agnew
Hice, Deceased:*
Bonds Nos. 399, 398, 363, 362, 361, 360, 359, 337,
336, 358, 357, 356, 397, 396, 395, 394, 393, 392, 391,
390, 389, 388, 387, 386, 385, 384, 383, 382, 381, 380,
379, 378, 377, 376, 375, 374, 373, 372, 371, 370, 369,
368, 367, 366, 365, with interest coupon due May 1,
1911, and all subsequent coupons,   45

*Agnes McG. Hice, Executor of Estate of Agnew
Hice, Deceased:*
Bonds Nos. 1402, 1403, 1404, 1405, 1406, 1407, 1408,
1409, with interest coupon due Nov. 1, 1911, and all
subsequent coupons,   8

*C. T. Brooks and F. J. Emeny, Executors of the
Estate of Annie M. Brooks, Deceased:*
Bonds. Nos. 1334, 1335, 1336, 1337, 1338, 1339, 1340,
1341, 1342, 1343, 1344, 1345, 1346, 1347, 1348, 1349,
1350, 1351, 1352, 1353, 1354, 1355, 1356, 1357, 1358,
1359, 1360, 1361, 1362, 1363, 1364, 1365, 1366, 1367,
1368, with interest coupon due Nov. 1, 1911, and all
subsequent coupons,   35

TABLE III

A Comparison of "Donations or Gifts" Granted Departing Members
of the Society and Lawyers' Fees Paid for Legal Services at
Various Periods of the Society's History

February 15, 1805
Working capital of Harmony Society at founding in USA $23,000
Approximate per capita wealth at this time $ 46
1832 Schism
Total departing gifts or separation pay granted to 250
departing members $105,000
Fee paid to Lawyer Forward alone for legal services in
this case $ 1,000
Ascertainable total number of years and months
of service which 99 of the above-mentioned members devoted to building the Harmony Society,

not considering their contributions to the common
treasury ....1,259 years and
                                       5 months.
(Time served by others could not be determined.)
Basic norm used to figure above separation pay to
withdrawing members: Men, per year $75
                     Women, per year $25
                     Men, per month $ 6
                     Women, per month $ 2
Estimate of time Lawyer Walter Forward served the
Society in above case, excluding assistance, fees for which
are not included above   1 month.
1846 to 1856 Joshua Nachtrieb Litigation
Donation received by Joshua Nachtrieb upon withdrawal $ 200.00
Years of his service devoted to building the Harmony
  Society   27 years
Amount allowed Nachtrieb by Circuit Court of the
  United States for the Western District of Pennsylvania $ 3,890
Amount allowed Nachtrieb by U.S. Supreme Court on
  appeal of the Society   Nothing.
Excluding previous lawyer's fees in this case amount
  ascertainable as paid to *one* of the lawyers alone for
  the Supreme Court Case $ 2,000
1903–1905 Ending of Duss Era
Donation received by John Duss upon withdrawal $500,000
Donation received by Mrs. John Duss upon withdrawal,
  including the Franz Gillmann donation which he
  willed her immediately $1,293,000
Amount paid Attorney J. T. Brooks alone for his legal
  services $105,000
Amount ascertainable as paid to Attorney D. T. Watson $ 95,000
Amounts paid other lawyers not available.

Epilogue

GEORGE RAPP'S HARMONY SOCIETY, AS IS DEMONSTRATED IN MY
first book on this subject, was the socioeconomic showplace of
America in the first half of the nineteenth century. Any for-
eigner traveling in this country who was genuinely interested
in what our country was doing in those days was sure to include
a visit to the Harmony Society in his schedule. The Harmonists
were famous for their industry and their skilled craftsmen not
only throughout America but throughout the Western world.
Harmony, Pennsylvania; New Harmony, Indiana; Economy,
Pennsylvania—all three of the settlements which they carved
out of the forest primeval became important American centers
of business, industry, and culture as long as the Harmonists
dwelled there.

The reasons for the success of the Society might be summarized as follows:

1. Excellent, honest, and inspired spiritual and economic
leadership.

2. A faithful, obedient, well-trained, and hard working group
of workers. A minimum of intellectuals and mere theorists.

3. Excellent organization of workers in various branches of
activity.

4. A homogeneous group consisting mostly of families which
had undergone the same religious experience.

5. Faith in special election by God for a special mission.

6. A nonmaterialistic attitude based on the Biblical com-
mands: Matt. 6:33: "But seek ye first the kingdom of God, and
his righteousness; and all these things shall be added unto you,"
and 1 Cor. 7:29–30: "But this I say, brethren, the time is short:
it remaineth, that both they that have wives be as though they
had none . . . and they that buy, as though they possessed
not."

7. A common goal and incentive which was kept fresh and of common interest by keeping on the move.

That they were mistaken in their faith and that Christ failed to claim their Society—the Philadelphia Congregation that kept the faith—as His Bride, was not their failing; rather, this strong faith was what Ibsen later called "the life-giving illusion." It was the Supreme Court of the United States that failed to bring the affairs of the Society to an orderly conclusion when appealed to in the Schwartz case. At that time justice did not prevail, as the opinion of Chief Justice Fuller showed, but we must accept the course that history followed in this matter.

There is one happy development in the tragic history of these great American pioneers. Although the American Bridge Company, which purchased the Harmony Society lands to develop the world's largest structural steel fabricating plant there, wiped out the very name of George Rapp's divinely established Economy (göttliche Ökonomie) and substituted the name Ambridge for it, it has from a worldly point of view become a worthy successor to George Rapp and his Harmonists. As we drive over America's excellent highways, we travel over beautiful bridges whose structural steel was produced in whole or in part on that land which George Rapp and his people first prepared for civilization.

We drive over structural steel produced at Economy-Ambridge all over the United States. In Louisiana we drive across the Mississippi over structural steel from Economy-Ambridge in the Huey P. Long or Sunshine Bridges; in California, the San Francisco-Oakland Bay Bridge; on the Maine State Turnpike, the Old Alfred Road Overpass, selected by Jury of Award, American Institute of Steel Construction, as the most beautiful Class III Bridge built in 1947. In New York City, the Marine Parkway Bridge, the Tappan-Zee Bridge, and the Verrazzano-Narrows Bridge; in Delaware, the Chesapeake City Highway Bridge and the Delaware Memorial Bridge near Wilmington, Delaware; in Pennsylvania, the Allegheny River Bridge on the Pennsylvania Turnpike near Pittsburgh—all built entirely or in part of structural steel from Economy-Ambridge.

At Economy-Ambridge, all or much of the structural steel was produced which also made these great buildings possible:

Empire State Building; Rockefeller Center, 9 buildings; Chrysler Building; Pan Am Building; United Nations Headquarters; Gateway Center, Pittsburgh; Terminal Building, Greater Pittsburgh Airport, Economy-Ambridge; Vehicle Assembly Building for NASA, Merritt Island, Florida (Cape Kennedy).

When George Rapp's faithful disciple Jacob Henrici saw the "gigantic ship" *The Great Western*, he wrote as follows to his fellow-trustee Baker:

The same is built entirely of iron and carries 25,000 tons, is almost 700 feet in length and from 80 to 120 wide and could carry 10,000 soldiers or 4000 passengers overseas. When one observes the magnificence of the entire structure, its tremendous steam engines and besides the outer majestic, giant size also the inner wonderful construction, where everything is so powerfully and well assembled that practically not a drop runs through . . . when one considers and admires all this, one cannot help but consider that this wonderful gigantic work with its entire splendor and magnificence had to exist first in finished and completed form in the mind of a fallen man, before it could be started. Who would not be compelled at such a sight to think of the greatness of man who can produce such miraculous works even now in his low, fallen state? What will he be able to accomplish then when he has been restored to his original dignity and when he will apply his sanctified and practiced powers of creation for the honor and glory of God his Savior and to the welfare and pleasure of his beloved fraternal family (Bruderfamilie).

Jacob Henrici later felt justified in using funds of the Harmony Society to help build the railroads that made Pittsburgh more accessible to the world because he believed he was thereby helping fulfill the prophecy of Isaiah 40:4. If George Rapp, R. L. Baker, and Jacob Henrici, three great American pioneers of the West, had lived to drive over these bridges and visit the buildings listed above—and this is only a small part of the production that has gone out of Economy-Ambridge—they would not have been shaken in their faith in Christ's promise that he would return to dwell with his people but would have looked upon the American Bridge Company as a humble servant in the fulfillment of that prophecy. And if they had studied the beautifully illustrated booklet *Plants and Products, American Bridge Division, United States Steel Corporation,* they would probably have said exactly what Baker and Henrici, on November 21, 1851, wrote to the President of the Ohio and Pennsylvania Railroad, General Wm. Robinson, about railroads being the commencement of the fulfilling of Isaiah 40:4. For Baker and Henrici, then, the long-range program of this vast corporation, the American Bridge Company, was written by Isaiah centuries ago in words which also formed the heart of the faith of George Rapp's Harmony Society:

Prepare ye the way of the Lord, make straight in the desert a highway for our God. Every valley shall be exalted, and every mountain and hill shall be made low; and the crooked shall be made straight, and the rough places plain; and the glory of the Lord shall be revealed, and all flesh shall see it together; for the mouth of the Lord hath spoken it.

Notes

Preface

1. Karl J. R. Arndt, *George Rapp's Harmony Society, 1785–1847* (Philadelphia: University of Pennsylvania Press, 1965; Rev. ed., Rutherford, Madison, Teaneck: Fairleigh Dickinson University Press, 1971).

2. Heinrich Luden, *Reise Sr. Hoheit des Herzogs Bernhard zu Sachsen-Weimar-Eisenach durch Nord-Amerika in den Jahren 1825 und 1826,* Herausgegeben von Heinrich Luden (Weimar: bei Wilhelm Hoffmann, 1828).

3. Karl J. R. Arndt, "The Harmony Society and Wilhelm Meisters Wanderjahre," *Comparative Literature* 10, No. 3, Summer 1958.

Chapter 1

1. Carl Wittke, *The Utopian Communist. A Biography of Wilhelm Weitling, Nineteenth-Century Reformer* (Baton Rouge: Louisiana State University Press, 1950).

Chapter 2

1. A. E. Zucker, *The Forty-Eighters, Political Refugees of the German Revolution of 1848* (New York: Columbia University Press, 1950).

Carl Wittke, *Refugees of Revolution: The German Forty-Eighters in America* (Philadelphia: University of Pennsylvania Press, 1952).

2. Gottfried Kinkel, *Gottfried Kinkels Selbstbiographie 1838–1848.* Herausgegeben von Richard Sander (Bonn: Verlag von Friedrich Cohen, 1931).

Adolph Strodtmann, *Gottfried Kinkel. Wahrheit ohne Dichtung.* Biographisches Skizzenbuch. Vols. I and II (Hamburg: Hoffmann und Campe, 1850–1851).

3. Francis and Theresa Pulszky, *White, Red, Black* (New York: Redfield, 1853). The quotation following is from 1:271–75.

4. Mrs. Pulszky deserves the title of Cassandra, as the one prophetess who foresaw exactly what happened, with this limitation: she did not even dream that this "worldly individual" would be of her sex.

5. The reader will be interested to know that the discoverer and publisher of Stephen Foster, Mr. Peters, was conductor of music and teacher of the Harmonist musicians. His own compositions were often performed there and he was a close friend of the Society. See Karl J. R. Arndt and Richard D. Wetzel, "Early Economy as Musical Center of the Pittsburgh Area," in *The*

Western Pennsylvania Historical Magazine, April and following issues, 1971.

6. See my article, "The Effect of America on Lenau's Life and Work," in *The Germanic Review,* April 1958.

7. New York Public Library has the papers of Weitling, including a set of his paper *Republik der Arbeiter* and a manuscript of *Organisations Gesetze der Gemeinde Communia.*

8. The physician was Dr. Benjamin Feucht.

9. See *Nachtrieb* v. *Baker.* Circuit Court of the U.S. for Western District of Pennsylvania, No. 28 of November Term 1849.

Chapter 3

1. E. O. Randall, *The Separatist Society of Zoar.* Ohio Archaeological and Historical Publications, vol. VIII (Columbus: Published in 1900 for the Society by Fred. J. Heed, 1900). They were also a direct influence on the establishment of Brook Farm.

2. *Lemmix* v. *Baker.* Circuit Court of the U.S. Western District of Pennsylvania, No. 2 of November Term 1852.

3. *Baker* v. *Nachtrieb* in U.S. Supreme Court. December Term, 1856.

Chapter 4

1. Bertha M. H. Shambaugh, *Amana, The Community Of True Inspiration* (Iowa City: The State Historical Society of Iowa, 1908).

2. Paul H. Giddens, *The Birth of the Oil Industry* (New York: The Macmillan Company, 1938). *The Beginnings of the Petroleum Industry. Sources and Bibliography.* Harrisburg: Pennsylvania Historical Commission, 1941), pp. 108, 128, 170. Commonwealth of Pennsylvania, Drake Well Memorial Park. *Pennsylvania Petroleum 1750–1872.* A Documentary History. (Titusville: Pennsylvania Historical and Museum Commission, 1947), p. 387. *Early Days of Oil. A Pictorial History of the Beginnings of the Industry in Pennsylvania.* (Princeton: Princeton University Press, 1948), p. 76.

3. Also see: "The 'Economite' Oil Company," *Petroleum Age,* March 1882.

Chapter 5

1. W. F. Workmaster, "The Frank H. Shiras Letters, 1862–1865." In *Western Pennsylvania Historical Magazine* 40 (Fall, 1957): 163–90.

2. *Scribner's Magazine* 19:160 (November 1879).

Chapter 6

1. Charles Nordhoff, *The Communistic Societies of the United States* (New York: Harper & Brothers, Publishers 1875), pp. 63–95.

2. Aaron Williams, *The Harmony Society* (Pittsburgh: Printed by W. S. Haven, Cor. Wood and Third Sts., 1866).

3. Karl Knortz, *Aus der transatlantischen Gesellschaft. Nordamerikanische Kulturbilder.* Ein Sonntag in Economy (Leipzig: Verlag von Bernhard Schlike, 1882), pp. 180–85. Karl Knortz, *Christian-communistic colony of Rappists in Pennsylvania* (Leipzig: Verlag Ernst Wiest (?) 1892); Karl Knortz, "Die Ansiedlung der Rappisten in Economy, Pennsylvanien," in *Amerikanische Lebensbilder, Skizzen und Tagebuchblätter* (Zürich: Verlags Magazin J. Schabelitz, 1884), p. 468. *Die christlich-kommunistische Kolonie der Rappisten in Pennsylvanien und neue Mitteilungen über Nikolaus Lenaus Aufenthalt unter den Rappisten. Vortrag* (Leipzig: Verlag Ernst Wiest, 1892).

4. Eduard Hemberle, "Erlebnisse und Beobachtungen eines deutschen Engenieurs in den Vereinigten Staaten. 1867–1885," in *Deutsch-Amerikanische Geschichtsblätter*, Jahrgang 2, Heft 1, Januar 1902.

Chapter 7

1. Christopher Hoffmann, *The Temple Work in Palistine.* Translated from the German by F. C. Fink and Paul J. Strohauer (Schenectady, N.Y.: C. Goetz, 1896). Christian Hoffmann was the author of an extensive cultural-historical study *Fortschritt und Rückschritt: oder Geschichte des Abfalls in den zwei letzten Jahrhunderten,* a kind of predecessor to Oswald Spengler's *Decline of the West.* He claimed that the world has been regressing instead of progressing.

2. Harold S. Bender, *Hutterite Studies.* Essays by Robert Friedmann. (Goshen, Ind.: Mennonite Historical Society, 1961). John W. Bennett, *Hutterian Brethren* (Stanford: Stanford University Press, 1967).

3. William A. Hinds, *American Communities and Co-operative Colonies.* 2nd rev. ed. (Chicago: Charles H. Kerr & Co., 1908), pp. 471–85.

4. William A. Hinds, *American Communities and Co-operative Colonies.* 2nd rev. ed. (Chicago: Charles H. Kerr & Co., 1908), pp. 456–63.

5. See Karl Goetz, "Das Deutschtum in Palestina" in *Mitteilungen der Akademie zur wissenschaftlichen Erforschung, und zur Pflege des Deutschtums,* Munich, November 1931, pp. 291–338.

6. William A. Hinds, *American Communities and Co-operative Colonies,* 2nd rev. ed. (Chicago: Charles H. Kerr & Co., 1908), pp. 412–21. A. J. F. Zieglschmid, *Die älteste Chronik der Hutterischen Brüder.* Ein Sprachdenkmal aus frühneuhochdeutscher Zeit (Ithaca: The Cayuga Press, 1943). *Das Klein-Geschichtsbuch der Hutterischen Brüder* (Philadelphia: The Cayuga Press, 1947). M. P. Riley: *The Hutterite Brethren.* An Annotated Bibliography with Special Reference to South Dakota Hutterite Colonies (Brookings, S. D.: South Dakota State University Press, 1965). John W. Bennett, *Hutterian Brethren* (Stanford, Calif.: University of California Press, 1967). Robert Friedmann, *Hutterite Studies* (Goshen, Ind.: Mennonite Historical Society, 1961).

7. *Christliche Zeitschrift für Christen* . . . Vom Geheimen Rath Hillmer. Dritter Jahrgang. Erstes Quartal. (Nürnberg, 1811). "Authentische Nachricht von den so genannten Hutterschen Brüdern in der Ukräne" (1802).

8. John Melish, *Travels in the United States of America in the years 1806–*

1811. 2 vols. (Philadelphia, Printed for the Author by T & G Palmer, 1812), vol. 2, pp. 64–83. "Journey to Harmony." A contemporary description of the original settlement at Harmony, often reprinted, e.g., *Society for Promoting Communities.* Reviewed at length in *Philanthropist* (London, 1815).

9. H. J. Chr. v. Grimmelshausen, *Der Abenteuerliche Simplicissimus.* Abdruck der ältesten Originalausgabe 1669 (Halle a/S.: Max Niemeyer, 1880). Book V, chapter 19.

10. For a history of this group, with whom the Harmonists had close relations, see: Bertha M. H. Shambaugh: *Amana, The Community of True Inspiration* (Iowa City: State Historical Society of Iowa, 1908). Amana still exists as a community, but recently gave up the communist system. They now manufacture the "Cadillac" of refrigerators.

Chapter 8

1. Ronald D. Gray, *Goethe The Alchemist.* A Study of Alchemical Symbolism in Goethe's Literary and Scientific Works (New York: Cambridge University Press, 1952).

2. Gottfried Arnold, *Das Geheimnis der Göttlichen Sophia oder Weisheit* (Leipzig: Bey Thomas Fritsch, 1700).

3. Julius F. Sachse, *The Music of the Ephrata Cloister* also *Conrad Beissel's Treatise on Music* as set forth in a preface to the *"Turtel Taube"* of 1747 (Lancaster, Pa.: Printed for the Author, New Era Printing Co., 1903). Joseph Bauman, *Das Leben und Wandel des in GOTT ruhenten und seligen Br. Ezechiel Sangmeisters; Weiland ein Einwohner von Ephrata* (Ephrata: Joseph Bauman, 1825). Walter C. Klein, *Johann Conrad Beissel. Mystic and Martinet 1690–1768* (Philadelphia: Pennsylvania University Press, 1942).

4. See also Hofrath von Ekhartshausen, *Die Wolke über dem Heiligthum, oder Etwas, wovon sich die stolze Philosophie unseres Jahrhunderts nichts träumen lässt* (n.p., probably Strassburg, 1802). Defense of Christianity against philosophy. Uses Kant in favor of Christianity. This book was an important force in the years following its publication. Was read by Czar Alexander and contributed to establishment of the Holy Alliance. It was read by the Harmonists. Copy in their library. The Harmonists also have many of his other publications, which reveals his great influence on the Society. Ernest J. Knapton, *The Lady of the Holy Alliance. The Life of Julie de Krüdener.* New York: Columbia University Press, 1939.

5. G. W. Featherstonhaugh, *A Conoe Voyage up the Minnay Sotor* (London, 1847), p. 83.

6. See Arndt, *George Rapp's Harmony Society, 1785–1847.* 1st ed., pp. 564–67.

Chapter 9

1. A copy of the full report is in my German-American collection.

Chapter 10

1. It is interesting to note that Junior Trustee Duss had already, on January 2, 1891, answered a direct inquiry about inheritance in this manner: "There is positively no chance for inheritance here for any person. The fact that some one is related to one who is or who has been a member of this Society, counts for naught; since members *themselves can not lay claim to any of the society's property*. Father Rapp disinherited himself and all his heirs (as did also all his associates with themselves and their heirs) at the time of the formation of the organization of the Harmony Society. How the relatives of Rapp are going to inherit property to which Father Rapp himself relinquished all right, claim and ownership, is more than I or any unbiased and unprejudiced person can understand."

2. This testimony is particularly important in view of the completely false reports of many modern writers who print and reprint the malicious story that Rapp castrated his own son when he found that his wife was pregnant. Celibacy was not adopted until after Gertrude's birth. For a particularly malicious recent version of this lie see Richard O'Connor, *The German-Americans* (Boston and Toronto: Little, Brown and Company, 1968), p. 222.

3. The *Speidel* v. *Henrici* case was taken all the way to the U.S. Supreme Court, where it was argued on December 14, 1886, and decided against him on March 7, 1887. Mr. Justice Gray delivered the opinion of the Court reasoning as follows: "The general rule that express trusts are not within the statute of limitations does not apply to a trust openly disavowed by the trustee with the knowledge of the cestui que trust. Implied trusts are barred by lapse of time. A court of equity will not assist one who has slept upon his rights, and shows no excuse for his laches in assorting them. If a bill in equity shows upon its face that the plaintiff, by reason of lapse of time and of his own laches, is not entitled to relief, the objection may be taken by demurrer. A bill in equity against persons holding a fund avowedly in trust for the common benefit of the members of a voluntary association, living together as a community and subject to its regulations, cannot, whether the trust is lawful or unlawful, be maintained by one who has left the community, and for fifty years afterwards taken no step to claim any interest in the fund." See United States Reports, vol. 120, October Term 1886, pp. 377–90.

4. I could not find a record of memorandum C or X. The record was not complete.

5. *Jacob Henrici,* by J. Twing Brooks. Harmony Society Historical Association. Published by Gilbert Adams Hays (Sewickly, Pa.: Press of the Village Print Shop, 1922).

Chapter 11

1. The name Feucht appears often as Feicht and similar variations because the Swabian pronunciation was nearer to Feicht and because names then were carelessly and often emotionally spelled.

2. See Howard, "Baker vs. Nachtrieb" in *Reports of Cases Argued and Adjudged in the Supreme Court of the US*. Vol. XIX December Term, 1856, pp. 126–30.

3. Duss kept up his friendly relations with Teed even later when he moved to Florida. They were quite similar in a number of ways and Duss certainly admired him.

Chapter 12

1. *Schwartz* v. *Duss*. U.S. Reports, Vol. 187, 8–41 (1902) —47 L. Ed. 52–23 S. Ct. 4 (1902).

Chapter 13

1. "Advertising Bandmaster Duss," in *Printers' Ink*, New York, August 27, 1902, pp. 14–15.

2. On June 15 Duss added interest to his show by issuing a special invitation to Lulu Glaser and members of the "Dolly Vaden" comic opera then running in New York. She came with most of her company, and Duss played airs from the comic opera to honor them. On June 18 Duss and his band marched up Broadway to attend the matinee of "Show Girl" and on the next Sunday all 50 of the "Show Girl" girls were his guests at Nicholas Garden. Next he invited the company of "King Dodo," and he continued this kind of advertising through the summer.

Chapter 14

1. As late as May 19, 1909, De Reszke owned ten Liberty Land Company bonds, which at par meant that he owned $10,000 of Harmony Society assets on that date. This suggests what kind of settlement was made, for these bonds had belonged to Duss.

Chapter 15

1. The Ambridge Plant, when built in 1903, was the largest structural steel fabricating plant in the world, and it still retains that distinction. Today the plant occupies an area of 140 acres, 16 of which are used as a park.

2. It is ironical that on this land which once belonged to people who left Germany partly because they were opposed to war, 123 LST vessels were built for the U.S. Navy, which were then floated down the Mississippi to be used in storming the beaches of the enemy in World War II, both in Europe and in the Pacific Theatre. Today the plant's principal products are: Barges, Boats, Bridges, Heroult Electric Melting Furnaces, Industrial, Mill and Office Buildings, Pipework, Subway Structures, Tanks, Turntables, Weldments of various types, Long and Short Span Joists, Steel Bridge Flooring, and Steel Swimming Pools. The plant ships and receives material by rail, water, and motor truck.

3. Francis R. Harbison, *D. T. Watson of Counsel* (Pittsburgh, Pa., Davis and Warde, 1945), pp. 188–209, especially page 200. This publication consists of "excerpts from the archives" of D. T. Watson. The fact that Watson was looked upon as "one of the English-speaking world's great lawyers and as one of the two greatest of his era" makes the numerous factual errors in his account all the more appalling and shocking, but they serve to further substantiate my conviction that any honest and capable lawyer having the sense and initiative to demand access to the Harmony Society archives could have torn Watson's carefully built house of cards to shreds.

Appendix A

Survey of the
Harmony Society Archives
at
Economy, Pennsylvania

Unbound documents and manuscripts

Most of the important source material is written in the German language and in old German script. A thorough knowledge of both is prerequisite for intelligent work in the Harmony Society Archives. Because of the great influence of German mystics on the life and thought of the Society, anyone contemplating serious research in the Archives should also be well versed in all the books of the Bible and the writings of the German mystics. Without such preparation most of the symbolism used in the letters of the leaders of the Society will be lost.

The manuscripts of the Rapp trusteeship: 1785–1847

In this period the letters of George Rapp, Frederick Rapp, and the Langenbachers (Bakers) are the most frequent and informative. There is a lively correspondence between these leaders of the Society because representatives of the Society were frequently away on business trips for the Society. The period of migration from Württemberg to Harmony, Pennsylvania, and from there to Indiana, and from Indiana to Economy, Pennsylvania, is covered in considerable detail by the correspondence between leaders building on the new frontier and those at the home base. Throughout this period there are also thousands of letters to the Society from all parts of the United States and Europe. The Indiana period contains some of the most valuable and most informative source material on the founding and development of Indiana into a State. There are letters from most of the prominent men of Indiana during the Indiana decade, also copies of letters from the Society to these men; there was also extensive correspondence with the pioneers of the English Prairie in Illinois for which the Harmonists did much work. Letters from Frederick and George Rapp and the Bakers are fairly representative of the entire period of their life. There are also many letters from relatives of members and from members who have withdrawn. The letter books covering this period of the Rapp trusteeship are well kept and contain copies of outgoing letters. Because they are bound, they are listed separately in the following section of bound records. Extremely important in this period are also the letters from the various agents of the Society, particularly the letters from Solms in Philadelphia. These letters give an excellent insight into current events and the business world of the time. Together with the letters from friends and relatives of members of the Society, they present a fine picture of life in America at that time and of immigration problems and procedures in the first half of the nineteenth century. There are very complete records of the silk manufacture of the Society and the mining and marketing of the Society's coal and oil.

The manuscripts of the Baker-Henrici Trusteeship: 1847–1868

There is a lively correspondence between Baker and Henrici during this period, which affords an insight into the social and business problems of the Society, particularly those dealing with the Society's pioneer work in drilling for oil wells. Beginning with this period there are also numerous, regular letters in German from Jonathan Lenz on Society affairs. These continue until his death. Again, the letters from the Agents of the Society are extremely important. There are letters from former members, relatives, and friends of members, highly interesting letters about the war between the states, and important letters from politicians and public officials. The German letters from Louise Weil, who lived in the Society for some time, are nonbusiness letters but valuable source material on life in the Society. There is a great variety of letters from persons from all walks of life to the leaders of the Society. Letters by the Feuchts and from Henning are especially revealing. There are also many legal records and interesting firsthand reports of life in Washington by Baker while attending U.S. Supreme Court trial of *Baker* vs. *Nachtrieb* (1856).

*The manuscripts of the Henrici-Lenz-Wölfel-Duss
Trusteeship: 1868–1892*

Most important in this period are the copies of letters written by Henrici. He dominates the picture. There are some valuable letters from Trustee Lenz and Wm. Merkle, the man in charge of the Economy Oil Company at Tidioute, Pennsylvania. The Merkle and Lenz letters give valuable information about the earliest days of the American oil industry. There is a very informative correspondence with other communist groups such as Amana, Ora Labora in Michigan, the order of the Temple and its work in the Holy Land, the Hutterian Brethren, Teed's Koreshanity, and others. There are many letters from outsiders seeking help or admission, or thanking for help received, also legal records of lawsuits, especially important the second time the Society appeared before the U.S. Supreme Court in *Speidel* vs. *Henrici* (1887).

*The manuscripts of the Duss-Siber-Riethmüller-Duss
Trusteeship: 1892–1905*

Most of the incoming letters of this period are pasted into bound books as they come in. There is a great variety of these—business, social, crackpot, religious, legal. Outgoing business letters were usually copied into bound books of thin copy paper. There are many files of legal papers covering the various lawsuits of the Society, e.g., *Feucht* vs. *Duss, Everitt* vs. *Duss, Schwartz* vs. *Duss, Todd* vs. *Duss* (*Quo warranto*). This is the period that is least adequately covered, because the affairs of the Society were handled out of legal offices in Pittsburgh, hence these records were not included in the Society Archives. The *Schwartz* vs. *Duss* case, argued in 1902, was the third time the Society appeared before the United States Supreme Court.

Although the Archives have some material on the pre-American period of the Society, most of this material is to be found in archives of Maulbronn, Ludwigsburg, Stuttgart, and Tübingen, Germany. For the American period of the Society the bulk of the material, also mostly German insofar as the really important records are concerned, is found in the Harmony Society Archives at Ambridge, Pennsylvania, near Pittsburgh. Other manuscript sources came into private possession after John S. Duss became trustee of the Society and sold much of the property at public auction. In this way a valuable collection came by purchase to Indiana University, Bloomington. Many things were also removed from Ambridge by the Dusses when they went to Florida. From there and from the descendants of seceders items have been finding their way into the hands of collectors and libraries. Fugitive pieces and smaller collections were located at New York Public Library, Historical Society of Pennsylvania, Library of Congress, Supreme Court Library in Washington, D.C., W. H. Smith Memorial Library, and Indiana State Library in Indianapolis, Darlington Library of the University of Pittsburgh, Chicago Public Library, Library Company of Philadelphia, Workingmen's Institute of New Harmony, Indiana, and various personal collections in Chicago, eastern Ohio, and western Pennsylvania. A large amount of manuscript material and what remained of a library belonging to the chief librarian of the City of Frankfort am Main during the time of Goethe was laboriously collected by me on many research field trips in Louisiana, Texas, Ohio, Indiana, Pennsylvania, and Württemberg. There still is an interesting collection of manuscripts and books which belonged to the seceders to be seen at Germantown near Minden, Louisiana, where Count Leon's people ultimately settled. Their most valuable manuscript, however, was sold to the Library of Congress by a Shreveport, Louisiana, dealer who had acquired it. I had two photostat copies made of this interesting record, which contains the legal code for the Millennium, and presented one to the descendants of Count Leon at Germantown and kept the other for my own archives. There are also Harmony Society records in the court houses in the areas where the Society did most of its business, particularly in the court houses of Butler County and Beaver County in Pennsylvania, and Posey County, Indiana. By this search many transactions, no longer to be found in the Harmony Society Archives, could be followed to their conclusion. Because of the important early connections with Columbiana County, Ohio, the court house archives there also contain valuable records on the Society and its former members, particularly the Gloss faction which broke away from Rapp rather early. There is a personal file for most members in the Archives from which personal biographical information may be obtained. Mention should be made of valuable maps of Pennsylvania and Indiana, many of these done by hand and showing the lands of the Society. Also, Ohio Historical Society.

I should like to conclude this survey of the unbound section of manuscripts and letters in the Harmony Society Archives with the hope that before long at least the letters of the leaders of the Society up to 1847 will be published in a bilingual edition to make this unique record of migration and pioneering on our frontier available to those who now enjoy the fruits of the Harmonist's pioneering.

These papers constitute a unique record because they give in the words of the pioneers themselves their day-by-day account of the labor, suffering, joy, and hope, and they show how in all this activity their greatest source of strength lay in the fact that they were always living in the presence of an Almighty God, whose glorious reign on earth was about to begin and whose advance guard their Society represented.

Bound Records

1790
Book of letters from George Rapp to Hagmäyer: 1793–1802. 29 letters from Rapp copied into a book. They show Rapp's pastoral activity in Württemberg and reflect his early influence among the people of Württemberg before coming to America. Also other individual unbound letters for this period.

1800
Numerous unbound letters from 1800–1810 written by Frederick and George Rapp and others in the Society and outside.

SCHOOL EXERCISE BOOK 6: 1802. School exercises. Arithmetic book written by John Rapp.

DAY BOOK 20: 1804–1805. Daily record of merchandise sold to individuals by Society.

INVOICE BOOK 21: 1804–1806. Merchandise purchased by Society from various individuals.

FAMILY BOOK 7: 1805–1807. Accounts of Society families.

DAY BOOK 13: 1806–April–Dec. Merchandise sold.

INVOICE BOOK 26: 1806–1812. Goods purchased by Society.

DAY BOOK 6: 1807–Jan.–Oct. Purchases and sales by the Society from individuals.

DAY BOOK 30: 1806–1807. Purchases of goods made by Society.

LEDGER BOOK 9: 1807–1811. Accounts with the Society. Merchandise.

DAY BOOK 29: 1808. Purchases of goods. Sales of goods by Society at Harmony store.

LEDGER BOOK 2: 1808–1812. Accounts with Society.

"BOOK OF LIFE": 1805–1890. Articles of agreements and signatures.

Tabel Buch der Nahmen der Kinder so in Harmony gebohren seyn: 1804–1820. (Family register)

1810

SCHOOL EXERCISE BOOK 14: c. 1810. School exercises. Arithmetic book, equivalence tablet, measures, weights, and currency.

SCHOOL EXERCISE BOOK 13: c. 1810. School exercises. Arithmetic book.

SCHOOL EXERCISE BOOK 15: c. 1810. School exercises. Dictionary, English-German.

SCHOOL EXERCISE BOOK 18: c. 1810. School exercises. French grammar and exercises.

CASH BOOK 22: 1810–1814. Daily accounts. Bank notes, cash receipts and expenditures.

LEDGER BOOK 3: 1810–1817. Ledger. Accounts with Society.

SCHOOL EXERCISE BOOK 7: 1811. School exercises. Arithmetic book written by David Ruff, Harmony, Butler Co.

LEDGER 29: 1811–1812. Accounts with Society. Income from enterprises.

LEDGER BOOK 31: 1811–1849. Ledger. Accounts with the Society. Note: Index in front.

DAY BOOK 7: 1811–1812. Sales by Society to individuals.

FAMILY BOOK 3: 1811–1815. Family ledger. Record of merchandise received by members of Society.

MEMORANDUM BOOK 4: 1811–1821. Record of harvests, dairy products, cattle, meat from Society farms. Record of produce and sundry merchandise bought.

INVOICE BOOK 5: 1812–1813. Purchases and sales with Isaac Bean, Pittsburgh, Joseph McFerran at Beaver Point.

CORRESPONDENCE BOOK 2: 1812–1818. Letters from Society written by Frederick Rapp.

FARM BOOK 6: 1812–1821. Sheep raising. Record of sheep and amount of wool produced.

ORDER BOOK 5: 1812–1823. Order book. Memorandum of orders on the manufactory in Harmonie.

CORRESPONDENCE BOOK 20: 1812–1824. Letters from Society.

INVOICE BOOK 2: 1813–1818. Purchases and sales with Mr. Isaac Bean and Co., Pittsburgh, Pa. Abishai Way Co.

CLOTH BOOK 14: 1813–1819. Color, quantity, price of dyes. Used by dyer for members of Society.

MEDICINE BOOK 11: 1814. Medicine book. Recipes of various medicines and their appliance.

DAY BOOK 2: 1814–1815—Oct.–Nov. Note exchange. Money transactions.

DAY BOOK 25: 1814–1885. Shoemaker's day book. Mathew Scholle.

DAY BOOK 2: 1814–1817. Daily entries of merchandise.

DAY BOOK 18: 1814–1819. Accounts with Society.

FAMILY LEDGER BOOK 5: 1815–1819. Family ledger. Accounts with wool, carter, carpenter, tartar, potter, doctor, weavers, dyers, nail-makers, shoemakers, saddler, blacksmith, tavern, tinner, distillery, stocking weaver, tanner, hatter, wagonmaker, brewery, soap. Memo. of soap and butter given out.

LEDGER 28: 1816–1819. Petty ledger accounts with Society.

LEDGER BOOK 31: 1816–1840. Harvests of Harmony Society. Records.

INVOICE BOOK 3: 1818–Sept. 14. Prices (wholesale) of articles manufactured in Harmony. Hats, saddles, bridles, stockings.

CASH BOOK 27: 1818–1819. Cash transactions of Frederick Rapp.

DAY BOOK 31: 1818–1819. Pittsburgh point brewery, purchases made, agreements, receipts and expenditures, individual accounts.

CORRESPONDENCE BOOK 6: 1818–1822. Letters from Society written by Frederick Rapp.

INVOICE BOOK 3: 1818–1830. Shipments by Society. Mostly by wagon.

WOOL BOOK 9: 1818–1834. Wool book, list of prices for dyeing of cloth. Harmonie, Indiana account.

DAY BOOK 24: 1819–1821. Day book. Produce Book.

SCHOOL EXERCISE BOOK 19: 1819–1822. School exercises. Composition Book used by Pauline Speidel during her school years.

FARM BOOK 4: 1819–1824. Record of land clearings. Grain sowed and grain harvested. Income and expenditures from each farm.

INVOICE BOOK 3: 1819–1825. Purchases and sales between companies and Society.

FAMILY BOOK 4: 1819–1826. Family ledger. Accounts with barber, carpenter, coopers, doctor, distillery, hatter, cloth, shoemaker, stocking, tavern, tailor, wool, carder, wagonmaker.

1820

SCHOOL EXERCISE BOOK 9: 1820. School exercises. Arithmetic book written by Christian Lenz.

SCHOOL EXERCISE BOOK 8: 1820. School exercises. Arithmetic book written by Phillip Becker, in Harmony.

SCHOOL EXERCISE BOOK 21: c. 1820. School exercises. French grammar exercises.

SCHOOL EXERCISE BOOK 22: c. 1820. School exercises. Physics and chemistry.

SCHOOL EXERCISE BOOK 15: 1820–1823. School exercises. German grammar written by Florena Stahl.

CLOTH BOOK 13: 1820–1855. Dye materials. Chemicals bought to make dyes. Dyes purchased.

SCHOOL EXERCISE BOOK 10: 1821. School exercises. Arithmetic Book written by George Weingartner.

CORRESPONDENCE BOOK 26: 1821–1823. Letters written by John Reichart and Gottlieb Langenbacher to Abishai Way and Co.

DAY BOOK 22: 1821–1823. Produce book. Produce bought by the Society. Sales and purchases by Society.

LEDGER BOOK 30: 1821–1826. Petty ledger. Accounts with the Society.

CLOTH BOOK 12: 1821–1827. Women's clothing. Distribution of women's clothing.

BLACKMITH SHOP BOOK 2: 1822–1824. Blacksmith shop. Production and distribution of new implements and repair work.

LEDGER BOOK 62: 1822–1825. Ledger of agriculture. Harmony Indiana. List of field marks:

Spring-field—44½ acres.	Poplar-field—69½ acres.
Walnut-field—30½ acres.	Creek-field—41 acres.
Sheep-field—44½ acres.	Lewis-field—48 acres.
Ranken-field—38 acres.	Lewis-middle—50 acres.
Wine-field—30½ acres.	Lewis-upper—57½ acres.
Grafing-field—60 acres.	Meiner-field—25 acres.
Graben-field—50 acres.	Althauser—50 acres.
Bridge-field—57 acres.	Althauser-field—87 acres.
Stallings-field—52 acres.	Hickory-field—36 acres.
Saal-field—50 acres.	Barn-field—22 acres.

Time of sowing and harvest, amount of crops harvested in bushels as: wheat, oats, corn, barley and rye.

1864–1875

Time of men and women working in fields.

CORRESPONDENCE BOOK 4: 1822–1825. Letters from Society written by Frederick Rapp.

CLOTH BOOK 5: 1822–1828. Cloth distributed to members.

FARM BOOK 2: 1822–1854. Record of livestock. Farm produce; grains in field; Harvested and stored. Distribution.

MEMORANDUM BOOK 3: 1823. Memo. book of store in Harmony.

MEMORANDUM BOOK 3: 1823. Memo. book of store in Harmony.

MISCELLANEOUS BOOK 4: 1823. Medicine given by Society. Hospital receiving medicines.

DAY BOOK 3: 1823–1825. Goods purchased by Society from individuals. Hides, grain, butter.

INVOICE BOOK 8: 1823–1827. Sales by Society to companies and individuals. Store at Shawneetown. Store at Vincennes.

CATALOGUE BOOK 4: 1829. Catalogue of books. List of books and prices.

STORE RECORDS BOOK 2: 1823–1832. Store records, receipts, expenditures and inventory for stores at Vincennes and Shawneetown.

ORDER BOOK 3: 1823–1841. Goods ordered from and by the Society.

LEDGER BOOK 63: 1823–1843. Textile production. Various types of cloth, weight, length in yards, kind of yarn used and name of weaver.

MEMORANDUM BOOK 3: 1824. Fruit trees sold.

MEMORANDUM OF DRAFTS AND NOTES SENT FROM HARMONIE. 1824–1827. Cash book. Receipts of cash from Frederick Rapp and R. L. Baker. Expenditures for goods bought. 1823.

INVOICE BOOK 10: 1824–1828. Purchases of merchandise by Society. Goods brought to Economy from Harmonie Indiana. Aug. 26.

DAY BOOK 32: 1824–1833. Merchandise put up and forwarded to Economy at different times and various transports.

LEATHER BOOK 2: 1824–1836. Purchases and expenditures by Society, store, saddlery, tanners, teamsters, wool factory, cotton factory and individuals for leather and deer skins. Causes of accidental death taken from the *Pittsburgh Observer* July 28, 1833, written in German.

ECONOMY OIL BOOK 24: 1825. Memorandum of goods shipped to Economy by William Penn. Samples of various bank-notes and money. Also oil wells oil account.

CASH BOOK 28: 1825–1826. Deposits and withdrawals by check.

LEDGER BOOK 59: 1825–1828. Accounts with the Society.

LEDGER BOOK 21: 1825–1828. Accounts with the Society.

CORRESPONDENCE BOOK: 1825–1828: Official letters sent out by Society Trustees.

LEDGER BOOK 32: 1825–1829. Accounts book.

CLOTH BOOK 6: 1825–1831. Orders packed.

CASH BOOK 29: 1825–1831. Deposits and withdrawals.

MEMORANDUM BOOK 3: 1825–1831. Road taxes paid with labor and material. Allegheny Co.

FAMILY BOOK 6: 1825–1832. Family ledger. Accounts of family of Society.

FREIGHT BOOK 5: 1825–1833. Record of shipments. Invoice of shipments.

MEMORANDUM BOOK 3: 1826. Prices of wool.

WOOL BOOK 5: 1826–1827. Purchases of wool by Society from individuals.

CLOTH BOOK 8: 1826–1830. Yarn spun. Spinning of yarn record of.

INVOICE BOOK 24: 1826–1831. Invoice of goods sent to Abishai. Way and Company by Society.

DAY BOOK 16: 1826–1831. Daily sales and purchases by the Society.

DAY BOOK 23: 1826–1831. Produce purchased by Society. Record of wheat, rye, corn, oats, flax seed, barley, beeswax, linen, shingles, rags, sugar, and hides.

WOOL BOOK 10: 1826–1836. List of individuals, amounts of wool and prices paid by Society.

CLOTH BOOK 3: 1826–1845. Record of cotton goods manufactured. Production of ribbons, satin vests, velvets, wool, handkerchief.

LEDGER BOOK 33: 1826–1853. Goods purchased by society for general use, blacksmith, brewery, cotton factory, cloth, cooper, doctor, distillery, dyer, glovemaker, hatter, joiner, flour mill, machinery, oil mill, potter, reel maker, saw mill, shoe maker, saddler, soap boiler, silk factory, tanner, tinner, turner, painter, tavern, tailor, wool factory, wagonmaker, museum, carpenter, weaver, cordwood, land cleaner, breechesmaker, barber, watchmaker. Cash receipts of various enterprises listed above. Index (incomplete) in front of book.

CASH BOOK 89: 1827. Cash book. Receipts of cash from Frederick Rapp and goods bought. Addresses of 200 merchants, bankers, consuls, printers, lawyers and physicians.

WOOL BOOK 7: 1827. Invoice book. Wool purchased by Society.

INVOICE BOOK 19: 1827–1830. Merchandise sold by Society.

INVOICE BOOK 25: 1827–1858. Commission book. Invoice of goods sent to agents on commission.

TRANSLATIONS OF HARMONY AGREEMENTS: 1827–1892. Mutilated.

MISCELLANEOUS BOOK 8: 1828. Summons, subpoena. Blank forms.

WOOL BOOK 3: 1828, March 15–December 31. Purchases of wool by Society from various individuals.

MEMORANDUM BUCH DES MUSIC BANDES DER OKON-OMIE: 1828–1831. Musical programs given and comments thereon.

WOOL BOOK 3: 1828–May 18–August 14. Cloth sold during wool season.

CORRESPONDENCE BOOK 5: 1828–1830. Letters from Society written by Frederick Rapp and R. L. Baker. English–several in German. (Index–Last page of book).

INVOICE BOOK 7: 1828–1832. Purchases by Society from various companies.

CLOTH BOOK 11: 1828–1840. Women's clothing. Distribution of clothing to women.

CASH BOOK 5: 1828–1847. Cash received and expended.

MEDICINE BOOK 10: 1828–1848. Medicine book. Recipes and prescriptions given to individuals.

LEDGER BOOK 64: 1828–1872. Textile mill. Accounts of production in linen, wool cloth, muslin, scarfs, cotton cloth, carpets and fustian (combination of cotton and linen) by various weavers).

THERMOMETER BOOK: 1829 (WR 11)

WOOL BOOK 8: 1829–1829. Invoice book. Wool purchased by Society.

CATALOGUE BOOK 4: 1829. Catalogue of books once held by the Harmony Society. List of books and prices.

CLOTH BOOK 10: 1829–1848. Distribution of cloth to members.

SHOE SHOP BOOK 5: 1829–1850. Shoe shop. Record of production and distribution.

LEDGER BOOK 19: 1829–1865. Petty ledger. Accounts with Society.

1830

WOOL BOOK 11: c. 1830. Wool book. Samples of woolen cloth. Different ways and colors in dyeing cloth.

WOOL BOOK 9: 1830. Wool purchased by the Society.

INVOICE BOOK 23: 1830–1843. Sales book. Merchandise sold by Society.

LEDGER BOOK 65: 1830–1852. Textile Mill. Daily production of textiles, material length and weight.

WOOL BOOK 2: 1831–1832. Purchases of wool from Society from various individuals.

CORRESPONDENCE BOOK 24: 1831–1835. Letters from Society. Written by Frederick Rapp, R. L. Baker, Jacob Henrici. Note: Index in front of book.

CLOTH BOOK 5: 1831–1838. Production of cloth.

DAY BOOK 26: 1831–1839. Frederick Rapp's day book.

CLOTH BOOK 4: 1831–1841. Cloth stored. Record of sales. Invoice of cotton goods sold to companies.

DAY BOOK 21: 1831–1841. Produce bought by Society. Record of grain, ashes, butter, tallow, feathers, pork, fur, and wool.

BOOK OF RECORD AND ACTS OF THE COUNSEL OF ELDERS: 1832–1850.

CASH BOOK 30: 1832–1837. Bank accounts, deposits and withdrawals.

INVOICE BOOK 6: 1832–1846. Purchases by Society from various companies.

MISCELLANEOUS 4: 1832–1875. Post Office transactions. Postmaster: R. L. Baker.

SCHOOL EXERCISE BOOK 11: 1833. School exercises. Arithmetic Book written by Nicander Wolfangel, also used by his son John Wolfangel.

CASH BOOK 31: 1833–1834. Deposits and withdrawals.

MEMORANDUM BOOK 2: 1833–1834. Record of sicknesses of members of Society. Recipes—Making of silk, cloth, cleaver, cements, varnishes, gilding, silvering, grindstones, chemical experiments, glue.

WOOL BOOK 12: 1833–1836. Wool purchased from individuals by Society and prices paid, agreements.

WOOL BOOK 4: 1833–1836. Purchases of wool by Society from individuals.

LADING BOOK 12: 1833–1838. Bills of Lading. Shipment by society on wagon.

FAMILY BOOK 2: 1833–1861. Ledger. Family account with Society.

CASH BOOK 31: 1834–1835. Deposits. Deposits and withdrawals.

CASH BOOK 32: 1834–1835. Deposits and withdrawals.

CASH BOOK 90: 1834–1835. Tax Book. List of individual and Society members taxed.

LEDGER BOOK 21: 1834–1839. Accounts with Society.

LADING BOOK 12: 1834–1839. Bills of lading. Shipments by Society on steamboat.

CASH BOOK 33: 1834–1840. Deposits and withdrawals.

DAY BOOK 17: 1834–1840. Daily sales at Baden store by E. Culberson.

CASH BOOK 34: 1835–1836. Deposits and withdrawals.

CORRESPONDENCE BOOK 19: 1835–1839. Letters from Society. Index in back of book.

SILK RECORDS: 1836–1841.

LEDGER BOOK 61: 1836–1841. Ledger. Accounts with Society by individuals. Amounts of stone coal used by blacksmith shop, wool factory, mill tavern, distillery store, hat shop, washhouse, barn and silk factory.

CORRESPONDENCE BOOK 3: 1836–1841. Letters from Society written by George Rapp and others.

CASH BOOK 35: 1836–1841. Deposits and withdrawals.

LAND AND MONEY BOOK 13: 1836–1852. Notes—Mortgages, stocks. Shares—interests, bonds. Judgments: loans, record of.

CASH BOOK 36: 1837–1839. Deposits and withdrawals.

SERMON BOOK: 1837–1863. Mostly Rapp's sermons.

WOOL BOOK 6: 1837–1877. Purchases of wool by Society from various individuals.

CASH BOOK 37: 1838. Deposits and withdrawals.

LEDGER BOOK 60: 1839–1840. Ledger. Accounts with Society.

SILK BOOK 2: 1839–1842. Silk book of cocoons, production, weight and reeled silk.

CORRESPONDENCE BOOK 23: 1839–1848. Letters from Society. Written by R. L. Baker, Jacob Henrici.

BILLS OF LADING BOOK 2: 1839–1852. Steamboat shipments by George Rapp later R. L. Baker.

DAY BOOK 15: 1839–1875. Merchandise sold by Society.

DAY BOOK 10: 1839–1875. Sales of merchandise by the Society.

1840

CASH BOOK 38: 1840. Deposits and withdrawals.

CLOTH BOOK 16: 1840–1843. Silk manufactured. Satin manufactured. Ribbons manufactured.

SCHOOL EXERCISE BOOK 17: 1841. School exercises. French grammar and exercises written by Conrad Feucht.

CASH BOOK 91: 1841. Tax book. List of individuals taxed in Economy township.

TAX RECORDS BOOK 24: 1841. Tax book. Taxes paid by individuals of Economy Township and Economy Society.

TAX RECORDS BOOK 25: 1841. Tax book. Taxes paid by individuals of Economy Township.

WOOL BOOK 13: 1841. Wool book, purchases and expenditures by Society for wool from individual prices.

WOOL BOOK 14: 1841. Wool purchases made by Society from individuals and prices.

CASH BOOK 40: 1841–1842. Bills and notes from Louisville, New Orleans and St. Louis.

CASH BOOK 39: 1841–1842. Deposits and amount of interest paid.

SILK BOOK 3: 1841–1845. Silk book, accounts of reeled silk, types and weight.

DAY BOOK 14: 1841–1845. Sales and purchases of grain. Hides. Wool. Daily records.

CASH BOOK 41: 1841–1847. Deposits and withdrawals.

CASH BOOK 41: 1841–1847. Deposits and withdrawals.

CLOTH BOOK 9: 1841–1881. Women's clothes. Clothes furnished to the women of society.

SILK BOOK 4: 1842. Cocoon book, daily accounts of various types of cocoons, amount and weight.

CORRESPONDENCE BOOK 21: 1842–1847. Copies of letters about silk business.

CLOTH BOOK 2: 1842–1853. Cloth shipments from mill to companies.

WINE CELLAR BOOK 2: 1842–1860. Whiskey book. Amount of whiskey distributed among various members listed. 1842–1859. Account of carpets and blankets received by members of Society for their own use.

SILK MFG. BOOK 8: 1843. Silk book. Reeling of silk from cocoons and weight.

SILK BOOK 5: 1844–1846. Silk book. List of various silk dyes, and how to use them.

LEDGER BOOK 34: 1844–1854. Contingent fund deductions. Donations to charities and individuals. Wagner Case expenses. Patterson (James) expenses.

DAY BOOK 5: 1844–1868. Sales by Society to individuals. Wine, whiskey, wool, grain. (miscellaneous merchandise)

SILK BOOK 6: 1845. Silk book. Samples and various ways of dying, different colors.

SILK MFG. BOOK 9: 1845. Silk book. Reeling of silk from cocoons and weight.

SILK BOOK 7: 1846. Silk book, accounts of cocoons, weight and production.

LEDGER BOOK 35: 1846–1890. Taxes, Road-Limestone Township. Expenditures and receipts. Warren County-Limestone Township.

SILK MFG. BOOK 10: 1847. Silk book. Reeling of silk from cocoons and weight.

SILK MFG. BOOK 11: 1847–1848. Silk book. Daily record for the cultivation of silkworms.

SCHOOL EXERCISE BOOK 12: 1847–1851. School exercises. Arithmetic book, tables, measures, weights and currency written by Wolfangel.

CASH BOOK 42: 1847–1857. Deposits and withdrawals.

INVOICE BOOK 11: 1847–1867. Purchases made by Society. Goods bought.

MEDICINE BOOK 7: 1847–1870. Medicine book. Recipes for various kinds of medicines.

DAY BOOK 4: 1847–1880. Purchases of merchandise by Society from individuals.

CORRESPONDENCE BOOK 25: 1848–1878. Letters from society. Written by R. L. Baker and Jacob Henrici.

MEMO BOOK 7: 1848–1849. Medicine. Prescriptions filled...... record.

LEATHER BOOK 3: 1849–1869. Saddle shop. Accounts of saddles, harnesses and leather straps and belts.

LEDGER BOOK 36: 1849–1883. Taxes-School-Limestone Township. Expenditures and receipts. Warren County-Limestone Township.

1850

MEDICINE BOOK 6: 1850–1853. Medicine book. List of various medicines.

FARM BOOK 7: 1850–1855. Farm book. Livestock accounts as hogs, cattle, calves and sheep, including market prices on meat and hides and domestic use.

MEDICINE BOOK 5: 1850–1858. Medicine book. Prescriptions of medicines given to various persons in Economy. How to use the medicine.

LAND AND MONEY TRANSACTION BOOK 2: 1851–1871. Money, loans, investments, stocks, mortgages, bonds. 1860–1863. Minutes of Oil Co. meetings.

INVOICE BOOK 9: 1851–1874. Purchases of medical supplies for Society by R. L. Baker. Record of medicine sold to individuals.

TAX RECORD BOOK 26: 1852. Tax book. List of taxables and

amounts in Harmony township, assessor Jacob Henrici including Society members.

TAX BOOK 2: 1852. Tax records for Harmony township and Harmony Society, list of state tax, county tax and militia fines.

CLOTH BOOK 15: 1852–1862. Muslin—linen given out to society families.

LADING BOOK 8: 1853–1855. Shipment of goods by railroad. R. L. Baker, Trustee.

WAGE BOOK 8: 1853–1861. Wages paid to workers in merchandise.

LEDGER BOOK 57: 1853–1864. Individual accounts, lands, stocks, mortgages, expenditures and receipts. Harmony Society.

TAX RECORDS BOOK 27: 1854. Tax book. List of taxables, occupations, assessments in Harmony township and Society. Assessor Jacob Henrici. General accounts of Society mortgages, judgments, notes, bonds, agreements, real estate, stocks, personal property number of deaf, dumb, blind and militia list.

LAND AND MONEY BOOK 16: 1854–1859. Accounts of receipts and expenditures of Ross land.

ECONOMY LUMBER BOOK 45: 1854–1864. Lumber book. List of individual accounts including, Sewickley Bridge, Mariata bridge and Darlington engine house accounts.

LEDGER BOOK 37: 1854–1882. Account with Society Logging Co., by various workers Hausen, J. P. Accountant, Limestone Twp. Warren County. Records of purchases and wage deductions. Work records in back of book.

CASH BOOK 6: 1854–1892. Money received by Society from baker, tavern, tanner, wagonmaker, etc.

TAX RECORDS BOOK 28: 1855. Tax book. List of taxables their occupations, assessments in Harmony township and Society. Assessor Jacob Henrici. General accounts of Society, mortgages, judgments, notes, bonds, agreements, real estate, stocks, personal property number of deaf, dumb, and blind and militia list.

CASH BOOK 43: 1855–1856. Deposits and withdrawals.

TAX RECORDS BOOK 29: 1856. Tax book. List of taxables their occupations, assessments in Harmony township and Society. Assessor Jacob Henrici. General accounts of mortgages, judgments, notes, agreements, bonds, stocks, real estate, personal property and militia list.

CASH BOOK 44: 1856–1857. Deposits and withdrawals.

TAILOR SHOP BOOK 4: 1856–1868. Tailor shop. Account of the distribution of coats, pants and other clothes to the Society members.

TAX RECORDS BOOK 30: 1857. Tax book. List of taxables their occupations, assessments in Harmony township and Society. Assessor Jacob Henrici, general accounts of mortgages, judgments, notes, agreements, bonds, stocks, real estate, personal and militia list.

CASH BOOK 45: 1857–1861. Deposits and withdrawals.

CASH BOOK 46: 1857–1865. Deposits and withdrawals.

FARM BOOK 5: 1858. Farm book. Names and acreage of the various fields in Economy.

TAX RECORDS BOOK 31: 1858. Tax book. List of taxables and their occupations, assessments, in Harmony township and Society, Assessor Jacob Henrici. General accounts of mortgages, judgments, notes, agreements, bonds, stocks, real estate, personal property and militia list.

MEMORANDUM BOOK 6: 1858–1877. Miscellaneous notations.

JUSTICE OF PEACE BOOK 2: 1858–1893. Cases heard by Justice of Peace. J. P. Houser, Limestone Warren County.

TAX RECORDS BOOK 32: 1859. Tax book. List of taxables their occupation, assessments in Harmony township and Society. Assessor Jacob Henrici. General accounts of mortgages, judgments, notes, stocks, real estate, personal property and militia list.

CASH BOOK 47: 1859–1860. Deposits and withdrawals.

CASH BOOK 48: 1859–1861. Deposits and withdrawals.

1860

TAX RECORDS BOOK 33: 1860. Tax book. List of taxables their occupation, assessments in Harmony township and Society. General accounts of mortgages, judgments, notes, stocks, real estate, personal property and militia list.

LADING BOOK 7: 1860–1862. Goods shipped by R. L. Baker by railroad.

LEDGER BOOK 38: 1861. Accounts with Economy Oil Co., by various workers. Lenz, Jonathan—Accountant. Tidioute. Record of purchases and wage deductions. Partial index in front of book.

LEDGER BOOK 38: 1861. Accounts with Economy Oil Co., by various workers. Lenz, Jonathan—Accountant. Tidioute. Record of purchases and wage deductions. Partial index in front of book.

TAX RECORDS BOOK 34: 1861. Tax book. List of taxables their occupation, assessments in Harmony township and Society. General accounts of mortgages, judgments, notes, bonds, stocks, real estate, personal property and militia list.

LEDGER BOOK 20: 1861–1862. Accounts with Society. Petty ledger.

ECONOMY OIL BOOK 16: 1861–1862. Cash book. Cash payments.

ECONOMY OIL CO. BOOK 28: 1861–1862. Economy Oil Co. Oil well accounts and amount of oil from each well. Orders filled.

CASH BOOK 49: 1861–1863. Deposits and withdrawals. Memorandum of checks made out to individuals.

WAGE BOOK 9: 1861–1868. Work book. Account in goods.

LUMBER BOOK 46: 1861–1881. Lumber book of individual accounts with the lumber mill. Wine accounts showing the amount of barrels. 1861–1881.

TAX RECORDS BOOK 35: 1862. Tax book. List of taxables their occupation, assessments in Harmony Township and Society. General accounts of mortgages, judgments, notes, bonds, stocks, real estate, personal property and militia list.

LADING BOOK 9: 1862–1864. Shipment of goods by railroad R. L. Baker, Trustee.

CASH BOOK 50: 1862–1865. Deposits and withdrawals. Memorandum of checks made out to individuals.

TAX BOOK 3: 1862–1866. Federal tax on whiskey, leather, rail roads, license and income tax for Harmony Society.

ECONOMY OIL BOOK 19: 1862–1866. Day book. Sale of merchandise at Tidoute. Payments.

STORE RECORDS BOOK 3: 1863–1870. Store records, list of individual accounts.

TAX RECORDS BOOK 36: 1863–1873. Tax book. List of taxables their occupations, assessments in Harmony township and Society. General accounts of mortgages, judgments, notes, bonds, stocks, real estate, personal property and militia list.

ECONOMY OIL BOOK 16: 1864. Ledger. Accounts with E. O. Co.

ECONOMY OIL BOOK 13: 1864–1865. Money paid out by Economy Oil Co.

ECONOMY OIL BOOK 18: 1864–1865. Accounts with E. O. Co.

ECONOMY OIL BOOK 21: 1864–1866. Day book. Sales, purchases of Economy Oil Co.

ECONOMY OIL CO. BOOK 30: 1864–1866. Economy Oil Co. Cash book. Receipts and expenditures.

ECONOMY OIL CO. BOOK 29: 1864–1866. Economy Oil Co. Expenditures of the Economy Oil Co.

LADING BOOK 4: 1864–1866. Shipments by railroad by Society. R. L. Baker, Trustee.

ECONOMY OIL BOOK 27: 1864–1868. Time and payroll book of the Economy Oil Co.

ECONOMY OIL BOOK 9: 1864–1868. Expense book. Cash expenditures of Economy Oil Co.

ECONOMY OIL BOOK 24: 1864–1872. Daily report of oil well production. Shipments.

ECONOMY OIL BOOK 2: 1864–1875. Oil sold by James Patterson.

LEDGER BOOK 62: 1864–1875. 1822–1825. Ledger of agriculture. Harmony Indiana. List of field marks:

Spring-field—44½ acres.	Poplar-field—69½ acres.
Walnut-field—30½ acres.	Creek-field—41 acres.
Sheep-field—44½ acres.	Lewis-field—48 acres.
Ranken-field—38 acres.	Lewis-middle—50 acres.
Wine-field—30½ acres.	Lewis-upper—57½ acres.
Grafing-field—60 acres.	Meiner-field—25 acres.
Graben-field—50 acres.	Althauser—50 acres.
Bridge-field—57 acres.	Althauser-field—87 acres.
Stallings-field—52 acres.	Hickory-field—36 acres.
Saal-field—50 acres.	Barn-field—22 acres.

Time of sowing and harvest amount of crops harvested in bushels as: wheat, oats, corn, barley and rye. 1864–1875. Time of men and women working fields.

ECONOMY LUMBER BOOK 24: 1864–1879. Sales of lumber.

WAGE BOOK 25: 1865. Wage book. Cash expenditures and wages paid out to individuals.

ECONOMY OIL BOOK 6: 1865–1866. Receipts of oil received by shipping agents.

CASH BOOK 52: 1865–1867. Deposits and withdrawals. Memorandum of checks made out to individuals.

CASH BOOK 51: 1865–1867. Deposits and withdrawals. Memorandum of checks made out to individuals.

CASH BOOK 52: 1865–1867. Deposits. Deposits and withdrawals. Memorandum of checks made out to individuals.

TAX RECORDS BOOK 37: 1865–1875. Tax book. List of taxables their occupations, assessments in Harmony township and Society. General accounts of mortgages, judgments, notes, bonds, stocks, real estate, personal property and militia list.

ECONOMY OIL BOOK 20: 1865–1878. Ledger. Accounts with Ralston and Economy Oil Co.

LAND AND MONEY BOOK 14: 1865–1880. Bills receivable. Receivable bills. Loans outstanding. Notes.

LADING BOOK 5: 1866–1868. Shipments by railroad by Society.

ECONOMY OIL BOOK 3: 1866–1868. Cash payments by Economy Oil Co.

ECONOMY OIL BOOK 22: 1866–1868. Receipt book. Money received from Economy Oil Co.

ECONOMY OIL BOOK 12: 1866–1869. Cash book. Payments in cash for wages, taxes, sundries. Cash receipts also.

ECONOMY OIL BOOK 14: 1866–1870. Daily accounts of E. O. Co. Day book.

POST OFFICE BOOK 4: 1866–1872. Newspaper and magazine subscription.

TAX RECORDS BOOK 38: 1866–1876. Tax book. List of taxables their occupation, assessments in Harmony township and Society. General accounts of mortgages, judgments, notes, agreements, bonds, real estate, personal property and militia list.

ECONOMY OIL BOOK 7: 1867. Oil sales.

INVOICE BOOK 9: 1867–1869. Medicine sold by Society to various individuals.

CASH BOOK 54: 1867–1869. Deposits and withdrawals. Memorandum of checks made out to individuals.

CASH BOOK 53: 1867–1869. Deposits and withdrawals. Memorandum of checks made out to individuals.

LAND AND MONEY BOOK 9: 1867–1873. Bonds held by Society against various individuals.

INVOICE BOOK 4: 1867–1877. Merchandise bought from various companies. Henrici and Lenz—Trustees.

ECONOMY OIL BOOK 8: 1867–1877. Daily record of oil tanks. Measurements of oil.

HOTEL BOOK 3: 1867–1881. Hotel book, list of workers and titles, accounts of meals, medicine and animal treatment.

ECONOMY OIL BOOK 6: 1868. Oil reports. Daily record of oil from wells and in tanks.

RECEIPT BOOK 7: 1868–1869. Receipts from Economy Oil Co.

CASH BOOK 55: 1868–1869. Deposits and withdrawals. Memorandum of checks made out to individuals.

CASH BOOK 12: 1868–1869. Cash receipts. Expenditures.

CASH BOOK 56: 1868–1870. Deposits and withdrawals. Memorandum of checks made out to individuals.

ECONOMY OIL BOOK 7: 1868–1870. Measurements of oil—daily. Oil received from wells.

WAGE BOOK 11: 1868–1872. Wage book. Individual wage accounts remittance in goods by Society.

CASH BOOK 57: 1868–1873. Deposits and withdrawals, memorandum of checks made out to individuals.

BILLS OF LADING BOOK 3: 1868–1877. Shipments by railroad from Society Henrici and Lenz, Trustees.

ECONOMY OIL BOOK 10: 1868–1878. Daily measurements of oil.

ECONOMY OIL BOOK 4: 1868–1878. Cash payments for expenses by Ralston and Economy Oil Co.

INVOICE BOOK 22: 1868–1878. Sales book. Merchandise sold by Society.

TAX RECORDS BOOK 39: 1868–1878. Tax book. List of taxables their occupation, assessments in Harmony township and Society. General accounts of mortgages, judgments, agreements, notes, bonds, real estate, stocks, personal property and militia list.

LAND AND MONEY BOOK 6: 1868–1884. Check book on Economy Savings Institution.

LEDGER BOOK 5: 1868–1887. Accounts with Society. Various merchandise.

WAGE BOOK 26: 1869–1870. Wage book. Cash expenditures and wages paid out to individuals.

RECEIPTS BOOK 9: 1869–1873. Receipts for Economy Oil Co. (for services and materials) .

CASH BOOK 58: 1869–1874. Bank book. Deposits and interest.

ECONOMY OIL BOOK 25: 1869–1876. Payments and receipts of Economy Oil Co.

STORE RECORDS BOOK 4: 1869–1886. Accounts of individuals and Society members. (Music in back of book)

1870

ECONOMY OIL BOOK 11: 1870–1871. Day book. Cash payments and receipts.

CASH BOOK 59: 1870–1872. Bank book. Deposits and withdrawals.

CASH BOOK 60: 1870–1874. Bank book. Deposits and withdrawals.

CASH BOOK 61: 1870–1875. Bank book. Deposits and withdrawals. Memorandum of checks made out to individuals. (Memo-Misc.)

ECONOMY OIL BOOK 23: 1870–1875. Day book. Daily sales and purchases of Economy Oil Co.

BEAVER FALLS WATER CO. BOOK 2: 1870–1887. Beaver Falls Water Co. List of commissioners, subscribers and shareholders. By-laws.

WAGE BOOK 27: 1871–1873. Wage book. Cash expenditures and wages paid out to individuals.

POST OFFICE BOOK 3: 1872–1875. Postage and subscriptions of newspapers.

ECONOMY OIL BOOK 26: 1872–1875. Daily reports of oil well production.

ECONOMY OIL CO. BOOK 5: 1872–1879. Record of oil well shipments.

LEDGER BOOK 10: 1872–1885. Accounts with Society.

JUSTICE OF PEACE BOOK 6: 1872–1885. Docket. Suits on mortgages.

RECEIPT BOOK 5: 1872–1890. Receipt book. Money paid out by Economy Oil Co.

WAGE BOOK 2: 1873–1877. Wages paid by the Society to the workers.

SCHOOL EXERCISE BOOK 20: 1875. School exercises. Key of stenography by Dr. Carl Albecht.

LEDGER BOOK 6: 1875–1878. Accounts with Society. Various merchandise.

CASH BOOK 62: 1875–1878. Bank book. Deposits and withdrawals. Memorandum of checks made out to individuals.

POST OFFICE BOOK 6: 1875–1889. Day book and journal. Transactions—Economy Post Office, Henrici, Postmaster.

CASH BOOK 7: 1875–1880. Money received and expended by Society. Day book.

LAND AND MONEY BOOK 8: 1875–1892. Notes, bonds and interest held by Society against various individuals.

TAX RECORDS BOOK 4: 1876. Tax records, list of individual accounts.

STORE RECORDS BOOK 5: 1876–1877. Store accounts of M. Nardie with Henrici and Lenz.

CASH BOOK 2: 1876–1879. Payments in cash by Society. Wages, help, sundry expenses.

CORRESPONDENCE BOOK 7: 1876–1882. Letters from Society written by Henrici and Lenz, Trustees.

DAY BOOK 10: 1876–1885. Day book. Goods sold and purchased by Society.

DAY BOOK 4: 1877. Price list of merchandise handled by Knox and Orrs.

WAGE BOOK 12: 1877–1887. Time book, list of workers hired, possible list of Society members working. (No wages listed.)

WAGE BOOK 6: 1877–1879. Merchandise sold to individuals by Society and taken out from wages.

MEMORANDUM BOOK 5: 1877–1886. Record of people working for Society. Arrival, departure, and behavior.

CASH BOOK 17: 1877–1892. Cash payments. Receipts by Society.

DAY BOOK 27: 1878–1879. Store, daily sales. Groceries, hardware.

CASH BOOK 63: 1878–1880. Bank book. Deposits and withdrawals. Memorandum of checks made out to individuals.

INVOICE BOOK 17: 1878–1880. Goods purchased by Society.

DAY BOOK 28: 1878–1881. Store, daily sales. Groceries, hardware.

RECEIPT BOOK 4: 1878–1882. Receipts. Henrici and Lenz—
Trustees.

FARM BOOK 3: 1878–1889. Record of grains; livestock; dairy
products at Society farms.

CORRESPONDENCE BOOK 17: 1878–1879. Letters to Society.

CASH BOOK 64: 1879–1890. Bank book. Deposits and withdrawals.
Memorandum on checks.

CORRESPONDENCE BOOK 18: 1879–1880. Letters to Society.

TAX RECORDS BOOK 40: 1879–1881. Tax book. List of taxables,
their occupation, assessments in Harmony township and Society.
General accounts of mortgages, judgments, agreements, notes,
stocks, bonds, real estate, personal property and militia list.

LAND AND MONEY BOOK 3: 1879–1881. Valuation of property,
real estate sales, holdings, bonds, houses.

LEDGER BOOK 15: 1879–1883. Accounts with Society.

CASH BOOK 11: 1879–1885. Income and payments.

SHOE SHOP BOOK 3: 1879–1888. Accounts with shoemaker. Shoe-
making and repairing.

LEDGER BOOK 4: 1879–1891. Accounts with Society.

1880

INVOICE BOOK 12: 1880–1881. Goods purchased by the Society.

RECEIPT BOOK 19: 1880–1882. Freight receipts.

MEMO BOOK 8: 1880–1883. Medicine accounts. Drugs sold.

ECONOMY OIL BOOK 15: 1880–1885. Daily accounts of E. O. Co.
Day book.

BLACKSMITH SHOP BOOK 3: 1880–1891. Blacksmith shop.
Record of blacksmith and mechanic shop.

WAGE BOOK 13: 1881. Time book, individual wage accounts.

DAIRY BOOK 4: 1881–1882. Accounts of milk, cream and prices.

CASH BOOK 65: 1881–1883. Bank book. Deposits and withdrawals.
Memorandum of checks made out to individuals.

WAGE BOOK 17: 1882. Time book, list of workers, titles and rates.

WAGE BOOK 16: 1882–1883. Wage book, list of teamsters and
workers hired.

WORK BOOK 15: 1882–1883. Time book, list of workers hired,
list of teamsters hired and rates.

WAGE BOOK 14: 1882–1883. Time book, list of workers hired (no
wages listed).

RECEIPT BOOK 16: 1882–1885. Freight receipts.

RECEIPT BOOK 2: 1882–1889. Receipt book. Henrici and Lenz—Trustees.

DAIRY BOOK 2: 1882–1892. Sales and shipments of milk and cream.

DAY BOOK 19: 1881–1883. Goods purchased from the Society by individuals.

ECONOMY LUMBER BOOK 28: 1881–1891. Sales of lumber. Coal.

CORRESPONDENCE BOOK 8: 1882–1895. Letters from Society by Henrici and Lenz, Trustees. Duss, Riethmueller, Woelfel.

DAIRY BOOK 5: 1883–1884. Accounts of milk, cream and prices.

LEDGER BOOK 13: 1883–1886. Accounts with Society.

DAY BOOK 12: 1883–1886. Blotter. Daily entry of merchandise sold.

DAY BOOK 12: 1883–1886. Record of postage stamps canceled.

WAGE BOOK 3: 1883–1886. Paid wages to workers for miscellaneous jobs.

RECEIPT BOOK 6: 1883–1886. Receipts. Money paid out on account. Henrici and Lenz—Trustees.

LEDGER BOOK 18: 1883–1887. Accounts with Society.

JOURNAL BOOK 6: 1883–1887. Society.

CASH BOOK 66: 1883–1891. Bank book. Deposits and withdrawals.

CASH BOOK 67: 1883–1891. Bank book. Deposits and withdrawals.

LAND AND MONEY BOOK 4: 1883–1892. Deed book of properties. Beaver Falls, New Brighton.

LAND AND MONEY BOOK 12: 1883–1894. Rent book. Rent, gas, bond accounts with various individuals.

HOTEL BOOK 4: 1884–1887. Hotel book, list of meals given to tramps and cost.

TAILOR SHOP BOOK 2: 1884–1887. Tailor book. Accounts of individual workers.

CASH BOOK 68: 1884–1888. Bank book. Deposits and withdrawals.

RECEIPT BOOK 25: 1884–1889. Receipts of payment for merchandise bought from Society.

RECEIPT BOOK 13: 1885–1886. Freight receipts.

ECONOMY LUMBER BOOK 47: 1885–1887. Lumber book, list of individual accounts for lumber and sawdust with Economy Lumber Co.

CASH BOOK 18: 1885–1890. Cash payments. Receipt by Society.

DAY BOOK 11: 1885–1893. Daily sales and purchases by Society. Deposits to Economy Saving Institution.

HOTEL BOOK 2: 1885–1893. Money received for lodging and meals.

BOOK OF CANCELED NOTES, INCLUDING DUSS PAYOFFS AND RECORD OF BONDS: 1885–1915.

TRANSIT READINGS 2: 1886.

WAGE BOOK 18: 1886–1887. Time book, list of workers hired, possible list of Society members working.

ECONOMY LUMBER BOOK 48: 1886–1887. Saw mill. List of orders and receipts.

TRANSIT READINGS 3: 1886–1887.

DAY BOOK 9: 1886–1888. Merchandise sold by Society to various individuals. Stamps canceled.

CLOTH BOOK 17: 1886–1888. Sewing. Amounts and items of needlework made for the Society, bedspreads, pillowcases, comforters and towels.

RECEIPT BOOK 12: 1886–1889. Receipts. Henrici and Lenz—Trustees.

ECONOMY OIL BOOK 17: 1886–1892. Cash book of E. O. Co.

LEDGER BOOK 39: 1886–1898. Zoar. Wages and expenses for workman at Zoar, Sewickley, and Economy.

LEDGER BOOK 39: 1886–1898. Wages and expenses for workman at Zoar, Sewickley, and Economy.

ECONOMY LUMBER BOOK 49: 1887. Lumber book. List of individual accounts and orders.

TAILOR SHOP BOOK 3: 1887–1888. Tailor book. Accounts of individual workers.

LEDGER BOOK 8: 1887–1888. Accounts with Society.

RECEIPTS BOOK 17: 1887–1888. Freight receipts.

CASH BOOK 69: 1887–1890. Bank book. Deposits and withdrawals.

WINE CELLAR BOOK 3: 1887–1890. Sale of wine, whiskey, cider. Full account for 1888.

ECONOMY LUMBER BOOK 33: 1887–1898. Lumber deliveries.

TAX BOOK 21: 1888. Tax records of individuals, Society members, titles, militia list and real estate accounts.

WINE CELLAR BOOK 3: 1888–1889. Sale of dried fruit and jellies.

ECO. LUMBER BOOK 20: 1888–1889. Lumber received from Tidioute.

ECONOMY LUMBER BOOK 50: 1888–1890. Lumber book. List of individual accounts, receipts and expenditures.

RECEIPT BOOK 18: 1888–1890. Freight receipts.

ECONOMY LUMBER BOOK 40: 1888–1890. Lumber shipments.

WAGE BOOK 28: 1888–1890. Wage book. Cash expenditures and wages paid out to individuals.

WINE CELLAR BOOK 5: 1888–1891. Sales of wine, whiskey, vinegar, cider. Donations from cellar to charity.

LAND AND MONEY BOOK 11: 1888–1892. Rent book. Collections of rent for houses at Economy, Fair Oaks, and Leetsdale. Gas collections.

LEDGER BOOK 17: 1888–1896. Accounts with the Society.

FLOUR MILL BOOK 2: 1888–1908. List of individual accounts. Production of flour, middling, bran, chopped corn, chopped feed, table meal, wheat, corn, oats, hay, straw, salt and prices on each.

LEDGER BOOK 16: 1889–1890. Accounts with Society.

BRICK WORK BOOK 49: 1889–1890. General accounts of sales, receipts and expenditures.

ECONOMY LUMBER BOOK 51: 1889–1890. Lumber book. List of individual accounts. Accounts with Economy Society and Harmony brickworks.

TAX BOOK 22: 1889–1890. Tax records of individuals, militia list and real estate accounts.

BRICK WORK BOOK 41: 1889–1890. Brick deliveries.

SHOE SHOP 2: 1889–1891. Sales and repairs of shoes.

BRICK WORKS 36: 1889–1891. Day book. Brick sales.

ECONOMY LUMBER BOOK 39: 1889–1891. Daily sales of lumber.

BRICK WORK BOOK 49: 1889–1890. General accounts of sales, receipts, and expenditures.

BRICK WORK BOOK 50: 1889–1892. Daily accounts of brick receipts.

LEDGER BOOK 27: 1889–1892. Accounts with Society.

RECEIPT BOOK 8: 1889–1892. Receipts. Henrici and Woelfel—Trustees. Henrici and Lenz—Trustees. Henrici and Duss—Trustees.

ECONOMY LUMBER BOOK 30: 1889–1893. Ledger.

WINE CELLAR BOOK 6: 1889–1898. Day book. Wine sales. Whiskey sales. Cider sales.

RECEIPT BOOK 3: 1889–1899. Receipts. Henrici and Lenz—Trustees. Henrici and Woelfel—Trustees. Duss and Siber—Trustees. Duss and Riethmueller—Trustees.

1890

ECO. LUMBER BOOK 20: 1890. Inventory of lumber.

ECONOMY LUMBER BOOK 5: 1890. Lumber inventory.

BRICK WORK BOOK 13: 1890—July to Nov. Dray book. Shipments of brick by railroad.

ECO. LUMBER BOOK 19: 1890–1891. Day book. Sales of lumber.

BRICK WORK BOOK 31: 1890–1891. Dray book. Shipment of brick by railroad.

RECEIPT BOOK 14: 1890–1891. Freight receipts.

ECO. LUMBER BOOK 12: 1890–1891. Lumber orders. Commission book.

ECONOMY LUMBER BOOK 3: 1890–1891. Record of lumber sawed at mill. Commission book. Lumber shipped to dealers.

ECONOMY LUMBER BOOK 52: 1890–1892. Lumber book. Price list of lumber accounts of individuals, Society and brickyard. Coal accounts.

CASH BOOK 15: 1890–1892. Cash payments. Receipts by Society.

CORRESPONDENCE BOOK 13: 1890–1892. Brickworks book. Letters from brickworks.

ECONOMY LUMBER BOOK 27: 1890–1892. Purchases and sales of lumber.

DAY BOOK 8: 1890–1893. Sales of merchandise. Daily entries by Society to individuals. Woelfel–Trustee.

ECONOMY LUMBER BOOK 32: 1890–1893. Cash book. Payments and receipts.

ECONOMY LUMBER BOOK 29: 1890–1894. Cash book.

ECONOMY LUMBER BOOK 38: 1890–1894. Journal book. Accounts with Economy Lumber Co.

BRICK WORKS BOOK 42: 1890–1898. Cash payments. Receipts.

ECO. LUMBER BOOK 22: 1891. Lumber order.

BRICK WORK BOOK 12: 1891, June–September. Dray book. Shipments of brick by railroad.

ECONOMY LUMBER BOOK 53: 1891–1892. Lumber book. Accounts of individuals and Society.

BRICK WORKS BOOK 10: 1891–1892. Dray book. Shipments of brick by railroad.

RECEIPT BOOK 15: 1891–1892. Freight receipts.

ECONOMY LUMBER BOOK 8: 1891–1892. Lumber sales accounts. Price list of molding.

ECONOMY LUMBER BOOK 26: 1891–1892. Lumber sales. Accounts.

BRICK WORK BOOK 15: 1891–1892. Shipments by railroad of brick.

LEDGER BOOK 26: 1891–1892. Accounts with Society.

TAX BOOK 23: 1891–1892. Tax records of individuals, real estate.

WAGE BOOK 10: 1891–1892. Wages paid to workers.

ECONOMY LUMBER BOOK 9: 1891–1893. Brick sales. Coal, lumber sales.

ECONOMY LUMBER BOOK 9: 1891–1893. Coal sales. Lumber, brick sales.

ECONOMY LUMBER BOOK 37: 1891–1893. Journal. Sales and shipment of lumber.

ECONOMY LUMBER BOOK 9: 1891–1893. Lumber Co., commission. Deliveries.

ECO. LUMBER BOOK 10: 1891–1893. Lumber commission and deliveries.

ECONOMY LUMBER BOOK 9: 1891–1893. Lumber sales. Coal, brick sales.

ECO. LUMBER BOOK 21: 1891–1893. Lumber shipments by railroad car.

ECO. LUMBER BOOK 17–A: 1891–1893. Shipments from a mill.

ECO. LUMBER BOOK 17: 1891–1893. Shipments of lumber and coal.

ECO. LUMBER BOOK 13: 1891–1894. Lumber orders.

WAGE BOOK 19: 1891–1895. Time book, list of workers, titles and rates, possible list of Society members working.

ECONOMY LUMBER BOOK 35: 1892. Journal.

POST OFFICE BOOK 2: 1892. Money order book. Money orders, Henrici, Postmaster.

POST OFFICE BOOK 5: 1892. Money order book. Record of money orders sent from Economy Post Office.

ECO. LUMBER BOOK 18: 1892. Production at planing mill.

LAND AND MONEY BOOK 15: 1892. Receivable bills. Bills. Payable bills. Supply account. Wine ledger accounts. Labor ledger accounts.

ECONOMY LUMBER BOOK 6: 1892–Feb.–Nov. Letters from Eco. Lumber Co. Estimates. Correspondence.

CASH BOOK 3: 1892–March–Nov. Payments: wages, supplies, miscellaneous.

RECEIPT BOOK 26: 1892–May–Dec. Freight receipts.

BRICK WORK BOOK 14: 1892–July to Dec. Dray book. Shipments of brick by railroad.

BRICK WORKS BOOK 8: 1892–1893. Dray book. Shipments of brick by railroad.

HARMONY SOCIETY MINUTES: 1892–1893.

BRICK WORKS 15: 1892–1893. Kiln production.

ECONOMY LUMBER BOOK 16: 1892–1893. Lumber shipments. Accounts.

ECONOMY LUMBER BOOK 25: 1892–1893. Lumber sold by Economy Lumber Co.

RECEIPTS BOOK 10: 1892–1893. Receipts. Henrici and Duss– Trustees.

BRICK WORKS BOOK 43: 1892–1893. Brick production.

CORRESPONDENCE BOOK 11: 1892–1893. Letters from Planing Mill Co.

HARMONY SOCIETY MINUTES (German) HSM2: 1892–1893.

INVOICE BOOK 13: 1892–1893. Goods purchased by Economy Planing Mill and Lumber Yard.

INVOICE BOOK 20: 1892–1893. Merchandise sold by Society to various individuals.

CORRESPONDENCE BOOK 16: 1892–1894. Brickworks book. Letters from Brickworks.

ECONOMY LUMBER BOOK 41: 1892–1894. Order book. Orders for lumber by various people.

ECONOMY LUMBER BOOK 54: 1892–1894. Lumber book. List of orders for lumber and brick by individuals.

ECONOMY LUMBER BOOK 4: 1892–1894. Orders of lumber. Deliveries of lumber.

ECONOMY LUMBER BOOK 43: 1892–1894. Sales journal.

ECONOMY LUMBER BOOK 44: 1892–1894. Day book. Daily record of lumber sales.

WAGE BOOK 20: 1892–1894. Time book, list of workers hired and rates.

ECONOMY LUMBER BOOK 42: 1892–1894. Order book. Lumber ordered from planing mill.

CASH BOOK 20: 1892–1894. Payments and receipts by Society.

ECONOMY LUMBER BOOK 36: 1892–1895. Purchase book and journal.

POST OFFICE BOOK 8: 1892–1895. Stamps and postal accounts.

ECONOMY LUMBER BOOK 23: 1892–1895. Cash book. Cash payments and receipts of Planing Mill.

ECONOMY LUMBER BOOK 34: 1892–1895. Journal.

FREIGHT REGISTER BOOK 3: 1892–1895. Record of shipments by freight.

LEDGER BOOK 25: 1892–1895. Accounts with Society.

LEDGER BOOK 56: 1892–1895. Harmony Society, list of general accounts.

CORRESPONDENCE BOOK 22: 1892–1896. Letters from Society. J. S. Duss—Trustee.

JOURNAL 3: 1892–1896. Society.

LEDGER BOOK 54: 1892–1896. General accounts of Harmony brickworks, receipts and expenditures.

ECONOMY LUMBER BOOK 2: 1892–1896. Time book. Payroll of Economy Lumber Co.

ECONOMY LUMBER BOOK 55: 1892–1897. Lumber book. Individual accounts. Inventory of capital and machinery. Economy Planing Mill Co. individual accounts.

BRICK WORKS BOOK 34: 1892–1897. Production of brick. Dry, setting, loading. Inventory of brick.

LEDGER BOOK 41: 1892–1898. General accounts of society receipts and expenditures for grist mill, dairy, cellar, including rents and supplies. A list of carpenters, painters, blacksmiths and wagonmakers.

LEDGER BOOK 40: 1892–1898. Accounts, general. Stocks, bonds, rent receipts, bills receivable, and bills payable. Balance sheets. Index in front of book.

LEDGER BOOK 23: 1892–1900. Accounts with Society.

LEDGER BOOK 42: 1893. Meat bought at Economy. Meat distributed to members. Also orders for Duss music, 1898.

TAX BOOK 4: 1893. Tax records, list of individuals taxed for Harmony township.

INVOICE BOOK 15: 1893–June–November. Goods purchased by Economy Planing Mill and Lumber Yard.

BAKE SHOP BOOK 2: 1893–1894. Bake Shop. Accounts of bakery. Number of loaves of bread received by various families and the cost amount of flour used.

BRICK WORK BOOK 11: 1893–1894. Dray book. Shipments of brick by railroad.

INVOICE BOOK 14: 1893–1894. Goods purchased by Planing Mill and Lumber Yard.

ECONOMY LUMBER BOOK 15: 1893–1894. Sawmill daily reports. Daily report of lumber sawed.

WAGE BOOK 21: 1893–1894. Time book, list of workers hired, titles and rates.

RECEIPT BOOK 21: 1893–1895. Freight receipts.

WAGE BOOK 21: 1893–1894. Time book, list of workers hired, titles and rates.

WAGE BOOK 22: 1893–1896. Time book, list of workers hired, titles and rates, possible lists of Society members working.

ECONOMY LUMBER BOOK 56: 1893–1896. Lumber book, daily reports, individual accounts, accounts of French Point Planing Mill Co., Harmony Society, Harmony brickworks, Economy Distillery Co.

BRICK WORKS BOOK 39: 1893–1896. Brick production.

JOURNAL BOOK 4: 1893–1897. Society.

MINUTES OF THE HARMONY SOCIETY: 1893–1897. (German) HSM.3.

CASH BOOK 19: 1893–1898. Payments and receipts of Society.

LEDGER BOOK 22: 1893–1898. Accounts with Society.

CORRESPONDENCE BOOK 9: 1893–1898. Letters from Economy Planing Mill. Letters from Society.

BRICK WORK BOOK 51: 1893–1899. Daily accounts of kiln production.

ECONOMY LUMBER BOOK 11: 1893–1899. Lumber sales accounts.

RECEIPT BOOK 11: 1893–1901. Receipts. Duss and Riethmiller—Trustees.

WAGE BOOK 7: 1893–1902. Rayroll and rent collections. Leetsdale and Economy.

TAX BOOK 5: 1894. Tax records, list of individuals taxed in Harmony township.

BRICK WORK BOOK 30: 1894. Hauling receipts.

LEDGER BOOK 58: 1894. Shares of stock (company not mentioned) sold to individuals.

ECONOMY LUMBER BOOK 14: 1894—April–October. Lumber sold by Society.

BRICK WORKS BOOK 2: 1894—April–October. Shipments of brick by railroad.

INVOICE BOOK 16: 1894—May to December. Goods purchased by Economy Planing Mill and Lumber Yard.

BRICK WORKS BOOK 17: 1894–1895. Hauling receipts for bricks.

BRICK WORK BOOK 18: 1894–1895. Hauling receipts for bricks.

BRICK WORK BOOK 20: 1894–1895. Hauling receipts for bricks.

BRICK WORK BOOK 21: 1894–1895. Hauling receipts for bricks.

BRICK WORK BOOK 25: 1894–1895. Hauling receipts for bricks.

BRICK WORKS BOOK 33: 1894–1896. Cash account book (cash transactions).

CASH BOOK 4: 1894–1896. Cash payments and receipts of the Harmony Society.

CORRESPONDENCE BOOK 15: 1894–1896. Brickworks book. Letters from Brickworks.

DAIRY BOOK 3: 1894–1896. Shipments of milk and cream.

LEDGER BOOK 11: 1894–1897. Accounts with Society.

LAND AND MONEY BOOK 5: 1894–1897. Collections of rent. Rent book.

JOURNAL BOOK 5: 1894–1898. Society.

STORE RECORDS BOOK 6: 1894–1898. Store records of individual accounts and receipts. (Reference to ledger by number.)

CASH BOOK 14: 1894–1898. Cash payments. Receipts of Society.

WAGE BOOK 5: 1894–1898. Wages paid by Society.

TAX BOOK 6: 1895. Tax record, list of individuals taxed, male and female of Harmony township.

BRICK WORKS BOOK 9: 1895–1896. Dray book. Shipments of brick by railroad.

ECONOMY LUMBER BOOK 25: 1895–1896. Feed, grain, delivered by Economy Grist Mill to members of Society. Cash accounts of Economy Grist Mill.

DAY BOOK 33: 1895–1898. Lists of receipts and expenditures.

RECEIPT BOOK 22: 1895–1898. Freight receipts.

BRICK WORKS BOOK 45: 1895–1900. Brick production. Loadings and sales. Inventory.

FREIGHT REGISTER BOOK 2: 1895–1900. Freight register. Record of shipment by freight.

BRICK WORK BOOK 19: 1896. Hauling receipts for bricks.

BRICK WORK BOOK 16: 1896—March–November. Hauling receipts for bricks.

BRICK WORKS BOOK 5: 1896, June to October. Dray book. Shipments of brick by railroad.

WINE CELLAR BOOK 2: 1892–1896. Wine inventory.

BRICK WORKS BOOK 3: 1896–1897. Dray book. Shipments of brick by railroad.

BRICK WORK BOOK 23: 1896–1897. Hauling receipts for bricks.

BRICK WORK BOOK 24: 1896–1897. Hauling receipts for bricks.

TAX BOOK 7: 1896–1898. Tax records, list of individuals taxed, male and female of Harmony township.

CASH BOOK 13: 1896–1900. Cash receipts. Payments.

ECONOMY LUMBER BOOK 7: 1896–1900. Lumber stock inventory.

LEDGER BOOK 14: 1896–1900. Accounts with Society.

LAND AND MONEY BOOK 7: 1897, May to October. Stubs. Money paid by the Society.

BRICK WORKS BOOK 35: 1897. Brick sales.

BRICK WORKS BOOK 38: 1897. Ledger. Accounts with Harmony Brick Works.

TAX BOOK 8: 1897–1898. Tax records, lists of individuals taxed in Harmony township.

BRICK WORKS BOOK 4: 1897–1898. Dray book. Shipments of brick by railroad.

ECONOMY LUMBER BOOK 57: 1897–1899. Lumber book. Individual accounts. Specifications to work done.

LEDGER BOOK 43: 1897–1899. General accounts for society including brick works, inventory, kilns, soles, French Paint Planing Mill Co., stocks, receipts and expenditures, partial index in front of book.

1900

HARMONY SOCIETY MINUTES: 1897–1903. (German) HSM.4.

CORRESPONDENCE BOOK 14: 1897–1899. Brickworks book. Letters from Brickworks.

WAGE BOOK 23: 1897–1900. Time book, list of workers hired, titles and rates.

INVOICE BOOK 18: 1897–1900. Goods sold by Society. Wine cellar products sales.

JOURNAL BOOK 7: 1897–1900. Society.

POST OFFICE BOOK 7: 1897–1900. Money order book. J. S. Duss, Postmaster.

BRICK WORKS BOOK 40: 1897–1900. Wage book. Wages paid by Harmony Brick Works.

CASH BOOK 10: 1897–1900. Money received and expended.

LEDGER BOOK 55: 1897–1901. General accounts of Harmony Brick Works including capital, receipts, expenditures, livestock, repairs, hauling, freight, salary, sales, cash, sidings, claims, fuel, clay rights, purchases.

BRICK WORKS BOOK 49: 1897–1901. Journal. Harmony Brick Works.

BRICK WORKS BOOK 47: 1897–1901. Record of brick production.

LAND AND MONEY BOOK 10: 1897–1901. Rent book. Collections for rent and sundries.

CASH BOOK 9: 1897–1902. Payments in cash by Harmony Society.

BRICK WORK BOOK 22: 1898. Hauling receipts for bricks.

TAX BOOK 9: 1898. Tax records of state and county tax paid by individuals in Harmony township.

BRICK WORK BOOK 26: 1898. Hauling receipts for bricks.

BRICK WORKS BOOK 7: 1898–1899. Dray book. Shipments of brick by railroad.

RECEIPT BOOK 23: 1898–1900. Freight receipts.

ORDER BOOK 6: 1898–1904. Order book. List of individual orders for books, prices included. Receipts.

WINE CELLAR BOOK 4: 1898–1909. Sales of wines, cider, vinegar from wine cellar.

TAX BOOK 10: 1899. Tax records of individuals taxed in Harmony township, bicycle tax and registry list.

BRICK WORKS BOOK 6: 1899. Dray book. Shipments of brick by railroad.

BRICK WORK BOOK 27: 1899. Hauling receipts for bricks.

BRICK WORKS BOOK 37: 1899, Jan.–June. Order book. Orders of brick from Harmony Brick Works.

CORRESPONDENCE BOOK 12: 1899–1900. Brick Works book. Letters from Brick Works.

BRICK WORKS BOOK 35: 1899–1901. Production of brick from various kilns.

LEDGER BOOK 44: 1899–1903. General account of oil and gas wells including general business.

LEDGER BOOK 45: 1899–1905. General accounts for society including capital, stocks, bonds, banks, rents, notes, taxes, maintenance, lands, mortgages, real estate.

LEDGER BOOK 46: 1899–1905. General account for society including general ledger, form and labor ledger, rent ledger, receipts, expenditures, maintenance, shrinkage, capital.

1900

ECONOMY LUMBER BOOK 58: c. 1900. Lumber book. List of individual accounts of lumber and coal.

TAX BOOK 11: 1900. Tax records of individuals taxed in Harmony township, bicycle and registry list.

BRICK WORKS BOOK 46: 1900–1901. Ledger. Accounts with Harmony Brick Works.

BRICK WORKS BOOK 46: 1900–1901. Ledger. Accounts with Harmony Brick Works.

CORRESPONDENCE BOOK 10: 1900–1901. Letters from Harmonie Brick Works.

RECEIPT BOOK 24: 1900–1902. Freight receipts.

CASH BOOK 8: 1900–1902. Money received and expended.

LADING BOOK 11: 1900–1902. Shipments by railroad by Society.

DAY BOOK 34: 1900–1903. Individual accounts and amounts with flour mill.

WAGE BOOK 24: 1900–1903. Time book for Harmony brick works, lists of workers hired and rates, possible lists of Society members working, including receipts and expenditures.

LEDGER BOOK 7: 1900–1903. Accounts with Society.

ORDER BOOK 2: 1900–1903. List of merchandise to be ordered.

CASH BOOK 23: 1900–1904. Cash book. Cash expenditures for:

Harmony Society, (general accounts) Harmony Brick Works. Water Company. Liberty Land Co.

JOURNAL 2: 1900–1904. Society.

LEDGER BOOK 12: 1900–1904. Accounts with Society.

TAX BOOK 12: 1900–1904. Tax records of individuals taxed in Harmony township for school tax.

FREIGHT REGISTER BOOK 4: 1900–1905. Record of shipments by freight.

DAY BOOK 35: 1900–1906. Western Grain and Products Co. Accounts and amounts of individuals. Index in front of book.

CASH BOOK 16: 1900–1920. Cash payments. Receipts of Society.

TAX BOOK 13: 1901. Tax records of individuals taxed in Harmony township, bicycle tax and registry list.

LEDGER BOOK 47: 1901–1904. General accounts of receipts and expenditures from Economy enterprises. Rent receipts from houses and farms.

LEDGER BOOK 48: 1901–1904. Account of feed purchased at Economy by various people and concerns.

TAX BOOK 14: 1902. Tax records of individuals taxed in Harmony township, for state tax, dog tax and poor tax.

WINE CELLAR BOOK 4: 1902. Nov. 27. Wine inventory.

BOOK OF CHECKS PAID: 1902–1903.

LADING BOOK 6: 1902–1904. Shipment of goods by railroad.

LADING BOOK 10: 1902–1904. Shipments by railroad by Society.

CASH BOOK 21: 1902–1905. Cash receipts and payments by Society.

CASH BOOK 24: 1902–1905. Cash expenditures for: Harmony Society, (general accounts).

LEDGER 24: 1902–1908. Memorandum of music sold.

RECEIPT BOOK 20: 1902–1909. Freight receipts.

TAX BOOK 15: 1903–1904. Tax records of individuals taxed in Harmony township for county tax, poor tax, dog tax and register list.

JOURNAL BOOK 7: 1903–1905. Daily account of purchases made by various people at the flour mill.

CASH BOOK 25: 1903–1909. Cash expenditures for: Harmony Society (general accounts). Dickson Land Account.

LEDGER BOOK 49: 1903–1909. General accounts for society including capital, stocks, bonds, banks, real estate, taxes, maintenance, lands, bills payable, bills receivable, insurance, mortgage.

WAGE BOOK 4: 1903–1910. Wages paid by Harmony Society.

MISCELLANEOUS BOOK 9: 1903–1910. Record of hearings before Justice of Peace. Docket.

CATALOGUE OF BOOKS 2: C-1904. Catalogue of books owned by John S. and Susie C. Duss, containing some of Harmony Society library. Date of earliest publication listed 1551. (Sir Thomas More, *Utopia*.) Number of books catalogued, 1661. Cutter classification for library of 1000 books used.

TAX BOOK 16: 1904–1905. Tax records of individuals taxed in Harmony Township, registry list.

ECONOMY FIRE CO. BOOK 2: 1904–1905. Economy Fire Co. general accounts. Index in front of book.

TAX BOOK 17: 1904–1905. Tax records of individuals taxed in Harmony township.

ECONOMY FIRE CO. BOOK 3: 1904–1906. Economy Fire Co. list of meetings and proceedings.

LEDGER BOOK 50: 1904–1908. General account of feed mill, warehouse, band, wholesale house, Economy Milling Co. Partial index in front of book.

ECONOMY FIRE CO. BOOK 4: 1904–1912. Economy Fire Co. list of receipts and expenditures.

TAX BOOK 18: 1905–1906. Tax records of individuals taxed in Harmony township.

ECONOMY LUMBER BOOK 31: 1905–1907. Ledger. Accounts with Economy Planing Mill.

CASH BOOK 22: 1905–1910. Income cash. Payments cash.

TAX BOOK 19: 1906–1907. Tax records of individuals taxed in Harmony township.

TAX BOOK 20: 1907–1908. Tax records of individuals taxed in Harmony township.

LEDGER BOOK 52: 1907–1910. General accounts of feed mill by various people and concerns. Index in front of book.

CASH BOOK 26: 1908–1912. Cash receipts and expenditures for Economy Milling Co. (General Accounts).

LEDGER BOOK 53: 1911–1914. General accounts recorded including capital, notes, loans, banks, deposits, mortgages, stocks, bonds, lands, receipts, taxes, cases, expenditures. Index in front of book.

CASH BOOK 16: 1900–1920. Cash payments. Receipts of Society.

Appendix B

The Library of the Harmony Society

Although the preceding survey of the Harmony Society Archives (Appendix A) reflects little of the cultural life within the community, it definitely was there and is documented in its musical, scientific, technical, and cultural library. The excellent and unique musical records of the Society have already been analyzed and catalogued by the musicologist Dr. Richard D. Wetzel, and his definitive and documented account of this neglected chapter of American music will soon be published. Title C 1904 in my survey of the Harmony Society Archives cites a catalogue of books owned by the Dusses, but this is not representative of the real library of the Harmony Society. The best insight into the real library of the Society is found in the following "List of German Books" compiled in 1829 by R. L. Baker, a list that will be of special interest to those familiar with German literature of the classical period of Herder, Goethe, and Schiller, especially in their younger years. Although many of these books were sold, given away, or taken to Florida by the Dusses, the fact that these titles were once in the library of the Society speaks for the cultural life within it. It is a library of which many a college in that time would have been very proud, especially when one considers the great number of scientific and technical works which the Society purchased but which are not included in this catalogue. It also does not include the extensive musical library. Although the Harmonists had many mystical and religious books, they always kept up to date in news coverage throughout the nation and in the most recent scientific and technological publications. They were also diligent readers of Nile's *Register,* which frequently reported their activities.

Verzeichnis der Deutschen Bücher

1. Schrökhs Lehr Buch der Weltgeschichte. L. N.	2	1.50
2. Chronik des 19ten Jahrhunderts von G. C. Bredow	13	13.00
3. [Left blank]		
4. [Left blank]		
5. Atlas Selectus von allen Reichen und Ländern der Welt	2	2.00
6. Geschichte der grossen Teutonen von Graf v. Wakerbarth	1	2.00
7. Das achtzehnte Jahrhundert von D. H. Stöber	8	4.00
8. Erdbeschreibung und Geschichte von Amerika von C. D. Ebling	1	" 50
9. [Left blank]		
10. Dr. A. F. Büschings Auszug aus seiner Erdbeschreibung	2	1.00
11. Beschreibung der Welt, Sternkunde und Natur Geschichte von E. L. Walz	1	" 75
12. ditto do do do do	1	" 75
13. Reise durch einige der Vereinigte Staaten von J. D. Schöpf	1	" 50
14. J. M. Hartmanns Erdebeschreibung und Geschichte von Afrika	1	" 75
15. Handbuch der Geographie und Statistik von Dr. Stein	1	" 50
16. Kleine Geographie oder Abriss der politischen Erd Kunde	1	" 50
17. Volkelts kurze Erdbeschreibung	1	" 25
18. J. D. Hartmans kurzer Abriss der neuesten Erdbeschreibung	1	" 25
19. Fragmente über Ostindien von Gloyer	1	" 50
20. Beiträge zur Bestimmung des Alters unsrer Erde von F. Gussmann	1	" 50
21. Geographie für Kinder von M. G. C. Raff	1	" 25
22. Deutsche Geschichte von T. G. Voigtel	1	" 75
23. Analen der Geschichte Frankreichs	1	" 25
24. Leitfaden zur allgemeinen Menschen-Geschichte sold Siglen	1	" 25
25. Historischer Bilder Saal von Lossius und Schulze	2	2.00

26. Suppius Weltgeschichte	1	" 25
27. Chronologisches Handbuch der neuesten Geschichte	1	" 25
28. Historisches Handbuch für die Jugend von Dyk	6	2.00
29. Schiksale der Französischen Eroberer	1	" 25
30. Allgemeine Welt Geschichte für die Jugend	1	" 50
31. Deutsche Geschichte und Deutschlands traurige Ereignisse	1	" 50
32. Johann von Lerys Reise in Brasilien	1	" 25
33. Clarks Reise durch Russland und die Tartarei	1	" 50
34. Betrachtungen u. Phantasien auf einer Reise durch Sachsen	1	" 25
35. Humboldts Reisen um die Welt	4	2.00
36. Die Entdekung von Amerika von J. H. Campe	1	1.00
37. L. W. Gilberts Handbuch für Reisende durch Deutschland	1	" 25
38. Gemälde von Westindien u. Süd Amerika	2	1.00
39. Tagbuch der Reisen von N. E. Kleemann	1	" 50
40. Kapitains James Cook Reise um die Welt	2	" 75
41. Le Vaillant neue Reise in das Innre von Afrika	1	" 25
42. J. P. Texiers Reise durch Spanien und Portugal	1	" 25
43. Merkantilische Notizen über England	1	" 25
44. ditto do do	1	" 25
45. Das Strassburger Münster	1	" 50
46. Kritische Geschichte der spanischen Inquisition	4	2.00
47. Die Schottische Maurerey	1	" 25
48. Leben und Thaten des Joseph Balsamo	1	" 25
49. Pokeach Irwin Allegorien u. Hieroglyphen	1	" 25
50. Hebräische Mysterien der Freimaurer	1	" 12
51. Abhandlung über Telegraphen von A. N. Edelkranz	1	" 12
52. do do do	1	" 12

No.		Qty	Price
53.	Verfassungs-Urkunde für das König-Reich Würtemberg	1	"12
54.	Zertrümmerung der grossen Planeten Hesperus und Phaethon	1	"12
55.	Abriss der Geschichte der Christlichen Religion Sold to Siglen	1	"50
56.	Neueste Religions Begebenheiten	1	"25
57.	Reformations-Geschichte von P. F. Roos Sold to Siglen	2	1.50
58.	Thiemes Grundlinien zu einer Geschichte aller Religionen	1	"75
59.	Religiöses Handbuch an Andreas Bergman geschenkt	1	"50
60.	Tägliches Handbuch von J. F. Stark (verkauft)	1	"50
61.	Passions-Spiegel von J. R. Hedingen Sold to Siglen	1	"25
62.	Evangelischer Lehr-Begriff von K. F. Hartmann Sold to C. Braun	1	"25
63.	Die neuesten Offenbarungen Gottes Sold	1	"25
64.	G. C. Riegers leichter Weg zum Himmel Sold to Siglen	1	"25
65.	Helmonts ungemeine Meynungen	1	"25
66.	Thomas Bromley Offenbarungen	1	"25
67.	C. A. Roemelings Ausgang aus Babel Sold Seibert	1	"25
68.	Finks Häusliche Andachten	1	"50
69.	Jakob Böhms Schriften	1	1.50
70.	G. L. Seiz. Catechismus Predigten Sold to Siglen	1	"50
71.	Riegers Predigten Sold to Casper Braun	1	"37
72.	Eines ungenanten Schriftforschers Betrachtungen Sold to Siglen	1	"50
73.	Riegers Passions Predigten Sold to Siglen	1	"50
74.	Seits Catechismus Predigten ditto	1	"50
75.	Predigten über Natur Texte von Ewald	1	"50
76.	Die Erziehung des Menschen Geschlechts von Ewald	1	"50
77.	G. J. Zollikofers Predigen (Caspar Braun)	1	"75
78.	Biblisches Erbauungs Buch von G. F. Seiler do	1	"75
79.	do do do	1	"75

No.	Item	Qty	Price
80.	Der Prophet Joel von C. W. Justi	1	" 25
81.	Der Prophet Amos von C. W. Justi	1	" 25
82.	" do Micha " do ditto	1	" 25
83.	Auserlesene Biblische Historien von J. Hübnem	1	" 75
84.	Blik in das Geheimnis Gottes über die Menschheit Sold to Siglen	1	" 50
85.	[Left blank]		
86.	Einleitung in die Bibel Sold to Siglen	1	" 25
87.	Leben heiliger Seelen ditto	1	" 25
88.	Christliches Erbauungs-Blatt	1	" 37
89.	" do do	1	" 50
90.	Offenbarungen der Jane Leade Sold to Siglen	1	" 25
91.	Lebens-Beschreibung einer Wittwe Sold to C. Braun	1	" 12
92.	Bemerkungen über die lezten Zeiten	1	" 25
93.	Reden von Hellsehenden Sold to Siglen	1	" 37
94.	Religion der Bibel do	1	" 50
95.	Das Geheimnis der Gottseligkeit von J. Ganz do	1	" 25
96.	Arnts wahres Christenthum	1	1.00
96 1/2	Brastbergers Predigten		
97.	Die Evangelische Missions Schule in Basel	1	" 75
97 1/2	Auserlesene Lebens-Beschreibungen Heiliger Seelen		
98.	Grundriss eines Systems der Anthropologischen Psychologie von Wezel	2	1.50
99.	Betrachtung des Menschen nach Geist, Seel und Leib Sold to Siglen	1	" 25
100.	Grosse Begebenheiten durch das Wort-Gottes Sold to Sigl	1	" 12
101.	Die sieben lezten Posaunen oder Wehen (Sold)	1	" 12
102.	Welt Alter, von Johann Albrecht Bengel Sold to C. Braun	1	" 25
103.	ditto do do	1	" 25
104.	Die neuesten Religions Begebenheiten	1	" 12

No.	Title	Note	Qty	Price
105.	Die Würtembergische Tabea	Sold to Siegl	1	" 25
106.	Bild Gottes an den ersten Christen	Sold to Siglen	1	" 37
107.	Gottfried Arnolds erstes Marterthum	Sold (Seibert)	1	" 37
108.	Erklährung der Offenbarung Jesu Christi	Sold to Siglen	1	" 25
109.	do do do dem Göhring geschenkt		1	" 37
110.	Theosophische Send-Schreiben von Gichtlen	here	1	" 50
111.	Der Weg des Lebens	Sold to Siglen	1	" 37
112.	Wissenschaft der ewigen und unsichtbaren Dinge	Sold to Siglen	1	" 50
113.	Gottes Gelahrtheit von Robt. Barclay		1	" 75
114.	Der göttliche Liebes Triumpf von Christoph Schütz		1	" 50
115.	Der drey Prinzipien und Welten von Gichtlen	Sold to Siegl	1	" 25
116.	do do do		1	" 25
117.	Schwedenburgs Philosophie	Sold to Siglen	1	" 75
118.	Der Weg zu Christo von Jakob Böhm		1	" 50
119.	Ein hundert und sieben und siebenzig Fragen von Jakob Böhm	Sold	1	" 50
120.	Auflösung der obigen	do	1	
121.	Betrachtung der sieben Tage Werke von Jakob Böhm	Sold to Siegl	1	" 25
122.	Beschreibung der drey Principien göttlichen Wesens	do do Siglen	1	" 50
123.	Von der Mensch Werdung Jesu Christi	do do Seibert	1	" 75
124.	Erklärung des ersten Buchs Mosis von Jakob Böhm	Sold to Sigler	1	1.00
125.	Betrachtung Göttlicher Offenbarung	do	1	1.00
126.	Vierzig Fragen von der Seele	do	1	1.00
127.	Von der Geburth und Bezeichnung aller Wesen do	do	1	1.00
128.	Die ganze Theologie der neuen Kirche von Schwedenborg	do (Weber)	1	1.00
129.	Geistliche Fama	Sold to Siglen	2	1.50
130.	Die Sieben lezten Posaunen von Armbruster, abgegeben an Georg Bentel, pr. R. L. Baker, June 9. – 40.	Sold to Siglen	1	" 50

131. Das Buch von der Nachfolge Christi von Sailer	1	"75
132. Das Christenthum von G. K. Horst	1	1.00
133. Das verborgene Leben mit Christo in Gott von Benier Sold to Mr. Vogel, Pittsb.	1	"50
134. Der Frau L. M. Guyon Beschäftigungen Sold to Siglen	2	1.00
135. Weg der Wahrheit von G. Terstegen Sold	1	"50
136. Geistliche Brosamen ditto " Sold to Casper Braun	2	1.50
137. Geistliche und erbauliche Briefe do	2	1.50
138. Die heilige Liebe Gottes do Sold	1	"50
139. Gottes Verehrungen von C. G. Salzmann	2	1.50
140. Michael Hahns Schriften Sold to Pfarrer Braun	6	6.00
141. Siona ein Beytrag zur Apologetik des Christenthums	1	"75
142. Handbuch der Religion von J. A. Hernes	2	2.00
143. Christliche Homilien	1	".50
144. Ein Buch für Christen und Juden	1	"50
145. Lehr-Buch der Sitten-Lehre	1	"37
146. Hades ein Beitrag zur Theorie der Geister Kunde Sold to C. Braun	1	"12
147. Christliche Zeitschrift für Christen	3	2.00
148. Unterhaltungen mit Gott in den Abend-Stunden	1	1.00
149. do do in den Morgen-Stunden	1	1.00
150. Magnus Fried. Roos, Christliches Haus-Buch Sold to Siglen	2	2.00
151. Stunden der Andacht	8	4.00
152. Emiliens Stunden der Andacht	1	"50
153. Nathanael oder die Göttlichkeit des Christenthums	1	"50
154. J. P. Millers Sitten Lehre Sold	1	"37
155. Religion für das Herz do	1	"37
156. Goldne Früchte, in Silbernen Schalen	1	"50

157. Gottfried Arnolds Kirchen u. Kezer Historie	Sold	2	6.00
158. Johann Tauler Predigten	Sold to Casper Braun	1	2.00
159. J. W. Peterson verklärtes Evangelium	Sold to Siglen	1	1.50
160. Betrachtungen der Augsburgischen Confession	ditto	1	1.00
161. Herrn Georgi von Wellings-Schriften	Kept here	1	
162. Brastbergers Predigten	Sold to Casper Braun	1	
163. Auserlesene Lebens Beschreibung Heilger Seelen	(Verkauft)	1	2.00
164. Algemeine Deutsche Garten Zeitung		3	3.00
164 1/2 Erbaulicher Christen Schaz in 300 Liedern	Sold to C. Braun	1	" 25
165. Würtembergisches Gesang Buch		1	" 50
166. ditto ditto		1	" 37
167. ditto ditto		1	" 37
168. Reformirtes Gesangbuch		1	" 50
168 1/2 Sammlung geistlicher Gedichte und Lieder		1	" 25
169. Ronsdorffs silberne Trompeten in Lieder		1	" 37
170. Kern geistlicher Lieder		1	" 25
171. Das Gesangbuch der Herrn Huter und andern		1	" 75
172. Einige Christliche Lieder und Gebete		1	" 12
173. Blumen aus der alten Geschichte		1	" 25
174. do do do		1	" 25
174 1/2 Rabeners Satiren		1	" 37
175. Die kleinen Freunde der Natur Gaschichte		1	" 25
176. Frau von Genlis Mythologie		1	" 50
177. ditto ditto		1	" 50
178. Romane aus der Christen Welt aller Zeiten		1	" 50
179. Jean Pauls Humanität und Menschen-Bildung	Sold Dr. Linenbrink	1	" 37
180. Gesundheits-Taschen Buch		1	" 25

No.	Title	Qty	Price
181.	Der Mensch und das Menschen Leben	1	" 25
182.	Familien Leben ein moralisches Unterhalt. Buch	1	" 12
183.	Thomas Wilkox Worte der Ermahnung Sold to Sieglen	1	" 12
184.	Die Amerikanische Gold Grube	1	" 12
185.	Beiträge zur Bestimmung des Alters unsrer Erde	1	" 25
186.	Versuche zu sehen (zweiter Theil)	1	50
187.	Geschichte der Christlichen Religion und Kirche	1	" 12
188.	Merkwürdige Begebenheiten aus der Welt Geschichte	1	" 25
189.	Kriegs-Schauplaz in Spanien	1	" 12
190.	Abuschelem oder die Weisheit Indiens	1	" 25
191.	Wahrheits-Spiegel und Höllenfarth	1	" 37
192.	Über den Umgang mit Menschen von A. F. Knigge	2	1.75
193.	Bibliothek für die gebildete Lese Welt	1	" 37
194.	Blumen aus der alten Geschichte	1	" 25
195.	Cabinet Trauer Gemälde und Schrekens Scenen	1	" 25
195 1/2	Die Kunst das menschliche Leben zu verlängern Hufeland	1	1.00
196.	Der Handlungs Kontorist	1	" 12
196 1/2	Anleitung zur Menschen Kenntnis	1	" 50
197.	Merkwürdige Lebens-Beschreibungen verschiedener Kauf-Leute	1	" 25
197 1/2	Früchte der Einsamkeit von Wilhelm Penn	1	" 25
198.	Der Greis	1	" 25
198 1/2	ditto	1	" 25
199.	Deutscher Plutarch	2	1.25
200.	Sprüche des Nordischen Weisen	1	" 25
201.	Sömmering, über die körperliche Verschiedenheit des Negers vom Europäer	1	" 25
202.	Leben und Schiksale des Grafen von Las-Casas	1	" 37
203.	Des Generals Mina Leben und Feld-Züge	1	" 25

No.	Title	Note	Qty	Price
204.	Platons Leben und Schriften	Sold to Dr. Linenbrink	1	1.00
205.	Leben Thaten, und Meynungen, merkwürdiger Männer		2	1.50
206.	J. K. Lavaters Lebensbeschreibung von Gessner (verkauft)		3	2.25
207.	Der Mensch und das Menschen Leben		1	" 25
208.	Das Leben von Georg Waschingten		1	" 25
209.	Leben Meynungen u. Schiksale Denkwürdiger Personen		1	" 50
210.	Fabius und Cato ein Stück der römischen Geschichte	Sold to Dr. Linenbrink	1	" 25
211.	Leben und Wandel von Sangmeister		1	" 12
212.	Das Geheimnis der Bosheit bis auf den Grund aufgedekt		1	" 25
213.	do do do do	do Sold to Seibert	1	" 25
214.	do do do do	do Sold to Seibert	1	" 25
215.	do do do do	do ditto	1	" 25
216.	Das hoch teutsche A.B.C, nebst einig. Lieder	ditto	1	" 12
217.	Evangelium Nicodemi		1	" 12
218.	Gespräch im Reich der Toden		1	" 25
219.	Forderung der Christenheit vors Gericht		1	" 25
220.	Edle Züge der Neu-Franken		1	" 12
221.	Lais und Theodor		1	" 12
222.	Betrachtung der Evangelischen Lehre der heiligen Schrift	Sold	1	" 25
223.	Fragmente über Menschen Bildung von E.M. Arndt		2	" 50
224.	Leben Alfred des Grossen Königs von England		1	" 50
225.	Auserlesene Romane		1	" 50
226.	Flemings Geschichte ein Denkmal des Glaubens		2	1.00
227.	Rath an meine Tochter, in Beispielen aus der wirklichen Welt		2	" 75
228.	Biographen, Skizzen, Scenen, und Gemälde aus dem menschen Leben		1	" 37
229.	Leben der Schwedischen Gräfin		1	" 25
230.	Peter Pistors Reiseabendtheuer zu Wasser und zu Land		1	" 25

No.	Title	Qty	Price
231.	Die Ritter der rothen Rose, von Wilhelmine von Gersdorf	1	" 75
232.	Das Blumen-Körbchen	1	" 25
233.	Woldemars Vermächtnis an seinen Sohn Sold to Dr. Linenbrink	1	" 75
234.	Kleine Romane für die Jugend	2	1.00
235.	[Left blank]		
236.	Hersiliens Lebens Morgen, oder Jugend-Geschichte	1	" 50
237.	Gumal und Lina eine Geschichte für Kinder	1	" 75
238.	Späne aus der Werk-Statt Meister Sachsens (sold)	1	" 37
239.	Die Seherin von Prevorst	2	1.00
240.	Das Räuber Mädchen mit Kupfer	1	" 37
241.	Johann Georg Zimmermann von der Einsamkeit	1	" 12
242.	Sammlung dem Nuzen, und dem Vergnügen der Jugend	1	" 25
243.	Die Kinder Welt von Krumacher	1	" 50
244.	Cabinet historischer Trauer Gemählde	1	" 25
245.	Rinaldo Rinaldini der Räuber-Hauptmann	1	" 50
246.	Das Goldmacher Dorf	1	" 12
247.	Der Philosoph für die Welt	1	" 50
248.	Schakespears Schauspiele	1	" 25
249.	Theudelinda von Baiern Königin der Langobarten	1	" 37
250.	Isidor Bauer zu Ried	1	" 50
251.	Ruinen der Vorzeit	1	" 50
252.	Omars Lehren, oder Biographen zur Menschen Kentniss	1	" 50
253.	Almusa der Sultans-Sohn	1	" 25
254.	Albert und Eugenie eine Bildungs-Schrift	1	" 75
255.	Konrad und Siegfried von Feuchtwangen	1	" 25
256.	Festbüchlein von Krumacher	2	" 75
257.	Robinson der Jüngere	1	" 50

No.	Title	Qty	Price
258.	Kleine Tugend Lehren	1	" 25
259.	Vom Magnetismus sold to C. Braun	1	" 12
260.	Rosamunde eine Geschichte für Kinder	1	" 50
261.	Matrialien zur teutschen Stilübungen	1	" 25
262.	Schreib materialist		
263.	Vater Burgheims Reisen mit seinen Kindern	2	" 75
264.	Farben Lehre von Göthe	1	" 50
265.	Die Garten Kunst	1	" 37
266.	Die Ekonomie oder Haushaltungskunst	1	" 50
267.	Volksbuch ein fasslicher Untericht	1	" 50
268.	Kurzer Lehr-Begriff Kosmologisch und anth.	1	" 25
269.	Reden über die Malerey	1	" 12
270.	Natur Geschichte für Kinder von G. C. Raff	1	1.00
271.	Johann Fibigs Handbuch der Mineralogie	1	" 25
272.	Anfangs-Gründe der Chemie	1	" 37
273.	Anfangs-Gründe der Metallurgie	1	" 50
274.	Anweisung zur Physik	1	" 25
275.	Anfangs-Gründe der Natur Lehre	1	" 25
276.	L. C. Schmahlings Natur Lehre	1	" 25
277.	Ziehns sämtliche Schriften der Revolutionen der Erde	1	" 50
278.	Abend-Unterhaltungen über die Technologie	2	" 50
279.	Versuche in Sokratischen Gesprächen über Geometrie	1	" 25
280.	Steins Grund-Lehren der reinen Geometrie	1	" 25
281.	Die Verhältnisse der Zahl nach der Pestalozzischen Methode	1	" 25
282.	Hand-Buch der gesammten Arithmetik 2 Theile in einem Band	1	" 25
283.	do do do do do do	1	" 25
284.	Bernhardts Vollständige Abhandlung vom Wiesenbau	1	" 50

No.	Title	Qty	Price
285.	Einleitung zur Kentnis der englischen Landwirtschaft	2	1.00
286.	Schilderungen des menschlichen Lebens von Lafontaine	2	"75
287.	do do do	2	"75
288.	Tinchen oder die Männer Probe von	2	"75
289.	Die Gefahren der grossen Welt	2	"75
290.	Die Moral-Systeme oder Ludwig von Eisach do	2	"75
291.	Das heimliche Gericht des Schiksals oder Rosaura von Lafontaine	3	1.12
292.	G. W. Rabeners Satiren	1	"50
293.	Schriften der schönen Geister in Teutsch-Land	3	1.00
294.	G. W. Rabeners Briefe Leben und Schriften	1	"50
295.	Geister Kunde von J. H. Jung Stilling sold to Casper Braun	1	1.00
296.	Geschichte Florentins von Fahlendorn von Stilling sold to Siglen	3	"75
297.	Der Mensch		
298.	Das hohe A.B.C.	1	"12
299.	Der Graue Mann, eine Volks-Schrift (sold)	3	1.50
300.	Stillings-Grauer Mann sold to Siglen	3	1.50
301.	Stillings-Menschen Freund (sold)	5	2.50
302.	Das Heimweh von Heinrich Stilling sold to Sieglen	1	"37
303.	Stillings kleine gesamelte Schriften sold to C. Braun	1	"50
304.	Gedichte von J. H. Jung genant Stilling do do	1	"50
305.	Erster Nachtrag zur Sieges-Geschichte von Stilling do	1	"50
306.	Theobald oder die Schwärmer von Stilling sold to Casper Braun	1	"50
307.	Stillings Antwort über Catholicismus und Protestantismus	1	"50
308.	Fenelons Lahr-Säze der alten Welt-Weisen sold to Siglen	1	"50
309.	[Left blank]		
310.	Klopstoks Werke	2	1.50
311.	do do		–50

No.	Title		Qty	Price
312.	Hand-Bibel für Leidende von J. C. Lavater	sold to C. Braun	1	" 50
313.	Eduard Jungs Nachtgedanken		1	" 75
314.	Das Christ-Fest von F. A. Krummacher		1	" 37
315.	Eduard Jungs sämtliche Werke		1	" 37
316.	Constants curiose Lebens-Geschichte		3	" 75
317.	Ideen zur Philosophie der Geschichte der Menschheit		1	" 50
318.	Der Himmel auf Erden von Salzmann		1	" 50
319.	Der Tod Abels, u.s.w. von Gessner	sold to Seibert	1	" 50
320.	Blätter höhrer Wahrheit von Mayer		1	" 50
321.	Herders sämtliche Werke		2	1.00
322.	Gessners sämtliche Schriften		2	1.00
323.	Der Tod Adams von Klopstok und die Herrmanns Schlacht L. N.		1	" 50
324.	Die Christliche Religion		1	" 25
325.	Todes Gesänge von Schubart		1	" 37
326.	Schubarts Gedichte	sold to C. Braun	2	" 75
327.	Urania Taschen Buch für Damen		1	" 37
328.	Elegieen und vermischte Gedichte von Tiedge		1	" 50
329.	Gedichte von Salis		1	" 25
330.	Urania ein Lyrisch-Didaktisches Gedicht		1	" 25
331.	Rheinische Flora		2	" 37
332.	Poetische Werke von Uz		2	" 75
333.	Sammlung Prosaischen Schrift-Steller und Dichter		1	" 25
334.	do do do		1	" 25
335.	Deutsche Anthologie oder Aus-wahl deutscher Gedichte		1	1.50
336.	Blüthen, dem blühenden Alter gewidmet		1	1.25
337.	Sammlung vorzüglicher Gedichte		1	" 25
338.	Blumen aus der alten Geschichte		1	" 25

No.	Title	Qty	Price
339.	Klopstok und Schiller	2	1.00
340.	Heide Blumen, vom Verfasser der Parthenais	1	" 25
341.	Angenehme Schulstunden und Gedichte	1	" 25
342.	Dichter Blüthen	1	" 25
343.	Noth und Hülfs-Büchlein für Bürger und Bauern	4	3.00
344.	Mittel zur Vertilgung schädlicher Thiere	1	" 25
345.	Anleitung zum Bleichen	1	" 25
346.	Vermischte Gedichte	1	" 25
347.	Biographien Skizzen und Gemälde	1	" 25
348.	Grundsäze der Volks-Arzneikunde sold to C. Braun	1	" 37
349.	Beschreibung der Mineral Wasser	1	" 25
350.	Gedanken von Gott und der Welt und der Seele des Menschen (sold)	1	" 50
351.	Gellerts Moralische Vorlesungen	2	1.00
352.	do do do	2	1.50
353.	Leben heiliger Seelen von Terstegen sold	1	" 25
354.	Geistliches Blumen Gärtlein sold	1	" 50
355.	John Kangans Reise nach der Ewigkeit sold	1	" 25
356.	Samlung bester deutscher Schriftsteller	1	" 50
357.	Geistliches Schazkästlein von Hillern	1	" 50
358.	Weg der Wahrheit von Terstegen (sold)	1	" 50
359.	Geistiges Blumengärtlein	1	" 50
360.	Das Verborgene Leben mit Christo in Gott, Bernier (sold)	1	" 50

Bibliography

THE MAIN BIBLIOGRAPHICAL INFORMATION IS GIVEN IN MY FIRST volume, *George Rapp's Harmony Society, 1785–1847,* but the following titles not found in that volume will prove valuable. I have worked primarily with firsthand material written by contemporaries of the events described and for that reason most bibliographical references are found within the text of the book. Those interested in further secondary titles should consult the following journals, particularly: *Indiana Magazine of History, The Western Pennsylvania Historical Magazine, Pennsylvania History,* and *The Pennsylvania Magazine of History and Biography.* The Harmony Society Archives at Old Economy in Ambridge, Pennsylvania, try to keep an up-to-date file on dissertations written on various aspects of the Harmony Society. These are increasing in number as the history of the Harmony Society becomes better known, but, unfortunately, the dissertations I have examined are inadequate because they are based either on hearsay, on secondary material, or on inadequate research caused by insufficient training in doing research with such unique and difficult manuscript material as is found in the Harmony Society Archives. These archives have been insufficiently cared for because of lack of funds to provide the specialists and the archivist with the thorough training in old German manuscripts needed for such an unusual collection. Even when funds are available, appointments are made by political considerations rather than objective review of scholarly training. If adequate facilities free from ever-changing political considerations cannot be assured at Ambridge, the Archives should be moved out and placed under the control of one of the excellent libraries in Pittsburgh where adequate professional care could be provided.

Anon. *Briefe aus den Vereinigten Staaten von Nord-Amerika*, Vol. II. Leipzig: Verlagsbuchhandlung von J. J. Weber, 1853. pp. 242–54 negative account of Harmony Society. Claims George Rapp came from the Schwarzwald and did not allow members to read newspapers or books. He obviously got his information from enemies.

Anon. *Erinnerungen an Johann Friedrich Maier, Schulmeister in Kornthal*. Zum Besten der Rettungsanstalten in Kornthal und Wilhelmsdorf, 1881. Kornthal was established to stop emigration of Separatists.

Arndt, Karl J. R., and Wetzel, Richard. "Harmonist Music and Pittsburgh Musicians in Early Economy." A series of articles in the *Western Pennsylvania Historical Magazine* starting April 1971.

Arndt, Karl J. R., and Brostowin, Patrick R. "Pragmatists and Prophets; George Rapp and J. A. Roebling versus J. A. Etzler and Count Leon," *Western Pennsylvania Historical Magazine*, 52 (January and April 1969) : 2–27 and 171–98. Röbling the builder of bridges and report on Count Leon.

Baedeker, K. *Nordamerika: Die Vereinigten Staaten nebst einem Ausflug nach Mexiko*. Leipzig: Verlag von Karl Baedeker, 1904. p. 265. 17 M. Economy, ein 1848 [*sic*] von den Harmoniten, den Anhängern Georg Rapp's (1757–1847), eines schwärmerischen Bauern aus Württemberg, gegründetes Dorf in hübscher Lage auf einem Plateau über dem Ohio.

Bennett, John W. *Hutterian Brethren: The Agricultural Economy and Social Organization of a Communal People*. Stanford, California: Stanford University Press, 1967. Excellent bibliography.

Brostowin, Patrick R., and Arndt, Karl J. R. "Pragmatists and Prophets: George Rapp and J. A. Roebling versus J. A. Etzler and Count Leon," *Western Pennsylvania Historical Magazine*, 52 (January and April 1969) : 2–27 and 171–98. Röbling builder of bridges and report on Count Leon.

Buley, R. Carlyle. *The Old Northwest Pioneer Period 1815–1840*. 2 vols. Bloomington: Indiana University Press, 1951. See 1:34–35 and 2:597–600 about Harmonists. The footnote on page 600 of volume 2 perpetuates a wrong reading and translation of Dr. Müller's letter. He did not write as quoted:

"The Wagner woman especially caused me some tribulation (or temptation?)," but "I was especially worried about the Wagner woman." He was the physician of the Society and was writing about his concern for the *health* of some members. Again, he wrote at the close of his letter of December 17, 1814: "Father, I am walking in the light"—not, as quoted: "Father, I am walking in the paths of lust."

Giddens, Paul H. *The Beginnings of the Petroleum Industry: Sources and Bibliography.* Harrisburg: Pennsylvania Historical Commission, 1941. See pp. 108, 128, and 170 about Harmony Society oilwells.

Giddens, Paul H. *Pennsylvania Petroleum 1750–1872: A Documentary History.* Titusville: Pennsylvania Historical and Museum Commission, 1947. See p. 387 about Harmony Society oil works.

Krouse, Rita Moore. *Fragments of a Dream: The Story of Germantown.* Ruston, Louisiana: Leader Press, 1962. Publishes document allowing Bernhard Müller to change his name to Maximilian Ludwig Proli. Also contains reproductions of Proli, Leon, and his wife.

Landenberger, Albert. *Johann Valentin Andreæ, ein schwäbischer Gottesgelehrter des siebzehnten Jahrhunderts.* Barmen: Verlag von Hugo Klein, 1886. Pietistic background of Harmonists.

Lang, Gottlob. *Michael Hahn: Ein Gottesmann im schwäbischen Bauerngewand.* Stuttgart: Calwer Verlag, 1962. A contemporary and rival of George Rapp who did not emigrate but remained in the church, where his influence is felt still.

Larner, John William Jr. " 'Nails and Sundrie Medicines': Town Planning and Public Health in the Harmony Society, 1805–1840," *Western Pennsylvania Historical Magazine* 45 (1962): 115–38. Publishes maps of Harmony, New Harmony, and Economy.

Miller, Ernest C. "Utopian Communities in Warren County, Pennsylvania," *Western Pennsylvania Historical Society* 49 (October, 1966): 301–17.

O'Connor, Richard. *The German-Americans: An Informal History.* Boston: Little, Brown and Company, 1968. pp. 219–29 a slanderous account of the Harmony Society based on hostile popular accounts not documented. Repeats slander that "John Rapp was crudely emasculated by the piggery, and bled to death." Claims John's wife disappeared and that her child was killed. The child concerned was the Gertrude Rapp discussed in this book.

Owen, Robert Dale. *To Holland and to New Harmony,* ed. J. Elliott. Indianapolis: Indiana Historical Society, 1969. Very well illustrated including an excellent reproduction of Lesueur's sketch of Economy in 1825. First hand account of meetings with Harmonists.

Pittsburgh Chronicle Telegraph 1893. Reports on Economy.

Pittsburgh Commercial Gazette, 1892 to 1893. Reports on Economy.

Pittsburgh Dispatch, 1892 to 1893. Reports on Economy.

Pittsburgh Leader, 1890. Reports on Economy.

Pittsburgh Times, 1892. Reports of Economy.

Riley, Marvin P. *The Hutterite Brethren: An Annotated Bibliography with Special Reference to South Dakota Hutterite Colonies.* Brookings, South Dakota: South Dakota State University, November, 1965.

Roessle, Julius. *Von Bengel bis Blumhardt: Gestalten und Bilder aus der Geschichte des schwäbischen Pietismus.* Metzingen: Verlag Ernst Franz, 1959. See pp. 290–91 about George Rapp's power as a preacher.

Scholtz, Harald. *Evangelischer Utopismus bei Johann Valentin Andreä: Ein geistiges Vorspiel zum Pietismus (Darstellungen aus der württembergischen Geschichte,* Band 42). Stuttgart: W. Kohlhammer Verlag, 1957. Important for background of Harmonists in Württemberg.

Schuster, Otto. *Schwäbische Glaubenszeugen: Gestalten und Bilder aus der württembergischen Kirchengeschichte.* Stuttgart: Calwer Verlag, 1946. Articles on Bengel and Hahn, who influenced George Rapp.

Steimle, Theodor. *Friedrich List Brevier.* Munich: Verlag von R. Oldenbourg, 1942. p. 51. Refers to List's articles on the Harmony Society in the *Readinger Adler.*

Wetzel, Richard. *History of the Music of the Harmony Society.* The first scholarly study of the extensive musical records of the Harmony Society was in process of publication as this volume went to press.

Wetzel, Richard. See Arndt, Karl J. R. and Wetzel, Richard. A series of articles in the *Western Pennsylvania Historical Magazine,* starting April 1971.

Zündel, Friedrich. *Johann Christoph Blumhardt: Ein Lebensbild.* Giessen: Brunnen-Verlag, 1922. Biography of the minister who was called to George Rapp's home town of Iptingen after his departure. See chapter 6: Iptingen.

Index

The purpose of this index is to assist in locating specific subjects, events, titles, or individuals when related to these. No attempt has been made to include all names that appear in this volume or to list them each time they appear, as one would in a vocabulary frequency list, which is not within the purpose of this index. Those interested in membership lists will find them referred to under that key word and in the first volume, which includes a reproduction of all signatures of the earliest members of the Harmony Society. A Biographical Dictionary of all members of the Society, whether they left the Society or died in membership, is now in preparation and will be published as one of the volumes of my Documentary History of George Rapp's Harmony Society. The index does not cover the Survey of the Harmony Society Archives or the Catalogue of the Harmony Society Library, which have their own arrangement.